LINCOLN'S
ATTORNEY GENERAL
EDWARD BATES OF MISSOURI

The First Reading of the Emancipation Proclamation before the Cabinet
STANTON, CHASE, LINCOLN, WELLES, SEWARD, SMITH, BLAIR, BATES

Lincoln's Attorney General
Edward Bates of Missouri

by MARVIN R. CAIN

UNIVERSITY OF MISSOURI PRESS

Columbia · *Missouri*

To my parents, Frank and Irma A. Cain

INTRODUCTION

P OLITICAL biographies of historical personalities involved in the American Civil War, while not as numerous as military studies of the same conflict, have been popular since Appomattox. Nearly all of the major figures of the period have been studied by nineteenth-century historians, who tended to glorify famous men, and by twentieth-century historians, who have searched for new and subtler interpretations of the causes of the Civil War. To both layman and professional alike, the verbal output describing the lives of those who were touched by the great conflict appears to have reached the saturation point.

For one reason or another, Edward Bates has merited no such published study, although his diary, kept during the war years, has long been exploited by historians as a rich mine of information and insight. Usually mentioned in studies of Abraham Lincoln and other contemporaries are Bates's role in the Republican presidential race in 1860 and his defense of Administration policies, both constitutional and unconstitutional, during the war. But apart from his supportive functions, he has not drawn the interest or attention of historians in their explorations of the Civil War period.

Many reasons could be cited for ignoring Bates, but I believe that his lack of color and his seeming unimportance in the Civil War cabinet are the main factors that have turned historians away from a study of his life. Viewed among the major figures of his lifetime—a period that saw Andrew Jackson, Henry Clay, Daniel Webster, Roger B. Taney, John C. Calhoun, Charles Sumner, William H. Seward, and, of course, Abraham Lincoln—Bates indeed pales in significance and interest; seen among his contemporaries, a colorful personality such as his political foe Thomas Hart Benton strikes the fancy and engages the energies of biographers as the dour Bates cannot.

Although Bates's position in American history during the first half of the nineteenth century does not appear to entitle him to the same attention as the giants who furnished both substantive achievement and fanciful legend to the written re-creation of their country's past, his significance as a transitional political figure drew me to him. Bates was of his generation—caught between the agrarian idealism of Jeffersonian society and the material promise of young America and facing the formidable problems engendered by slavery, sectionalism, and the industrial awakening. Also, I believe that Bates played a more effective role in Lincoln's cabinet than has heretofore been thought. Moreover, Bates, the young Virginian transplanted to a frontier region where everyday life held lesser expectancies and employed cruder means than those of his native state, arouses one's anticipations. The development of Bates the man of professional standing and of property into a conservative political leader almost overwhelmed by the sweep of Jacksonian Democracy; the formation of the Whig party of Missouri under his guiding hand; the growth of his interest in railroads and other internal improvements; and finally, toward the end of his life, his confrontation of the slavery question, all blend into a story of transitional times seen through the eyes of a participant.

Despite his involvement in a time of change, Bates's basic attitudes never changed; he remained inflexibly loyal to a past he never fully understood or knew. His doctrinaire beliefs, alongside his pragmatic and often guilt-ridden attempts to solve constitutional problems during the Civil War, held him to the consistency that led to his fight against the arbitrary power of Stanton's Army and, in part, to his break with Lincoln and most of the Cabinet.

Perhaps, then, Bates, more than Calhoun or Lincoln, epitomizes the time in which they all lived. His conservative image, his almost admirable position on the extension of slavery, his Machiavellian feats as a local political leader, and his dogged adherence to a Constitution he was prepared to violate for expediency, mark him as a complicated and somewhat formidable figure. His rejection of the "new democracy" of Jacksonianism and his eventual defense of many of its precepts have engaged my interest, since I believe that lesser men in important stages of history often reflect more of their time and its forgotten hours than do those whom we recognize as great.

I am grateful to several people who have made this study pleasurable. I am especially indebted to Dean James L. Bugg, Jr., of the University of Missouri at St. Louis, who suggested the topic for this book and has guided and inspired its completion from a doctoral dissertation; it is hoped that his standards of excellence and his rich scholarship are sometimes evidenced in its pages. I owe much also to Professor Gilman M. Ostrander of the Department of History, Michigan State University, and to Dean James Neal Primm of Hiram College, Hiram, Ohio, for reading the manuscript and offering valuable and needed suggestions. Both of these scholars have also encouraged the writer in more ways than in the completion of this work. I should like to acknowledge and thank the staff of the State Historical Society of Missouri at Columbia, Mrs. Ernst Stadler of the Missouri Historical Society at St. Louis (an excellent guide for any researcher), the staffs of the Manuscripts Division of the Library of Congress and of the Diplomatic, Fiscal, and Legal Division of the National Archives, Mr. David Drury, Miss Toni Costly, and Mrs. Jean Marr McDonald of Michigan State University, and my wife, who has helped in countless ways of which she might not know. All of these people and several others, working in various manuscript depositories and university libraries, have made appreciated contributions. None of them is responsible for the errors in this work; only I may lay claim to them.

M. R. C.

Michigan State University
September, 1964

CONTENTS

CHAPTER I   FRONTIER POLITICIAN   1

CHAPTER II   FORMATION OF A PARTY   40

CHAPTER III   REQUIEM FOR WHIGGERY   58

CHAPTER IV   A REPUBLICAN VICTORY   90

CHAPTER V   DAYS OF CRISIS   128

CHAPTER VI   THE FALL OF TWO GENERALS   162

CHAPTER VII   THE FIERCEST PASSIONS OF OUR NATURE   182

CHAPTER VIII   THE ATTORNEY GENERAL AND SLAVERY   212

CHAPTER IX   THE LEGAL QUESTIONS OF WAR   239

CHAPTER X   AFFAIRS IN MISSOURI   269

CHAPTER XI   AT THE BOTTOM OF THE CUP   285

CHAPTER XII   A GENERATION THAT HAD PASSED AWAY   316

BIBLIOGRAPHY   334

INDEX   353

CHAPTER I

FRONTIER POLITICIAN

ON APRIL 29, 1814, Virginia-born Edward Bates arrived in the frontier town of St. Louis, Missouri. The small, sturdy youth of twenty-one had finally completed the arduous journey from his birthplace in Virginia, nearly a thousand miles eastward. His massive forehead, large Roman nose, and firm mouth and chin presented a facial solemnity enlivened by piercing black eyes. Five feet, seven inches in height, he strode through the streets of the Mississippi River settlement, seeking the office of his brother Frederick, Secretary of the Missouri Territory.[1]

Many years had passed since Edward had said farewell to his brother at the family home in Belmont, near the James River in Goochland County, Virginia. There they had grown up as part of a large family of five daughters and seven sons.

[1] Edward Bates to Elihu Shepard, July 1, 1866, Edward Bates Papers (Missouri Historical Society, St. Louis, Missouri). Hereafter cited as Bates Papers; other collections to be noted. John F. Darby, *Personal Recollections*, 400.

Edward was the youngest son of Thomas Fleming and Caroline
Matilda Woodson Bates. He was born in 1793, a decade after
his father had left the Continental Army, following the Battle
of Yorktown. Although the family held a reputable social
position in class-conscious Goochland County, his father had
great difficulty providing for his large family. The elder
Bates had enjoyed better days before the Revolution, having
attended school in England, from whence he returned to Virginia to start a successful career as a merchant and local
official. When the Revolutionary War began, he abandoned
his business and his Quaker faith to serve in the American
army. He received little reward for his patriotism; the
Revolution left him in debt and without a permanent occupation. Young Edward therefore grew up in straitened circumstances, although a few negro slaves worked several acres
of land on their Belmont estate.

Because his elder brothers left home in young manhood,
Edward came under the tutelage of his mother and older
sisters. By the time he was five, their devoted and persistent
instruction had produced results; he could spell several words
and before he reached the age of eight had composed verse.[2]
But the death of his father in 1805 forced the family to send
him to live with his brother in Northumberland, Virginia.
Two years later, as a youth of fourteen, he moved to the
home of his cousin Benjamin Bates in Hanover, Maryland.
His cousin proved to be an excellent tutor who provided Edward with a background in philosophy, history, and natural
science. The young man also enrolled in Charlotte Hall
Academy in St. Mary's County. Long reliance on private study
and his cousin's erudition made him dissatisfied with formal
schooling, however. He spent many of the long, lonely hours

[2] Edward Bates, "Frederick Bates Biographical Sketch," *Michigan Pioneer and Historical Society Collections*, VIII, 563-64.

away from his family reading historical treatises and composing poems.[3]

For a while, Edward contemplated a career in the Navy. Although Congressman James Pleasants of Virginia, a family friend, promised him a commission, he eventually decided against a Navy career because his mother disapproved. Surprisingly, in politically conscious Virginia, where Thomas Jefferson, James Madison, James Monroe, and John Randolph lived, the young man gave little consideration to entering public life. The outbreak of the War of 1812 temporarily made the decision for him; arming himself with the old English Tower musket his father had carried at Yorktown, Edward enlisted in the Virginia militia. He saw brief service in his native state, but was mustered out before the end of the war, late in 1813. His military commitment at an end, and faced with an uncertain future, he decided to undertake the long journey to St. Louis to join Frederick.[4]

Years earlier, Frederick had left for the Northwest and a position as quartermaster in the Army. After brief service with the military, he settled in Detroit, where he became the first postmaster of the city and a prominent merchant. In 1805 family connections as well as recognition of his abilities brought him an appointment from President Thomas Jefferson to the judgeship of the territorial court. He quickly gained local reputation as a talented administrator, serving as a land commissioner also, and in the following year Jefferson named him Secretary of the Louisiana territory and recorder of land titles in St. Louis, succeeding Joseph Browne, Aaron Burr's brother-in-law; Jefferson wanted a loyal public official in the West. Also, Frederick had a firsthand knowledge of

[3] Thomas to Frederick Bates, August 21, 1798, Edward Bates Papers (State Historical Society of Missouri, Columbia, Missouri).

[4] Conversation with Miss Caroline Bates Singleton, December 4, 1958; Edward Bates, "Frederick Bates Biographical Sketch," *op. cit.,* 563; Caroline M. Bates to Frederick, December 28, 1807, Bates Papers (State Historical Society of Missouri).

the complicated land claim cases growing out of the Spanish cession of the Louisiana territory to France and the subsequent American purchase in 1803. At first Frederick felt ill at ease among the mixed Spanish-French-English population of St. Louis. However, he soon established himself on the land-hungry Missouri frontier as a judge, speculator, businessman, and friend of the large landholder. Also, under the Jefferson and Madison administrations, he exercised considerable patronage power. In 1808 he compiled and published the first set of territorial laws and, for a while, served as acting governor. By the time young Edward arrived in the town in 1814, Frederick was a well-known and prosperous citizen of St. Louis.[5]

Edward found that Frederick's closest associates, professional and social, were the wealthy French residents of St. Louis who held titles to vast areas of land, the key to political success in early Missouri. Frederick owned land west of town on the Dardenne Prairie, and north of St. Charles, near Bonhomme, where he had settled on a 1,000-acre farm. In addition, the enterprising Secretary had leased mineral land in the southeast part of the territory, along the Mississippi River. His social graces as well as his political position gave him entree to the powerful circle that had formed about the Chouteaus, the founders of St. Louis. Frederick also numbered among his intimate friends the merchants of the town and, particularly, the territorial lawyers, some of whom were making outstanding reputations.

Among the frontier lawyers Edward Bates thought Rufus Easton to be the most eminent. Easton had served as territorial judge, postmaster, United States district attorney,

[5] Frederick Bates to August B. Woodward, June 18 and October 20, 1807, and February 23 and March 26, 1808, *Michigan Pioneer and Historical Society Collections*, VIII, 558-63; Caroline M. Bates to Frederick, September 6, 1810, Bates Papers (State Historical Society of Missouri).

and territorial delegate to Congress. Also, he enjoyed considerable success as a land speculator and as representative for the small land claimants, who were abundant on the frontier. Therefore, the impressionable young man was overjoyed when Easton allowed him to read law in his office. After years of family and personal insecurity, he at last had a stable situation through which he could achieve the ambition that burned brightly in him; he had found a profession. For two years he pursued legal studies under the man he later characterized as "a wiser man than he passed for, and a better man than his adversaries chose to admit."[6]

Edward quickly learned law and its frontier usage, under both Easton and his brother Frederick. As he studied, he became acquainted with the members of the St. Louis bar, the center of political as well as legal activity in the territory. By the close of 1816 he had successfully completed his legal training and the bar examinations. He entered practice at a time when claim lawyers, representing titleholders or claimants of grants issued by the Spanish before the Louisiana Purchase, were rising to prominence. Before the United States had taken over the territory, Spanish governors had sold or given away land grants indiscriminately. Most of these titles were held now by the wealthier large landholders, who often were reluctant to go to court to obtain legal confirmation. Thus, as settlers moved onto the land, disputes arose over pre-emption rights as opposed to original grants issued under the Spanish regime, and the question became one of public as opposed to private interests. Also, the property clause in the Treaty of Cession, signed by the United States and France, came under examination because it required all land claims to be validated if the legality of the original grant was proven. To expedite the settlement of the complicated and often conflicting claims, Congress appointed a board of land commissioners for the upper Louisiana territory to hear

[6] Edward Bates to Elihu Shepard, July 1, 1866, Bates Papers.

disputed cases and to render decisions. People holding land titles therefore needed skilled lawyers to represent them in claim litigation.[7]

Bates did not specialize as a claim lawyer, as did Thomas Hart Benton, David Barton, Rufus Easton, Edward Hempstead, and others. He preferred, instead, to handle legal affairs for the officials in Governor William Clark's administration and for the wealthy businessmen of the town. Moreover, Frederick often called on him to help run his various business interests. Among other things, Edward became involved in managing a steam mill company. Often he made trips to other places for his brother. In 1817, at Frederick's request, he undertook a journey to Virginia to settle the family estate in Belmont and the personal affairs of his brother Tarleton, who had been killed in a duel in Pittsburgh. Tarleton, a protégé of Judge Hugh M. Brackenridge and a staunch Jeffersonian, met his death after a quarrel with a Federalist newspaper editor over a political matter.[8]

At Belmont the reunion with his mother and elder sister was not a completely happy occasion. The death of Tarleton, their financial difficulties, and the dispersion of the family saddened what otherwise might have been a joyous homecoming for the young man. An older brother, James Woodson Bates, a graduate of Princeton, recently had left the family home to join Frederick and Edward in St. Louis.[9] It did not

[7] J. Thomas Scharf, *History of St. Louis, City and County*, I, 1449; Lemont K. Richardson, "Private Land Claims in Missouri," *Missouri Historical Review*, L, 391-92, 394-95.

[8] Edward to Frederick Bates, September 1, 1817, Bates Papers; Walter B. Douglas, "Manuel Lisa," *Missouri Historical Society Collections*, III, 387; Thomas M. Marshall, *The Life and Papers of Frederick Bates*, I, 296.

[9] Edward to Frederick Bates, October 30, 1817, Bates Papers (State Historical Society of Missouri); Edward to Frederick Bates, September 29 and October 13, 1817, Bates Papers. James Woodson Bates moved to Arkansas in 1819, became the first territorial delegate, and served in Congress from 1819 to 1823. He was also a lawyer, circuit court and probate judge, and land commissioner.

require much persuasive skill for Edward to induce his mother and sister to accompany him back to Missouri. Not until June of 1818, however, were the financial affairs settled and the family, along with seventeen slaves, ready to leave Virginia. The return trip to St. Louis was made by way of Pittsburgh in order to make final disposition of the unfortunate Tarleton's estate, a negotiation which took longer than Bates had anticipated.[10] A year had passed by the time he returned to St. Louis and resumed his practice.

After his return from Virginia, Bates, as many did, speculated in land, using as capital his share of the family estate. Although Frederick's material and political success gave Edward a decided advantage when he resumed his own dual career as a lawyer and businessman, by now he desired to make his own way. Eagerly he accepted appointment as circuit attorney in St. Charles, St. Louis, and Washington counties, and he formed a partnership with Joshua Barton, younger brother of David Barton, who was a noted territorial lawyer and political figure. Bates soon gained a reputation as a forceful and talented counsel with the ability to combine frontier language and classical learning into persuasive argument that he delivered in a soft, appealing voice. People who heard him in the circuit courts of St. Charles, St. Louis, and Washington counties recalled, later, the charm of the slightly built, gifted speaker. In 1818 Governor William Clark appointed him attorney for the Northern District of Missouri.[11]

These beginnings of a successful career brought Bates more and more into contact with the older French families. He soon was accepted as one of the lawyer-politician group favored by the town's business and landholding elements.

[10] Edward to Frederick Bates, June 15 and July 10, 1818, Bates Papers.

[11] St. Louis *Missouri Gazette*, September 4, 1818; Darby, *op. cit.*, 396; William V. N. Bay, *Reminiscences of the Bench and Bar of Missouri*, 130-31; footnote citing an address by Colonel Thomas T. Gantt in Scharf, *op. cit.*, I, 1466.

Among his new associates Bates counted Alexander McNair, David Barton, and the flamboyant Thomas Hart Benton. He was among the more learned and cultured of the group, the social graces of Virginia and the erudition of a cultivated family standing him in good stead. He easily found a place among wealthy, conservative, frontier entrepreneurs, such as Auguste and Pierre Chouteau, Manuel Lisa, Bernard Pratte, and Bartholomew Berthold, who had made fortunes from fur and merchandising empires, and among prominent governmental figures, such as William Clark, Charles Gratiot, John B. C. Lucas, and William Christy, all of whom had held public positions. Mostly interested in profitable enterprise and professional opportunity, these men looked with eager anticipation to the rich mining regions of Missouri's southeast, to the future sales of the large tracts of land they held, to the fur trade along the reaches of the upper Missouri, and to the establishment of a commercial and banking community in St. Louis where the natural wealth of the Louisiana territory could be converted into capital, land, and fortune.

Gradually, and without any display of enthusiasm, Bates entered politics by joining the crusade for Missouri statehood. Several reasons lay behind the movement that was launched in 1817 amidst a flurry of petition-writing and public meetings. Many people, including most of the agrarian settlers, wanted improved transportation and communication facilities. Not a few desired stabilization of land policies and of land prices, which were being driven ever upward by steady immigration into the territory and the unresolved status of thousands of acres of land that had been reserved from public sale. Still others thought that a state government would protect and promote their speculative and commercial enterprises. Many townsmen, enjoying the prosperity brought by the high prices of agricultural products and the accessibility of easy credit, looked forward to having a state legislature that could charter banks and corporations. A few, concerned over the unchecked land speculation and the influx of settlers with slaves, thought that a state government could better cope with these problems. Whatever their motivation, all these residents desired statehood.

In 1818 John Scott, Missouri's lone territorial delegate, presented to Congress several petitions requesting that his territory be admitted as a state under the provisions of the 1803 Treaty of Cession. In the debate that followed, Representative James Tallmadge, Jr., of New York, offered a resolution aimed at curbing southern political dominance in general and slavery in particular. Tallmadge proposed that Missouri be admitted to the Union after providing for the manumission of all children of slaves who had reached their twenty-first birthday. Among the voices raised in protest against the Tallmadge Resolution was that of Missouri's Scott. However, the resolution passed as an amendment to the House bill of admission. The Senate struck out the clause that restricted slavery, leaving the debates on the future of slavery and on the constitutional foundation of the Union at an impasse.

As were many of his colleagues, Bates was angered at attempts made by antislavery congressmen to place restrictions on Missouri's admission to the Union. He believed that the Tallmadge Resolution violated the Constitution because it laid restrictions on a state beyond those calling for "a republican form of government." Therefore, he aligned himself with the popular antirestrictionists, who opposed, also, Senator Jesse B. Thomas' compromise amendment of 1820, which prohibited slavery in all the Louisiana Purchase north of the 36° 30', with the exception of the proposed state of Missouri. Congress had no right, Bates felt, to impede statehood by raising the slavery question. He still clung to a strong belief in State rights and a strict construction of the Constitution, principles fundamental to the disciples of Thomas Jefferson and dear to the young man from Virginia.

The Thomas Amendment passed, and the Maine-Missouri statehood bills were combined after a heated debate in Congress. In April, 1820, President James Monroe issued a proclamation authorizing Missouri to form a state government and to draft a constitution that would permit the inclusion of slavery.[12]

Attracted by the prospect of a political career, Bates became a leading contender for a post as delegate to the state constitutional convention to be held in St. Louis. He campaigned actively on the platform of suffrage for free, white, adult male residents and of unrestricted importation of slaves into Missouri. Also, unlike his more democratic mentor Easton, he came out for a property qualification for both voters and officeholders. In the election he received a total of 881 votes from the four townships in St. Louis County and was one of the many antirestrictionists elected to the convention.[13]

As a delegate-elect, Bates demonstrated a philosophical immaturity and a political inflexibility that later marred his reputation for consistency. Despite some Jeffersonian tendencies, his personal morality made him turn from the democratic implications of the famous Virginian's all-encompassing faith. The rapid transition he had made from unsettled adolescence to security and recognition among the propertied class on the frontier also influenced his outlook and conduct. His association with wealthy men such as the Chouteaus heightened his concern for the preservation of property rights and for political and social stability. Though he did not become a frontier squire, he had little faith in mass democratic rule; he felt that a natural aristocracy of

[12] St. Louis *Missouri Gazette*, May 19, 1819, and April 5, 1820; Glover Moore, *The Missouri Controversy, 1818-1821*, 48; Floyd C. Shoemaker, *Missouri's Struggle for Statehood, 1804-1821*, 110.

[13] St. Louis *Missouri Gazette*, May 10, 1820; Richard Edwards and M. Hopewell, *Edwards' Great West*, 322-23.

talent and ambition directed the course of any society. Son of a Quaker father, his political views were more akin to eighteenth-century Whiggery than to the Jeffersonian faith he professed. His outlook was as much of the Revolutionary period as the old blue coat with gilt buttons and the ruffled linen that he loved to wear. Occasionally, he did represent claimants who occupied land on which they had paid no taxes against speculators who paid the tax due and sued for the title. However, he considered defense of such cases an exercise in simple justice and a professional challenge rather than a demonstration of belief in democracy. His ambition and his close relationship to the banker-merchant class of St. Louis made him a member of the conservative group at the state convention.[14]

Bates belonged to the lawyer faction that had led the way to statehood and intended to dominate the constitutional convention. Among the more prominent members of the frontier bar at the convention were Easton, Benton, Scott, Hempstead, McNair, and the Barton brothers. Towering above all was David Barton, a Kentucky-born lawyer who had migrated to Missouri in 1809 and had served as attorney general and speaker of the territorial legislature. Bates greatly admired the suave, good-looking lawyer, whose charm in court was legendary. Ten years older than Bates, Barton too was a man of classical learning and easy grace, whose success in the frontier courts often was difficult to understand. The cultivated Barton had led the statehood movement; he therefore stood unquestionably at the head of the lawyer group in the convention.

The constitutional convention began on June 12, 1820, in the Mansion House in St. Louis. The forty-one delegates from fifteen counties first had to consider the propositions in the congressional enabling act. However, in order for

[14] Darby, *op. cit.*, 400; *St. Louis Globe-Democrat*, February 26, 1926. A biographical sketch appeared in this edition.

the new state to accept the five propositions, two congressional stipulations had to be met: The state could not collect taxes on public lands nor could it collect taxes on bounty lands. The delegates voted to accept these conditions and to receive, in return, the sixteenth section of each township for the use of public schools, twelve salt springs with six sections of land adjoining each spring, 5 per cent of the net proceeds from the sales of public land for the building of public roads and canals, four sections of land for the establishment of a state capital, and thirty-six sections of land for a seminary of learning.[15]

Bates deviated little from the strict State rights pattern followed by the St. Louis lawyer group in the debates. As the rest, he astutely observed the thin line between appeals for certain federal guarantees and advocacy of state self-determination. It is significant that men of strict State rights persuasion, such as Duff Green of Howard County, land speculator and merchant extraordinary, could unite with Barton, William Christy, and others who favored broad powers for the central government. Bates opposed the proposition that allowed Congress to regulate river navigation; he believed that federal regulation of the waterways would discourage improvement of rivers by incorporated companies and, accordingly, would restrict private enterprise. Also, he proposed to modify another of the propositions by requesting Congress to relinquish control of the state's share of the proceeds from the sale of public lands. His suggestion that this money be controlled by the state legislature was evidence of another hope held by the lawyer clique that planned to guide Missouri's new government. If these funds were available to the legislature, the state might initiate its own internal improvements and educational policies.[16]

[15] *Journal of the Missouri State Convention*, 9. Hereafter cited as *Convention Journal*.

[16] Franklin *Missouri Intelligencer*, July 1, 1820; St. Louis *Missouri Gazette*, June 29, 1820; *Convention Journal*, 5.

Appointed to the Committee on the Judiciary by the convention's president David Barton, Bates worked tirelessly. He was much pleased with his new role and with that of his profession which, he believed, was to provide Missouri with a proper constitution. The lawyers at the convention, he thought, would see to it that the judiciary had in its hands the power to interpret all forms of civil, common, and constitutional law. To prove his point, he drafted a section endorsing a strong, independent judiciary. Vigorously he opposed the provisions that would give to the legislature the power to remove judges of the state supreme and circuit courts; he advocated, instead, lifetime tenure and minimum salaries for all court officers. In addition to his other duties he spent many hours writing the preamble to the constitution while serving on the Committee on the Judiciary.[17]

While he favored a strong judiciary, Bates and most of the lawyer clique hoped to curb the powers of the legislature, in the event that body received a democratic mandate. Bates himself proposed a clause restricting the legislature's powers of incorporation. He also voted against other resolutions that would permit legislative regulation of dueling and of slavery. Finally, in his zeal to draft a conservative constitution, he recommended a general review of all state legislation every three years. As did most of the Barton group, he stood in opposition to Rufus Easton and Alexander McNair, who wanted popular election of judges, white manhood suffrage, and broad powers for the legislature.[18]

Gradually, the Barton group exerted its control over the convention. Altogether, Bates introduced eight major proposals during the course of the proceedings. In addition to those dealing with the judiciary, he proposed the prohibition of religious corporations. He led a number of debates in

[17] Louis Houck, *History of Missouri*, III, 252.
[18] *Convention Journal*, 15.

open session, and he wielded great influence in the internal councils of the Barton faction. With Barton, Henry Geyer, John Rice Jones, John Cook, John Scott, and Jonathan Findlay, he emerged as one of the principal authors of the constitution. By the time the convention adjourned on July 19, 1820, the young lawyer had added greatly to his reputation.[19]

In the summer days that followed, however, he learned about the uncertainties of state politics. He discovered much, too, about economic influences on political conditions. Missouri was in the throes of a depression, the delayed effect of a national panic that had begun the year before. Sensing a change in the public's mood, Alexander McNair deserted his colleagues in the law to become the gubernatorial candidate of the democratic faction opposed to minimum salary guarantees for state officials, life tenure for judges, restriction of the legislature's powers, and a complicated process for the amendment of the constitution. Barton immediately combined forces with Benton, now the editor of the *St. Louis Enquirer,* and Frederick Bates. The three men selected hero-explorer and former territorial governor William Clark as their candidate to oppose McNair. But McNair had the better case with the voting public, especially with those in outlying rural areas where feeling against the constitution was strong. On August 19, 1820, he received a 3,923-vote majority over Clark in Missouri's first state election.[20]

Honoring the myth of the time that no party conflict existed, McNair named Bates as the state's first attorney

[19] Charles van Ravenswaay, "The Tragedy of David Barton," *Bulletin of the Missouri Historical Society,* VII, 39-41; Shoemaker, *op. cit.,* 195, 204; St. Louis *Missouri Gazette,* June 29, 1820.

[20] Franklin *Missouri Intelligencer,* August 26, 1820; *St. Louis Enquirer,* September 19, 1820; William N. Chambers, *Old Bullion Benton: Senator from the New West,* 96-97; Walter B. Stevens, "Alexander McNair," *Missouri Historical Review,* XVII, 10; Shoemaker, *op. cit.,* 258-59.

general and Joshua Barton as its first secretary of state.[21] With an anticonstitution group in the majority, the legislature, inclined at first to veto Bates's appointment, eventually granted belated confirmation because of McNair's urging. To help placate the legislature, the popular and democratic-minded William Christy was made state auditor. Friends of Frederick Bates requested him to run for the office of United States senator, but after some political bargaining, the lawyer junta chose David Barton and Thomas Hart Benton as candidates for the new state's most important positions. Except for McNair's election to the governorship, the two factions fared equally well in obtaining public office.

The economic crisis in Missouri dictated the course of the new state administration. As a result of the Panic of 1819, immigration into Missouri had steadily declined, leaving in desperate straits speculators who had bought land when credit had been easy to obtain and merchants who had overstocked their stores. Missouri was sunk in a depression brought on by the collapse of the cotton market in Europe, the influx of cheaply produced manufactured goods from England, the revival of European agriculture after the Napoleonic Wars, and the creation of trade barriers against American commodities. The state's predicament was made worse by the liberal credit policies of the Second United States Bank and the chartering of local banks with insufficient capital. Missouri was affected, as were her western and southern sisters, by the abrupt end of the land and cotton booms. In each of these states, elasticity of credit and the proliferation of banks and loan agencies eager to finance almost any profit-minded enterprise had brought the state to the brink of financial ruin. A critical shortage of the specie necessary to bolster the once optimistic speculation made

[21] Buel Leopard and Floyd C. Shoemaker, eds., *The Messages and Proclamations of the Governors of the State of Missouri,* I, 40.

matters worse. With financial credit drastically restricted, the Bank of Missouri was forced to suspend specie payment. When depression struck the rural areas of the state in the summer of 1821, McNair was forced to summon a special session of the state legislature to consider remedial measures. Responding to his pleas, the legislators passed a loan office act that authorized the issuance of state certificates of credit through loan agencies. The General Assembly also passed a stay law that allowed to debtors who owned land additional time to redeem it.[22]

Bates hardly had settled in his new office before the legislature put through the relief program. At the same time, the legislature, reflecting the popular reaction against the constitution, was considering amendments concerning tenure of office and minimum salaries—touchy political subjects in the midst of an economic depression. Greatly shaken by these developments, Bates analyzed the relief legislation from a constitutional standpoint. He looked upon the loan office certificates as "rag money," paper currency that states, constitutionally, could not issue. He also felt that the stay law, which allowed debtors a certain period of time to pay taxes on foreclosed property, violated the sanctity of contracts and made all property legal tender in payment of debts. Knowing that what he did was unpopular, he nevertheless decided that all the relief legislation was unconstitutional. Since he felt that he could not support McNair's program, he resigned his office as attorney general in late 1821. Besides, he had received a lucrative private offer from the Chouteaus, and profits from land he owned outright kept him free of financial difficulty; his taxes that

[22] James N. Primm, *Economic Policy in the Development of a Western State: Missouri, 1820-1860*, 2-6; Bray Hammond, *Banks and Politics in America from the Revolution to the Civil War*, 258-59.

year amounted to $1,000, placing his name high among the taxpayers of St. Louis.[23]

Fascinated, however, by the excitement of public life, Bates did not remain politically inactive for long. In the summer of 1822 he announced his candidacy for the Missouri House of Representatives. He based his campaign on an antirelief platform that proved to be antilegislature as well. He denounced the relief legislation as an outrageous violation of individual rights and an unconstitutional interference with property rights, the very basis of republican government. An active campaigner, he generalized eloquently on the legislature's assaults on the constitution, warning that they threatened the true shield of the people—the judiciary. Since public opinion had, by this time, begun to turn against relief legislation, Bates had little difficulty in winning election in August. Many observers acknowledged that the younger brother of Frederick Bates truly had mastered the art of frontier politics.[24] Moreover, in his successful campaign for office, he had not compromised his principles.

Bates obviously did not fit the role of popular and successful politician. Consistently he had demonstrated his respect for the always unpopular judiciary and his concern for its interest, which he associated with the interest of the banking and commercial community. When, in November, 1822, he took his seat as a member of the House of Representatives in Missouri's Second General Assembly, he represented the landed and mercantile society of St. Louis as opposed to the agrarian majority of the state. Paradoxically, the young

[23] Primm, *op. cit.*, 21, 54; Bates to Colonel Pierre Chouteau, July 30, 1821, Bates Papers; Olive Baker, "Paper Read before Montgomery County Club of St. Louis," *Missouri Historical Review*, VII, 203; John Paxton, "St. Louis Directory and Register, 1821," *St. Louis Directory for 1854-1855*, 260; Scharf, *op. cit.*, I, 359; W. J. Hamilton, "The Relief Movement in Missouri," *Missouri Historical Review*, XXII, 81-82.

[24] St. Louis *Missouri Republican*, May 15 and July 31, 1822.

man, once so indifferent to politics, had advanced himself
by repudiating much of the Jeffersonian tradition he had
once espoused. His Hamiltonian view of the legislature's
main problems—the relief laws and the proposed constitutional amendments—had not changed from what they had
been in 1820, only now the ten amendments that provided
for more legislative control over the state judiciary and for
popular election of judges and court officers were more dis-
tasteful to him. He regarded the amendments as designed to
augment the powers of an inexperienced legislature elected
by ill-informed rural voters. Openly, he expressed his fear
that the attempts being made to restrict the judiciary were
instigated by self-seeking politicians. Popular election of
judges and legislative determination of their salaries bothered
him especially. The judiciary was to him the protector of
individual and property rights, and he opposed its being
entrusted to hands more accustomed to the plow than to the
quill.[25]

To hasten the end of the loan office certificates, which
had become unpopular because of their devaluation, Bates
introduced a bonding proposal to withdraw the notes from
circulation, to fix a rate of depreciation and value, and to
provide for their replacement by acceptable bank paper.
The passage of his resolution was one of the first steps
toward reversing the unsuccessful relief program which, by
now, was receiving mixed support from both creditors and
debtors in the state.[26]

Despite the efforts of Bates and like-minded members of
the legislature, seven of the proposed constitutional amendments were ratified. Irritated, Bates recommended that in
the future the vote on ratification of proposed amendments
to the constitution be recorded. He also insisted on a popular

[25] *House Journal, Second General Assembly of the State of
Missouri,* 69, 71.

[26] *Ibid.,* 77.

referendum in the future on proposals for constitutional changes, whereby the voters would determine whether or not to summon a convention. He knew that such a measure would impede the amendment process and make less likely any tampering with the constitution on the part of the legislature. It would be up to the convention when called, he said, to decide upon the proposed amendments. The freshman representative maintained that such measures were necessary to keep the legislature from altering the constitution without first informing the people.[27]

After the session of 1822-1823 ended, Bates reached an important point in his life. On May 29, 1823, he married Julia D. Coalter, the daughter of David and Ann C. Coalter. He had first courted her sister, Caroline, but he became more attracted to Julia on his frequent visits to their home. The Coalters were a distinguished family. Julia's brother John D. Coalter, a talented young lawyer, was also a state legislator. One of their sisters, Marie, had married William Harper, Judge of the Chancery Court, while Caroline, whom Bates first had wooed, later married Virginia-born and -educated Hamilton Rowan Gamble, a prominent lawyer. Nine months after their marriage, the attractive young Julia, whom Bates idolized, presented him with his first son, Joshua Barton Bates.[28]

His marriage temporarily altered his political plans. Bates decided against running for re-election and devoted full time to the law practice with his partner Joshua Barton. This decision, however, ultimately involved him deeply in political affairs and changed the course of his career. David Barton and Benton, Missouri's two senators, stood at the head of separate factions that were vying for political control of

[27] *Ibid.*, 99, 149.

[28] Edward Bates to Frederick, May 15, 1823, Bates Papers; William S. Bryan and Robert Rose, *A History of the Pioneer Families of Missouri*, 139.

the state. An intense personal rivalry had developed between the two shortly after the constitutional convention when Benton had turned toward the problems of internal improvements and land. To make the West a model of an agrarian society, Benton, though he enjoyed the support of powerful mercantile and banking interests, devised a plan to reduce the price of public land to the point of eventual donation of unsold tracts to poor settlers who could not afford the purchase price. Barton bitterly disagreed. He thought the land should be held by the central government as a source of national revenue. As the hostility deepened between the two on the land question, other issues arose to separate them further. Benton supported Senator Henry Clay of Kentucky for President, while Barton favored Secretary of State John Quincy Adams.[29] Dismayed by Benton's growing patronage power, Barton also attacked the spirit of political factionalism that he accused his senatorial colleague of fomenting.

An unexpected event led to a complete break between Missouri's two senators and toward the consolidation of parties in the state. In the conduct of his practice, Joshua Barton uncovered evidence that William C. Rector, Surveyor-General of the Missouri land district, had let contracts to members of his family and, subsequently, had profited by falsifying his financial records. Barton accused Rector of corruption in a letter published in the *Missouri Republican* under the pseudonym "Philo." Thomas Rector, brother of the Surveyor-General, discovered the identity of William's accuser. While he indicated that much of the charge was true, Rector nevertheless challenged Barton to a duel, in which he, an expert duelist, killed Barton. Rector's shot precipitated the clash that had been impending and that determined political conditions in Missouri for years.[30]

[29] Chambers, *op. cit.*, 89, 116-18.
[30] St. Louis *Missouri Republican*, July 23, 1823.

Barton's tragedy stunned Bates. Immediately after his partner's death, he published an acrid letter in which he repeated Barton's charges and to which he demanded an answer from William Rector. In addition to this demonstration of physical courage, he also challenged the Rectors to an open court hearing of the whole affair. Though his audacious course was motivated mainly by grief over Joshua's fate and by his intense dislike of the Rectors, the incident immediately produced political reactions. William Rector was close to the McNair administration and was a personal friend of Benton, a relationship both David Barton and Bates denounced, implying that a conspiracy had been hatched between them. By this time, Governor McNair and John Scott, now a representative in Congress, were involved because of their ties to Benton and the Rectors.[31]

So determined was the Bates-Barton confrontation of their opponents that many friends of the Rectors thought it best to abandon them to their fate. Bates called on an old Virginia acquaintance, Nathaniel Beverly Tucker, now a judge in nearby Jefferson County, and requested him to write William Wirt, Monroe's attorney general, with the demand that all of William Rector's accounts in Washington be examined and, if found fraudulent, that prosecution proceedings be brought against him. Conscious of the political aspects of the affair, Tucker wrote Wirt with the suggestion that Bates's demands be considered. After an official investigation, most of the accusations against Rector were found to be true, and, in 1824, President Monroe removed him from office.[32]

The tragic duel thus split David Barton and Benton on the eve of the 1824 presidential election. Barton rallied his

[31] *Ibid.*, August 27, 1823.

[32] John O'Fallon to Smith, July 27, 1823, General Thomas Smith Collection; Franklin *Missouri Intelligencer*, August 2, 1824; Tucker to Wirt, October 6, 1824, William Wirt Papers.

followers, composed largely of the urban merchants and
large landholders, around the candidacy of John Quincy
Adams, while Benton led the small farmers and rural businessmen, who were attracted by his graduation-donation
plan, into Henry Clay's camp. Each group became a dis-
ciplined organization, intent on winning and holding public
office. Benton made a serious attempt to defeat Barton in
1824, but the Senator's popularity in the legislature ensured
his re-election. The two factions therefore devoted their attention to the gubernatorial race. Frederick Bates, who had
married Opie Ball and had moved to Thornhill, his estate
in Bonhomme Township, ran for governor as the Barton
candidate. The Benton-McNair coalition chose as their representative William Henry Ashley, wealthy owner of the Rocky
Mountain Fur Company.

Naturally, Bates aligned himself with the Barton group.
He had abandoned his private practice to take the post of
United States district attorney, but he decided his new
official duties could wait until after the campaign. He had
certain reservations concerning the Barton platform on the
major questions of the day. He had regarded Crawford as
the best presidential candidate and was reluctant to support
the Easterner Adams. Too, he had some private doubts about
Barton's nationalistic views. Only on the supremacy of the
judiciary did Bates fully agree with the Senator, who espoused
a federal system of internal improvements, a protective tariff,
a restrictive land policy, and the gradual abolition of slavery.
However, Bates put aside his differences with Barton and
worked to put his brother in the governor's chair.[33]

Bates used the Rector-Barton affair in his campaign against
the Benton-McNair party. Following the elder Barton's lead,

[33] Edward Bates to Frederick, August 24, 1824, Bates Papers;
U. S., *Congressional Debates*, 21st Cong., 1st Sess., VI, 146-49.
Though Barton delivered this speech in 1830, it reviewed the
formation of Missouri political groups prior to the election of 1824.

he identified McNair with the corrupt Rectors. His attacks stung the incumbent governor so keenly that he heatedly answered them in newspaper replies. McNair denied ever having granted favors to the controversial family and repudiated any political connection with them. Although Bates had discovered a technique so effective that he would use it again, how much he harmed Ashley's candidacy by attacking McNair remains speculative.[34]

In August, 1824, Frederick Bates won the gubernatorial election by a total of 6,165 votes to 4,631 for Ashley. Soon afterward, Frederick named Gamble as his secretary of state. The election appeared to be a victory for the Barton men, though Frederick earnestly maintained he was an old Jeffersonian republican who stood above party. Edward was delighted with the outcome. His future now appeared bright indeed, for the recently promulgated Land Act of 1824 permitted claimants to take cases to the district courts. As well as the promise of a political future, he now had an opportunity to conduct land claim cases "handsomely," and to earn lucrative fees.[35]

Bates voted for John Quincy Adams in the presidential election, though he felt a great admiration for Henry Clay. The Kentuckian, however, was defeated in the popular contest, and William Harris Crawford, Andrew Jackson, and Adams were soon locked in the struggle in the House of Representatives. Jackson's rise had been swift, following his military career and his brief term as senator from Tennessee. The fragmentation of parties during Monroe's administrations, the paralytic stroke that incapacitated Crawford, and

[34] St. Louis *Missouri Republican,* August 2, October 25, and November 15, 1824; John O'Fallon to Smith, November 18, 1824, General Smith Collection.

[35] Edward Bates to Frederick, June 30, 1824, Bates Papers. As recorder of land titles, Frederick had declined to register unsettled claims for public sales. As a result, many acres of land were withdrawn from public sales.

Clay's elimination at the polls placed the Hero of New
Orleans foremost in the presidential race. Next to Clay,
Jackson had received the highest number of votes in Mis-
souri.[36]

In defiance of his constituents, however, John Scott, Missouri's only congressman, decided to cast his ballot and,
therefore, his state's vote, for Adams. Apparently he did so
because Adams had made a vague promise concerning Scott's
brother, whose judgeship was in jeopardy as a result of a duel
in which he had fatally wounded his opponent. Before
making his decision, the disturbed Scott took the precau-
tion of asking both Benton's and Barton's advice as well as
that of several members of the state legislature. Having
abandoned Clay, Benton had taken up Jackson's standard,
and Barton continued to stand behind Adams. Scott found
also that many of the legislators could not agree on any one
candidate. Thus, he decided to vote for Adams, who won
the election and became the country's sixth President. Scott's
action marked another turning point in the course of Missouri
politics.[37]

Denouncing Scott's deed as perfidy, Benton and his followers unfurled Jackson's banner even as Adams entered the
White House. Now the Benton men had a popular candidate
to add to their other popular causes, cheap land and universal
free education. Also, the Bentonites joined the Jacksonian
outcry against Clay and his "corrupt bargain," charging that
the Kentuckian had swung votes he commanded in Congress to Adams in return for an appointment as secretary
of state. Finally, the Benton men raised the cry of "Eastern
domination" against the nationalist Adams. Such shouting

[36] Scharf, op. cit., I, 566.

[37] Charles F. Adams, ed., Memoirs of John Quincy Adams, VI,
474.

of slogans was to become a customary part of the state, congressional, and local elections for years to come.[38]

After the state elections, Bates devoted nearly all of his time to his responsibilities as district attorney. In early 1825 he successfully defended Judge Richard S. Thomas in his trial before the Missouri House of Representatives for discharging a court clerk and replacing him with his own son. Bates also represented several land claimants who were applying for grants under the New Madrid Act. During the New Madrid earthquake of 1811, much property had been damaged or lost. Congress provided that New Madrid claimants might relocate on any public lands not sold and would receive certificates verifying their titles. Bates represented persons who had filed on unconfirmed land and persons who had transferred their certificates to others in payment of debts. Such practices had led to much unsavory speculation on the part of wealthy St. Louisans who bought up the certificates at a cheap price, but Bates, as did his brother, interpreted the law liberally. Ironically, in court he sometimes found himself confronting old friends, such as the Chouteaus, who had speculated in the New Madrid grants.[39]

Just as it appeared that he was well on the way to success, Bates was dealt a stunning blow. On August 4, 1825, after a brief illness, Frederick Bates died. To his younger brother who idolized him, his death was a severe loss. Edward did not recover from his shock in time to participate in the political maneuvering for the office vacated by Frederick's death. Even the hopes of his old tutor Rufus Easton did not stir him to action, nor did he campaign against the Benton candidate, John Miller. Not only did the death of Frederick

[38] St. Louis *Missouri Republican*, March 23, April 11, and July 18, 1825; Chambers, *op. cit.*, 115-16.

[39] Franklin *Missouri Intelligencer*, February 1, 1825; Bates to George Graham, August 23, 1824, Wirt to Richard Rush, October 10, 1825, *American State Papers, Public Lands*, IV, 813.

leave a vast void for the young man who for more than ten years had been his companion and aide, but it also limited Edward's newly gained prestige.[40]

By early 1826, however, Bates once again succumbed to the lure of public life. Early in the year, he perceived that Scott had been so discredited by the wrathful Benton that it would be impossible for him to be re-elected. "I belong to no party," Bates declared, as Frederick had, in announcing his candidacy for Missouri's congressional seat. He professed only a tender regard for old republican principles, including that of state sovereignty. Assuming a position of compromise on the American system, he denied Congress the power to regulate internal improvements and proposed that surplus Treasury funds be distributed annually to the states for construction of transportation and educational facilities. Keeping his Jeffersonian creed in mind, he advocated the liquidation of the national debt and proclaimed the virtues of strict constitutional government. Also, he publicized the fact that he favored the right of instruction, which was championed also by Benton. Undoubtedly he was recalling Scott's apostasy when he said that a vote cast by a representative in a presidential election should be in accordance with the popular will or with the legislature's instructions. Lastly, he endorsed a system of state control over public lands and mineral areas.[41]

His well-planned campaign, which avoided partisan extremes, appealed to a great variety of voters. Some of his friends in the Barton faction, however, thought he sounded too much like a Jacksonian. Benton, in fact, abandoned the idea of running another candidate against Scott and threw his support to Bates. Somewhat surprised, the candidate carefully skirted the areas of disagreement between

[40] Electioneering circular, Rufus Easton Papers; Jackson *Independent Patriot*, August 20, 1825.

[41] Franklin *Missouri Intelligencer*, June 29 and July 6, 1826.

himself and the Benton-Jackson party. However opportunistic his conduct may have been, it was not altogether inconsistent with his notion that extreme partisan politics was bad. Too, though his animosity toward Benton once had been bitter, Bates had not yet reconciled his Western sectionalism with his conservative outlook on land and internal improvement policies. The election proved surprisingly close, Scott polling 4,155 votes to 6,000 for Bates. Significant to observers was the fact that even with Benton's support, Bates ran a close race.[42]

Bates left his family in late November for the long trip to Washington. He arrived in time to attend the opening session of the Twentieth Congress on December 3, 1827. Among those present in the House of Representatives were Silas Wright of New York, George McDuffie of South Carolina, George R. Gilmer of Georgia, William C. Rives of Virginia, Edward Livingston of Louisiana, and three soon-to-be-famous Americans, John Bell, David Crockett, and James K. Polk, all from the state of Tennessee.

Bates soon realized that the men who championed Jackson controlled most of the committees in Congress. Upon his own appointment to the Private Land Claim Committee, he resolved to follow a nonpartisan course as neither an administration nor a nonadministration man. He had begun to suspect that both the philosophy and the organization of the current political parties were only transitory. It therefore would be a mistake, he concluded, to enlist under any banner. Instead, he decided to act impartially, as a devoted representative of his state.[43]

[42] Gamble to Smith, August 26, 1826, General Smith Collection; Boggs to Gamble, July 24, 1826, Hamilton R. Gamble Papers; Franklin *Missouri Intelligencer*, September 21, 1826; Elihu Shepard, *The Early History of St. Louis and Missouri from Its First Exploration in 1773 to 1843*, 84.

[43] Edward Bates to Fleming Bates, May 20, 1827, Bates Papers (State Historical Society of Missouri).

True to his pledge, Bates's first action in the new Congress was to prepare a bill calling for the sale of lead mines in Missouri that, heretofore, had been leased out by the government. The Enabling Act of 1820 had reserved mineral lands in the state for the central government, which leased them out to individuals, thus providing revenue. In his bill Bates proposed sale of the land and construction of a road in the lead regions to be paid for out of the proceeds. Some months before, Barton, reporting for the Senate Public Land Committee, had recommended that the sale of these mineral areas be postponed. Since that time, however, pressures had risen within Missouri for public sale of these lands. Responding to the popular demand, Bates called for an official report on the cost of maintaining the mines and on the amount of revenue the government derived from leasing them. His efforts soon produced favorable results, and the Public Land Committee reported a bill calling for the sale of the lead mines.[44]

Despite his intention to represent Missouri impartially, political interest and private convictions soon dictated a course for Bates that was not in keeping with popular sentiment in his state. After years of frustration, Benton's graduation-donation bill, reintroduced in December, appeared attractive enough to be voted into law. The bill would reduce the price of land from $1.25 an acre, the minimum price established by the Act of 1820, to outright donation of unsold lands to actual settlers. Benton predicted that the measures of the bill would have a salutary effect on the whole country. He contended that cheap land would bring cultivators from the East to settle western areas and would stop the flow of specie to the East, thereby eliminating the necessity for a tariff on imports. Also, the Missouri senator declared that, once the bill was enacted, it would curb land

[44] *American State Papers, Public Lands,* IV, 864; U. S., *House Journal,* 20th Cong., 1st Sess., 1-2.

speculation, which profited only a few. Barton immediately replied to Benton's argument. Graduation-donation, he said, would encourage speculation instead of eliminating it. The legislation, according to Barton, would only depreciate land values and damage western economy. Not enough settlers would migrate to the West to occupy the cheap land, and the speculators eventually would enrich themselves. At the same time, Benton's plan threatened a valuable source of government revenue for the sake of a few settlers. Nor would the bill prevent the draining of specie from the West, Barton maintained, for there was no money there. He therefore offered a compromise proposal to reduce the price of land to $1 an acre minimum and after five years to donate unsold land to settlers who had cultivated it for five more years.[45]

The Benton-Barton exchange left Bates facing a problem. The Jacksonian majority in the Missouri General Assembly endorsed Benton's plan and sent instructions to Missouri's representatives in Washington to support it also. If he followed Barton, who was the only senator from the western states who opposed Benton's bill, Bates would violate the principle of instruction he was pledged to honor. Also, three years earlier, the General Assembly had sent a memorial, signed by Governor Frederick Bates, asking for a reduction in public land prices to fifty cents an acre. Yet Bates did not like Benton's idea or agree with his contention that it would increase the level of prosperity in the West. He also felt a sense of political and personal debt to Barton, who had recently secured a judgeship in Arkansas for his brother James Woodson Bates. Quickly he made his decision. Cheap lands, he said, did not attract the sturdy, more dependable cultivators from the East. Instead of letting it go so cheaply, the government should evaluate the western land carefully and give priority to residents of Missouri. In thus taking a

[45] U. S., *Congressional Debates*, 20th Cong., 1st Sess., IV, 23-27, 28-29, 484, 494, 497.

stand against Benton's graduation-donation bill, Bates identified himself with an argument that was unpopular in his
own state.[46]

When the question of the removal of Indians from the area
came up, however, Bates moved to the side of the frontiers-
men. Interest of Missourians in the removal of Indians had
heightened when President Adams declared that a treaty
of cession, negotiated by the State of Georgia, had defrauded five Creek Indian tribes of vast acreages of land.
The southern state, however, defiantly insisted it would force
the migration of Indians to the trans-Mississippi region, and
the people in the West became alarmed at the prospect of
Indian tribes being settled on lands they claimed and occupied.

In Congress, Bates pleadingly described the effects of "a
large body of Indians . . . set down in our midst." To prevent
the relocation of the tribes near his state, he recommended
the creation of an Indian territory between Canada and
the upper Missouri River. Though he hoped to prevent the
settlement of Indians in or near his state by extinguishing
their land titles south of the Missouri River, he recommended
fair treatment for the displaced tribes. As did many Jacksonians, he thought the practice of negotiating with the
Indian bands as separate nations unwise, but he agreed that
it helped protect them from unscrupulous white officials.
Carefully he avoided the constitutional question involved
in the clash between Georgia and the Adams administration.[47]

[46] *American State Papers, Public Lands*, V, 36, 588; Bates to
M. M. Marmaduke, February 2, 1829, Dr. John Sappington Manuscripts; U. S., *Congressional Debates*, 20th Cong., 1st Sess., IV,
678; Barton to Adams, April 6, 1828, in Clarence E. Carter, ed.,
The Territorial Papers of the United States, Arkansas Territory,
XX, 640, 683; Hattie M. Anderson, "Frontier Economic Problems
in Missouri," *Missouri Historical Review*, XXXIV, 192-93.

[47] U. S., *Congressional Debates*, 20th Cong., 1st Sess., IV, 1948-
50; Bates to Gamble, January 24, 1828, Gamble Papers.

In his thinking on national issues, the tariff appeared to Bates to be the most controversial issue confronting the Twentieth Congress. At first he evinced little interest in the question except to introduce a resolution calling for increased duties on lead, an important mineral in Missouri. His cursory examination led him to believe that the tariff debate was a Jacksonian scheme to maneuver New England wool interests into opposing duties on raw materials, thereby placating the antitariff South and making the party position on the tariff ambivalent. Actually, this was not the case, but Bates did not believe that Jacksonian Silas Wright had authored the bill to protect agriculture. Also, he was angry because his amendment concerning duties on lead was voted down without formal discussion. This action, he maintained, was an affront to his state, which would bear an unjust share of the financial burden. The measure, he thought, was the work of "sinister influences," intent on duping the people of the West, who "are not deeply versed in mercantile calculations." He voted against the tariff because it would "give moral offense to a large part of the United States without affording protection to the rest." In justification, he pointed to the vote of many Jackson men in the West who had reversed their original positions and voted for the tariff and to the New Englanders who had taken a stand against it. Except for the bill's "supposed connection" with the coming elections, he wrote Gamble, it would have been defeated in the House.[48]

The long-debated question of internal improvements also came up in the House. Bates clung to his conviction that

[48] U. S., *House Journal*, 20th Cong., 1st Sess., 116; U. S., *Congressional Debates*, 20th Cong., 1st Sess., IV, 2353-56; Bates to Gamble, April 30, 1828, Gamble Papers; Fayette *Missouri Intelligencer*, June 6, 1828; John A. Garraty, *Silas Wright*, 52-53, 56-57. James K. Polk, a staunch Jacksonian, opposed the tariff on the same grounds as did Bates. See Charles G. Sellers, Jr., *James K. Polk, Jacksonian, 1795-1843*, 118-19.

dividing the Treasury surplus among the states was the best way to provide for the improvements. However, as Barton, he voted for the Cumberland Road bill and the Chesapeake and Ohio Canal bill, both of which centralized internal improvements under the federal government. Congress, he wrote the editor of the Fayette *Missouri Intelligencer,* must have "internal improvement control over the soil and citizens of the state which they must assume in order to govern, protect and manage roads and canals through the several public states." His views pleased Missouri constituents who wanted internal improvements but had no preferences between a federal or state system.[49]

Bates's interest in the proposed judiciary bill was centered on its effects on the courts of the state as well as of the nation. The bill was aimed at extending the federal circuit system to the western and southern states and at reforming the Supreme Court in general. Actually, the move to revise the judicial system was a complicated one, representing in part the state-federal conflict over the jurisdiction of the courts. Most pressing was the volume of business in all of the circuit courts, where United States Supreme Court justices and district judges sat together, and in new states where the district judge, often sitting alone, decided on circuit cases. Proposals to remedy the situation were as varied as the reasons behind them. Several congressmen, among whom was Daniel Webster, wanted to maintain the supremacy of the federal court and, therefore, proposed three additional circuits and three additional justices on the bench of the Supreme Court. Advocates of state sovereignty, incensed at Marshall's assertion of supremacy over state courts and the judiciary's disruption of state relief legislation, sought only to curb the powers of the federal bench. Many called for a repeal of the twenty-fifth section of the Judiciary Act of

[49] Fayette *Missouri Intelligencer,* April 11 and July 11, 1828; U. S., *Congressional Debates,* 20th Cong., 1st Sess., IV, 1818.

1789, which provided for concurrence by a large majority among Supreme Court justices on all matters affecting state laws or court decisions. Also, most of these same advocates wanted a bill to amend the process acts of 1791 and 1792 and to make circuit courts conform to procedures followed in local courts or to those outlined in state legislation.

The complicated struggle in Congress resulted in curious coalitions of representatives of opposite views who believed the same solution would have entirely different consequences. For example, many thought that the expansion of the judiciary would increase its authority and jurisdiction, while State righters counted on the same plan to diffuse the Court's strength and decentralize its power. Some adherents on both sides of the question jointly favored a separate circuit court system for new states, each group hoping that it would achieve the contrasting results. But underneath all proposals was the fundamental question involving the expansion or reduction of the federal judiciary's power. Most Jacksonians, from Martin Van Buren of New York to Benton of Missouri, joined those who would make courts and judges more responsive to the popular will, whether it be through regulation by the state legislature or through congressional measures designed to dissipate the power of the bench and of the men who sat on it.[50]

Although the debate on the judiciary in the Twentieth Congress had many aspects, Bates concentrated on two features. First, he opposed the modification of the federal system that would place Missouri in a circuit with Kentucky or in one with Illinois, Indiana, and Ohio. Second, he spoke out against the proposal to make the processes in federal courts conform to those used in state courts or specified in state laws. He knew that many of the measures were aimed at ending ju-

[50] U. S., *Annals of Congress*, 17th Cong., 2d Sess., 29; U. S., *Congressional Debates*, 20th Cong., 1st Sess., IV, 31-35, 36-71, 90-91, 94-95, 201, 327.

dicial interference with relief legislation and at making the federal courts and judges conform more closely to local notions of legal process and justice. If the judicial process bill passed, he argued, it would decentralize the federal system and force suitors into courts that were responsive to popular sentiment and not to fundamental law. The bill, he concluded, deprived the federal tribunals of the power of execution and dangerously relegated their proceedings to the level of inferior state courts.[51]

A new aspect of the controversy over public land involved Bates in another issue of national importance during the first session. George McDuffie, John C. Calhoun's trusted lieutenant in the House, proposed the suspension of legal proceedings on all unconfirmed land claims in Missouri and Arkansas. McDuffie's suggestion came at a time when the House was reconsidering the time limitation of the act of 1824 that permitted the settlement of French and Spanish land claim cases in the district courts. Months later, Benton charged that Bates had advised McDuffie to make his proposal in order to keep the lands under government control or in the hands of wealthy landholders, and, in either case, to sell them at high prices. Bates denied these allegations in a pamphlet and explained his position on the unconfirmed land claims as one of expediency. As he saw it, many of the titles would never be confirmed, and he merely thought it ill-advised for the district court to stay in session while appeals were being made to the Supreme Court. He had recommended to McDuffie only that land claim litigation, which involved considerable expense, be suspended until the Supreme Court reached a decision on the claims. His proposed bill would allow claimants more time to file petitions instead of, as Benton charged, placing obstacles in their way. He had always supported legislation that would

[51] *Ibid.*, 2649, 2651; Bates to Gamble, February 29, 1828, Bates Papers.

grant pre-emption rights to those settlers who actually occupied the land. Deeply angered by Benton's statements,
he challenged the Senator to appear in court.[52]

His dispute with Benton over land claimants and land
came at a very inopportune time. When his pamphlet attacking Benton appeared in Missouri, he was preparing to
return to his home state and campaign for re-election in the
summer. Ignoring the possibility that Benton might have deliberately provoked him, Bates had fired a thinly disguised
volley to open the campaign. But Benton moved swiftly and
skillfully. He selected one of his staunchest followers, Spencer
Pettis, an advocate of cheap land, to oppose Bates in the
1828 race.

On his return to Missouri, Bates was not yet fully aware
of the fact that his honeymoon with the Jacksonians was
over; he decided to repeat his strategy of 1826 by campaigning
again as a "no-party" candidate. He spoke approvingly of
President Adams, but maintained that he was "no Jackson
reviler" and was "a nonpartisan in the party controversy."
Other than this appeal to the same electorate that had sent
him to Congress two years before, he had little to say until
Pettis confronted him with the question concerning public
land.[53]

Benton brought the land issue to the fore because he
thought it was Bates's most vulnerable weakness in Missouri.
In mid-July, Pettis engaged Bates in open debate at Fayette,
Missouri, revealing to him for the first time the strategy of
the Benton opposition. To Bates's dismay, Pettis delivered a
polemic on the graduation bill that delighted the largely
rural crowd. Forced on the defensive, Bates haltingly agreed

[52] U. S., *House Journal*, 20th Cong., 1st Sess., 682; Edward
Bates, *Edward Bates Against Thomas Hart Benton*, 3, 7, 11; U. S.,
Statutes at Large, IV, 52-54, 298; Bates to Gamble, April 30, 1828,
Gamble Papers.

[53] Fayette *Missouri Intelligencer*, June 20 and July 11, 1828.

to the proposition that free land might be given to those settlers who could not afford the purchase price. This obvious bit of electioneering was inconsistent with his previous statements and his identification with both Frederick Bates's and Barton's views on the subject. He was not, however, resorting to pure demagoguery. Frequently in the past he had defended claimants who pleaded "squatters' rights," and on at least one occasion he had approached President Adams about the plight of a poor landholder.[54]

Opposition from the Benton forces proved too formidable for Bates, whose record on internal improvements, Indian removal, and the right of instruction was inconsistent. His purported nonpartisanship came into question also when voters recalled his strong ties to David Barton and his obvious dislike of Benton, the Jacksonian leader in Missouri. No doubt some citizens remembered the conservative of 1820-1822 who had supported minimum salaries and life tenure for judges, and many had read or had heard of his scathing pamphlet that charged Benton with corruption. These factors practically ensured his loss of the election. The final result, however, was no humiliation, for he received 5,127 votes to 7,813 for Pettis. The 2,686-vote margin in large part represented voters who stood behind Benton's causes and candidates.[55]

Downcast, Bates returned to Washington in November, 1828, as a lameduck congressman. The Jacksonians had swept both the state and the presidential elections in Missouri, Jackson receiving 8,272 votes out of a total of 11,672. Benton now reigned as the political king of Missouri, although he

[54] *Ibid.*, July 11, 1828; C. F. Adams, *op. cit.*, VII, 546.

[55] Fayette *Missouri Intelligencer*, July 25 and August 1, 1828; James O. Broadhead, "Recollections," in A. J. D. Stewart, ed., *Bench and Bar of Missouri*, 16; John B. C. Lucas, ed., *Letters of Honorable John B. C. Lucas from 1815 to 1836*, 181; St. Louis *Missouri Republican*, September 16, 1828.

confronted the same bitter enemies. The Jacksonian victory in the state represented a revulsion against the Easterner Adams and against the "corrupt bargain" charge rather than a public expression on specific issues. Nevertheless, Bates despaired of his political future, only recently so bright. He rose in the House to proclaim, "My days on this floor are numbered and are few as a member of this body, therefore, I cannot be greatly affected by a new course that may now be adopted."[56]

In spite of his rancor, he did not slacken his efforts in the second session. Aided by both Barton and Benton, he first attended to his bill on mineral lands in Missouri. His efforts were rewarded when, in March, 1829, Congress passed a bill allowing the President to place lead mines on sale. This act resulted in the sale of lead regions in Missouri at $2.50 an acre and ended the federal policy of reserving mineral lands. It was the only major legislative victory for Bates as a member of Congress. He also introduced some new bills providing for the expeditious settlement of land claims, the adjustment of the western boundary of Missouri, and the completion of litigation of Spanish land grants involving his state.[57]

As a member of the Committee on Private Land Claims, Bates submitted a report in behalf of the St. Louis schools. Under the provisions of an act of 1812, revenue from all unclaimed, surveyed land belonging to the town was to be used

[56] Washington *National Intelligencer*, August 26, 1828; Bates to Julia, December 1, 1828, Bates Papers (State Historical Society of Missouri); U. S., *Congressional Debates*, 20th Cong., 2d Sess., V, 262.

[57] U. S., *House Journal*, 20th Cong., 2d Sess., 77; U. S., *Congressional Debates*, 20th Cong., 2d Sess., V, 8-9; Bates to John D. Coalter, January 22, 1829, Bates Papers (State Historical Society of Missouri); Bates to Gamble, February 9, 1829, Gamble Papers; Fayette *Missouri Intelligencer*, July 11, 1828; U. S., *Statutes at Large*, IV, 364.

to support the St. Louis public schools. Often, however, the St. Louis Board of Trustees had difficulty in determining which were common lands, since titles were still vested in the central government. Therefore, the board wished to hold title to all lands mentioned in the act of 1812. Bates recommended that Congress relinquish title to the tracts, and two years later, Congress passed a bill that gave the state legislature control of all the unappropriated land in St. Louis.[58]

Bates's last effort in Congress involved him in the debates over the Oregon question. Because of his rather parochial views on expansion, he joined a group of congressmen who opposed a territorial bill that would have provided for the occupation and settlement of Oregon. He objected particularly to an amendment that would give a New Orleans fur company the right to establish a colony in Oregon on land granted by the government. In the House he attacked the amendment, calling it a grant of special privilege to a private company. He pointed out that the defenseless colony would need to have military protection for its commercial operations, otherwise it would invite foreign encroachment. He suggested the dispatch of a military expedition to explore the Northwest but not to establish a settlement. It was unwise, he said, for the country to overreach itself into the Far West before the more settled areas were sufficiently populated for material growth. After presenting his arguments against the bill, he joined with a majority of the House in voting to defeat it.[59]

Bates prepared to leave Washington in March, 1829, almost convinced that at the age of thirty-six he was abandoning public life forever. On one of his last days in Congress he engaged in a fiery exchange with George McDuffie, who had ridiculed him while he was speaking. He turned, dramat-

[58] U. S., *House Reports*, 20th Cong., 2d Sess., Report 12, 1-2; U. S., *Statutes at Large*, IV, 435.

[59] U. S., *Congressional Debates*, 20th Cong., 2d Sess., V, 126-29, 192.

ically faced his tormentor, and challenged him to a duel. Surprised, McDuffie declined the duel and apologized for any conduct that might have offended the Congressman from Missouri. Trivial as the incident may have been, it indicated a return of Bates's feeling of insecurity among the forces of political upheaval. He returned home, little damaged in professional reputation, but almost an anachronism because of the recent political changes.[60]

Bates had completed his early development. His gradually formed consolidated-creditor-court beliefs marked him as a conservative nationalist of the 1820's, whether he professed Jeffersonianism or Hamiltonianism. Too, he had combined Whiggish sentiments with a spirit of western sectionalism, and both were engraved in his personality. A Westerner, Bates had no concept of state sovereignty bound to slavery, nor was he overly antagonistic toward a supposedly wicked central government. Instead, he nurtured a philosophy of economic sectionalism and conservatism on a belief in a unified constitutional system and the innate wisdom of the federal judiciary as opposed to the majority will of the uneducated masses. To him, Jacksonian Democracy represented but a brief halt in the nation's growth that nevertheless threatened the courts, the Constitution, and the harmonious relationship between federal and state governments—all parts of a mechanistic order in which he firmly believed.

[60] Bates to Julia, December 4, 1828, and January 4 and February 23, 1829, Bates Papers (State Historical Society of Missouri).

CHAPTER II

FORMATION OF A PARTY

*B*ATES returned to Missouri, concerned about his professional future and uncertain as to his political course. He moved his family, which now included six-year-old Joshua and two-year-old Nancy, to the farm in St. Charles. The occasion was not a joyous one, for the recent death of their fourth child Fanny Means Bates, who had lived only eleven months, had saddened the family. Since his political future appeared too unpromising to pursue, Bates at first decided to re-establish his practice in St. Charles and St. Louis. However, as he learned more about the unsettled political conditions, he did not long remain inactive. Within a few short months he announced his candidacy for the state senate in the elections of 1830.[1]

Because of the inchoate nature of Missouri politics and Benton's inability to consolidate completely his group's victory

[1] Columbia *Missouri Intelligencer*, August 7, 1830. Holmes Conrad Bates, the second child, died in infancy in July, 1826.

of 1828, the Jacksonian revolution had not been as widely sweeping as many had anticipated. Party organization was undergoing transition. The anti-Jackson group lacked effective leadership, but it remained vocal. Naturally, Bates stood high among those opposed to the Benton Democrats, in spite of his recent defeat for re-election to Congress. Stimulated by his own ambition and by a new realization of opportunity, he vigorously campaigned against his Jacksonian rival, Dr. Hardage Lane, for a seat in the state senate. The two major issues, the proposed constitutional amendments and the re-election of Barton, seemed almost insignificant in view of the political upheaval of 1828. Nevertheless, Bates took a strong stand against the constitutional amendments that represented the popular assault on the courts. His victory over Lane, a few weeks later, signified a personal triumph given him by voters who elected many Benton men also to the General Assembly. While lacking a real program upon which to rally a viable opposition, the young man (he was now thirty-seven years old) nonetheless inherited the responsibility of leadership without a party.[2]

Once elected, Bates surveyed the political scene in Missouri. It was indeed perplexing. David Barton, the once-powerful leader of the anti-Benton group since the days of the Missouri Compromise, now stood little chance of re-election. The Jackson men—or Democrats, as they called themselves—had 45 votes in the General Assembly as compared to 27 for those loyal to Barton. As Bates realized, the real key to Missouri politics was Benton himself. Ever since the election of 1828, the Senator's opposition had acted only in response to his public acts and positions. When Benton entered the historical 1830 Webster-Hayne debate, which began on

[2] Fayette *Western Monitor*, August 25, 1830; Thomas H. Benton to Finis Ewing, August 20, 1830, Thomas Hart Benton Papers; Bates to Julia, December 4, 1830, Bates Papers (State Historical Society of Missouri).

the public land question and ended on a comprehensive discussion of the constitutional nature of the Union, he committed his followers to the advocacy of cheap land, political alliance between the South and the West, and reduction of the tariff. Added to the Missouri Democratic platform was the Jacksonian principle of legislative supremacy, especially over the judiciary. On each of these issues, Benton and Barton had clashed repeatedly. Therefore, Barton was identified with a group that favored a restrictive land policy, a high tariff, a strong national union, and an independent judiciary. Bates found himself in the same political category, campaigning, as Barton had, against policies that Benton advocated.[3]

Turning his attention to new Democratic efforts to pass several proposed amendments that provided for more legislative control over the state supreme court, for the popular election of circuit court judges and clerks, and for the abolishment of life tenure appointments of court officials, Bates began his new career in the General Assembly. His strategy, directed from a position on the Committee on the Judiciary, sought to restrict the powers of both the pro-Jackson assembly and Governor John Miller, a close friend of Benton. While censuring the Jacksonian program as an attack on the state judiciary and on constitutional government, Bates devised an obstructionist strategy that would delay the ratification of the proposed amendments. First, he introduced a bill to increase the membership of the state supreme court and to give the justices jurisdiction of the circuit court. Again, in early December he reported out a bill to increase the number of judicial circuits. He argued both these bills on the floor as a main tactic in preventing the Jacksonians from achieving their goals.[4]

As the contending groups concentrated on the senatorial

[3] Fayette *Western Monitor,* September 15, 1830.

[4] *Senate Journal, Sixth General Assembly of the State of Missouri,* 27, 41-42, 62, 64.

race, Bates initiated a rear-guard action. Using his influence, he lined up most of the anti-Benton men behind Alexander Buckner, a declared Jacksonian who favored a protective tariff and federal regulation of internal improvements. With Buckner as candidate, Bates had little trouble persuading independents, anti-Administration men, and conservative Democrats to vote against Benton's choices.[5] He thus emerged with an impressive victory, having driven a wedge into the ranks of the Jacksonians by recruiting a conservative candidate from among them.

Bates had grown concerned over the voters' reactions. The Jacksonian movement in Missouri, he believed, grew out of the issues of the 1820's that had directed popular reaction against banks, federal tariffs, and court decisions that seemingly favored creditor groups. For Bates, Henry Clay, the Kentucky champion of the American system, symbolized the prospect of a better future much more than did the Jacksonians. For this reason Bates had attached himself to the national Republicans. Yet, he realized that the majority of voters in Missouri were attracted by the old frontier hero Andrew Jackson.

The congressional campaign of 1831 therefore presented difficult problems for a leader without a party or a platform. Many of the old opponents of Benton thought that Barton should campaign against the incumbent, Pettis. Bates was undecided. Chronic alcoholism had consumed the abilities of Barton, leaving him with little of his once great personal magnetism; another close friend, Abiel Leonard, a Fayette conservative, had many supporters in the state legislature; finally, several of the anti-Jacksonians were urging Bates himself to run. His one defeat in 1828, however, had made Bates wary. Resolutely he maintained that the rising nullification spirit in South Carolina and the tenuous South-West

[5] J. C. Edwards to Daniel Dunklin, May 16, 1831, Daniel Dunklin Collection.

alliance would split the Missouri Democratic party, thus
making victory by the opposition easy. Meeting in July in
the St. Louis town hall, Bates, along with John F. Darby,
his brother-in-law Gamble, and other anti-Jacksonians, nominated Barton as their congressional candidate in hopes that
his once great popularity was not forgotten. His platform, as
outlined by the rump convention, was the American system—
a protective tariff for domestic industries and a federal program of internal improvements. Barton accepted the nomination which placed him in the congressional race against
Pettis.[6]

Time proved that Bates had miscalculated the effects of
internal strife in the Democratic party, however. Benton's
strong Unionist stand united the factions within his own
party. By the time of the election, the Senator and other
prominent Jacksonians in the state were supporting the
President against the incipient secessionist movement in South
Carolina. Contrary to Bates's expectations, the rising cloud
of nullification proved a blessing rather than a curse to the
Missouri Democrats. It gave them the opportunity to act as
the party of national unity, aligned solidly behind the Hero
of New Orleans.

The campaign between Barton and Pettis centered on the
question of rechartering the Second Bank of the United
States, which the Clay men had pushed to the fore in Congress. Pettis attacked Nicholas Biddle, director of the bank,
while Barton defended both Biddle and the controversial
institution. Pettis' vilification of the Director angered his
brother Thomas Biddle, president of the bank's branch in
St. Louis, so violently that he challenged Pettis to a duel.
Though Pettis won the election, he had to face the younger
Biddle on the dueling field. The victory the Jacksonians had

[6] Bates to Leonard, April 4, 1831, John Stapp to Leonard, May
8, 1831, Abiel Leonard Papers; Frederick A. Culmer, "Abiel
Leonard," *Missouri Historical Review*, XXVII, 320-21.

won at the polls was taken away suddenly by Biddle's lethal bullet.[7]

The death of Pettis gave Bates an opportunity to place himself at the head of the anti-Jacksonians. He did so quickly, and in an astute move he offered William H. Ashley the opposition's endorsement in his campaign for the now vacant congressional seat. The wealthy fur baron, as Bates knew, defended the United States Bank and favored the protective tariff in spite of his Jacksonian professions. Confronted with such an aspirant on the Democratic ticket, Benton was forced to put another candidate, Robert W. Wells of Columbia, in the field. Helped by the St. Louis vote, however, Ashley had little difficulty in defeating his rival.[8] Again, Bates had scored an election victory.

Changes in the social and economic make-up of the state were, in large part, responsible for the transitional and often perplexing state of politics demonstrated in Ashley's election. By the early 1830's Missouri was growing more prosperous daily as its products found new markets. People from the East and South moved into agricultural and mineral areas of the state, making these regions more powerful politically and more sensitive to state and federal policies. St. Louis, by absorbing its share of immigrants, was changing from a town on the Mississippi River into a huge, regional market place. As it became more urban, the characteristics of the city's politics changed also, frequently in favor of those who opposed Benton's party.

Bates did not let conditions move too far ahead of him. In the General Assembly he introduced bills calling for a new penal system in the state—ironically, a reform sponsored

[7] Elihu Shepard, *The Early History of St. Louis and Missouri from Its First Exploration in 1773 to 1843*, 99-101.

[8] Miller to Dunklin, August 22, 1831, Dunklin Collection; Columbia *Missouri Intelligencer*, October 1, 1833; William N. Chambers, *Old Bullion Benton: Senator from the New West*, 179.

by the Jacksonian governor, Daniel Dunklin—and for the creation of state boards and commissions that would be responsibilities of elective county officials. Also, he grudgingly supported a measure that provided for popular election of judges and court clerks.[9]

In his community he took part in the curious temperance movement, considered by many to be one of the leading reform efforts of the day. Inspired, perhaps, by the Quakerism of his youth, he became a leading opponent of hard liquor. By 1833 his activities in the Missouri Temperance Society led to election as president of the state organization. Under his guidance the society publicized a policy of moderation toward the consumption of liquor. Bates also made the improvement of public education one of his community goals. He continued to represent the St. Louis schools in court, securing for them a twentieth share of the common lands within the city limits. Even the antislavery crusade claimed him as an active, if cautious, participant. Since the early 1820's he had been a member of the American Colonization Society. More recently, he had joined a gradual emancipationist group in St. Louis, where he frequently held long discussions on the slavery question with Elijah Lovejoy, the noted abolitionist, and Joseph Charless, the antislavery editor of the *Missouri Republican.* Though he never evidenced great enthusiasm for the antislavery cause, Bates was torn between humanitarianism and Western indifference to the moral aspects of the Negro's plight. He also considered the constitutional and economic factors involved in slavery to be very important. But the popular feeling in Missouri concerning the controversial institution lacked fervor toward the abolition of slavery. In contrast, when the anti-Masonic movement swept over Missouri at about the same time, Bates,

[9] *Senate Journal, Sixth General Assembly,* 87, 96, 142-43; James R. Sharp, "Governor Daniel Dunklin's Jacksonian Democracy in Missouri, 1832-1836," *Missouri Historical Review,* LVI, 218.

perceiving the public reaction, advised his own lodge, of which he had been elected Worshipful Grand Master for eight terms, to "cease its labors."[10]

On the major political issues of the day Bates aligned himself with Clay, whether on slavery or on the tariff. The overriding issue of 1832, however, was President Jackson's veto of the bill to recharter the Second United States Bank. The impending presidential election heightened the drama of the veto, for it created a vital national issue between those who supported Jackson and those who fell in behind Clay. By summer Bates discerned that the political excitement that flared in the halls of the Missouri General Assembly and throughout the state had momentous promise. Religiously he attended public gatherings called to discuss the burning political question between the Jacksonians and their foes. At an August meeting of the anti-Jacksonians in St. Louis, he was elected chairman of the Committee on Resolutions. His committee drafted a petition demanding that Congress override the President's veto of the bank bill. Bates wrote much of the petition directed at Benton's "hard money" platform, imputing villainy or lunacy to anyone who opposed rechartering the bank. In the petition Bates extolled the commercial advantages of the bank and its function of regulating a currency of both specie and paper money. He concluded that the continued operation of the bank was advantageous "to the commercial prosperity and individual comfort of the Western people."[11]

Realizing that the Democratic party had many pro-bank men among its members and that it had a vulnerable spot

[10] John F. Darby, *Personal Recollections,* 244-45; Henry M. Brackenridge, *Recollections of Places and Persons in the West,* 232; Garland C. Broadhead, "A Few of the Leading People and Events of Missouri History," *Missouri Historical Review,* I, 289; J. Thomas Scharf, *History of St. Louis, City and County,* II, 1778-79.

[11] Columbia *Missouri Intelligencer,* August 4, 1832.

in Benton's hard-money doctrine, Bates fully expected the Jacksonians' defeat in Missouri. Democrats, such as Governor Miller, thought a state bank the answer to Missouri's needs, while other strong partisans of Benton, such as Daniel Dunklin, clung to their faith in specie as a panacea for all financial problems. Bates decided that Benton's defeat was at hand because of this split in his own party.[12] And, the anti-Jacksonians now had some semblance of national organization. Using Henry Clay's American system as their platform and Jackson's veto of the bank bill as a call to arms, the "National Republicans" nominated the Kentucky senator to run against Jackson in the 1832 presidential election.

The results of the elections, however, gave Bates little encouragement. Because of the rural vote, outspoken Jacksonian and agrarian-minded Daniel Dunklin received a sizable majority of votes in the gubernatorial contest. A few weeks later, the pro-Democratic General Assembly convened to decide whether Benton should be re-elected to the Senate. Bates quickly devised his strategy. Since the 1820's he had developed an intense dislike for the bulky egotist who now commanded all the Jacksonian forces in his state. Bates felt that Benton was a demagogue who irresponsibly espoused popular causes like cheap land and hard money to appeal to uneducated rural voters. Too, Bates regarded Benton's interest in politics as mainly for private gain rather than for public service. He therefore selected a sensational topic. He charged that "Old Bullion," as he was called because of his advocacy of hard money, had defrauded the government in mileage allowance and had spent public funds to pay personal debts. Benton, he also alleged, had embezzled money from the Bank

[12] Miller to Dunklin, March 8, 1832, John Steele to Dunklin, April 24, 1832, William Wright to Dunklin, May 12, 1832, John Miller to Dunklin, August 27, 1832, Dunklin Collection; Clarence H. McClure, *Opposition in Missouri to Thomas Hart Benton*, 12; Sharp, *op. cit.*, 228.

of Missouri when he had been a director of that institution. Without evidence, these accusations had little effect. The Jacksonians, on the contrary, added to their triumphs. Benton received 46 votes, while the anti-Jacksonians scattered their votes among three unsuccessful candidates.[13] The presidential election dealt Bates's hopes for a sweeping anti-Administration victory a severe blow. Jackson won an impressive victory at the expense of Henry Clay and his followers who had misread the signs of popular support for the bank.

By the time of the congressional elections in 1833, Bates determinedly had regrouped his forces. Three candidates, Dr. John Bull, George Strothers, and George Shannon, all professing to be Jacksonians, were running for Missouri's seat in the Congress. Bates wrote pro-bank and protectionist-minded Bull, promising him support in the election. The contest narrowed down to Bull, whom the Democrats regarded as a "counterfeit" Jackson man, and Strothers, Benton's candidate. Having no choice of their own who could share the magic of Jackson's name, the Bates group rallied to Bull. By dividing their Democratic opponents they were able to provide Bull enough support to win the election. Bates again had outgeneraled the Bentonites.[14]

Curiously, death once more offset the political balance. In late 1833 Missouri's United States Senator, Alexander Buckner, died suddenly of cholera. Governor Dunklin immediately named Dr. Lewis Linn of Ste. Genevieve to the vacant seat in the Senate. A novice in politics, Linn, who was loyal to the principles espoused by Benton, entered his new career as a devoted ally of the Jacksonian senator.[15]

[13] *St. Louis Beacon,* November 24, 1832.

[14] Columbia *Missouri Intelligencer,* June 1, 1833; J. C. Edwards to Dunklin, May 13, 1832, Miller to Dunklin, September 16, 1832, Dunklin Collection; Jefferson City *Jeffersonian Republican,* September 7, 1833.

[15] Jefferson City *Jeffersonian Republican,* September 21, 1833.

A few weeks before, Bates had decided to test the Jack-sonian strength by campaigning for the Missouri House of Representatives. His strategy called for him to gain a seat in the lower house while his old friend Barton successfully campaigned for one in the state senate. If both won election, the old leader and the new would each sit in a house of the legislature.

During his campaign, Bates excoriated Jackson for his veto of the bank bill and attacked state Democrats for proposing the constitutional amendments. Although his farm was in St. Charles, a Democratic stronghold, he wisely reg-istered as a resident of St. Louis County, an area of anti-Jacksonian strength; he had learned more of the art of politics since his earlier experience. As a young man profess-ing the Jeffersonian faith, he had belonged to no organized party. Now, he sensed it was time to join a party, and he chose the Whigs, the followers of Henry Clay who hoped to organize the opposition against "King Andrew." Bates sincerely believed Clay's paternalistic American system offered more to the West than the Jacksonian notion of free, relatively unregulated enterprise that had produced, in his opinion, a plethora of unchecked land speculation, unsound banking activity, and political demogoguery.[16]

Bates won by a comfortable margin, but the election re-sults proved disappointing for his party. Ashley was re-elected, although Benton's candidate Albert G. Harrison de-feated his rival for the other congressional seat. In the General Assembly the Whigs gained barely one-third of the seats. Of some consolation were the victories of Bates, Henry Geyer, Abiel Leonard, and other influential Missouri Whigs, which

[16] Columbia *Missouri Intelligencer*, January 25, 1834; National Historical Company, *History of St. Charles, Montgomery and War-ren Counties, Missouri*, 193.

gave their party more strength than their numbers warranted.[17]

The first problem confronting the new session of the legislature was the election or replacement of Lewis Linn, who occupied a temporary seat in the Senate. Bates and his followers could do little to prevent Linn's election, partly because the selection of ultra-conservative Lewis Bogy to oppose him was poor. The Whigs also suffered a setback when the General Assembly turned to consider the proposed constitutional amendments. In spite of predictions that Bates would "make the Jackson boys jump," the Whigs again found their efforts futile before a numerically superior opposition. It was impossible for Bates to bring together any coalition strong enough to outvote the Jacksonians on these amendments that he thought were so unwise.[18]

To Bates, one of the most undesirable of the constitutional amendments made the popular election of circuit and state supreme court justices mandatory. His admiration for John Marshall, Joseph Story, and James Kent had grown. He had long considered a strong, independent judiciary, as championed by these jurists, a necessary ingredient of constitutional government. He viewed political interference with decision-making in judicial matters a desecration of the principle of government by law. In early 1835 he thought an example of partisan law had been revealed in a decision by popularly elected Circuit Judge Luke E. Lawless. Because of his long-held aversion to political interference with the judiciary, Bates launched a major attack on Lawless and on what he thought was the Judge's loose interpretation of the state libel law.

[17] Jefferson City *Jeffersonian Republican,* February 14, 1835; Darby, *op. cit.,* 243; Columbia *Missouri Intelligencer,* December 13, 1834.

[18] *House Journal, Eighth General Assembly of the State of Missouri,* 50, 60, 61-62, 64, 92; Jefferson City *Jeffersonian Republican,* November 20, 1834.

The climactic case producing the Lawless decision denoted the changing political conditions in Missouri. In the 1820's Lawless, then an enterprising lawyer, had unsuccessfully represented land claimants before Judge James H. Peck, a fierce admirer of John Marshall. After Lawless attacked Peck's decisions in newspaper articles, the Judge jailed Lawless and disbarred him from practice. Lawless, however, had powerful political friends, including Thomas Hart Benton. In 1830, congressional impeachment proceedings were initiated against Peck. By now the controversy had become a political matter, with Benton supporting Lawless and David Barton and Bates defending Peck. Ably represented by William Wirt, former attorney general, Peck was acquitted by a close vote in the Senate. The Judge returned to Missouri, a hero to the anti-Jacksonians, but a symbol of unpopular judicial supremacy in a frontier state. Therefore, Lawless had his day when the Democrats consolidated their power, and he was elevated to a circuit judgeship a few years later.[19]

From his new station Lawless ruled against the admissibility of truth as evidence, in a particular libel case. Charging that the old measure that permitted prosecution of defendants in libel cases, though they proved their statements were true, was unconstitutional, Bates began his attack on the Democratic judge and on what he thought to be his manipulation of justice. In a speech to the House he referred to the Lawless decision and demanded legislation protecting defendants from criminal libel indictments when they were on trial for publishing or speaking the truth. He insisted that legislation was necessary to ensure the freedom "of the pen and the press" against such instances of Jacksonian demagoguery. Attempting to make all the political capital he could out of the matter, he ignored the fact that Lawless merely had interpreted a law that long had been controversial. A constitutional amendment concerning libel would have been more

[19] U. S., *Congressional Debates*, 21st Cong., VII, 3, 45.

appropriate, but Bates and the rest of the Whigs resisted any change in the constitution.[20]

The failure to win these major political battles made Whig strategy one of obstructionist delay in the state legislature. Unable to alter the Jacksonian program and increasingly alarmed over the reduction of his party's strength, Bates turned his wrath again on his old foe. He recirculated his handbill on Benton and, along with others, hired a newspaperman to write a series of articles in the *Missouri Republican*, attacking the Missouri Democrats. Beyond the issuance of periodic reports to local party leaders, however, he had little to offer. The Whigs' minority position and their frequent tirades against the popular Benton materially damaged their public image and left them with an unimaginative program. Ironically, the positions of both parties on major issues, such as on the state bank and internal improvements, were much the same.[21]

Discouraging political signs and an illness that left him physically exhausted decided Bates against campaigning for re-election in 1835. Instead, he returned to St. Charles and resumed his law practice. Interested Democrats noticed with a sense of relief his temporary retirement from politics. Beyond a doubt, confessed the editor of the St. Louis *Missouri Argus*, he was the most powerful leader of the anti-Jacksonian party in the state. His retreat from the field of political combat signified a major defeat for the Whigs in Missouri.[22]

As he had before, however, Bates played a clever game

[20] *Ibid.*, 389, 429, 465; Jefferson City *Jeffersonian Republican*, March 14, 1835.

[21] Wilson Primm to Darby, January 31, 1835, John F. Darby Papers; John Davis to Leonard, January 16, 1835, Leonard Papers; Columbia *Missouri Intelligencer*, March 21, 1835; Jefferson City *Jeffersonian Republican*, March 7, 1835.

[22] St. Louis *Missouri Argus*, June 19 and July 17, 1835.

with his foes. By late summer he again appeared in the
thick of the fight, organizing his party to defeat Harrison,
who ran against the apostate Ashley. Again, too, he divided
the Democrats by sponsoring a third candidate acceptable
to many Jacksonians. Consequently, the conservative Ashley
was re-elected. A few weeks later, Bates's enemies attributed
to him a rumor campaign against ex-Governor John Miller,
the announced Benton candidate for Congress in 1836. Bates
had also initiated a petition movement aimed at the administration of incumbent Governor Dunklin.[23]

In 1836 Bates acted as party adviser on the issue of chartering a state bank. He journeyed to Jefferson City in an
attempt to persuade legislators that the chartering of a
state bank was unwise. He argued that such an institution
would become an irresponsible fiscal agency of the Democratic
party and that it would issue worthless paper. Also, he maintained, the chartering of new state banks weakened the
cause of those who were struggling to re-establish a national
bank. While he directed his appeals mainly to Whig legislators, he hoped they would have a desired effect on hard-
money and antibank Democrats. Without the help of their
votes, he knew, the Whigs were powerless to prevent the
chartering of a state bank.[24]

Before a decisive vote was reached on the state bank, the
Whigs suffered a defeat in the late summer elections. Lilburn
Boggs, a Benton Democrat, was elected governor, and John
Miller won the congressional seat. In November the legislature
returned Linn to the Senate. It was apparent how much the
Whigs' inability to agree on a party stand concerning the
state bank affected the outcome. The urban merchant group
looked on a state bank as a source of needed credit and had

[23] Dunklin to A. G. Harrison, August 1, 1835, Abiel R. Corbin
to Dunklin, September 18, 1835, Dunklin Collection.

[24] St. Louis *Missouri Argus,* January 22 and June 24, 1836.

little use for constitutional arguments against the institution.
Governor Boggs had added to the Whigs' discomfiture by
advocating a specie-paying bank that would issue no notes
in denominations under $20.[25] This popular plan, which
attracted many voters, also contributed to the defeat suffered
by the Whigs.

Bates now found little of immediate interest in the Whigs'
fortunes. He helped draft a party platform calling for much-
needed railroad construction in the state, but he did not
attend the Whig nominating convention. Throughout the
rest of 1836 and into 1837, he rode the circuit and devoted
most of his time to his growing law practice. Even the depression of 1837 created little in the way of political issues,
because of the state's financial stability. The scheme to
establish a subtreasury, proposed by Van Buren, stirred up
some interest because Benton championed it during the campaign. Bates's friend Abiel Leonard finally received his
chance to run against Benton, but the incumbent received
123 votes to 48 for the Whig from Fayette.[26]

More youthful leadership did give the Whigs a fresh
appeal in the 1838 elections to the General Assembly. Wilson
Primm, Abiel Leonard, William Campbell, and Charles D.
Drake—all younger Whigs—now replaced the old Barton-
Bates-Gamble hierarchy. To improve party unity, the younger
politicians eagerly organized Whig vigilante committees and
committees of correspondence throughout Missouri. In 1839
the St. Louis Committee of Correspondence produced a
useful report on state voting. According to its analysis,
300 votes had kept the Whigs from a majority position in the

[25] James N. Primm, *Economic Policy in the Development of a
Western State: Missouri, 1820-1860*, 22-24.

[26] St. Louis *Missouri Argus*, April 22, 1836, September 8, 1837,
and June 21, 1838; William V. N. Bay, *Reminiscences of the
Bench and Bar of Missouri*, 217; Thomas L. Anderson, "Autobiography"; Chambers, *op. cit.*, 231-32.

state legislature. The committee also concluded that much of the public had misunderstood Whig principles in the past. However, their platform appeared little changed from that of the Bates Whigs.[27]

The "new" Whig program of 1839 in fact affirmed the durability of the minority party as organized by Bates almost a decade earlier. Opposition to executive power, support for a national bank, federal control of internal improvements, and maintenance of an independent and stronger judiciary were virtually the principles the anti-Jacksonians had supported in 1830-1831. Some goals had been modified; for example, the new Whigs agreed to support a state bank and to settle for state-sponsored internal improvements. Many of them compromised on these issues because they felt that Bates's tactics of delay and division had stigmatized their party as one of obstruction. The defeats on specific questions outweighed the election victories, now forgotten, of those conservative candidates who had professed Jacksonianism but had acted as Whigs.

The rather severe judgment of the younger Whigs caused Bates much anguish; therefore, in 1839-1840 he grew more estranged from the party that, in Missouri, had been largely of his inspiration. He did not attend the state convention, nor did he actively participate in any of the state campaigns. Prior to the presidential election, he set out on a speaking tour in Lincoln, St. Charles, and Warren counties on behalf of the Whig candidate General William Henry Harrison. He visualized Harrison as the frontier-hero successor of Jackson and, therefore, a strong candidate. His brief return to politics ended, however, at a large Whig meeting in St. Louis at which he supported a resolution calling for the re-establishment of a national bank. After this appearance

[27] A. G. Harrison to Dunklin, March 8, 1838, Dunklin Collection; Scharf, *op. cit.*, I, 665; Palmyra *Missouri Whig*, August 3 and October 12, 1839.

he had little to do with the campaign that brought Harrison and the Whigs a much-sought-after victory and strengthened the party in Missouri.[28]

It appeared that Bates would not re-enter public life again. His sensitivity to defeat and criticism and his little-remembered reluctance to enter politics at all made his retirement appear permanent. In addition, two more children had been born into his family, and he now had to provide for a brood of four sons and three daughters. In 1842 he sold his homestead Cheveaux in St. Charles and moved into St. Louis, purchasing a larger house on North Sixth Street. He now found he had more time for his profession, his family, and community activities and became an ardent worker in the First Presbyterian Church of St. Louis. Often he displayed his talents for public speaking to various civic and religious groups.[29] It seemed almost certain that his days as an influential and active politician had ended. His leadership in the Whig ranks had been personal and opportunistic, never organizational, and he had followed Barton's strategy of responding to the policies of Benton without advancing a popular program of his own. On major issues, such as the national bank, internal improvements, and the integrity of the judiciary, he had remained steadfast. As the party increased in strength, however, his popularity waned because he could not match the more active leadership provided by the younger Whigs. At the age of forty-nine Bates already seemed the spokesman of a past generation when one successfully could hold Hamiltonian beliefs while honoring the memory of the Jeffersonian tradition.

[28] St. Louis *Missouri Argus*, May 30 and June 5, 1840.

[29] Onward Bates, *Bates et al of Virginia and Missouri*, 28; conversation with Miss Caroline Singleton Bates, December 4, 1958; Scharf, *op. cit.*, II, 1465.

CHAPTER III

REQUIEM FOR WHIGGERY

$\mathcal{D}$URING the years 1842 to 1856 Edward Bates emerged from his situation as a forgotten man in political retirement to that of a national figure purportedly of the rank of statesman. Old parties broke up, and new ones dedicated to a variety of causes were formed during these years, yet Bates clung steadfast to the Whig party. Instead of fading into obscurity, paradoxically he rose to prominence amid sectional controversy over a question he attempted to avoid—slavery and its status in the territories. Thus, Bates, the opponent of change, emerged as a nationally known politician who was sometimes mentioned for the Presidency. No great ideological struggle claimed him as a leader, and no party found in him a philosopher of distinction, yet he achieved recognition among men who led historic causes.

From 1842 to 1847 Bates worked diligently at his law practice, little noticed except by colleagues and friends. Ill fortune in land speculation and the ever-increasing demands of a large family had created considerable financial difficulty for him. Gone was the time when his success in business promised a secure future. In June of 1846 he sold much of his property in St. Charles and moved his family into a large three-story house on the corner of Sixteenth and Chestnut streets in St. Louis. Christened "Grape Hill'" because of its owner's fondness for growing grapes, the new residence accommodated his family, now grown to six sons and three daughters.[1]

At the time of his decision to relocate his family and concentrate on a more lucrative law practice in St. Louis, the Mexican War had just begun, fulfilling Bates's prediction made two years earlier. He had concluded that President James K. Polk would follow an expansionist program while adhering to a strict State rights, Jacksonian view of government. He had followed the movement to annex Texas with great misgivings and applauded Henry Clay's stand against it. Long opposed to territorial annexation, he now regarded the beginning of the war as a national calamity. He took an introspective look at what appeared to be the expansionist goals of the slaveholding South and saw the war as part of their plan. In such a scheme he envisioned a threat to the tranquillity of the Mississippi Valley.[2]

Although Bates regarded the debates in Congress on the Oregon bill through partisan eyes, he had consistently attacked designs of territorial expansion. Since his days as a congressman he had looked on advancement into the unsettled areas as a direct and unnecessary route to sectional clash over slavery. He interpreted the Mexican War as an attempt by Southern Democrats to offset the balance of political power

[1] Land Deed, April 15, 1844, Bates Papers; Bates Diary (1846-1852), June 3, 1846, Bates Papers. Bates purchased the site for the new house in 1844. When he moved, he sold his last slave.

[2] *Ibid.*, February 8, 1849; St. Louis *Daily Union*, February 25, 1847.

against them by carving out new territory that would add
slaveholding states to the Union. Much to his surprise, he
discovered his old foe Benton had similar thoughts. In early
1847, he heard his former antagonist ascribe selfish motives
to the men who supported the Mexican War. Afterward, he
reflected at length over the views of his former rival and
concluded they were his own.[3]

Bates looked on the actions of the Polk administration,
including the decision for war, as the apex of the Southern
Democratic conspiracy to gain political power. He railed at
the "mass ignorance" and at what he believed to be the
tragic shortsightedness of the Democratic party. Most important, he thought that Polk had acted unconstitutionally in
the execution of his office. "Can any reflecting man," he
asked, "fail to see that this usurpation of the war power, if
submitted to by the nation, and drawn into practice by future
presidents, is, of itself, a civil revolution?"[4] The failure of
the truce in August, 1847, convinced him that Polk planned
to use the war to make himself and his party omnipotent
in domestic and foreign affairs as well as to advance the
cause of the southern slavocracy. Presidential agent Nicholas
P. Trist's peace terms at Guadalupe Hidalgo, he prophesied,
would end in the acquisition of an American territorial empire
built on the limited and amoral aspirations of Democratic
slaveholders. Polk's unjust war of conquest portended a
threat to the constitutional balance of American government
and, moreover, a distinct blow to sectional tranquillity.[5]

The political rise of Army generals during the war also
caused Bates concern. He feared that they would be used as
figureheads in the grandiose scheme of territorial conquest.

[3] Bates Diary (1846-1852), May 16, 1847.

[4] Bates to Henry Asbury and others, September 30, 1848, Justin
H. Turner Collection.

[5] Bates Diary (1846-1852), October 12, 1847, and March 13,
1848.

With a minority of his party, he saw little to celebrate in the military victories of even the Whig generals, Winfield Scott and Zachary Taylor. If the Whig party should support military leaders who were involved in carrying on a war of selfish nationalistic purpose, he reasoned, the party would be no better than the despised Democrats who had brought about a political revolution under General Andrew Jackson.[6]

Bates's views on the war concurred fully with those held by Henry Clay's faction of the Whig party; Clay, too, believed that the Whigs should have united against expansionism. If the Whigs had stood behind Clay on the annexation of Texas, Bates was convinced, they could have carried the issue to the country and emerged victorious over their Democratic rivals. Instead, he observed, the Whig division over the annexation of Texas had contributed more to national discord than had the goals of the expansionist-minded Democrats. He deplored the Mexican War because he clearly saw that it had at once disrupted the party of Clay and excited public interest over new territories.[7]

His reviving interest in party affairs, as a result of the Mexican War, coincided with the interest in internal improvement that gained force in 1847. He accepted an appointment from the Whigs' State Central Committee as a delegate to the River and Harbor Convention held at Chicago in 1847. Called for the first week in July, the convention was the final product of nationwide discussions over measures for improvement of inland transportation and communication. Delegates from the North and West, particularly, thought the gathering necessary, as Polk had vetoed the bill for the appropriation for rivers and harbors the previous year. Knowing that Missouri Whigs were interested in a federal program of aid in improvement of the rivers and in the development of mineral resources, Bates agreed to attend the convention

[6] *Ibid.*, March 3 and May 16, 1847, and March 13, 1848.
[7] *Ibid.*, March 13 and November 12, 1848.

and help articulate Western concern. Too, he would speak
as a party man on the central issues.[8]

At first his role among the two thousand delegates from
seventeen states and territories was inconspicuous. Around
him were several nationally prominent men. Thurlow Weed,
contending for leadership of the national Whig party, was
there with his protégé William H. Seward, Senator from
New York. Horace Greeley, eccentric editor of the *New York
Tribune,* came to report the convention's activities. From the
prairie country adjacent to the Mississippi arrived rancorous
Elihu Washburne and Congressman Abraham Lincoln of
Illinois. The presence of Thomas Corwin, the Ohio Whig
leader, whom Bates personally admired, lent the gathering
still more prestige.

Bates seemed insignificant among the distinguished assem-
blage, but agreements reached in the back halls of the convention brought him recognition early; on July 5, 1847, the
delegates elected him as their presiding officer. Although the
convention members, desiring a Westerner, had settled on
him as a compromise choice, Bates could not have been more
astonished or pleased.[9] Indeed, he found it difficult to com-
pose himself as he was conducted to the platform. Making a
few introductory remarks, he haltingly pleaded for a national
program of internal improvements similar to Clay's American

---

[8] Mentor L. Williams, "The Chicago River and Harbor Con-
vention, 1847," *Mississippi Valley Historical Review,* XXXV, 607;
St. Louis *Daily Union,* March 23 and June 25, 1847; James N.
Primm, *Economic Policy in the Development of a Western State:
Missouri, 1820-1860,* 93-94; George Penn to E. D. and W. B.
Sappington, August 16, 1847, Dr. John Sappington Manuscripts;
J. Thomas Scharf, *History of St. Louis, City and County,* II, 1826-
27.

[9] Bates Diary (1846-1852), July, 1847; Robert Fergus, *Chicago
River and Harbor Convention,* 173-74.

system. His speech made little impression on the gathering, but the delegates had not expected a great oration.[10]

In his brief tenure as president of the convention, Bates attempted to expedite business by appointing executive and resolutions committees. As expected, he had to contend with several delegates who used the convention as a public forum; Abraham Lincoln, for one, delivered a speech on the constitutional basis for congressional regulation of internal improvements. Although sectional feeling touched all who spoke, the convention united to repudiate the doctrines of the convention held in 1845 at Memphis, at which the delegates had declared the territories to be possessions of individual states, not of the federal government.[11] Bates, however, thought the convention lacked central direction because of the delegates' varied local interests and private political hopes.

For his final convention speech Bates therefore decided to expound two of his favorite topics—national unity and western expansionism. He depicted the country as caught in a critical state between sectional disruption and unbounded prosperity, and he warned of the insufficiencies of party dogma in arriving at final decisions. All sections must speak for themselves, he said, but they should do so in voices of moderation and compromise, for only by statesmanlike concession could problems of slavery and territorial acquisition be solved so the nation could move on to material greatness. He advocated the building of a central transcontinental railroad as an initial step toward a national policy of improvement of communications and transportation. Obliquely he praised the position of the Whig party, but he sympathized with those

[10] John F. Darby, *Personal Recollections,* 398-99; Charles Gibson, "Edward Bates," *Missouri Historical Society Collections,* II, 54; Williams, *op. cit.,* 609; *New York Tribune,* July 17, 1847; Fergus, *op. cit.,* 50.

[11] Williams, *op. cit.,* 610; *Hunt's Merchant Magazine and Commercial Review,* XVII, 217; *American Review,* VII, 120; Donald W. Riddle, *Congressman Abraham Lincoln,* 17.

who stood on constitutional grounds against a federal system of internal improvements.[12]

Bates made a lasting impression on many of the delegates with his speech. John F. Darby, a former mayor of St. Louis, saw the short, squat man, whose bearded jaw thrust forward from a face distinguished by a gleaming, broad forehead, as the undeniable leader of the West. Horace Greeley thought that Bates would be one of the foremost candidates in the next presidential election. Wealthy New Yorker Philip Hone described the Missourian's performance as "beautiful beyond description, brilliant and tasteful as Crittenden, seductive and captivating as Clay, powerful and convincing as Webster. I never heard ideas expressed in language so appropriate." Thurlow Weed wrote, "We [the delegates] look forward with confidence to the political revolution which will restore Edward Bates to public service. The nation cannot afford to be deprived of so much integrity, talent, and patriotism." Bates himself concluded that his speech had gained him a "higher standing in the nation."[13]

Immediately after the convention was adjourned, Bates, excited over his newly acquired prestige, decided to accompany several delegates on a cruise of the Great Lakes. On board the pleasure boat *Saint Louis,* they talked for hours while consuming large quantities of chicken, lobster, and trout, washed down with ample portions of champagne. Bates told Weed, Corwin, Hone, and the others that he had felt compelled to make a significant speech at the convention because of the importance he attached to internal improve-

[12] St. Louis *Daily Union,* July 15, 1847; *New York Tribune,* July 15, 1847.

[13] Bates Diary (1846-1852), July, 1847; Horace Greeley, *Recollections of a Busy Life,* 247; Paul M. Angle, ed., "The Western Trip of Philip Hone," *Journal of the Illinois State Historical Society,* XXXVIII, 287; Fergus, *op. cit.,* 174; Blaine B. Gernon, "Chicago and Abraham Lincoln," *Journal of the Illinois State Historical Society,* XXVII, 249.

ments in preserving national peace. This topic and the vigor of other animated conversations kept the Missouri Whig outdoors too long, however. He became ill with a severe head cold and was forced to retire to his cabin.[14]

Bates returned to St. Louis and enthusiastically resumed his practice of law. Inspired by his national recognition at the Chicago convention, he began writing a series of newspaper articles denouncing the Mexican War and the Polk administration in pacifistic terms. Because he now felt more personally involved in political developments, he made frequent trips to attend state supreme court sessions in Jefferson City and talked with prominent legislators about the issues of the day.[15]

Early in 1848 news reached him that the Whigs were once more about to abandon their old hero Henry Clay to make way for the popular Whig of the day, Zachary Taylor. Clay's indecisiveness on the annexation of Texas had alienated many in both wings of the Whig party. After reflecting on the new development, Bates prudently decided to sacrifice principle for expediency and switched his support to Taylor, the victorious general of the Mexican War. In speaking at public gatherings, he avoided the whole question of "military dictatorship" by quoting Taylor's views on government and citing his publicized respect for Congress. He frequently pointed out that Taylor was a moderate on the questions of slavery and territorial expansion and, because of his popularity, an asset to the Whig party in its struggle against the Democrats. Apparently, he did not wish the voters to recall that only a year before he had criticized Clay's enemies as the war group.[16]

[14] St. Louis *Missouri Democrat,* January 17, 1861; Angle, ed., *op. cit.,* 287; *New York Tribune,* July 23, 1847; Fergus, *op. cit.,* 170, 174.

[15] Bates Diary (1846-1852), October 12, 1847.

[16] *Ibid.,* February 8, 1847, and January 30, March 13 and 14, and April 23, 1848; Columbia *Missouri Statesman,* March 3, 1848.

Convinced of the wisdom of his choice, Bates presided over several Taylor meetings in Missouri during the 1848 campaign. Frequently, he attacked Polk's "constitutional violations" and expansionist policies and implored his audiences to vote for Taylor in order to save the country from power-hungry Democrats. His vigorous efforts did not long go unrecognized by many of his fellow Whigs, who hoped he could be lured back into politics. In late April, the Whig state convention took the first step in reviving Bates's political career by nominating him as their vice-presidential candidate.[17]

In addition to lending his oratorical talent to the Taylor cause, Bates wisely had aligned himself with the younger element of the national Whig party. He thought the new leaders, such as Seward, Weed, Corwin, and Alexander Stephens, were opposed to making slavery a national question and thus presenting the voters with a divisive problem. Privately, he felt these Whig men of distinction had to clarify the issue of congressional supremacy, as opposed to State rights, in the territories. If congressional right to exclude slavery from the territories could not be established, he believed the southern slaveholding expansionists would interdict free, white migration into the West and ultimately arouse hostility in the North. Therefore, he endorsed the Wilmot Proviso to prevent slavery, either in the form of an abstract argument or a historical force, from making the territorial West an exclusive rural domain of southern slaveholders who, he thought, would deny it the benefits of modern progress. He looked hopefully to the younger leaders to

[17] Columbia *Missouri Statesman,* April 14, 1848; Bates Diary (1848-1852), February 22 and April 5, 1848; *Liberty Weekly Tribune,* April 21, 1848.

implement a plan of controlled expansionism and constitutional containment of slavery.[18]

By the end of the campaign his public speaking efforts had strengthened the voice of the Missouri Whigs and had advanced the party image of national unity. He transformed the Whig Central Committee from an ineffective, resolution-making body into an active, influential junto and persuaded prominent Whigs, such as Abiel Leonard, James S. Rollins, and John F. Darby, to exert greater efforts in the party's behalf. By the time of Taylor's victory, many politicians, including Thurlow Weed, were recommending Bates for a post in the Cabinet because of his leadership in Missouri. The Missouri General Assembly forwarded a petition to President-elect Taylor virtually demanding the honor for the western Whig leader.[19]

Though he openly joked about a Cabinet post for himself, Bates privately encouraged young Charles Gibson to organize a "Bates-for-the-Cabinet" drive. Gibson, an ardent admirer and close political adviser of Bates, had been one of several young men who had studied law in Bates's St. Charles office-home. Also, he had become a member of the immediate family by marrying one of Hamilton R. Gamble's daughters. Eagerly he accepted his task, for he was determined to bring about Bates's appointment to the Taylor cabinet and, perhaps, advance his own political fortunes. The hopes of both Gibson

[18] Bates Diary (1846-1852), August 5, 1848; Bates to Justin H. Turner and others, September 30, 1848, Turner Collection; Bates to George H. Stone, September 6, 1848, in *New York Tribune*, April 28, 1860. This letter came to light twelve years later, when Greeley published it to aid Bates in his attempt to win the Republican presidential nomination.

[19] John Richardson to Leonard, December 11 and 15, 1848, Abiel Leonard Papers; Bates Diary (1846-1852), December 2, 1848, and February 3, 1849; Jefferson City *Jefferson Inquirer*, December 9, 1848; C. F. M. Noland to Darby, December 25, 1848, John F. Darby Papers; Columbia *Missouri Statesman*, December 29, 1848; *Liberty Weekly Tribune*, January 5, 1849.

and Bates proved fruitless, however. Reflecting on the incident years later, Gibson concluded that Bates was ignored by Taylor because the President-elect was dominated by eastern Whig politicians with strong antislavery leanings. Bates himself commented sourly on Taylor's final Cabinet selections, noting that the President had failed to include anyone from the Mississippi Valley. Privately, he realized that this failure had done great damage to the Missouri Whigs, who sought a mediator to reconcile the warring factions of their party.[20]

In spite of Taylor's rejection, Bates re-entered politics. The impending split in the Democratic party had created the most dramatic setting in Missouri politics since Jackson's election in 1828. Thomas Hart Benton now faced a group of intransigent and organized Democratic rivals who were determined to discredit him in his own party. His opposition to the Mexican War and his support of the Wilmot Proviso, accompanied by severe attacks on proslavery expansionists, had precipitated a disruption of the Democratic party in Missouri. Prior to his campaign in 1850 for re-election to the Senate, Benton's enemies launched a slanderous, vitriolic crusade against him. Led by Claiborne Fox Jackson, the slaveholding elements in the legislature adopted a series of resolutions that denied the constitutional power of Congress to exclude slavery from the territories. The legislators demanded endorsement of these resolutions by Missouri's congressmen and senators. As many knew he would, Benton refused to obey the legislature's edict and appealed directly to the people.[21]

Grudgingly, Bates acknowledged his admiration for the Senator in the intraparty struggle. Benton's preference for a

[20] Gibson Diary (1848-1897), Easton R. Gibson, ed., "Gibson Autobiography," Charles Gibson Papers; Bates Diary (1846-1852), March 3, 1849.

[21] William N. Chambers, *Old Bullion Benton: Senator from the New West*, 341-42, 348-52.

central railroad route over a northern or southern one and
his avid concern for western commercial growth as a solution
to the sectional conflict closely paralleled his own views. In
October, 1849, Bates again made a special trip to the rotunda
of the St. Louis Courthouse to hear the Senator deliver the
speech that ended in his famous peroration on a western "passage to India." Pleased by what Benton said, Bates approached
him afterward and for the better part of an hour talked to
him about the proposed railroad terminus in Missouri with
branch lines extending into the South and the West. He also
sounded out Old Bullion on the growing sectional crisis in
order to learn more about his views.[22]

The mounting controversy in Missouri between freeholders
and slaveholders, resulting from the debates in Congress over
admission of California and organization of New Mexico
and Utah as territories, motivated Bates to consider a Whig-
Benton alliance. For a while he thought of actively campaigning for Benton in his race for the Senate, hoping to defeat
the proslavery group in the state legislature. However, he
realized that he still had differences with Old Bullion, and
he could not easily forget the bitterness of their former struggles. Much to Bates's dismay, Benton denounced the proposed
compromise bill every time he spoke in public. Bates favored
the controversial bill, partly because it was sponsored by
Henry Clay, but mainly because he felt that it would still
the agitation that was rising over slavery and allow the country to get on with material progress. The omnibus bill, reported out of committee, provided for the admission of California as a free state, for the territorial organization of New
Mexico and Utah, for the settlement of the Texas-New Mexico
boundary line, for the passage of a federal fugitive slave law,
and for the abolition of slavery in the District of Columbia.
Bates believed these proposals offered a program on which

[22] Bates Diary (1846-1852), January 11, February 15, and
October 24, 1849; Chambers, *op. cit.*, 353.

both northern and southern moderates might compromise and, more important, eliminated the chief causes of sectional agitation. If Benton continued to object to the bill, he thought there could be no *rapprochement* between the moderates in their respective parties.

Taylor's insistence on the admission of California as a free state before any other compromise measures were considered, delayed action on the compromise bill. Clay and Webster, the Whig giants who with Calhoun had dominated the Senate for decades, were making one last effort to put the compromise bill through. Talk of secession and the demands of southerners for federal protection of slavery in the territories, however, served as warnings of an impasse.[23] In mid-July, as the debate raged, Taylor suddenly died. Vice-President Millard Fillmore, an old-line Whig who favored the bill, stepped into the Presidency. More at home among the conservative element of his party, Fillmore began to reorganize the Cabinet. Recognizing Bates as the party spokesman in the West and a champion of the compromise moderate enough to be accepted in the North, Fillmore offered him the position of Secretary of War.[24]

Bates seriously considered the advice of both Gamble and Gibson to join the new Cabinet in order to help revive the moribund party in Missouri. He had many private reservations, however, over the consequences of the pending compromise and the legislation on fugitive slaves. The salary for a member of the Cabinet was only $6,000 a year, an amount hardly sufficient to provide for a large family. Beyond these considerations, Bates believed that his political fortunes appeared to be better on the state level than on the national

[23] Bates Diary (1846-1852), August 23, 1849, and March 6, 1850.

[24] J. B. Crockett to Darby, July 27, 1850, Darby Papers; William O. E. Griffis, *Millard Fillmore*, 57-59.

level. These factors outweighed his friends' urgings, so he declined Fillmore's offer.[25]

Bates did not abuse Fillmore's graciousness, however. In late July, he, Julia, and the younger members of the family departed for White Sulphur Springs, Virginia. An infant daughter had died a short time before, so Bates decided to combine his political mission with a vacation for Julia. After a brief visit to the old Bates homestead in Goochland County, they traveled on to White Sulphur Springs. Here Bates left his family and went quickly to Washington to see Fillmore. The President gave him a cordial reception, and to Bates's mild surprise, offered him the post of Secretary of the Interior. Although he found this position even more difficult to refuse than that in the War Department, Bates declined again. Nevertheless, he assured Fillmore of his personal loyalty as well as that of the Missouri Whigs.[26]

Upon his return to Missouri Bates found the Whigs' situation deteriorating in the midst of Benton's fight for his political life. Privately he had feared as much, but he had prepared no plan of action. "If the Whigs of the West would only be true to themselves, and refuse firmly to take sides in the sectional controversies," he wrote in his diary, "they might soon have disposed of the main questions of government in their own hands."[27] Unwilling to make a sudden decision, he implored the moderate Whigs to "stand firm and reject an alliance with the Southern Democrats." As was to be expected, his admonitions had little effect on the anti-Benton Whigs in the legislature, who regarded Bates as a senior

[25] "Gibson Autobiography," Gibson Papers; Bates to Fillmore, August 1, 1850, Millard Fillmore Papers; St. Louis *Missouri Intelligencer*, August 12, 1850.

[26] Bates Diary (1846-1852), August 27, 1850; Bates to J. Kennedy Furlong, June 25, 1856, Horace Greeley Collection; *New York Times*, February 17, 1860.

[27] Bates Diary (1846-1852), November 27, 1850.

orator rather than as a party leader. The Whigs chose Henry
S. Geyer to face Benton, and the proslavery Democrats placed
James S. Green in nomination for the Senate seat. Factional
balloting resulted in a three-way tie between Benton, Geyer,
and Green. Hopelessly deadlocked, the legislative session carried over into 1851.[28]

Unfortunately, Bates had learned little from Clay's failure
to resolve within his own party the question of slavery.
Bates's decision to treat the slavery issue as a limited, sectional one was unfortunate, coming at a time when he might
have persuaded his own state party to coalesce and to deal
a severe blow to the Democratic proslavery forces in Missouri. Instead, he failed to assume effective control of party
organization, in the face of proslavery opposition, and resorted to an outmoded tactic: He sent a wordy memorandum
to Whig representatives, urging them to abandon Geyer and
vote for Benton. But he acted too late and with too little
conviction. After the thirty-ninth ballot, Geyer sent out a
public letter repudiating congressional control over the territories. The move brought proslavery Democrats to his support, and on the fortieth ballot, he received a sufficient number of votes to end Benton's thirty-year tenure in the Senate.[29]

The election dealt the moderate Whigs a stunning blow.
Bates fatalistically accepted it as a decisive defeat of the
entire Whig party by proslavery forces, but he remained
silent. Any hope he might have entertained for a moderate
Democrat-Whig coalition appeared lost. The Whigs now were
left with a schism within their party ranks and with leaders
who either hoped to maintain the Union with slavery or were
willing to make the sectional issue the basis of a new political
organization. Geyer, who proved to be completely in sym-

[28] *Ibid.*, December 22, 1850, and January 11, 1851; St. Louis
Missouri Republican, December 3, 1850.

[29] Bates Diary (1846-1852), January 23, 1851; William Mc-
Pherson to Darby, January 3, 1851, Darby Papers.

pathy with Southern Democrats, alienated the moderate Whigs so seriously that the demise of the whole party seemed certain.[30]

Bates quickly consulted with other Whig leaders of Missouri who were concerned over the party's future. Soon after the election he attended a meeting called in St. Louis by James O. Broadhead, one-time law pupil under Bates and now a prominent member of the bar and a state legislator from Pike County. Bates attended the meeting in order to urge the establishment of an orthodox party newspaper in St. Louis in the hope that the old Whig unity could be restored. By now he was completely disillusioned with the Whig "bargain" that had resulted in Geyer's election, and he was in a fighting mood. Staunch Geyer Whigs, he counseled, must be made to appear as proslavery Democrats, out of step with the Fillmore administration. If the moderates remained united and firm on accepted party principle, however, the breach between many of the proslavery and antislavery Whigs might be closed. This unrealistic hope represented as much optimism as he could generate over a gloomy situation. It also indicated that Bates, whether he realized it or not, had passed the point of compromise.[31]

The one issue on which Bates felt the Whigs must unite was the transcontinental railroad. As did Clay, he based much of his hope for the nation's future on the material prosperity of the West and on the promise of a burgeoning population of free white laborers migrating from both the North and the South. Realizing that the development of a great national economy was taking place, he envisioned a manufacturing and commercial society in the Mississippi Valley. Somewhat incongruously he set a course against the territorial expansionism that had resulted from the Mexican War,

[30] Bates Diary (1846-1852), January 11, 1851.

[31] R. E. Terry to Leonard, March 3, 1851, Broadhead to Leonard, March 16, 1851, Leonard Papers; Darby, *op. cit.*, 398.

for he still feared the spirit of "manifest destiny" as a dangerous frenzy that stirred up sectional hostilities. As did most Whigs, he believed in an organic concept of popular sovereignty bestowed upon a government to act on its own initiative in behalf of the people. He proposed what he had long considered a practical solution: The federal government must check territorial annexation, exclude slavery from the western areas, and embark on a program of internal development to restore national prosperity and tranquillity.[32]

Bates clarified his views in 1851 in a speech delivered on the Fourth of July in Jefferson City, celebrating the beginning of the Pacific Railroad. "Liberty cannot exist except under government of law," he said. But theory had to have practical application, he told his listeners,

> for it is idle to talk about law to hunger and nakedness, it is a waste of argument to reason about order to men who have just enough light to see the darkness of their path and just enough liberty to feel the degradation of their lot. Constitutions and statutes cannot fill their bellies, nor cover their beds, nor moralize their hearts, nor humanize their manners. . . . Our nation . . . stands a giant among the nations of the earth. Our flag floats with honor in every port. Our commerce whitens every sea and the love of our country is published in thunder around the globe and all these blessings are the fruits of that glorious Constitution.

Here, at the end, he made his thematic point: Constitutional government was threatened by secession and war; if the Mississippi Valley, united and prosperous, developed its resources, it would have enough political and economic power

[32] Bates to John Law and others, in St. Louis *Missouri Republican*, December 3, 1850; Bates Diary (1846-1852), January 1, June 29, July 1, and December 31, 1850.

to command the easing of tensions and the elimination of prejudices peculiar to the "old Eastern world."[33]

Eloquence did not provide enough suitable leadership in the sectional conflict that was rapidly approaching a climax over the questions of fugitive slaves and territorial expansion. Before he spoke at the Fourth of July celebration, the Supreme Court of Missouri had listened to arguments presented in the crucial Dred Scott case. Scott, a slave living in Missouri, claimed his freedom on the grounds that he had once resided with his owner in the free state of Illinois and in the Minnesota Territory, both north of the Missouri Compromise line. The case set in motion a series of events that were to make Bates's words almost meaningless and his views on slavery conservative.

Bates perceived that the proslavery justices of the supreme court intended to use Dred Scott's case as a *modus vivendi* to overrule previous decisions that granted freedom to slaves under the provisions of the 1787 Northwest Ordinance. Hamilton R. Gamble, who now sat on the court after having dissolved his partnership with his brother-in-law, furnished Bates with firsthand reports of the case. Gamble's analysis convinced Bates that the case involved a bargain between two of the justices and the anti-Benton Democrats and Geyer Whigs. Aroused, Bates urged his former partner to act. Gamble thereupon wrote a memorable opinion that advocated adherence to precedents in similar cases in which slaves had been granted their freedom, but he was the lone dissenter. The other two members of the court ruled that Scott was subject to the laws of Missouri and not of Illinois or of the Minnesota Territory.[34]

[33] Edward Bates's speech at Pacific Railroad Celebration, July 4, 1851, Bates Papers; Jefferson City *Jefferson Inquirer,* July 19, 1851.

[34] Bates Diary (1846-1852), January, 1852; Vincent C. Hopkins, *Dred Scott's Case,* 16-18.

Bates realized the probable consequences of the Dred Scott case: It would focus national attention on the most basic point of slavery. He knew he must speak out in late April when the Whig state convention met in Columbia to decide on party nominees for both local and national offices. In a bold attempt to prevent Bates's nomination, the Geyer Whigs introduced a resolution that would have compelled all candidates to endorse the principle of slavery extension or, as the Dred Scott decision indicated, the right of southern slaveholders to take their property with them wherever they chose. Led by Broadhead, the moderate Whigs refused to accept the resolution and, as a counterstroke, placed Bates in nomination for Vice-President on the national ticket. Floor debates between the opposing factions shifted quickly to the proposed candidate's views on the Compromise of 1850. Dramatically, Benjamin Tompkins, a St. Louis Whig, produced a letter Bates conveniently had sent him and read it to the convention. It proved to be an unqualified avowal of the right of Congress to legislate for the territories and a reaffirmation of both the Missouri Compromise and the Compromise of 1850. Hoping not to frighten away conservative delegates, Bates denied that he was a free-soiler, and he castigated the efforts of Northern "ultras" to increase the North's political dominance over the South. Although a calculated risk, the letter swayed the doubtful delegates and gave the moderate Whigs enough votes to nominate Bates for the Vice-Presidency. The convention fight, however, had clearly divided the Whigs over the dangerous question of slavery extension.[35]

Bates's private sentiments were more complex than those he set forth in his letter to Tompkins. He feared more than

[35] Palmyra *Missouri Whig*, March 25, 1852; Columbia *Missouri Statesman*, April 30, 1852; Bates Diary (1846-1852), addition to entry of April 20, 1852; James Winston to Leonard, May 18, 1852, Leonard Papers.

ever that southern extremists had fashioned, beginning with the Mexican War, a conspiracy to establish a slave confederation. He thought the radicals were so heartened by their continued success that many of them planned to seize control of the federal government and nationalize slavery. If they could repudiate the right of Congress to legislate over the territories, it would be the crucial step in their grand design. What concerned him most was the absence of a strong national party to prevent such a calamity. One must be formed, or the moderate Whigs revitalized, he felt, in order to support the right of Congress to exclude slavery from the territories.[36]

Bates left Missouri in May on another political journey, well camouflaged as a vacation in South Carolina for Julia and Richard. After a pleasant stay in the Palmetto State, where he attempted to gauge the extent of southern radicalism, the three traveled to Virginia. Following a familiar pattern, Bates left his wife and son to call on Fillmore in Washington. His visit was preceded by that of a St. Louis friend, Dr. William Carr Lane, and his self-appointed agent Charles Gibson, who had toured the South to talk to various political leaders before going to Washington for a conference with Senator Thomas Corwin. The aim of Lane, Gibson, and Bates was to determine the level of Whig strength in the South and to learn what the reaction in Washington would be to Bates's candidacy for the Vice-Presidency in 1852. Apparently all found that conditions afforded a degree of hope. On his return to Missouri, Bates appeared happier and "much improved in health."[37]

[36] Bates Diary (1846-1852), March 6, June 29, and July 1 and 29, 1850, and May 31, 1851.

[37] Bates Diary (1846-1852), June 5, 1852; Bates to Fillmore, May 29, 1852, Fillmore Papers; Bates to Corwin, June 17, 1852, Thomas Corwin Papers; J. H. Means to John D. Coalter, January 8, 1853, Coalter to Mrs. Claudia Means, September 17, 1852, Bates Papers.

Bates's bid for second place on the Whig national ticket was consistent with his belief that only Fillmore and others like him could preserve national harmony and the Compromise of 1850. As Fillmore, Bates thought that the slavery issue eventually could be solved by the colonization of Negroes who would be freed gradually. James O. Broadhead took these thoughts with him when, at the head of the Missouri delegation, he journeyed to Baltimore in June for the Whig national convention. However, William H. Seward, directing the strategy of the antislavery wing, outmaneuvered Fillmore's followers and secured the presidential nomination for General Winfield Scott. Even then, Broadhead and his friends managed to keep Bates's name before the convention and win 97 votes for him on the first ballot in the vice-presidential contest. Revealingly, only delegates from Arkansas, Kentucky, Missouri, and Virginia, among the southern states, voted for Bates, a scant 20 per cent of the total count he received. Many of the delegates felt, however, that a reconciliation with the Fillmore men had to be reached. On the second ballot William A. Graham, Fillmore's secretary of state from North Carolina, was unanimously chosen as the party's vice-presidential candidate.[38]

Bates displayed little enthusiasm for General Scott at the head of the Whig ticket. The subsequent election of the Democrats' dark horse Franklin Pierce and his "young America" followers made Bates all the more fearful that the spirit of southern expansionism had won, and that a territorial conquest of Cuba, Puerto Rico, and the West Indies would begin. Furthermore, he thought that the Democratic victory meant political domination by the forces of southern slavery and the loss of federal internal improvements to strengthen the country's unity. Instead of the fulfillment of his Hamilton-

[38] *New York Tribune,* June 17 and 26, 1852.

like vision, he darkly pictured a fierce sectional struggle for economic and political supremacy.[39]

The Whigs' failure in 1852 also altered Bates's plans for the future. Happily, he hit upon a project that would require both his professional and his political skills by deciding to run for the judgeship of the St. Louis Land Court in the summer of 1853. His services as an elder in the Central Presbyterian Church and as president of the Missouri Colonization Society had added to his prominence in social and professional circles, which in turn enhanced his chances in the local election. Realizing how well qualified Bates was for the land court, the Democrats hurriedly selected Franklin A. Dick as the opposition candidate and launched a campaign against their old nemesis. They declared Bates disqualified because of his involvement in nineteen of the twenty cases pending before the land court, a fact the Whig candidate could not deny. But Bates wisely had not sought a party's nomination; he ran as an independent, campaigning vigorously among the German voters in St. Louis, who generally opposed large landholding interests. In August he won easily and joined five other Whigs in victory, his party having captured six of eight county offices.[40]

In early fall the new judge convened the land court in its small room above the county collector's office on Chestnut Street. He heard many cases involving land claims, often of staggering complexity. It did not take him long to establish a reputation as a fair jurist who carefully circumscribed the land court's jurisdiction. On one occasion be exercised his authority to reverse an old decision by the circuit court that judgment could be entered against the contractor for the property as well as against the property. But he avoided

[39] Bates Diary (1846-1852), November 3, 1852.

[40] St. Louis *Missouri Democrat*, May 9, 10, 18, and 21, July 13 and 30, and August 3, 1853; A. Todd to Darby, July 28, 1853, Darby Papers; Bates Diary (1846-1852), March 17, 1852.

political entanglements; in later years he looked on his experience in the land court as one of the most rewarding of his life.[41]

Bates's involvement in the land court did not deter him completely from engaging in the party controversy over the transcontinental railroad issue, which had now grown more heated. In Missouri, the Whigs advocated a federally subsidized program to aid private companies in constructing the route, while the Democrats wanted state appropriations for financially deficient railroad enterprises. The controversy involved more than partisan politics. After the legislature chartered the Pacific Railroad Company in 1849, many of Bates's Whig friends bought up land that had been set aside by Congress for the construction of their railroad, hoping to resell it for a large profit. Bates, however, was not involved in the scheme; he supported the program of federal funds in order to assure the construction of a railroad route to the Pacific.[42]

By the time of the 1854 elections, the railroad question had outgrown the bounds of local political and pecuniary interest and had become part of the complex question of territorial organization. Senator Stephen A. Douglas of Illinois introduced early in the year a bill to organize the Nebraska Territory, reputedly in order to facilitate the construction of a central railroad route and to push the settlement of western lands. Originally, he hoped to avoid the question of slavery extension, but he had to recognize it in an amended version of the bill that respected the sensibilities of antislavery men in regard to the Missouri Compromise and of proslavery men in regard to property rights of southerners. Douglas pro-

[41] St. Louis *Missouri Democrat*, October 14, 1853; Bates Legal Memorandum Book (1849), Bates Papers.

[42] Roy E. Riegel, "The Missouri Pacific Railroad until 1879," *Missouri Historical Review*, XVIII, 9; Richard Edwards and M. Hopewell, *Edwards' Great West*, 415.

posed to leave the problem of slavery to the territorial legislatures—the famous doctrine of "popular sovereignty"— thus allowing the inhabitants of an area to decide for or against slavery. This ambiguous portion of the bill led to lengthy debates and counterproposals, including one by Missouri's Senator David Rice Atchison on federal protection of slavery in the territories and against its prohibition there, a guarantee he himself claimed for his proslavery constituents. Under pressure, Douglas introduced amendments that in effect would establish the rule of local determination and thus void the understanding reached in the Missouri Compromise.[43]

As did many leaders in Congress, Bates looked upon the Douglas bill and its subsequent alterations as monumental errors of judgment. He predicted that the Douglas measure, if passed, would split Democrats and Whigs by abrogating the principles of both the Missouri Compromise and the Compromise of 1850. Thus, it would lay the emotion-packed issue of slavery before the people as the most basic national question, and the delegation of power to local legislatures would render Congress helpless to solve it. Commercial and geographical expansion would become a struggle for political and economic supremacy between the North and the South. Therefore, a deep despair filled him when the Kansas-Nebraska Act, as it came to be called, became law in May. As if on cue, proslavery political forces united dramatically in Missouri, leaving the free-soil Whigs stultified and Bates confronted with an issue he had hoped to avoid.[44]

[43] Frank H. Hodder, "The Railroad Background of the Kansas-Nebraska Act," *Mississippi Valley Historical Review*, XII, 11; St. Louis *Missouri Democrat*, June 13, 1853; Primm, *op. cit.*, 109-10, 112-13; William E. Parrish, *David Rice Atchison of Missouri: Border Politician*, 138; Roy F. Nichols, "The Kansas-Nebraska Act: A Century of Historiography," *Mississippi Valley Historical Review*, XLIII, 204-5.

[44] *Liberty Weekly Tribune*, February 20, 1854.

Bates was tired, his nerves frayed by anxious days of worry over the national political vacuum and over what he believed to be the conspiratorial designs of the proslavery radicals. In his efforts to avoid the choices presented by the territorial act, he chanced on an extreme solution. As did many other Whigs, he turned temporarily to the embryonic American or "Know-Nothing" party as the only way to prevent the controversy over slavery from becoming the most important issue in American national life.[45]

Although the eastern wing of the American party preached racial and ethnic intolerance, Bates was no bigot. He had in fact held the "Know-Nothings" partly responsible for breaking up the Whig party in the late 1840's. While he had exhibited a mild distrust of foreigners and foreign institutions, he had never become a fanatical nativist. His purpose in joining the party was one of sheer political expediency. He saw himself joining a fusion of Whigs and Know-Nothings that would help make the American party in the West a force opposed to the extension of slavery. If conservatives who opposed the principles of the Kansas-Nebraska Act wished to call themselves Americans and champion a nativist cause, he had few objections. The feelings of ethnic minorities mattered little when the larger issue of national union was at stake. By enlisting with the Know-Nothings, however, he was committing a political blunder which was to be costly a few years later.[46]

Bates found perplexing the needs to take a stand against slavery—without appearing to do so—and to formulate a party position—without an organization. He had to think of his own future as well. With his tenure in the land court at an end, he needed to weigh seriously the proposals that he run for the Senate. Once there, some of his friends suggested,

[45] Bates to John A. Bross, July 31, 1854, Abraham Lincoln Collection (Chicago Historical Society).

[46] Bates Diary (1846-1852), February 25, 1847, and February 22, 1848; St. Louis Missouri Democrat, August 1, 1854.

he might exercise real leadership over his Missouri followers. His political situation was not clear, however. A private poll of Whig legislators in Jefferson City, conducted by Gibson, revealed that many were opposed to Bates because of his alleged free-soil tendencies. This knowledge confirmed Bates's own conclusions that he could not risk being identified with the rising antislavery Republican party, still quite unpopular in Missouri. He knew several Whigs preferred the more conservative Know-Nothings. The old Whig Central Committee, in fact, remained distinctly cool to a senatorial seat for their one-time leader.[47]

For a while, though, Bates acted suspiciously like a candidate, retaining the support of staunch Whig friends, such as Abiel Leonard and James S. Rollins. By early 1855, however, he reached the conclusion that the risks involved in a race for the Senate were too great and the odds too high against him. Dramatically, Bates ruled out his candidacy for the Senate. "The captains of tens and the captains of hundreds," he announced, "may lead its dismembered fragments in marauding guerrilla warfare but nevermore shall we fight an honorable pitched battle."[48] He would not even accept a draft, he informed his supporters, knowing that his refusal to run left the legislature in an impasse; no coalition could muster enough votes for any one nominee. The General Assembly adjourned without re-electing Atchison or electing his successor.

Bates considered abandoning the Know-Nothings altogether

[47] Gibson to Gamble, January 2, 1854, Hamilton R. Gamble Papers; D. R. Risley to Leonard, October 23, John Richardson to Leonard, October 23, James J. Lendley to Leonard, December 7, 1854, Leonard Papers; St. Louis *Missouri Democrat,* November 24, 1854.

[48] Samuel T. Glover to Leonard, September 15, 1854, John Davis to Leonard, January 1, 1855, Leonard Papers; St. Louis *Missouri Democrat,* November 16, 1854; *Liberty Weekly Tribune,* September 29, 1854; Bates to Whig Committee, January 5, 1855, in *Liberty Weekly Tribune,* February 9, 1855.

and attempting to create an alliance between the Whigs and antislavery Democrats. He called on Benton to discuss their mutual problems. Privately, he entertained the idea of proposing to his old foe a fusion of Democratic and Whig moderates. The ex-Senator proved to be friendly, almost cooperative. Bates spoke cautiously, however. He worried lest Benton use the Whigs to make a last desperate bid for a Senate seat. Too, he feared the revival of Benton's once great popularity, as he knew his own needed strengthening. If he should run in tandem with the old hero he would come off second best in any victory the two might share. Therefore, after his talk with Benton he decided against a Whig-Democrat fusion for both personal and party reasons. He would hang doggedly onto a half-formed plan to "nationalize" the American party along Whig lines and attempt to rally the electorate against the abrogation of the Missouri Compromise.[49]

Bates realized that there were many forces temporarily at work against the creation of a party that might embody the old Whig principles. Factional controversies on various issues, ranging from slavery to internal improvements, made it virtually impossible to reconcile or rally displaced politicians. The state elections severely damaged the moderate Whigs, making it possible for the Kansas-Nebraska element of the party to seize control of the Central Committee. The party of Henry Clay had little hope of success in Missouri when it convened on November 30, 1855, in Jefferson City. In a last attempt, the delegates tried to join a coalition of the American and the Benton-Democrat parties, but when this failed, the disillusioned men left the capital city to vanish into political obscurity.[50]

[49] James M. Hughes to Atchison, July 13, 1854, David Rice Atchison Papers; John Scott to F. Kennett, April 4, 1855, Kennett Family Papers.

[50] Walter H. Ryle, "Slavery and Party Realignment in Missouri in the State Election of 1856," *Missouri Historical Review*, XXXIX, 321-25, 327-29.

Bates obdurately refused to concede defeat to the proslavery group although he knew the breakup of the Missouri Whigs meant the end of party organization. He entertained a euphoric vision of Whigs, Americans, and antislavery Democrats uniting behind former President Millard Fillmore to win the 1856 election. Fillmore already had been nominated by the American party's national council and again at its hastily called Philadelphia convention in February, 1856. Filled with a new hope, Bates looked on this development as the beginning of a national conservative movement dedicated to preserving a union "bound together by ties of blood and kindred."[51]

In the spring he undertook a series of trips in Missouri and Illinois to speak in Fillmore's behalf. Often, it meant that he addressed crowds more attached to Know-Nothingism than to the idealistic cause of saving the Union, but he spoke to them nevertheless. As he approached the end of his campaign efforts, he hit upon an idea that he thought would help promote a conservative national party. In Palmyra, Missouri, on the warm afternoon of July 2, he addressed the large crowd that had gathered to hear him. Dramatically, he repudiated Know-Nothingism and attacked, in order, the Democratic presidential candidate James Buchanan and the newly created Republican party as examples of extremism on both sides. The Democrats, he said, were making two serious mistakes. They were supporting an extension of the southern slave empire, and they were unwittingly aiding the militant Republicans by making slavery a central issue. Ignoring the contradiction in this statement, he went on to tell his delighted audience, many of whom had once helped make Palmyra a stronghold of Missouri Whiggery, that the Republicans threatened to violate property rights by disobeying the Fugitive Slave Act and the Constitution itself. Act now with Fillmore as leader, he begged his listeners, to form a

[51] Palmyra *Southern Sentinel*, September 3, 1856.

national conservative alliance that would reject Democratic and Republican radicalism and save the country.[52]

In spite of his apparent sacrifice in leaving the American party, Bates had long been disenchanted with the Know-Nothings and their political ineffectiveness. He realized they lacked a party rhetoric, an ingredient that he knew was essential to political victory. By the time he delivered his speech at Palmyra, he regarded the Missouri Know-Nothings with open scorn because of their wavering on the slavery question and their inclination to select venal politicians as candidates. It also was clear to him that the free-soil Democrats preferred to stand alone, without Whig or American allies, in both the city and state elections.[53]

Hoping that it could be the genesis of a revitalized national party to oppose the extension of slavery and the growth of sectional extremism, Bates decided to accept an appointment as delegate to the Whig national convention in Baltimore. Too, he liked the image some created of him as a national figure capable of unifying the country. But he either made a poor choice or misjudged the consequences of the Baltimore convention. His obvious lack of communication with national leaders suggests the former.[54]

He arrived in Baltimore in mid-September at the head of a nine-man delegation from Missouri. Before him lay a disheartening scene. Some faithful members of the wrecked party, it seemed, had gathered to commiserate with each other over the cruelty of history. The *New York Tribune* characterized the convention as a "collection of fossils" committed to nominating a Know-Nothing who would be "too transparent a humbug to be more than mildly amusing."[55]

[52] *Ibid.*, July 2, 1856; *Liberty Weekly Tribune*, July 11, 1856.

[53] Jefferson City *Jefferson Inquirer*, August 26, 1856; *Hannibal Messenger*, September 4, 1856.

[54] *Liberty Weekly Tribune*, September 12, 1856.

[55] *New York Tribune*, September 17, 1856.

Bates, however, mustered a little hope when he saw in attendance old Whig stalwarts like William A. Graham of North Carolina, John J. Jones of Georgia, James H. Matthews of Illinois, Wyndham Robertson and Alexander Rives of Virginia, and Washington Hunt of New York. They were experienced hands who had helped guide their party in happier times, now meeting in a last desperate attempt to salvage the old political power that they had enjoyed.

Although he may have anticipated it, Bates acted mildly surprised when on the first day of the convention, September 17, the delegates elected him their presiding officer. Standing beneath a large portrait of George Washington, he thanked the convention and cautiously pledged the Whigs that he would work toward a reorganization along the old lines of "power and success." He urged the delegates to turn for inspiration to national heroes Hamilton, Jefferson, and Clay, an imposing range for a party that was purportedly setting out on a new course. Otherwise, he had little of note to say to the convention.[56]

On the second day of proceedings, after a plethora of committee reports and memorials, Bates spoke on the Kansas-Nebraska Act. He attributed the success of the measure to Atchison's cupidity and Douglas' ambition for the Presidency. Again, he raised the charge of conspiracy on the part of proslavery Democrats and carried his argument to the untenable ground of denying that the Territorial Act had abrogated either the Missouri Compromise or the Compromise of 1850. The Kansas-Nebraska Act had propagated the unhealthy doctrine of "popular sovereignty," he said, and left great moderate majorities in both parties without a political organization.[57]

[56] Baltimore *Sun,* September 18, 1856; *New York Times,* September 18, 1856.

[57] Baltimore *Sun,* September 19, 1856.

In spite of his initial oratory, Bates had difficulty in furnishing leadership. Few could agree on a platform, and fewer still seemed to share Bates's vision of a reorganized national party. The platform that emerged was little more than a series of clichés and an appeal for national unity. As that of four years before, this platform contained no resolution on the slavery question or on the power of Congress to legislate for the territories; no call to arms was sounded. Disillusioned, Bates gradually lost his will to fight, and the convention turned into a dull, painful routine. The Whigs nominated Millard Fillmore as their candidate for the Presidency and stumbled out of history repeating innocuous slogans of a day long passed.[58]

On September 19, the last day of the convention, a disappointed Bates delivered his final address. He made a last attempt to rally a disorganized political body by sheer rhetoric spewed out in short, declarative sentences:

> I am neither North nor South; I repudiate political geography. . . . I call no man a Whig . . . who does not revere the Constitution and laws of his country. . . . I am a man believing in making laws and then whether the law is exactly to my liking or not, for enforcing it— whether it be to catch a runaway slave and bring him back to his master or to quell a riot in a disordered territory. . . .

With this last, fatalistic plea, he terminated his practical relationship with the party he had loved so much. He desired to return home, in order to see his new-born son.[59]

The convention had tired the sixty-four-year-old Bates. Before returning home, he journeyed to Virginia with his

[58] *Ibid.*

[59] *Liberty Weekly Tribune,* October 17, 1856. This was the last of seventeen children born to Edward and Julia Bates. In two years, the youngest Bates child was to die and thus become the eighth in the family who did not survive early childhood. Only five of the seventeen children lived to an advanced age.

friend Wyndham Robertson for a short rest and for reflection upon his political career. After a few days in the Virginia countryside, he traveled to Washington for a meeting with Fillmore. He delivered the convention's decision to him and pledged his support in the coming election. His official duties completed, he left for St. Louis, a partial haven from his torment and doubt.[60]

In 1856 the Whigs in Missouri, standing on old party grounds, received their final, crushing defeat by the Democrats. Buchanan carried Missouri, and proslavery Democrats swept the state elections. Bates observed the eclipse of the Whig party without an outward show of emotion, but he revealed his private thoughts to the Indiana journalist-politician Schuyler Colfax. He was, Bates wrote, "a mere remnant of the old Whig Party—only a little more lonely now."[61] The statement was a mixture of truth and simplicity and of self-deception and misjudgment of purpose. Bates had reached a low ebb when his party was at its peak and then had been catapulted to national prominence when the Whigs were falling from power. This phenomenon occurred because he lacked forceful leadership and, thus, was looked upon as a statesman by those who confused compromise with vacillation.

[60] Bates to Robertson, October 4, 1856, Wyndham Robertson Collection.

[61] St. Louis *Missouri Democrat,* November 6, 1856; Bates to Colfax, May 31, 1858, Schuyler Colfax Collection.

CHAPTER IV

A REPUBLICAN VICTORY

H IS PARTICIPATION in lost causes in politics forced Bates temporarily to turn again to his law practice—and a new and successful partnership with John R. Shepley of St. Louis. Political events in Missouri, however, appeared to be headed toward a climax. The Benton Democrats had rallied around free-soil Congressman Frank Blair, son of old Jacksonian Francis P. Blair, and B. Gratz Brown, editor of the St. Louis *Missouri Democrat*. Both men championed gradual emancipation and the exclusion of slavery from the territories. But the Bentonites suffered a temporary setback in the 1858 elections, a fate Bates privately felt they deserved because of their agitation of the slavery issue. On the other hand, the rising strength of a militant pro-Southern group in the state alarmed him. With his old antagonist Benton, he believed in the Union and in the right of Congress to regulate slavery in the territories. He distinguished, however, between interference by Congress and its right to legislate.[1]

Through newspapers and conversations in court, Bates became increasingly aware of the approaching crisis over slavery. It was now clear to him that the gradual emancipationists led by Blair and Brown were gaining strength, possibly as forerunners of a third party, as the increase of white migration and the decline of the slave population coincided. He stood on the periphery, anxious to re-enter politics, but unsure of public opinion on the contentious question of the restriction of slavery.

Bates feared an eventual struggle between extremist groups in Missouri. He favored neither the proslavery Democrats nor the Republicans, now determined to enlist the support of all free-soil and antislavery men. When the self-styled New York Whig Committee, early in 1859, offered him an opportunity to express his views, he wrote a public letter on the major issues. Bates realized that his reply to the committee would place him on public record, so he made it moderate in tone, avoiding specific references to the slavery issue itself. The government had to "advance the interests of the people," he maintained, by protecting all economic and sectional groups. It must undertake a national development, including the building of roads and the improving of harbors, so as not to favor one type of property interest over another. He scorned the Buchanan administration for having set class against class, section against section.[2] He proposed that all moderates join together in an effort to

---

[1] St. Louis *Missouri Democrat*, August 9, 1858; Bates to Colfax, June 7, 1859, Schuyler Colfax Collection.

[2] Howard K. Beale, ed., *The Diary of Edward Bates, 1859-1866*, The Annual Report of the American Historical Association for the Year 1930, IV, 2, 6. Professor Beale's edition of Bates's diary is a compilation of five volumes, one kept in Missouri through early 1861, and four volumes recorded in Washington and Missouri through July, 1866.

preserve the Union through a program of internal development and cease agitating the slavery question.

Although he fully felt the weight of his sixty-five years, Bates experienced another surge of enthusiasm when Schuyler Colfax wrote him, asking for his views on national questions. Upon learning of Colfax's interest in Bates, Frank Blair reacted quickly, for he had thought, ever since the 1858 elections, of putting Bates at the head of a combination free-soil and gradual emancipationist ticket in Missouri. He arranged a conference with Gibson, who now acted as Bates's personal agent. The two decided to invite Colfax to St. Louis for a talk with Bates. A few weeks later Colfax arrived, as a representative of midwestern Republicans, to ascertain whether or not the Missourian had qualifications sought in a presidential candidate. Privately, he had reservations because of Bates's letter to the New York Whigs and his continuous diatribes against slavery agitation. Colfax realized that few Republicans were willing to relegate slavery to secondary importance or to follow a man who was reluctant to declare himself fully on the subject. He came, anyway, to interrogate the man who might easily represent similar Whig and Republican views regarding the tariff and the transcontinental railroad and who possibly might unite an opposition against the Democrats.[3]

Bates perceived at once how uneasy Colfax was when he, along with Blair and Gibson, conferred with him in St. Louis on April 27. He guessed that Colfax was trying to settle in his own mind whether a Bates ticket might be strong enough for the antislavery voters of the Northeast and yet moderate enough for the citizens in the border states. Aware of Colfax's predicament, Bates assured him of his opposition to the extension of slavery. He did so reservedly, for he thought little of Colfax's plan to con-

[3] *Ibid.*, 11; O. J. Hollister, *Life of Schuyler Colfax*, 141-43; Bates to Colfax, February 24, 1859, Colfax Collection.

solidate an anti-Seward faction in the Republican party and, along with Blair, to strengthen the free-soil element in Missouri. The possibility of alienating the border states, including his own, greatly bothered Bates. The interview with Colfax, however, marked out a new course for him. He was almost overwhelmed by the thought of his nomination for the Presidency.[4]

Enamored again of public life, Bates abandoned his beloved grape arbors to devote his hours of leisure to social and public activities. One of the long-time residents of St. Louis, he had a wide range of friends and acquaintances, although most of his immediate friends were ministers, merchants, and professional colleagues who regarded him now as one of the true pioneers of the community. He spent a great deal of time with professional people, particularly ministers and physicians like the Reverend James H. Brooks of the Second Presbyterian Church; Dr. William M. McPheeters, a prominent surgeon; Dr. John B. Johnson of the St. Louis Medical College; Reverend Enoch C. Wines, a minister-professor in the short-lived City University; and his own pastor, Samuel A. P. Anderson of the Central Presbyterian Church. Although he valued the political and intellectual views of these men highly, he did not neglect his relationship with other groups of professional people in the city. Among his friends were Roswell M. Field, a wealthy attorney who had pleaded for Dred Scott before the circuit court; Judge William T. Wood of St. Louis; and James O. Broadhead, a rising young lawyer. He also entertained widely assorted groups in his home, including Samuel G. Goodrich of New York, the famous "Peter Parley" of children's books fame; James B. Eads, inventor-engineer; William G. Eliot, minister and chancellor of Washington University in St. Louis; Asa S. Mitchell, editor of the St. Louis *Evening News;*

[4] Bates to Colfax, June 16 and 25, 1859, Colfax Collection; Beale, *Bates Diary,* 11-12.

Sol F. Smith, theatrical producer and lawyer; and youthful
Lieutenant J. E. B. Stuart of the United States Army.[5]

Circulating among these prominent friends, he naturally
engaged in many public activities. He spoke often at church
or other local gatherings, served on the board of trustees
for the new City University, and acted as political and
professional adviser to many visitors in his office. And, in
the belief that intellectual attainment was important to his
success as a political candidate, he began to read avidly.
In a period of a few weeks he digested Thomas Carlyle's
Frederick the Great and Adam Smith's *Wealth of Nations*
as well as contemporary works on science and political
economy. He also became a regular reader of the Washington
National Intelligencer and the London *Times* and *News*.[6]

Local adulation gave Bates new confidence also. In mid-
1859 he agreed to sit for a portrait by William Cogswell
of New York. A few months later he commissioned Chester
Harding, another well-known New York artist, to paint a
second portrait. He took much pride in the fact that both
paintings, when finished, were exhibited in St. Louis where
the public might gaze upon his likeness. It seemed to Bates
that the light of local and national attention had been turned
on him. With an uncharacteristic immodesty, he liked to
repeat a story, told him by a friend, concerning some small
boys in Sunday-school class in St. Louis. The boys had
been asked who the next President would be. "There was
a dead pause for a few seconds," Bates would relate, "when
a bright-faced little boy on a back seat, cried out—'Yes sir,
I can tell you—Mr. Bates—Pa says he ought to be, and
I reckon the people will do right.' And then there was
a general shout for the little politician, who had so much
faith in his father's judgment and the people's virtue."[7]

[5] *Ibid.*, 32, 34, 36, 51, 54, 63, 66, 78, 83, 87, 94, 99, 100, 126.
[6] *Ibid.*, 10, 24-25, 33, 48, 67.
[7] *Ibid.*, 30, 45-46, 90-91, 96.

Actually, he was taking stock of an evident Bates-for-President movement in certain sections of the country. Signs of popular support seemed all the more significant to him when he considered his refusal to campaign actively for the nomination and his steadfast, but implausible, denial of presidential aspirations. The indications, therefore, impressed him. Orville Hickman Browning, Illinois congressman and close friend of Abraham Lincoln, had journeyed to St. Louis at Bates's invitation and had returned to his constituency ready to campaign for the Missourian. Samuel Bowles, editor of the Springfield *Massachusetts Republican,* John D. Defrees of the Indianapolis *State Journal,* and Charles A. Dana of the *New York Tribune* all endorsed Bates editorially for the Republican candidacy. Unpredictable Horace Greeley, in spite of his reservations on Bates's position on slavery, had added the greatest journalistic weight by extolling the virtues of the eloquent Chairman of the Chicago River and Harbor Convention.[8] Free-soil newspapers in the Middle West, including the Quincy *Republican* and the St. Joseph *Free Democrat,* and conservative journals, such as the Richmond *Whig,* alike hailed Bates as a promising candidate of the "opposition" party. Anti-Administration groups in Connecticut, New Jersey, and Rhode Island also endorsed the former Whig. Winter Davis and Governor Thomas Hicks of Maryland had declared their support, too. It appeared that many influential men had settled on Bates because they

[8] *Ibid.,* 36-38, 54, 77; Bates to Gibson, September 1, 1859, Abraham Lincoln Collection (Chicago Historical Society); Columbia *Missouri Statesman,* October 21, 1859; Theodore C. Pease and James G. Randall, eds., *The Diary of Orville Hickman Browning, 1850-1881,* I, 380-81; Horace Greeley, *Recollections of a Busy Life,* 389-90; Glyndon G. Van Deusen, *Horace Greeley, Nineteenth-Century Crusader,* 241-43.

agreed with James O. Broadhead, who said he "was not touched with Northern fanaticism."[9]

The undeclared candidate was turning over in his mind some perplexing thoughts. It seemed wholly consistent for him to appear as a drafted choice, a man who did not seek the office but who would assume its responsibilities. He thought, too, that an open campaign probably would identify him as a sectional candidate. Therefore, he decided against making a formal declaration concerning his availability. He even declined to attend anti-Administration meetings, both local and in other states, where his presence might signify an acceptance of the role others wished him to play.[10]

From reading the newspapers, Bates concluded that he must act cautiously in his own state. Some Missouri newspaper editors warned against his consorting with the "black Republicans," while others maintained that antislavery men planned only to exploit Bates. After analyzing the editorials, Bates decided to make a public announcement on the major questions when the Missouri opposition party convened in late December. Seeking all the information he could obtain, he dispatched Gibson to various local meetings where ex-Whigs, Americans, and antislavery Democrats gathered. He was heartened somewhat by word that the local St. Louis delegates who would attend the state convention favored him as the presidential candidate. Also, he counted on most state Republicans supporting his candidacy when they held their convention in December.[11]

[9] Bates to Gibson, September 1, 1859, Robert Todd Lincoln Collection; Beale, *Bates Diary*, 45, 54, 89; St. Louis *Missouri Democrat*, November 9, 1859; Leonard to Robert Wilson, December 12, 1859, Abiel Leonard Papers; Broadhead to William Newland, December 6, 1859, James O. Broadhead Papers.

[10] *Liberty Weekly Tribune*, September 16, 1859; Beale, *Bates Diary*, 47.

[11] *Ibid.*, 50; Columbia *Missouri Statesman*, November 11, 1859; *Hannibal Messenger*, November 12, 1859; *Liberty Weekly Tribune*, November 18, 1859; Pease and Randall, *op. cit.*, 380-81.

For the first time, he and Gibson actually began planning strategy. Both men realized how difficult it would be to coalesce the dissident groups without alienating at least one. Bates felt he had to subordinate the slavery question until all the groups had agreed to unite. He especially wished to avoid offending local Republicans, who appeared more and more responsive to joining the rest of the opposition and supporting his candidacy. When rumors reached St. Louis that Whig and American representatives in the legislature were opposed to a coalition with the Republicans, Gibson left hurriedly for Jefferson City. There he worked diligently to reconcile the various groups and managed to keep alive plans for a united opposition convention by postponing it until the following February. He even persuaded the former members of the Whig party to join with Americans in the legislature in drafting a letter naming Bates as their candidate for the Presidency. But mutual distrust and the recollection of old divisions made the plans of Bates and Gibson tentative at best.[12]

Bates realized that he could not offer himself as a Republican candidate and win a majority following in Missouri. While he was being actively courted by antislavery men or free-soilers like Blair, he was expected by old conservative friends like Rollins and Henry T. Blow to adopt a "no-position-on-slavery" stand. Therefore, he had to reconsider at length his relationship with Missouri Republicans. If he could form a coalition of ex-Whigs, Americans, and antislavery Democrats, he might present himself to the Republican party at the head of a strong minority faction. This plan conceived of no philosophy, but served as a strategic guide to a "dual party" agreement. He might attempt to reconcile the nationalists in his and other states and then ask the Republican party to accept him as its

[12] Beale, *Bates Diary*, 70-72, 80-81, 83-84.

agent as well as the leader of the opposition outside its organization.[13]

In spite of his hopeful ideas, many leaders looked on Bates as an ultraconservative, reluctant to declare himself on slavery. Bates had attempted to clarify his position on the extension of slavery and yet avoid identification with some of the more radical views expressed by such Republican leaders as Seward and Lincoln. He clung obdurately to his argument that the slavery issue had assumed an unnatural importance in American politics. But he had become more specific on his slavery stand since the abrogation of the Missouri Compromise. He now carefully distinguished between slavery as an institution in the territories under the control of Congress, and in the states under local statute. Focusing his attention on the territorial issue, he insisted now only on the right of Congress to prohibit slavery outside of state boundaries and to deny it federal protection in those areas. Bates always had considered slavery a local institution under municipal or state law where it existed, and he opposed immediate steps to legislate it out of existence. Therefore, when he applied this doctrine to the prolonged debates over the admission of Kansas under the proslavery Lecompton Constitution, he maintained that any new state had the right to accept or prohibit slavery. The fine point he made was that if a convention proposed to draft a state constitution and establish a state government it could exclude or sanction slavery. Conversely, an old state had the right to protect slavery by guaranteeing slaveholders their rights under the Fugitive Slave Act, provided they did not accept literally the dictum of the Dred Scott case and become part of what Bates believed to be the growing conspiracy to nationalize slavery.

Actually, Bates's position on slavery was somewhat similar to that of Douglas who, in response to Lincoln's "Freeport

13 *Ibid.*, 55.

question," had insisted that the people of a territory had the right of choice on slavery. Yet Bates never ceased alluding to a pro-Southern plot headed by Buchanan and the Senator from Illinois and designed to perpetuate slavery and ensure its extension. After reading Douglas' article in *Harper's Magazine* on the separation of federal-state jurisdiction in the territories, he commented severely on the tortured construction used by the protagonist of popular sovereignty. As much as did Seward and Lincoln, he deplored the principle applied in the Dred Scott decision and upheld congressional intervention in the territories in the face of Southern intransigence, but his objections sounded more political than constitutional. Dred Scott's case, he reasoned, had determined only that Scott was not a citizen and therefore could not bring suit in a federal court; it did not carry slavery into the territories or anywhere else. Congressional control over the territories must be maintained. In the vast western areas, he believed, no compromise need be made with slavery, and slogans such as "squatter sovereignty" could not dictate otherwise if the national legislature exercised its powers and prohibited the extension of slavery. However, his concern for individual property rights and his belief in the right of a state to determine its own institutions and provide for its own police power never ceased to disturb his thoughts.[14]

As the only way to preserve a country of white men, Bates was content to wait for the natural demise of slavery. He favored Henry Clay's doctrine of forcible deportation when slavery should be overwhelmed by the tide of free white labor. Hopefully, he envisioned a program of gradual, compensated emancipation and colonization. However, thematic to his plan was the restriction and contraction of slavery by merely prohibiting slaveowners from taking their

[14] *Ibid.*, 27-29, 75, 79, 105, 111-13; Bates to Colfax, June 16, 1859, Colfax Collection.

human property into national territories. But Bates posted certain scruples around his pragmatic plan. "I have always thought and often said," he wrote in a statement designed to placate both North and South, "that slavery is an evil, social and moral and political; but I have never said that it was inconsistent with Christianity." His strong conviction of the inequality of whites and blacks and his realistic appraisal of history led him more logically to the conclusion that it was unfair to both races to keep the Negroes in America. "A government," he declared, "whose fundamental principle is the legal equality of all its citizens, ought to confine itself to regions where the citizens can do all the labors of life; and ought not to accept as a right any country whose productive labor, must of necessity be done by slaves."[15]

Unquestionably, Bates's hopes for a cautious approach to resolution of the slavery question received a blow when John Brown raided Harpers Ferry in October, 1859. Observing the public reaction to the unfortunate event, Bates concluded that Brown must be punished. However, he was incensed when a jury in Norfolk, Virginia, jailed a man who had praised Brown's deed. "It must be," he wrote, "that the slave states live in constant dread; and fear will make wise men foolish and kind men cruel." Obviously, he was calling attention to the evil results of slavery while subduing a call for its immediate eradication. This patent and conservative approach might placate citizens in the border states, but it did not endear him to politicians in the North who realized the political value of public emotion on the slavery issue.[16]

To gain popular response, however, Bates never let his adherents lose sight of the fact that he was pledged to a protective tariff and a central railroad to the Pacific. Less

[15] Beale, *Bates Diary*, 63, 65-66, 68.
[16] *Ibid.*, 65.

readily did he accept the Republican proposal to grant land for railroad construction, since it conflicted with his old Whiggish belief that the public domain was a source of revenue. He was reluctant also to accept their plans for an internal improvement program sponsored by the federal and state governments. These plans increased his doubts on a loose construction of the Constitution. Bates was rapidly approaching, nevertheless, a point where he could no longer espouse the economic platform of Henry Clay and, at the same time, champion state sovereignty. He could no longer suggest federal action on a transcontinental railroad and yet defend the dogma of local determination. Mainly, he desired to see the West expand and prosper into a region rich in opportunities and political power. Therefore, he would attempt to turn public attention away from agitation for slavery, implement a neo-Whiggish economic program, and, as he wrote Colfax, set himself before the public as a candidate of true national proportions "on whom there is any chance of uniting all parts of the nation."[17]

In spite of his confident public statements, Bates fully realized the problems of holding together an opposition party in his own state. He hoped that an effective attack on the Buchanan administration would make anti-Democratic factions forget certain differences. All his charges against the Administration were made with feeling, for he had detested Buchanan ever since the President had ventured to suggest, in his inaugural speech of 1857, that the Supreme Court should void the Missouri Compromise in its deliberations on the Dred Scott case. By declaring that the Missouri Compromise unconstitutionally prohibited slavery in territories belonging to all of the United States, Buchanan, Bates concluded, had reversed his narrow Jacksonian concept of the Supreme Court's role and had exercised a corruptive influence on the

[17] Bates to Colfax, January 30, 1860, Colfax Collection; William E. Baringer, *Lincoln's Rise to Power*, 202-3.

justices in order to win a decision for the slaveholders in his party and preserve his own political position. Aligned with Buchanan as obvious culprits, he said, were the rest of the leaders of the Democratic party, notably Jeremiah S. Black, the Attorney General, and Douglas. The greatest danger to the Union, he declared, was that "corrupt and dangerous party, the Democracy," because of its insistence on keeping the slavery issue in public view.[18]

Since local support in Missouri was a primary factor in Bates's plans, he anxiously awaited the outcome of the opposition's convention in Jefferson City. Others also felt that the convention might prove to be the crucial test. Rollins, speaking for the conservative ex-Whigs, speculated on a possible Bates "sell-out" to the Republicans. Indeed, Bates secretly had pledged to Colfax that he would make no statement that might irritate or confuse the Republicans. Gibson hurriedly returned to Missouri from the Republican convention in Indiana, where he and Peter L. Foy, editor of the pro-Bates *Missouri Democrat,* had been soliciting delegates' votes for their candidate. After a brief consultation with Bates, Gibson left immediately for Jefferson City, where he began to bargain with reluctant Whigs and Americans.[19]

On March 1, Bates received the cheering news that Gibson had done his work well. The convention had nominated him for the Presidency in an all-party demonstration of unity. Their "declaration," Bates noted, "embraced Protective tariff— Internal Improvements, Pacific Railroad, a Free Homestead— and denounced the 'Heresies' of the Democracy on slavery in the Territories." In spite of the political hazards of such a comprehensive program, he was gratified. "This is the first State Convention," he exulted, "in which all parties

18 Beale, *Bates Diary,* 52, 68-69, 89-90.
19 Broadhead to Rollins, February 1, 1860, Broadhead Papers; Bates to Colfax, February 2, 1860, Colfax Collection; Beale, *Bates Diary,* 104-6; St. Louis *Missouri Democrat,* February 24, 1860.

in opposition . . . all united in one body and acted harmoniously for the attainment of one object. It is at once the sign and the means of harmonious action on a larger scale." Ten days later he received news of additional support; meeting in the same city to choose their delegates to the convention at Chicago, the Republicans of Missouri gave him a solid vote of confidence.[20]

Having now the support of Missouri Whigs, Know-Nothings, and Republicans, Bates attempted to correct impressions harmful to his candidacy. Many still recalled his inopportune remarks about the foreign-born as well as his brief association with the innocuous American party. Though his loyal supporters insisted that Bates could carry Missouri and the rest of the border states, he needed to appeal to a national audience. Eastern journalists could help. Bates attempted to win over the editor of the *New York Times*, Henry J. Raymond, who called on him in St. Louis. Immediately afterward, Charles H. Van Alen, Greeley's personal agent, arrived from the East for a personal conference with Bates. After a pleasant visit, Van Alen returned home to inform Greeley that the Missourian's apparent lack of support among the antislavery Germans actually would be an asset in the conservative border states.[21]

More and more, though, Bates realized that the Republicans were seeking an avowed party man. He hesitated to become so because he disapproved of the extremists within the party; he thought he could best win the support of the South as a "national" rather than as a party candidate. But Chase and Seward were openly antislavery, and Lincoln,

[20] Beale, *Bates Diary,* 106-7, 108; Frank I. Herriott, "The Conference in the Deutsches Haus, Chicago, May 14-15, 1860," *Transactions of the Illinois State Historical Society,* XXXV, 135-37.

[21] Van Alen to Greeley, February 5, 1860, C. J. Corwin to Snyder, February 18, 1860, Horace Greeley Collection; Beale, *Bates Diary,* 86, 96-97; Reinhard Luthin, *The First Lincoln Campaign,* 64-66.

another contender, had stirred up interest in the East by
discussing the moral aspect of slavery in his Cooper Union
address. If Bates was to be a Republican candidate, therefore, he had to satisfy members of the party. It fell to the
Missouri delegation to the Republican convention at Chicago
to obtain from him a more specific declaration of his policies.
On the committee were friends and supporters, such as Foy
and Blow, who, nevertheless, put specific questions to him,
allowing for little equivocation. Mainly, the committee wanted
his views on the extension and constitutionality of slavery,
on colonization, on a homestead bill, on a railroad to the
Pacific, and on the issue of statehood for Kansas.

Realizing the urgency of their request, Bates gave them
a point-by-point reply. Slavery, he said, had always been
an evil that was destined for a limited existence. In the
states, slavery was controlled by the domestic law, in the
territories by Congress. Specifically, then, slavery could
not be carried into the territories nor implemented by a
territorial legislature, nor acted upon in a judicial way, as
the Supreme Court mistakenly had done in the Dred Scott
case. The final end of slavery and of the race question, he
said, would come with the adoption of colonization. As to
the Pacific railroad and the homestead bill, he endorsed
both with mild reservations about the possible activities of
land speculators. Finally, he expressed mild approval of
Kansas statehood under an antislavery constitution.[22]

His answers, expectedly enough, did not please all. Old
Whig friends Abiel Leonard and Richard C. Vaughan felt
he had gone too far in appeasing the Republicans. Some
believed that he had even placed himself with the other
Republican candidates, notably Seward. Bates sensed the
political uncertainty his reply to the committee had created,

[22] St. Louis *Missouri Democrat,* March 21, 1860; Beale, *Bates
Diary,* 111-14, 117; Clarence E. MacArtney, *Lincoln and His
Cabinet,* 67.

especially in his own state, and privately depreciated his chances at Chicago. However, if he were to declare himself a full-fledged Republican candidate, he decided, it might deal a mortal blow to his chances in the border states and indeed in others.[23]

In eastern party circles, Horace Greeley, who bitterly opposed Seward, defended Bates's pronouncements as the political wisdom of a citizen of a slave state. Bates was neither too timid nor too bold, Greeley wrote, but intent upon unifying old-line Whigs, western free-soilers, eastern protectionists, and northern Democrats. Nor had the Missourian been a Know-Nothing, Greeley assured his reading public. It seems unlikely, however, that Greeley's columns materially aided Bates in the East; in the West they might have made his moderation appear as indecision and reminded German voters he once had been a Know-Nothing.[24]

Whether he realized it or not, Bates's national strength among Republicans was fairly impressive. A rival candidate, Abraham Lincoln, discovered that both Bates and Seward had some support in his own state of Illinois. In fact, Orville H. Browning, Lincoln's close friend, had sent an astounding letter to Gibson, promising that the Illinois delegation would vote for Bates after it cast a favorite-son ballot for Lincoln. Browning also implied that Lincoln himself anticipated this turn of events and was willing to support Bates![25] Other

[23] Bates to Colfax, March 28, 1860, Colfax Collection; Bates to Hanna, March 24, 1860, John Hanna Collection; Beale, *Bates Diary,* 118-19; Richard C. Vaughn to Leonard, March 29 and April 6, 1860, Benjamin Howard to Leonard, March 29, 1860, Garth to Leonard, March 29, 1860, Leonard Papers.

[24] *New York Tribune,* February 20 and March 27, 1860.

[25] Lincoln to Trumbull, March 1, 1860, in Roy P. Basler, ed., *The Collected Works of Abraham Lincoln* (8 vols.; New Brunswick, New Jersey, Rutgers University Press, 1953), IV, 47; Browning to Gibson, February 8, 1860, Orville H. Browning Letters. For a brilliant explanation of Lincoln's position, see Don E. Fehrenbacher, *Prelude to Greatness: Lincoln in the 1850's,* 150-54; Baringer, *op. cit.,* 204.

predictions contained similar notes of almost unbelievable optimism. Chase men in Ohio looked on the Missouri judge as one of the most formidable candidates. Gibson had learned earlier that at least twenty of Indiana's twenty-six delegates to the convention would vote for Bates. A former law pupil and friend of Bates, Pennsylvanian Titian J. Coffey, declared that his state delegation favored his old mentor. Signs of Bates's popularity were evident also in the border states of Kentucky and Tennessee, and in Connecticut, Minnesota, and Ohio. Even some of the Missouri Germans, influenced by the clever editorials of the St. Charles *Democrat,* had decided to endorse the former Whig leader.[26]

Bates did not worry greatly about the German vote, for he thought it much less important when compared to that of the former Whigs and Americans. He felt safe in declaring the "moral and political status of slavery" to be an issue only when applied to the extension of the institution into the territories. Unlike Lincoln and Seward, he looked on the extreme antislavery Republicans as largely an alien German element. He did not deem a vigorous antislavery stand, taken to please the Germans, politically wise. In contrast to Carl Schurz and other Germans, he continued to diagnose slavery agitation, and not the constitutional or moral question of slavery itself, as the chief malady dividing the country.[27]

In early spring, Horace Greeley, Frank Blair, and Gibson agreed to act as Bates's campaign managers at Chicago. These three represented varying shades of opinion on party positions and the question of slavery. Although they cam-

[26] Beale, *Bates Diary,* 99, 102, 107, 114; St. Louis *Missouri Democrat,* March 6 and 21, 1860; Avery Craven, *The Growth of Southern Nationalism, 1848-1861,* 343; Sceva B. Laughlin, "Missouri Politics During the Civil War," *Missouri Historical Review,* XXIII, 417; Albert B. Hart, *Salmon Portland Chase,* 182-83, 187.

[27] Beale, *Bates Diary,* 37-38, 117; Bates to Colfax, April 9, 1860, Colfax Collection.

paigned actively with Chicago-bound delegates, as did Bates himself, the three managers made little attempt to work out a co-ordinated strategy. Instead, they prepared to go to the convention in May in the midst of rumors about the Blairs' scheme to make the Republicans respectable in Missouri by using Bates's name and about Greeley's private support of Lincoln for the nomination. B. Gratz Brown thought Bates was merely the "stalking horse" of the Springfield lawyer and was convinced that he had no real chance as an independent.[28] Doubtful as these stories might have been, it was obvious how little unity existed among those who intended to direct the Bates movement at the convention.

During the weekend of May 12-13, the incongruous trio of Greeley, Gibson, and Blair arrived in Chicago. Blair had rented a suite of rooms in the Tremont House, in which they established a Bates headquarters. At their first conference, the three men planned their convention strategy.[29] Thurlow Weed, in charge of the Seward forces, visited the Bates headquarters to suggest a promise of support for the Missourian if the Senator from New York failed in the early balloting. Actually, Weed worried about Bates's popularity in the border states. He had heard reports that had reached Greeley and Blair also. Encouraging news from the Indiana, New Jersey, Pennsylvania, and Virginia delegations gave the Bates forces so much confidence they decided to reject Weed's

[28] Walter B. Stevens, "Lincoln and Missouri," *Missouri Historical Review*, X, 69; Alexander McClure, *Recollections*, 396; St. Louis *Missouri Republican*, May 22, 1860. Stevens maintains that Bates had no expectation of being nominated and allowed the use of his name only to help prevent Seward's nomination. This is completely false.

[29] "Gibson Autobiography," Charles Gibson Papers; William E. Smith, *The Francis Preston Blair Family in Politics*, I, 475-76.

vague offer.[30] To capitalize on their candidate's rise in popularity, Blair and Greeley circulated a pamphlet which depreciated Seward's qualifications and enumerated Bates's political virtues.

Acting on the premise that most of the delegates had not made up their minds, Gibson, Greeley, and Blair planned to campaign mainly among the delegates from crucial states. Their strategy had some merit. The Indiana delegation rejected Seward and remained divided on other candidates. Key delegates, such as John A. Kasson of Iowa, David Dudley Field of New York, Henry Winter Davis of Maryland, Colfax of Indiana, and Browning of Illinois, all appeared to be for Bates. Kasson apparently had made much headway in his plan to swing his delegation to Bates if there should be and Oregon also evinced an interest in Bates.[31]

After a hurried assimilation of these reports, the Bates camp decided that he would run second to Seward if he received the votes of the uncertain delegates. Many had prolonged balloting. Several Pennsylvania delegates still regarded the Missourian favorably because of his tariff views. Led by the patriarchal Francis Preston Blair, the Maryland representatives as well as those of Delaware, Connecticut, concluded that whoever ranked second to Seward in the balloting eventually would win the decisive votes and the nomination.

[30] Charles C. Coffin, "Reminiscence," in Allen T. Rice, ed., *Reminiscences of Abraham Lincoln,* 164; *Chicago Tribune,* May 14, 1860; *Boston Evening Transcript,* May 15, 1860; Glyndon G. Van Deusen, "Thurlow Weed's Analysis of William H. Seward's Defeat in the Republican Convention of 1860," *Mississippi Valley Historical Review,* XXXIV, 104; Baringer, *op. cit.,* 237-38, 246. Baringer refers to Weed's offer as a "fairy tale"; see Van Deusen, *Greeley,* 247-48.

[31] *Boston Evening Transcript,* May 14, 1860; Alexander McClure, *Abraham Lincoln and Men of War Times,* 30, 31; Thomas H. Dudley, "The Inside Facts of Lincoln's Nomination," *Century Magazine,* XL, 477; James G. Blaine, *Twenty Years of Congress,* I, 167.

vague offer.[30] To capitalize on their candidate's rise in popularity, Blair and Greeley circulated a pamphlet which depreciated Seward's qualifications and enumerated Bates's political virtues.

Acting on the premise that most of the delegates had not made up their minds, Gibson, Greeley, and Blair planned to campaign mainly among the delegates from crucial states. Their strategy had some merit. The Indiana delegation rejected Seward and remained divided on other candidates. Key delegates, such as John A. Kasson of Iowa, David Dudley Field of New York, Henry Winter Davis of Maryland, Colfax of Indiana, and Browning of Illinois, all appeared to be for Bates. Kasson apparently had made much headway in his plan to swing his delegation to Bates if there should be prolonged balloting. Several Pennsylvania delegates still regarded the Missourian favorably because of his tariff views. Led by the patriarchal Francis Preston Blair, the Maryland representatives as well as those of Delaware, Connecticut, and Oregon also evinced an interest in Bates.[31]

After a hurried assimilation of these reports, the Bates camp decided that he would run second to Seward if he received the votes of the uncertain delegates. Many had concluded that whoever ranked second to Seward in the balloting eventually would win the decisive votes and the nomination.

[30] Charles C. Coffin, "Reminiscence," in Allen T. Rice, ed., *Reminiscences of Abraham Lincoln,* 164; *Chicago Tribune,* May 14, 1860; *Boston Evening Transcript,* May 15, 1860; Glyndon G. Van Deusen, "Thurlow Weed's Analysis of William II. Seward's Defeat in the Republican Convention of 1860," *Mississippi Valley Historical Review,* XXXIV, 104; Baringer, *op. cit.,* 237-38, 246. Baringer refers to Weed's offer as a "fairy tale"; see Van Deusen, *Greeley,* 247-48.

[31] *Boston Evening Transcript,* May 14, 1860; Alexander McClure, *Abraham Lincoln and Men of War Times,* 30, 31; Thomas H. Dudley, "The Inside Facts of Lincoln's Nomination," *Century Magazine,* XL, 477; James G. Blaine, *Twenty Years of Congress,* I, 167.

In order to place Bates within reach of Seward, the Blairs and Gibson had to overcome the formidable obstacle of midwestern German opposition. Fred Muench and C. L. Bernays, prominent St. Louis Germans, supported Bates, but they had little success in persuading their fellow German-Americans to do likewise. The candidate's former affiliation with the Know-Nothings alienated most of the German delegates, and his moderate and mixed views on slavery irritated nearly all of them. Theodore Hielscher, editor of the Indianapolis *Freie Presse*, bitterly denounced Bates, as did Dr. Canisius of the *Staats-Anzeiger* and Gustave Koerner, who already had convinced many Pennsylvania and Indiana delegates that a vote against Bates was a vote against slavery.[32] Beyond a doubt, many of the midwestern Germans preferred either Seward or Lincoln to the border-state moderate who had defended the 1856 Know-Nothing naturalization resolution.

Anxious to repudiate Bates publicly as a nativist, the Germans met in the Deutsches Haus on the night of May 14, two days before the convention was to begin. There, German Republicans from Connecticut, Illinois, Iowa, Kansas, Massachusetts, Michigan, Missouri, New York, Ohio, and Wisconsin placed themselves on record as opposing any candidate with nativist leanings. Primarily, of course, their resolutions were aimed at Bates's candidacy. Although he had support in the conference, his followers needed some of the German delegates' strength. Later, the importance of the Deutsches Haus conference to Bates's cause would not be disputed. At the time, however, Gibson and Blair chose to ignore it.[33]

After the Deutsches Haus conference, the Blairs, Greeley, and Gibson continued to concentrate their attention on the Indiana and Pennsylvania delegations. They hoped to obtain

[32] Herriott, *op. cit.*, 117-19, 153; Thomas J. McCormack, ed., *Memoirs of Gustave Koerner, 1809-1896*, II, 85, 88-89.

[33] Herriott, *op. cit.*, 186, 190.

enough support from these two pivotal states to give Bates a total of 65 votes on the first ballot.[34] Intent on keeping their candidate second to Seward in the early stages, the Bates men failed to discern the quiet efforts of Lincoln's strategists, who solicited only second-ballot votes for their candidate. "We let Greeley run his Bates's machine but got most of them for a second choice," Leonard Swett, a Lincoln manager, later recalled. With the aid of Carl Schurz, Koerner, and other obdurate Germans, the Lincoln men outmaneuvered Bates's followers, who depended on the political conservatism of the Middle West and the votes of the Pennsylvania and Indiana delegations.[35] On May 15, the eve of the convention, it seemed possible that they did not hope in vain.

On Wednesday, May 16, 2,000 Republicans gathered at the corner of Market and Lake streets in the huge Wigwam built to house the convention. Former free-soiler David Wilmot first addressed the gathering. Montgomery Blair then almost incited a riot by declaring that five more delegates, known to be Bates supporters, should be seated with the Maryland delegation. After considerable argument, the issue was resolved by giving Maryland the requested seats. No more important business followed during the day, and the convention adjourned. That night, with the Missouri delegation serenading in the background, old Francis Preston Blair freely predicted that Bates would sweep the convention.[36]

Regardless of the elder Blair's optimism, the Bates forces

[34] "Gibson Autobiography," Gibson Papers; St. Louis *Missouri Democrat*, May 14, 1860.

[35] Frank I. Herriott, "Memories of the Chicago Convention of 1860," *Annals of Iowa*, XII, 451; "Gibson Autobiography," Gibson Papers; Leonard Swett, "An Insider on the How of Mr. Lincoln's Nomination," in Rufus R. Wilson, ed., *Intimate Memories of Lincoln*, 293-95; *New York Tribune*, May 22, 1860.

[36] Charles W. Johnson, *Proceedings of the First Three Republican National Conventions, 1856, 1860, and 1864*, 96, 111-12; *New York Tribune*, May 17, 1860; Smith, *op. cit.*, I, 476.

realized how sharply the convention was dividing between those who favored an extreme antislavery man and those who desired to nominate a moderate. The majority of the latter group preferred a nominee who had not taken an equivocal stand on slavery as a moral issue. Bates's practice of treating slavery solely as a political incubus was too realistic for many of those who felt that they must support a moral crusade. Gloom settled over Bates's headquarters as many of the Indiana and Pennsylvania delegates found new interest in either Seward or Lincoln because the Missourian's willingness to challenge the proslavery forces seemed dubious.

During the day meeting on May 15, little change occurred in the convention procedure, but a new development came that night. Still indecisive as to a course of action, the Pennsylvania and Indiana delegates decided to caucus jointly in the Cook County Courthouse. Frank Blair attempted to speak on behalf of Bates, but loud voices in the back of the courtroom interrupted him. Lincoln men, led by Orville Browning and Koerner, swarmed into the building. Addressing the assembly, Koerner loudly questioned Bates's ability to carry Missouri or any other state with a large German population. Browning listed Lincoln's virtues, including his firm opposition to slavery.[37] Stunned by this sudden turn of events, Blair and Gibson witnessed helplessly the alienation of the two delegations that were vital to their plans. As the meeting broke up, leaders of the groups talked briefly with the dejected pair, but Bates's cause was lost in the two key states.[38]

Some hope still remained for the Bates forces, however. If the convention should deadlock on Lincoln and Seward, the latter might, as Weed had indicated, throw his votes to Bates. In addition, Delaware, Oregon, Maryland, and Connecticut

[37] Bates to Browning, June 11, 1860, Justin H. Turner Collection; Beale, *Bates Diary*, 129; McCormack, *op. cit.*, II, 89.

[38] *New York Tribune*, May 22, 1860; Bates to Colfax, May 25, 1860, Colfax Collection; Allan Nevins, *The Emergence of Lincoln*, II, 257.

still stood with the Missouri Republicans, and other delegations talked of Bates as the only third choice. Greeley worked incessantly, attempting to persuade delegates that prolonged balloting would give the nomination to Bates as the only candidate who symbolized national unity. All depended, Greeley realized, on floor decisions of several unpledged delegates who might be attracted to a compromise choice between Lincoln and Seward.[39]

On the morning of May 18, the third day of the convention, the nominations began. Amid the din of the overfilled Wigwam, William Evarts of New York nominated Seward for the Presidency, and Norman P. Judd placed Lincoln's name before the convention. After an arranged demonstration for the Illinois candidate, Frank Blair nominated Edward Bates. In turn, other speakers presented to the convention the names of Simon Cameron, Salmon P. Chase, William Dayton, and John McLean.[40]

The awaited hour had arrived. The convention clerk began the roll call of the states. Connecticut's chairman announced 7 votes for Bates, and Delaware immediately added 8 more. By the end of the roll call Iowa, Maryland, Missouri, Rhode Island, and Oregon had registered an additional 27 votes for Bates. His first ballot total was 42 votes—23 less than Gibson and the Blairs had hoped for. More discouraging, however, was the fact that no pivotal state had gone for Bates, and the sought-after votes of the Iowa, Kentucky, Minnesota, and Ohio delegations had not been delivered.[41]

The second ballot resulted in decisive changes. Connecticut dropped to 4 votes for Bates, and Delaware switched all 6 votes cast on this ballot to Lincoln. Only Maryland, Oregon, and Missouri voted for Bates, giving him a mere 35 votes

[39] Baringer, *op. cit.*, 274-75; McClure, *op. cit.*, 30.

[40] Johnson, *op. cit.*, 148-49; Swett, *op. cit.*, 295.

[41] Johnson, *op. cit.*, 149; *New York Tribune*, May 18, 1860.

as compared to 181 for Lincoln and 184½ for Seward. Lincoln's gain had sealed the fateful outcome.[42] Grimly, the Missouri delegation resolved to hold firm, but the increased Lincoln strength left them little hope. On the third ballot Massachusetts, New Jersey, and Pennsylvania cast 64 votes for Lincoln, and Maryland deserted the Bates column. At the conclusion of the balloting, Lincoln, at 231½, needed only 2 more votes; dramatically, the Ohio delegation announced a switch of 4 votes to the Illinois politician.[43] An uncontrollable wave of shouting proclaimed the end of the balloting and the nomination of Abraham Lincoln.

Ironically, the development for which the Bates men had worked had defeated them. They had hoped for prolonged balloting and a convention deadlock. However, the Missourian's managers had counted eventually on the delegations bound to Seward and had assumed that there would be no significant increase in Lincoln's strength after the first ballot. Misunderstanding the temper of the Republicans, Bates's lieutenants campaigned for their "nationalist" candidate in spite of the convention tactics employed by the Lincoln men. Afterward, Bates admitted that their plans had been based on the premise that he and Seward would be the only serious contenders for the nomination. He concluded,

> that the convention would take the one or the other, as it might determine the question whether the party should act independently upon its own internal strength, both as regards numbers, locality and moral support, or modify its platform and mollify its tone, in order to win a broader foundation and gather new strength, both numerical and moral from outside . . . if the party felt strong enough to go along, Mr. Seward appeared to me its legitimate leader and true exponent and I thought

[42] Johnson, *op. cit.*, 152; *New York Tribune*, May 18, 1860.

[43] Johnson, *op. cit.*, 153; *Boston Evening Transcript*, May 19, 1860.

. . . that if they waived Mr. Seward there would be
almost a political necessity to fall back on me.[44]

Bound to an unrealistic "internal-external" view of the Republican party, Bates had clung to fusion principles that were
outdated by the time of the convention. In the crucible of
the convention, many delegates decided that his appeals for
national unity and harmony were merely the pathetic gestures
of a misguided candidate.

Another weakness in the Bates campaign had been the
candidate's own overestimation of the strength of the border
states and of his personal involvement in Missouri politics.
He had been certain that the border states would stand behind
him as a bloc if he proved that he had the support of his own
state.[45] Actually, the events of 1859-1860 had revealed how
divided the border states were, so that no one candidate could
command a unified majority. Capitalizing on this disruption,
the Lincoln forces had reaped a fruitful harvest at the convention by aligning dissident groups, particularly the midwestern Germans, on their side. After the convention opened,
the unification of the border states behind Bates proved a
myth.

Furthermore, the tempting prize of the highest office in
the country had blurred Bates's political vision. Reflecting
on the convention, he concluded that an artificial stampede
had produced Lincoln's nomination. By their hasty action of
nominating the Illinois lawyer, he wrote, the Republicans
had "denationalized" their party. Since he thought of himself
as the only true national candidate who might have overshadowed radicals in Republican ranks and rallied moderate
groups in both the North and the South, he regarded his

[44] Beale, *Bates Diary*, 128-29.

[45] Bates to Browning, June 11, 1860, Turner Collection; Bates
to Greeley, May 27, 1860, Greeley Papers; Beale, *Bates Diary*, 129.
Bates felt that Lincoln was as "far North" as Seward; Fehrenbacher,
op. cit., 154-59.

defeat as a public tragedy. Privately, he felt the same as did Horace Greeley, who concluded that Bates's nomination would have been a farsighted act, beyond the mandate of the convention. But more prominently than their misgivings stood the never-answered question on the way Bates treated the slavery issue. Had he been willing to take a firm stand on slavery, he might have convinced practical politicians and abolitionists alike that he could be a strong candidate, who would have gained far more votes than he would have lost.[46]

To Orville H. Browning fell the task of persuading Bates to campaign for Lincoln. Journeying to St. Louis, Browning met with his old friend and the dejected Gibson at the Planters House. Browning found Bates understandably aloof and somewhat reluctant to make any commitment. Browning soon deduced that it might be difficult to get Bates into the campaign for the Republicans. Unknown to Browning, however, was the result of a meeting Bates had previously had with Gibson, Broadhead, and other friends. At the urging of this group that he campaign for Lincoln, he had agreed to support the Republican cause.[47]

Naturally disappointed over the results of the convention, Bates analyzed the Republican platform as a concession to a minority of the antislavery extremists. "It hugs in the lofty generalities of the Declaration of Independence," he said, "for no practical object that I can see, but needlessly exposing the party to the specious charge of favoring Negro equality." However, after weighing the advice of his friends, he decided to remain silent on the platform and to endorse Lincoln openly.

> But after all, what better can be done than support Lincoln? Personally unexceptionable; his integrity un-

[46] Beale, *Bates Diary*, 129, 130-31; *New York Tribune*, May 22, 1860.

[47] Pease and Randall, *op. cit.*, I, 410-11; Baringer, *op. cit.*, 320-21; Willard L. King, *Lincoln's Manager: David Davis*, 146-47.

impeached; his talents known and acknowledged; and his
industry and moral courage fully proven, politically,
(aside from the Negro question) all his antecedents are
right—square up to the old Whig standard. And as to
the Negro question . . . his doctrines as laid down for
use, are, in my judgment, substantially right.[48]

By June 11, Bates emerged partially from his self-imposed
isolation. He had surveyed the political scene. The Democrats
were split between the northern wing, which nominated
Douglas and Hershel V. Johnson of Georgia, and the southern
radicals, who had chosen John C. Breckinridge of Kentucky
and Joseph Lane of Oregon. In addition, a conservative Constitutional Union party had been formed, with John Bell of
Tennessee and Edward Everett of Massachusetts at the head
of its ticket. Writing to Browning, Bates announced his decision to support Lincoln's candidacy. As the Republican party
had pledged itself to uphold the Constitution and the Union,
he would endorse its cause and its presidential nominee, who
had "a high reputation for truth, courage, candor, morals and
amiability." He concluded in his letter,

> I consider Mr. Lincoln a sound, safe, national man. He
> could not be sectional if he tried . . . all his feelings
> and interests are identified with the great valley of the
> Mississippi. That valley is not a section, but conspic-
> uously the body of the nation . . . it is not capable of
> being divided into sections. It is one and indivisible,
> and the North and South are alike, necessary to its com-
> fort and prosperity. Its people too . . . love the nation
> as a whole. . . . The valley is beginning to feel its power,
> and will soon be strong enough to dictate the law of
> the land.[49]

In addition to his lofty generalization on Lincoln's position
both geographically and politically, Bates again attacked the

[48] Beale, *Bates Diary*, 129, 131.

[49] *Ibid.*, 132; Bates to Browning, June 11, 1860, Turner Collection.

Democratic party. Already, he said, the Democrats had unlawfully expanded the President's powers, had degraded the
judiciary, and had openly corrupted the national legislature.
Worse still, he charged, the Democrats had forced the voters
to take a sectional position on slavery. By their machinations,
they had "changed the status of the Negro slave, by making
him no longer mere property, but a politician, an antagonist
power . . . a power to which all other powers are required
to yield, under the penalty of a dissolution of the Union."
All true patriots, he declared, must stand behind Lincoln and
the Republicans.[50]

He decided against active campaigning, however, for after
the frustrations he had experienced at the convention, politics
seemed only a recrudescent exercise to him. In late June he
planned a vacation. He borrowed $2,000 from the Boatmen's
Bank and with Julia departed for South Carolina to visit
relatives. There he occasionally attempted to gauge the temper
of the people on the issues confronting the nation, but most
of the time he spent quietly relaxing. Julia enjoyed the visit
so much that they stayed longer than they had planned. Not
until mid-August did Bates and his wife return to Missouri.[51]

Convinced that his days in public life were over, Bates
turned diligently to his profession. He spent his private hours
at home with his family or working in his garden. Somewhat
reluctantly he helped his younger son Richard to form a law
partnership with his cousin, Richard G. Woodson. He was
worried about Richard's inordinate fondness for hard liquor.
Often, while drinking, the young man remained away from
home for long periods of time, neglecting both his family and
his practice. Bates's own financial problems made the burdens
of a large family increasingly difficult; the prospect of his
son's becoming independent promised some relief. He had

[50] Bates to Browning, June 11, 1860, Turner Collection.

[51] Beale, *Bates Diary*, 138, 141.

to borrow an additional $4,000 from the Boatmen's Bank on a six-month loan to repay debts incurred the previous year. Beyond that, he had to rely in part on financial support from both Barton and Julian, who were rising in the fields of law and medicine, respectively.[52]

Not until the eve of the election did Bates display his old interest in politics. He wrote to Republican committees in Missouri and in other states, encouraging their efforts in behalf of Lincoln. He also conferred with political leaders who were passing through St. Louis. One of these, the venerable congressman John J. Crittenden, urged him to use his influence to get Mr. Lincoln to make "a soothing address." But privately Bates had little patience with friends in the South who threatened secession if Lincoln was elected.[53]

Bates, in fact, had very definite ideas on the mounting disunionist threat in the South and on the possible election of Lincoln. Writing to his friend Wyndham Robertson three days before the election, he fully explained his views.

> I am grieved to find that you seem to be of that large and amiable class of patriots . . . who have allowed themselves to be scared into the belief that the *existence* of the Union is in danger—I do not participate in that fear. I know that even small factions . . . may stir up troubles . . . and thus force the government, against its will, to measures of stern necessity. I knew that the Democracy would struggle hard to retain its long-abused power to misgovern the country, and that, whenever the crisis should come, it would "die hard." I think the crisis *has come,* and . . . it must die out. The threat of dissolution is only the last stratagem of the Democratic party to transfer the government from the many to the few; and we dare not submit to it, for that submission would be a clear surrender of the one only principle of representative government—the right of the majority to

[52] *Ibid.,* 140, 145.

[53] *Ibid.,* 155.

govern the country; according to the forms of the constitution.

Thus, Bates did not eschew the use of coercive power to preserve the Union against the onslaught of radical secessionists. He wrote,

> I knew not who started the cant phrase that our government cannot be maintained by force: But I am tired of hearing it repeated . . . why should our national government be the solitary exception to the universal rule of mankind. Every other government . . . is armed with force to repress evil and punish crime. . . . This *no force* doctrine is very convenient for the few who are scheming after nullification and secession, as it may enable them to delude the more ignorant of their followers, into the false belief, that treason is safe.[54]

It was evident that Bates had formed a definite opinion on the course of the federal government since his painful interview with Browning in June. Moreover, as he indicated to Robertson, his doubts about Lincoln had been dispelled.

> You assume that Mr. Lincoln will be elected and I think he will; so I will speak of his election as a fact. I am not convinced that circumstances make it proper for him to make any public address declarative of his opinions and principles. . . . Should I become convinced that such a declaration on the part of Mr. Lincoln would tend to promote peace and good order, I would not hesitate to advise him to that course. . . . My own views and opinions of Mr. Lincoln; and his probable course in the Presidency, I think I know him very well, and I solemnly declare to you that, in my opinion; he is as true a conservative, national Whig as can be found in Missouri; Virginia or Tennessee (and that includes you and me and Mr. [John] Bell). He will fulfill his oath to the letter, by taking care that the laws (all the laws) be faithfully executed. He will studiously endeavor to restore peace and harmony; and to that end, will avoid,

[54] Bates to Robertson, November 3, 1860, Wyndham Robertson Collection.

as far as he can, all those exciting subjects which have so mischievously agitated the country, for some years past. He believes, as I do, that slavery in the states, belongs exclusively to the states that choose to have it; and that Congress has not; and ought not to have, any power over it there. And; as to the Territory, bought or conquered by the U. States, he believes, as I do, that Congress has full legislative power over it and may, at discretion, permit or forbid slavery therein.

If any thing like justice is done to Mr. Lincoln, and he is allowed quietly to organize his administration, and make a fair start, I have no doubt that he will set out the principles above indicated, in a mild and conciliatory spirit. His character is marked by a happy mixture of amiability and courage; and while I expect him to be as mild as Fillmore, I equally expect him to be as firm as Jackson.[55]

The early election results in the states of Indiana, Ohio, and Pennsylvania encouraged Bates, for he believed that Republican victories in these key states meant the end of the Democratic party. He hopefully speculated that the Republican party, now "made up chiefly of old Whigs, and professing in the main Whig policies will soon absorb all the Whigs who have not already fully identified themselves with one or the other of the Democratic factions, and will also absorb the greater part of the Northern Democrats."[56]

Bates also realized how the fall election results might augur well for Unionist followers of Clay and Webster and for one who saw eye to eye with the Republican presidential candidate. He openly asserted that "everyone expects Mr. Lincoln to offer me one of the Departments, and everybody seems to expect that I will accept it, as a matter of course." He appeared, however, to have an answer ready if disappointed again. If Lincoln filled "the place designed for me; with the

[55] *Ibid.*

[56] Beale, *Bates Diary,* 152.

right sort of men from the right section, . . . then I will certainly refuse."[57]

On November 6 Bates and the rest of the country received the results of the fateful election. Missouri overwhelmingly went for Douglas and Bell, giving Lincoln a total of only 17,028 votes. Even the Southern Democrats, with John C. Breckinridge at their head, received 31,317 votes in the border state. Of much significance, however, was the Republican gain since the election held the previous August. Southerners now talked more of secession because of the outcome, Bates reflected, but "if we must have civil war, perhaps it is better now, than at a future day."[58]

In Springfield, Illinois, on election night, Lincoln had listed a tentative Cabinet which included Seward, Montgomery Blair, Chase, and Bates. On November 22 he journeyed to Chicago for a conference with Hannibal Hamlin, the Vice-President-elect. Hamlin suggested the addition of ex-Democrat Gideon Welles of Connecticut to the Cabinet, and Lincoln agreed. On the President-elect's return to Springfield he, therefore, had five names. Thurlow Weed, however, arrived on a hurried visit in an attempt to persuade Lincoln of the necessity for a pro-Seward Cabinet. To his dismay, he found the President-elect intent on naming an all-parties Cabinet that included men who had no great admiration for Seward. Nevertheless, when asked by Lincoln, "What objection have you to Edward Bates of Missouri?" Weed replied, "None, not a shadow or a shade of an objection. . . . The political record of Mr. Bates is proverbially consistent."[59]

[57] *Ibid.*, 152-53; Bates to Worthington G. Snethen, October 27, 1860, William H. Seward Papers.

[58] Beale, *Bates Diary,* 158.

[59] Howard K. Beale, ed., *The Diary of Gideon Welles, Secretary of the Navy under Lincoln and Johnson,* I, 81-82; Harriet A. Weed, ed., *Autobiography of Thurlow Weed,* 608, 611; Charles E. Hamlin, *The Life and Times of Hannibal Hamlin,* 568-70.

On December 13 Bates received Frank Blair in his office.
The gaunt, hard-drinking Blair had just returned from Springfield with a message from Lincoln. The President-elect desired
to offer Bates a post in his Cabinet; he planned to come to St.
Louis in person to confer the honor. A bit startled, Bates
summoned Gibson. The three men agreed that it was demean-
ing for Lincoln to come to St. Louis, and that Bates instead
should go to Springfield. He told neither Blair nor Gibson
what his decision would be, but he already had considered
his own future. Weeks before, on election day, he had conferred at length with a relative of Mrs. Lincoln who planned
to visit the now-famous couple in Springfield.[60]

On December 15 Bates traveled the ninety-odd miles from
St. Louis to Springfield and went immediately to Lincoln's
office in the State Capitol. Early in the afternoon, the two
men adjourned to Bates's hotel room in order to have more
privacy. There Lincoln offered him a Cabinet post, but Bates,
a bit awed by the bustle of activity around the President-elect,
apparently misunderstood which one. He thought Lincoln was

> troubled about Mr. Seward; feeling that he is under
> moral, or at least party, duress, to tender to Mr. Seward
> the first place in the Cabinet. By position he seems to
> be entitled to it, and if refused, that would excite bad
> feeling, and lead to a dangerous if not fatal rupture of
> the party. And the actual appointment of Mr. Seward
> to be Secretary of State would be dangerous in two ways:
> 1. It would exasperate the feelings of the South, and . . .
> 2. That it would alarm and dissatisfy that large section
> of the Party which opposed Mr. Seward's nomination,
> and now think that they have reason to fear that, if
> armed with powers of the high place, he would treat
> them as enemies. . . . He [Lincoln] said that if this
> difficulty were out of the way, he would at once offer
> me the State Department—but, failing that, he would

[60] "Gibson Autobiography," Gibson Papers; Beale, *Bates Diary*,
156, 164.

offer me the Attorney Generalship, and urge my acceptance.[61]

He was unaware of Lincoln's message to Seward, delivered
the week before to the Senator from New York, asking him
to accept the coveted post. "He assured me," Bates wrote,
"that I am the only man that he desired for the cabinet, to
whom he has yet spoken a (or) written a word. . . ." He
thought himself best qualified for the office of Attorney General, but mistakenly assumed the State Department was to
be his. In any case he accepted—partly as compensation for
his frustration a few short months before—an appointment to
Lincoln's cabinet, the first man west of the Mississippi to
be so honored.[62]

Upon his return to St. Louis, Bates wrote to Lincoln, suggesting a public announcement in the Missouri newspapers.
Although he was not certain which Cabinet post was to be
his, he felt the news would be well received in the border
states. Lincoln immediately complied, instructing him to "let
a little editorial appear in the *Missouri Democrat*," publicizing
the appointment. This quick response made Bates feel a close
kinship to the tall, emaciated-looking man. He decided that
Lincoln might easily prevent secession, and preserve the Union
without war.[63]

[61] Lincoln to Seward, December 8, 1860, Basler, *op. cit.*, IV,
148-49; Beale, *Bates Diary*, 164-65.

[62] Pease and Randall, *op. cit.*, I, 440; "Gibson Autobiography,"
Gibson Papers; Beale, *Bates Diary*, 165. Browning spoke of "Mr.
Bates appointment as secretary of state." For the interpretation
that Bates was duped by Lincoln, see David M. Potter, *Lincoln
and His Party in the Secession Crisis*, 154. An opposite point of
view is presented in Helen Nicolay, "Lincoln's Cabinet," *Abraham
Lincoln Quarterly*, V, 260-68. Thurlow Weed conveys the impression that Bates was considered only for the position of Attorney General; H. Weed, *op. cit.*, 610.

[63] Beale, *Bates Diary*, 171; James G. Randall, *Lincoln the President*, I, 263; Lincoln to Bates, December 18, 1860, in Basler,
op. cit., IV, 154.

On December 30 Bates made a second trip to Springfield, at Lincoln's request. For weeks the lanky Illinois lawyer had endured hordes of patronage-seekers, party workers, political advisers, and sincere but unthinking friends who consumed his precious time. These prosaic matters, however, seemed insignificant in view of the fact that South Carolina had seceded from the Union. Moderates in Congress were attempting desperately to keep other southern states from following. Some Republican leaders demanded peaceful coercion against those states who threatened to secede. Seward, Charles Francis Adams, Charles Sumner, and other disparate voices in the Republican party presumed to speak for Lincoln in the void created by tragic vacillation. Thus, Lincoln had many things to consider during these anxious days.[64]

Bates ascertained the degree of Lincoln's discomfiture as soon as he arrived in Springfield. Conferring in the hotel room of Simon Cameron, who was in Springfield to secure a Cabinet position, he learned of the pressures being exerted on the President-elect. Both the moderates, who would compromise with South Carolina and her sister states below the Mason-Dixon line, and the extremists, who demanded a policy of coercion against the southern states, made demands of Lincoln. As he listened, it became clear to Bates how difficult it was for Lincoln to choose a cabinet. Seward and Chase represented opposing points of view toward secession, and the former presumed he would be the "prime minister," in the Cabinet. Impulsively, Bates suggested to Lincoln a way out of the dilemma, by offering to decline his appointment. Lincoln sharply refused, saying he needed his advice, not his resignation.[65]

[64] Phelps to Treat, December 18, 1860, Judge Samuel Treat Papers; Bates to Hanna, December 22, 1860, Hanna Collection; Bates to Colfax, December 24, 1860, Colfax Collection; Weed to Davis, December 26, 1860, David Davis Papers.

[65] Beale, *Bates Diary*, 171-72; Nevins, *op. cit.*, II, 438.

After his second visit to Springfield, Bates surveyed the make-up of the new administration and the policies it might be expected to follow. It appeared that he had analyzed well the Lincoln policies in his letter to Robertson a few weeks before. Lincoln desired in the Cabinet, Bates noted, men who would "entertain no proposition for a compromise in regard to the extension of slavery." Also, he perceived that the President-elect hoped to have a council of advisers who represented diverse elements in the Union. Opposed to this plan were many Republicans who thought Lincoln should take into his Cabinet men who were all of one persuasion or another. The consideration of Alexander Stephens of Georgia, James Guthrie of Kentucky, and John Gilmer of North Carolina created a furor in the party ranks. After the first two declined any appointment, Bates became the man who was "as far South" as Lincoln could go.[66]

Bates thought Seward would be by far the most controversial person in the Cabinet. He felt a strong revulsion toward Seward because of his "higher law" doctrine, his eastern background, and what Bates believed to be his goal of turning the Republican party toward fanatical antislavery goals. He thought, too, that Seward might be able to dictate a policy of coercion toward the South. But Bates had scant information on which to base his judgment. Had he known how diligently

[66] Lincoln to John A. Gilmer, December 15, 1860, Lincoln to Seward, January 12, 1861, Basler, *op. cit.*, IV, 151-52, 173; *New York Tribune*, January 17, 1861; Henry Adams to Charles F. Adams, January 2, 1861, in Worthington C. Ford, ed., *Letters of Henry Adams, 1858-1891*, I, 75; Chase to Henry B. Stanton, January 7, 1861, "Diary and Correspondence of Salmon P. Chase," *The Annual Report of the American Historical Association for the Year 1902*, II, 490; "Recollections of John P. Usher," in Wilson, *op. cit.*, 354; Arthur C. Cole, "Lincoln's Election an Immediate Menace to Slavery in the States?" *American Historical Review*, XXXVI, 756; Swett to Davis, January 11, 1861, Davis Papers. Swett wrote, "Lincoln's whole theory of uniting the elements of our party by coupling in a cabinet rival chiefs is a very bad one."

Seward was working in Washington to effect a compromise to avoid secession and war, he might have been more kindly disposed toward his future Cabinet colleague.

As Bates had speculated shortly before the election, it probably would be best for Lincoln to remain silent on the major issues. Bates himself revealed nothing of the President-elect's plans. Actually, he felt a great responsibility as a border-state representative in the Cabinet, but he believed that any statement Lincoln made was certain to be denounced in some quarter of the country. He felt a certain smugness in being in proximity to Lincoln, and thought that the President-elect already had confided much in him and seriously accepted his advice. Reports in newspapers, speculating on his position in the Cabinet, and statements of politicians like Jeremiah S. Black, Buchanan's Attorney General, predicting his future role, elevated his feeling of self-importance. Lincoln and his counselors, he felt, must keep silent.[67]

Because of the policy of silence, Lincoln's other Cabinet selections remained something of a mystery. He had to invite the venal Simon Cameron of Pennsylvania and Caleb Blood Smith of Indiana to join the Cabinet because of convention agreements. Speaking to a group of Republicans from Pennsylvania late in January, Lincoln revealed some of the reasons for his known selections. Bates and Seward had been asked to take Cabinet posts because they were old-line Whigs and "men whose characters I think the breath of calumny cannot impeach." On the other hand, Cameron had been appointed because of political considerations. If anything, the three men shared in common a moderate viewpoint on most public questions.[68]

[67] Beale, *Bates Diary,* 171-72; Black to Bucklaw, January 28, 1861, Jeremiah S. Black Papers.

[68] Remarks to the Pennsylvania Delegation, January 24, 1861, Basler, *op. cit.,* IV, 179-81.

Lincoln's obvious reluctance to discuss publicly his Cabinet appointments stemmed from his knowledge of politics and politicians and from his vacillation on the secession crisis. As soon as he discovered who was to join him in the Cabinet, Seward denounced both Chase and Montgomery Blair. In turn, Blair protested the inclusion of Cameron in the Cabinet. Seward insisted that Chase withdraw and proffered his own resignation in an effort to force Lincoln's hand.[69] To complicate matters, congressmen from the South circulated a rumor to the effect that Bates had been named to the Supreme Court at the last minute and Gilmer appointed to the Cabinet. A few congressmen opposed Blair and Bates on the ground that residents of slave states ought not to hold office under a Republican President. Lincoln, however, remained adamant on the confirmation of his original choices—Seward, Chase, Blair, Cameron, Smith, Welles, and Bates.[70]

In February, 1861, Bates prepared to make the long journey to Washington. Julia and Matilda were to come later, so only he and Richard would go early enough to attend the inauguration. As a state convention had been called in Missouri to debate the question of secession, he declined an offer to accompany the presidential party to the capital. Instead, he remained in St. Louis a few days in order to give last-minute advice to Missouri Unionists attending the convention. Finally, on February 26, he and Richard left for Washington and an unknown future. At the age of sixty-eight, he would be the oldest member of the Cabinet.[71]

[69] Washington *Evening Star,* February 26, 1861; New Orleans *Daily Picayune,* February 28, 1861; Washington *National Intelligencer,* February 28, 1861; *New York Times,* March 6, 1861.

[70] New Orleans *Daily Picayune,* March 7, 1861; Burton J. Hendrick, *Lincoln's War Cabinet,* 421; Laura A. White, "Charles Sumner and the Crisis of 1860-1861," in Avery Craven, ed., *Essays in Honor of William E. Dodd,* 177.

[71] Nicolay to Bates, February 5, 1861, Bates to Nicolay, February 9, 1861, R. T. Lincoln Collection; Beale, *Bates Diary,* 175.

CHAPTER V

DAYS OF CRISIS

On march 4, 1861, a blustering day in Washington, Edward Bates took the oath of office that made him Attorney General of the United States. The oath was administered in the State Department Building by Justice Samuel Nelson of the Supreme Court of the United States. After the brief ceremony, Edwin M. Stanton, his predecessor in Buchanan's cabinet, conducted him through the rooms in the southwest wing of the Treasury Building on Pennsylvania Avenue. New quarters were to house the entire section—Bates, an assistant attorney general, six office clerks, and a colored laborer.[1]

Bates's first few days in office were spent in unceasing labor. Along with other members of the Cabinet, he confronted great throngs of office seekers. He worked sixteen or seventeen

[1] Bates to John F. Potter, July 16, 1861, Attorney General Letterbooks, B, IV; Bates to Julia Bates, March 15, 1861, Bates Papers; Constance M. Green, *Washington: Village and Capital, 1800-1878*, 238-39.

hours a day, mostly in dispensing patronage.[2] Much of the administrative responsibility fell upon an old friend from Pennsylvania, Titian J. Coffey, whom Bates had appointed Assistant Attorney General, and upon Richard Bates, recently given a job as a clerk in his father's office, replacing a Southerner who resigned. Bates had tried to persuade Charles Gibson to join his staff, but his Missouri friend obtained a more lucrative position as Solicitor of the Court of Claims. Satisfied that Coffey and Richard could interview the patronage seekers, Bates retreated in exhaustion to his room in the National Hotel for a few days of rest. He interrupted his repose only long enough to attend services at the New York Avenue Presbyterian Church.[3]

The character of his office was ill-defined. He had no fixed pattern to follow in appointing district court judges, attorneys, and federal marshals, but he made several of the appointments. The President, other Cabinet officers, and some prominent politicians shared with him some of the patronage power.[4] Frequently, when no advice was given, he acted on his own authority and requested Lincoln to endorse the appointment he desired. He surprised many people by offering the office of Attorney for the District of Columbia to Edward C. Carrington, former Virginia state legislator, rather

[2] Bates to Broadhead, March 26, 1861, James O. Broadhead Papers.

[3] "Gibson Autobiography," Charles Gibson Papers; Howard K. Beale, ed., *The Diary of Edward Bates, 1859-1866,* 176, 181; Henry J. Carmen and Reinhard H. Luthin, *Lincoln and the Patronage,* 113.

[4] Lincoln to Bates, March 9 and 18, 1861, in Roy P. Basler, ed., *The Collected Works of Abraham Lincoln,* IV, 278, 290; Bates to Barton Bates, March 22, 1861, Bates Papers; Vincent C. Tegeder, "Lincoln and the Territorial Patronage: The Ascendancy of the Radicals in the West," *Mississippi Valley Historical Review,* XXV, 85.

than to Edwin M. Stanton.[5] However, his dispensing of patronage to old friends in Missouri, irrespective of their previous party affiliations, followed the customary practice.

In March the first formal meeting of the Cabinet distracted Bates from the problems of patronage. He measured his colleagues with a shrewd eye. Four men interested him especially: small and aloof Seward, with whom he had talked privately; ponderous and pontifical Gideon Welles; pretentious Salmon P. Chase; and, finally, Lincoln's second "convention bargain," phlegmatic Caleb B. Smith of Indiana. He had little time to evaluate those around him, for the President brought news of Sumter; military advisers had warned that the fort would fall within the month if no relief came.

Bates's reaction to the Sumter crisis, based on precious little information, seemed much like Lincoln's. If holding the fort meant war, he was against it.[6] He still believed the sentiment for secession to be a temporary blindness of Southern extremists that would soon be repudiated by a majority of responsible Unionists below the Mason-Dixon line. In his own state, he felt the movement was being fomented by a small minority whose strength would soon dissipate. Because the proslavery General Assembly seemed on the verge of voting Missouri out of the Union, he denied the primacy of the legislature in the controversy—it could not pass an ordinance of secession if opposed by a majority. He now maintained openly that secessionists were nothing less than a small, traitorous minority.[7]

[5] *New York Times*, April 18, 1861; Bates to Montgomery Blair, May 4, 1861, Blair Family Papers; Bates to Lincoln, May 21, 1861, Robert Todd Lincoln Collection. One correspondent, Jesse R. Grant, wrote to Bates, recommending his son "Captain Grant" for a commission. Grant to Bates, April 25, 1861, Abraham Lincoln Collection (Chicago Public Library).

[6] Beale, *Bates Diary*, 177-78.

[7] Bates to General Robert W. Wilson, January 16, 1861, Abiel Leonard Papers. Bates was convinced that the conventions called by state legislatures in the South were unrepresentative.

Before his departure for Washington in late February, Bates had conveyed again his innermost thoughts on the secession crisis to Wyndham Robertson. Like Lincoln, he confided to Robertson, he had been greatly misrepresented. Many persons, he wrote, "seem to think it is good policy to represent me as harsh and bigoted in my support of the Union and unwilling to compromise the present difficulty and to concede anything." It was not a question of preserving the Union, Bates went on. "In my conscience, I believe that the Union is absolutely necessary to the peace and prosperity of the people, in all the states. . . . I have never imagined a contingency in which I would assent to a dissolution of the Union. That being, in my deliberate opinion, the worst calamity that can befall the country." However, he would not unnecessarily run the risk of war. He continued,

> I am an advocate for liberal compromise, for mutual concession, for friendly settlement of all quarrels among the states and sections. . . . Indeed it seems to me, that this is the only mode by which violence and war can be prevented among states and sections which differ about their respective rights, and yet have no common and authoritative arbiter between them.

His brief experience in tension-ridden Washington had not altered at all his reflections of a few weeks before.[8]

Actually, Bates had little use for the compromise plans that had been proffered. He rejected both the Crittenden Compromise, calling for the extension of the 36° 30′ line to the Pacific, and the efforts of the Washington Peace Conference, which had assembled in February. Earlier in the year he had revealed to his friend Orville Browning, who had journeyed to Grape Hill to discuss the secession question, his intention to uphold federal laws in spite of Southern hostility. He believed, as did Lincoln, that secession and its advocates would

[8] Bates to Robertson, February 23, 1861, Wyndham Robertson Collection.

fade away and that "firmness, decision and moderation on the part of the Government will soon compel submission."[9] The action of the hastily assembled Missouri state convention in late February reinforced his belief in firmness. Moderate Unionists led by Gamble, who had returned to Missouri after residing a few years in Pennsylvania, voted to keep the state in the Union and to preserve order and peace in the divided border region. Only on the Sumter crisis did Bates advocate cautious delay.

In Cabinet council he learned more of the Administration's deepening quandary at Sumter as Major Robert Anderson's supplies ran low. He carefully followed the proceedings of the Virginia state convention, called to decide whether the Old Dominion should join the Confederacy. Even more than Lincoln, he was aware of Virginia's influence among the states of the South; therefore, he proposed a policy of delay in reprovisioning Sumter. Anderson had three weeks' supplies left; by the time they were exhausted, Virginia might have decided to remain in the Union. He was "willing to yield" and evacuate Fort Sumter, "while, at the same time, . . . strengthening the Forts in the Gulf, so as to look down opposition, and guarding the coast, with all our naval power, if need be, so as to close any port at pleasure."[10]

Though Bates did not sympathize at all with South Carolina's position or with the attitudes of the other Southern states that comprised the newly formed Confederacy, he wished to avoid a conflict at Sumter. He wrote,

> True, war already exists by the act of South Carolina; but this Government has thus far, magnanimously forborne to retort the outrage. And I am willing to forbear

[9] Theodore C. Pease and James G. Randall, eds., *The Diary of Orville Hickman Browning, 1850-1881,* I, 457; David M. Potter, *Lincoln and His Party in the Secession Crisis,* 237.

[10] Beale, *Bates Diary,* 178; memo to Lincoln, March 29, 1861, R. T. Lincoln Collection.

yet longer, in the hope of a peaceful solution of our present difficulties. I am most unwilling to strike—I will not say the first blow, for South Carolina has already struck that—but I am unwilling "under all the circumstances" at this moment to do any act which may have the semblance before the world of beginning a civil war, the terrible consequences of which would, I think, find no parallel in modern times.

To preclude such a disastrous encounter, he favored the plan of Assistant Secretary of the Navy Gustavus V. Fox to relieve Sumter on the ocean side. Also, he suggested the possibility of a commercial blockade.[11]

Two days later, on March 18, Bates attended another Cabinet council. As the situation seemed to have worsened, Lincoln requested the Attorney General's opinion on the collection of Southern taxes on shipboard. Ten days later Bates gave his reply which, in effect, denied the President the power to force collection in ports of seceded states. However, he suggested a congressional act prohibiting the use of Southern harbors as ports of entry.[12] Because the President and his Cabinet had not taken action on federal property or customs offices seized by the Confederacy and faced a possible evacuation of Sumter, plans for such actions took on a new meaning.

While Republicans in Congress demanded a firmer Administration policy, Anderson's supplies were running low. Seward's talks with the Confederate commissioners had been aimless and unofficial, and the dispatch of Lincoln's old friend and bodyguard Ward H. Lamon, as well as Gustavus V. Fox and Stephen Hurlbut, to Charleston for a conference with Governor Francis Wilkinson Pickens proved fruitless. Finally, on March 27, General Winfield Scott recommended, much to Lincoln's consternation, that Fort Pickens be aban-

[11] Beale, *Bates Diary,* 178-79, 181.

[12] Lincoln to Bates, March 18, 1861, Basler, *op. cit.,* IV, 290; Allan Nevins, *The War for the Union: The Improvised War,* 46; New Orleans *Daily Picayune,* March 30, 1861.

doned. The failure of unofficial discussion and the commanding general's defeatist attitude mitigated against any positive
policy. All signs pointed toward evacuation of Sumter and
humiliation of the new administration.

On March 29 Lincoln adopted Bates's suggestion that Cabinet members submit written opinions on the Sumter crisis.
Bates felt that his own ideas were understood, but he nevertheless set to paper recommendations on reinforcing regardless of "whether Fort Sumter be or be not evacuated." He
also advised that fast sloops capable of running the Confederate blockade be outfitted for military use. Military readiness
would underscore the Administration's determination to oppose secession, he concluded, and ultimately to enforce its
will.[13] His colleagues held varying positions. Scott's gloomy
advice and the specter of national disgrace prompted Blair
to recommend the provisioning of Sumter; Welles praised the
President's growing firmness, while Cameron and Smith
maintained a respectful silence; only Seward argued openly
against the relief of the fort.[14] Thus, in a matter of two weeks,
the Cabinet members had materially changed their minds on
the growing crisis. Encouraged, Lincoln mildly reproved his
Secretary of State for his suggested surrender of the fort
and issued an order for the preparation of relief expeditions
for both Sumter and Pickens. Following confusion concerning
the fleet to relieve Pickens on April 5, Welles directed the
expedition for Sumter to rendezvous off Charleston Harbor
on the morning of April 11. On April 6 Lincoln notified both

[13] Memo of Salmon P. Chase concerning Bates's views in Cabinet
meeting, March 29, 1861, R. T. Lincoln Collection; Beale, *Bates
Diary*, 180.

[14] Howard K. Beale, ed., *The Diary of Gideon Welles, Secretary
of the Navy under Lincoln and Johnson*, I, 14; David Donald, ed.,
*Inside Lincoln's Cabinet: The Civil War Diaries of Salmon P.
Chase*, 10; John G. Nicolay and John Hay, *Abraham Lincoln: A
History*, III, 394-95.

Major Anderson and Governor Pickens of the Administration's intention to provision Sumter.[15]

Hearing of the planned expedition on the same day, Bates noted that the Administration appeared ready to confront the issue.

> This adm[inistratio]n has kept its own counsel pretty well, yet, its general purpose to preserve its authority as far as possible, in the South, seems to be known by the press, though its particular means are still only guessed at. For some days, the public is much excited with rumors of military expeditions to various points, tho' most of the guesses point rather to the Gulf than to Charleston.
>
> In fact, at this moment, the matter stands thus—An expedition to provision fort Sumter, well appointed, consisting of light-draft, rapid steamers (drawing only 5 or 6 feet, so as to pass Charleston bar) commanded by Mr. Fox, leaves N. York to day or tomorrow, and will reach Charleston on the 11th., or 12th., at farthest. If Maj. Anderson hold out till then, one of two things will happen—either the forts will be well provisioned, the Southrons forbearing to assail the boats, or a fierce contest will ensue, the result of which cannot be foreseen— The fort may be demolished or the City burned—In either case there will be much slaughter.
>
> The President has sent a private messenger to Govr. Pickens, notifying him that provisions only and not men, arms or am[m]unition, will be landed, and that no attempt will be made to reinforce the fort, unless the provisions or the fort be fired upon.
>
> From the first, I have insisted that it was a capital error to allow batteries to be built around fort Sumter— the erection of those batteries being an assault, equal to the throwing of shells. In answer to my direct question today, the Secy. of War (Genl. Cameron) told me that the erection of batteries to assail fort Pickens w[oul]d

---

[15] Lincoln to Seward, April 1, 1861, Basler, *op. cit.*, IV, 316-17; Beale, *Welles Diary*, I, 25-32; Kenneth M. Stampp, *And the War Came: The North and the Secession Crisis, 1860-1861*, 273-74.

not be allowed—if attempted the Fort would prevent it with shot and shell.

A large naval force is ordered to the southern coast, and, in 3 or 4 days, either there will be some sharp fighting, or the prestige of the Government will be quietly reestablished.[16]

While waiting for the fateful decision on war or peace, Bates had a brief respite from official cares. Julia arrived in Washington, and he moved from his hotel room to more spacious quarters in their recently rented house at 459 "F" Street in the north part of the city. The Cabinet did not meet while the expeditions prepared to sail to Sumter and Pickens, so he devoted much time to moving his household. He did talk with the authorities sent by Virginia to interview Lincoln, and he held brief conversations with Lincoln, Seward, and John Minor Botts.[17] The rest of the time he spent in settling Julia, Richard, and two daughters, Matilda and Nancy, in their new home.

On the evening of April 11, Bates joined a dinner group at General Scott's headquarters on Pennsylvania Avenue. Among the guests were Seward and the eminent British journalist William H. Russell. As the evening wore on, Scott regaled his guests with old campaign stories, mostly of the Mexican War. In the midst of this conviviality, a messenger arrived with a dispatch. Scott quickly read the telegram and handed it to Seward. In turn Seward gave it to Bates, who read it impassively. Yet Russell detected a sudden surge of emotion among the three Americans. He soon learned that the telegram was a Confederate ultimatum: Anderson must surrender Sumter or be bombarded. The evening came to a hurried close, and

---

[16] Beale, *Bates Diary,* 181.

[17] Henry T. Shanks, *The Secession Movement in Virginia, 1847-1861,* 194.

each man rode home in the company of his own troubled thoughts.[18]

The next day war became a reality. In the gray dawn of April 12 the bombardment of Sumter began. Suddenly, the untried and not yet fully organized Lincoln administration found itself confronted with the most serious crisis in the country's history. Most immediately pressing was the question of whether it was a war or a domestic rebellion with which they had to deal.

The day after the firing on Sumter, Bates wrote to his young Army friend Lieutenant J.E.B. Stuart, who was stationed with the First Cavalry in St. Louis. Bates had learned from the War Department of Stuart's promotion before being assigned to recruiting service, and he wished to give the promising young officer some advice. Also, he hoped to assure the Virginia-born Stuart of his future in the Union Army. All officers ordered to fight traitors, he wrote, must not think of deserting their country because of state or sectional feeling. The struggle would be one to restore order and the Union. He presented a similar argument to another friend: the Government's action had been warranted, he explained to Virginia Unionist John Minor Botts; Lincoln had no constitutional power to summon a "Peace Convention," and the "reckless misleaders" of the South would never have consented to reunion on the basis of the *status quo* anyway.[19]

In Cabinet meeting on April 15, Bates revealed his hopes for a limited and brief war. He urged the closing of all Southern ports, and he suggested that the mouth of the Mississippi be sealed off at New Orleans by the Navy. He recommended that Washington be fortified for siege and that strategic points

[18] Potter, *op. cit.*, 264-65; Charles W. Elliott, *Winfield Scott, The Soldier and the Man*, 709-10.

[19] Bates to Stuart, April 13, 1861, Abraham Lincoln Collection (Henry E. Huntington Library); Bates to Botts, April 29, 1861, Bates Papers.

such as Harpers Ferry, Chesapeake Bay, and Gosport Naval Yard be strengthened immediately. His plan, he believed, would give "the least occasion for social and servile war . . . to disturb as little as possible, accustomed occupations of the people."[20] Once isolated and cut off from her markets, Bates reasoned, the Confederacy would soon capitulate. If not, the Mississippi could be protected and bases prepared along its banks for a Union overland offense into the South. To help accomplish this plan, he recommended that his inventor friend in St. Louis, James B. Eads, be given a contract to construct an armed flotilla of gunboats for use on the Mississippi. In a short time he saw the fruition of this latter suggestion.[21]

What Bates hoped for was the seizure of ports along the Mississippi River and the Atlantic seaboard, isolating the South completely and preventing the conflict from spreading into the West. At the Cabinet meeting on April 29, he solemnly outlined his plan to hold Gosport Naval Yard and Fortress Monroe, adjacent to Newport News at the mouth of the Chesapeake Bay, while initiating a campaign in the Mississippi Valley, aimed at New Orleans.[22]

Since the early days of the secessionist movement, Bates had worried about the security of St. Louis and the federal arsenal there. After arriving in Washington, he kept in touch with the Unionist Committee on Safety in St. Louis. It had

[20] Memo of Cabinet meeting, April 15, 1861, R. T. Lincoln Collection. For similarity to Lincoln's ideas, see Tyler Dennett, ed., *Lincoln and the Civil War in the Diaries and Letters of John Hay,* 11.

[21] *Ibid.;* Beale, *Bates Diary,* 183-85; Bates to Eads, April 17, 1861, James B. Eads Papers; Eads to Welles, May 8, 1861, Gideon Welles Papers; James B. Eads, "Recollections of Foote and the Gun-Boats," in Robert U. Johnson and Clarence C. Buel, eds., *Battles and Leaders of the Civil War,* I, 339.

[22] Beale, *Bates Diary,* 187; Bates to Broadhead, May 3, 1861, Broadhead Papers.

been formed by Unconditional Unionists such as Frank Blair and Conservative Unionists like Gamble before the state convention in February.[23] Much to Bates's relief, the committee appeared determined to keep Missouri on a pro-Union course, prepared to meet secessionist invaders.

After calling up 75,000 militia troops, Lincoln declared a blockade of Southern ports on April 19. Utilizing the extraordinary war powers of the Executive, he disregarded Southern belligerency, thereby making the conflict one between the government and insurgents. Parts of Alabama, Florida, Georgia, Louisiana, Mississippi, South Carolina, and Texas were proclaimed to be under blockade; any vessel attempting to enter a port in these areas was liable to seizure as a prize of war. Lincoln declared it a state offense to seize or interfere with a United States ship. Persons caught in such action would be guilty of piracy and subject to admiralty law.[24]

On the questions of blockade and belligerency, Bates, supporting Lincoln's actions, adopted the idea that the war was a domestic rebellion waged by internal enemies. He therefore suggested that local officers be given authority to seize and condemn Confederate vessels and contraband of war, but he warned Lincoln that all proceedings on prizes in admiralty courts must be conducted with caution. His advice ran parallel to the instructions Seward gave Charles Francis Adams, Minister to the Court of St. James's. Blockade was a measure taken to deny goods to those in revolt who had seized ports belonging to a sovereign power. Therefore, the nature of the Union blockade need not depend on interna-

[23] Bates to Lincoln, January 30, 1861, R. T. Lincoln Collection; Bates to Charles Bernays, February 24, 1861, Salmon P. Chase Collection; James O. Broadhead, "St. Louis during the War," manuscript, Broadhead Papers.

[24] Proclamation of a Blockade, April 19, 1861, Basler, *op. cit.*, IV, 338-39. For British reaction, see Ephraim D. Adams, *Great Britain and the American Civil War*, I, 83-90.

tional recognition of its effectiveness; it served only as a means to force insurrectionists into submission.[25]

Bates perceived the difficulty of treating the blockade as the enforcement of a municipal regulation. He wrote the district attorney in Key West of possible diplomatic repercussions if he seized and condemned neutral vessels. To the district attorney in St. Louis, who had inquired about the status of a Southern ship confiscated by General Nathaniel Lyon, Bates sent instructions directing him to take possession of the vessel, proceeding under lawful circumstances. Contradictory precedents left undetermined the relationship of municipal to international law, and his inexperience in these matters prevented him from solving the vital question of whether breach of blockade represented a violation of public law or constituted an act of belligerency on the part of a recognized power.[26]

If the word "blockade" had to be interpreted in its legal sense, Bates wrote Francis Lieber, it applied to action in a war between two independent powers. He had begun corresponding with the famous political economist of Columbia College when his son John Coalter Bates, newly commissioned, was assigned to the 11th Massachusetts Infantry, the same regiment in which Lieber's son was serving. To draw information from his new, illustrious friend, Bates expressed his own opinions on the questions of the day. He therefore ventured, in writing to Lieber, that the term "blockade" could be used in regard to the rebellion. Also, he indicated to the professor

[25] Alexander McClure, *Recollections*, 420; revision of William H. Seward to Charles F. Adams, May 21, 1861, Basler, *op. cit.*, IV, 378-79; Bates memo, April 23, 1861, R. T. Lincoln Collection; Norman A. Graebner, "Northern Diplomacy and European Neutrality," in David Donald, ed., *Why the North Won the Civil War*, 54.

[26] Bates to Thomas J. Boynton, June 25, 1861, Attorney General Letterbooks, B, IV; David R. Deener, *The United States Attorneys General and International Law*, 187-91, 368-69.

that he regarded as true the theory that "in the law of nations only supposition and the will of a single nation is distinct and positive." On the controversial issue of belligerency he sought refuge in the Constitution; it did not, he asserted, grant insurgents the right to be considered as a warring element.[27]

Bates's seeming ambiguity on the question of belligerency underscored official concern over the political ramifications of Lincoln's acts and over the danger of European recognition of the Confederacy. With this possibility in mind, Lincoln informed Congress on July 4 that the government would continue to close "the ports of the insurrectionist districts by proceedings in the nature of blockade." Even so, the President and the Cabinet worried about neutral involvements as the result of blockade, which might not be effective enough to meet the requirements of international law. The Navy was hard pressed to cover the hundreds of miles of shore line stretching from Charleston to New Orleans; it appeared doubtful that maritime countries would respect a mere verbal closing of Southern ports.[28]

On July 13 Congress authorized the President to close ports in insurrectionist areas and to condemn Confederate vessels in federal court proceedings. Another measure, passed on August 5, provided for the punishment of privateers as pirates. Under this act, all vessels intended for use by the Confederacy were to be seized by United States marshals. In spite of these steps, however, both Lincoln and Bates regarded the "doubtful question of blockade" and Confederate belligerency as cardinal problems in the early months of the war.[29]

[27] Bates to Lieber, August 23, 1861, Francis Lieber Collection; Bates to Asa A. Jones, May 8, 1861, Attorney General Letterbooks, B, IV.

[28] Message to Congress in Special Session, July 4, 1861, Lincoln to John M. Carlisle, July 10, 1861, Basler, *op. cit.*, IV, 428, 444.

[29] Pease and Randall, *op. cit.*, I, 489; Beale, *Bates Diary*, 193; U. S., *Statutes at Large*, XXXVII, 256-57, 314-15.

On the inevitable question of the conduct of prize cases in admiralty courts, Bates was even more ambivalent. By May, 1861, Great Britain had recognized the Union blockade as effective, but she withheld her recognition of the Confederacy. However, neutral vessels that were seized while violating the blockade or carrying contraband of war created international problems. In late July the New York District Court held that the *Petrel*, a former revenue cutter put to use by the Confederacy, was violating the blockade. Under the laws of war it was declared subject to seizure. The state court ruled that its domestic enemies were, in fact, waging war against the United States and were therefore subject to retaliatory measures. Bates, however, considered the court's decision irregular and politically dangerous. In early fall he directed district attorneys to avoid controversial points in preparing government cases in prize proceedings. The war against seceded states, as well as the blockade, was to be viewed as a measure against insurrection.[30]

On April 27 Lincoln, in an extraordinary display of executive power, had delegated authority to Winfield Scott to suspend the writ of habeas corpus on a military line between Washington and Philadelphia. The President thus touched off a constitutional explosion that reverberated throughout the war as to the Executive's right to suspend the writ, an act that many heretofore had held to be solely a legislative privilege. At the time of the suspension all in the Government apparently believed the capital was in great danger, following secessionist riots in Baltimore. It was in this atmosphere that

[30] Bates to J. Hubley Ashton, October 5, 1861, Bates to Danice Lord, October 8, 1861, Attorney General Letterbooks, B, IV; *Appletons' American Annual Cyclopaedia*, I, 72, 586; James P. Baxter, "The British Government and Neutral Rights, 1861-1865," *American Historical Review*, XXXIV, 12-14.

Lincoln ordered the suspension of the writ that protects one of the basic principles of American constitutional liberty.[31]

On May 10 the President extended the suspension of the writ to include Florida. In time, as the Army apprehended growing numbers of persons suspected of disloyalty or treason, it became axiomatic that officers possessed the authority to arrest and hold suspects without formal charges. To facilitate orderly detention of prisoners, they were placed in custody of the Department of State until their trial or release. Consequently, prisoners were seized by both military authorities and agents of the State Department. District attorneys were required to report the progress of trial proceedings to both the Secretary of War and the Secretary of State, and frequently United States marshals who took custody of the prisoners prior to trial had to account to both departments and to the Attorney General. Eventually, military authorities and the State Department reached an agreement that prevented most jurisdictional conflicts, but military arrests, inadequate administration, and the misguided efforts of prominent citizens created an incredible maze of inefficiency and arbitrary restraint over which no one person appeared to have control.

Having little authority, Bates did not often intervene in local affairs involving district attorneys and federal marshals. As the Government's legal adviser, he hoped to avoid questions that might involve the loyalty of the Administration's actions. He turned his attention instead to defending the Chief Executive's suspension of the writ of habeas corpus. His approach was necessarily prudent, for he knew that both judicial and legislative precedents for suspending the writ were based on the assumption that only Congress had this right when the public safety was threatened. He realized, too, that enforcement by the Army amounted to an announcement of general

[31] James D. Richardson, *A Compilation of the Messages and Papers of the Presidents, 1789-1897*, V, 321.

martial law, but he had started to think as Lincoln was thinking: Crush the Confederacy by a swift, ruthless concentration
of power and purpose. In defense of his actions, therefore, he
chose to regard treason on the part of Confederates as a
public crime to be tried in civil courts and settled with as
little publicity as possible. Also, he insisted on the elements
of treason being established under the provisions of the Constitution and the federal statutes.

Two incidents complicated Bates's task. The arrest of Maryland secessionists and members of that state's legislature produced a public outburst which compelled Lincoln to issue a
memorandum on May 17, limiting arbitrary imprisonment to
extreme cases. Worried over this turn of events, Bates cautioned the marshal of the Southern District of Illinois that
treason proceedings would be initiated only in those cases in
which prosecution was likely to be successful.[32] On May 25,
however, another incident occurred that focused even more
attention upon the President's questionable right to suspend
the writ.

John Merryman, a Maryland secessionist of means and position, had been arrested and imprisoned in Fort McHenry on
order of General George Cadwalder, in charge of the Maryland Department. On May 25 Chief Justice Roger B. Taney,
acting in his capacity as Circuit Judge of Maryland, issued a
writ of habeas corpus to effect Merryman's release. Acting
on instructions from Washington, Cadwalder refused to release Merryman and ignored Taney's request to appear in
court. In a stinging appraisal of the proceedings, Taney protested the President's right to suspend the writ of habeas
corpus while civil courts were functioning and Congress in
recess. Certainly, the Chief Justice concluded, Lincoln had
no power whatsoever to delegate such authority to the mili-

[32] Memo on Arbitrary Arrests, May 17, 1861, Basler, *op. cit.*,
IV, 372; Bates to D. L. Phillips, May 18, 1861, Attorney General
Letterbooks, B, IV.

tary. Taney appeared to have seized on the Merryman incident to challenge directly Lincoln's constitutional powers in the time of war.[33]

On order from Lincoln, Bates conferred with Reverdy Johnson, a former attorney general, before drafting the Administration's reply to Taney. Bates realized that if the Chief Justice's action cast doubt upon executive authority, it might seriously hamper the Executive's power. He approached his task cautiously, for he stood in awe of Taney and had little desire to make him an enemy. Too, he had received word from the district attorney in Baltimore that the Government's arbitrary action was no longer necessary, as the city was quiet.[34]

Admittedly, Bates had expressly withheld decisions on questions concerning habeas corpus in correspondence with district attorneys and had procrastinated on the questions of military arrests and detention.[35] He had feared the judicial ramifications of suspending the writ ever since the arrest of Emmett McDonald, shortly after the hostilities began, by military authorities in St. Louis who refused to release him on order of District Judge Samuel Treat. As had Taney, Treat, in reviewing the case before the district court, had questioned the Administration's right to enlarge the power of the federal

[33] 17 *Federal Cases, 1789-1879,* 144-53; Carl B. Swisher, *Roger B. Taney,* 550, 553-54.

[34] Lincoln to Bates, May 30, 1861, Basler, *op. cit.,* IV, 390; Addison to Bates, June 3, 1861, Attorney General Papers, B, IV. At least two of Taney's colleagues, James M. Wayne and John Catron, disagreed with the Chief Justice's position. See David M. Silver, *Lincoln's Supreme Court,* 17-18.

[35] Bates to Cameron, May 25, 1861, in Richard Rush and others, eds., *The War of the Rebellion: A Compilation of the Official Records of the Union and Confederate Armies,* Ser. 2, II, 8. Hereafter cited as *O.R.* Bates to W. M. Addison, May 7, 1861, Corbin A. Maupin Papers; Bates to Addison, May 10, 1861, Attorney General Letterbooks, B, IV.

government. He demanded to know by what constitutional power the Government so acted.[36]

Proceeding cautiously, Bates underscored his position in Cabinet meetings, in judicial proceedings, and in an official opinion in early June. First, he explained, the Attorney General had no control over litigation in the lower courts. Next, in an official opinion, he deferred to the embittered Taney by citing the Chief Justice's conclusion in a previous case, which defended substantive recognition as procedure based on congressional enactment.[37] Realizing that his line of argument incurred many perils, he confided to George A. Coffey, United States District Attorney at Philadelphia, his tortured private thoughts on habeas corpus:

> The President is required by the Constitution and the Statutes to suppress insurrection. The manner of doing it is not prescribed. The means of doing it are expressly given. Viz: The Army, the Navy, and the militia—draw your own inferences.

To Asa A. Jones in St. Louis he sternly advised, "Better let twenty of the guilty go free of public accusation than to be defeated in a simple case." Do not, above all, he cautioned the government prosecutor, "beget the idea of persecution."[38]

As Lincoln, Bates had little wish to argue constitutional authority and law, particularly with the Supreme Court. Neither had much legal experience in matters of constitutional

[36] R. B. Taney to Treat, June 5, 1861, Samuel Treat Papers; *Appletons' American Annual Cyclopaedia*, I, 356; 16 *Federal Cases*, 17-33.

[37] T. J. Coffey to Edward Jordan, May 8, 1861, Attorney General Letterbooks, B, IV; *Opinions of the Attorneys General of the United States*, X, 50-55.

[38] Bates to Coffey, June 4, 1861, Bates to Asa A. Jones, July 1, 1861, Attorney General Letterbooks, B, IV. In his letter to Jones, Bates advised him to prosecute persons charged with treason as common criminals rather than for "romantic treason."

law. Yet Bates had to entertain the question of whether or not the suppression of rebellion, or a state of war, was a legitimate political goal worth the sacrifice of certain constitutional precedents. He hoped the Army could restore order speedily in Baltimore and thus re-establish civil processes without coercive power. Until then he would defend the Administration's policies, forgetting entirely the central principle of Whig political thought—the weak executive.[39] Much as he disliked it, Bates concluded he must run the risk of incurring the wrath of the redoubtable Chief Justice by defending the executive's actions. He rationalized his position as a preference for the suspension of habeas corpus over the exercise of martial law, and he maintained this argument to the end of his life.[40]

By July 5 Bates had readied his opinion on the suspension of the writ of habeas corpus. He defended the assumption of extraordinary powers by the President and repudiated the Republican doctrine on the nullification of judicial pronouncements. In his opinion he outlined the three departments of the government—executive, legislative, and judicial—as being "co-ordinate branches" possessing equal sovereignty. According to the Constitution, as interpreted by Bates, the President was charged by his oath of office to protect and preserve the sacred instrument of government. Therefore, of all the departments of the government, the executive is the most active and most constant in action. Borrowing the Jacksonian concept of an "active" executive, he theorized on the President's assumption of responsibilities as the "primary guardian" of the Constitution and the country. Under the Militia Acts of 1795 and 1807, he pointed out, the President might use the

[39] Bates to Major General N. P. Banks, June 16, 1861, *ibid.*; James G. Randall, *Constitutional Problems under Lincoln*, 58; J. G. Randall, "Lincoln in the Role of Dictator," *South Atlantic Quarterly*, XXVIII, 245, 247.

[40] Beale, *Bates Diary*, 513-14.

Army or any other means at his disposal, such as the suspension of the privilege of the writ of habeas corpus, to suppress an insurrection.[41]

Bates had to concede to Congress the constitutional power to prevent the issuance of the writ of habeas corpus. However, he portrayed the President as a civil magistrate who could suspend the privilege of the writ when persons under arrest endangered the public safety. It was logical, therefore, for him to reason that "the President has the legal discretionary power to arrest and imprison persons who are guilty of holding criminal intercourse with men engaged in great and dangerous insurrection." If the Chief Executive, in exercising these extraordinary powers, violated the faith placed in him by the Constitution and by the oath of office he had taken, he might be removed by Congress, but Bates questioned the grounds upon which the President could be impeached for using implied powers and judicial precedent when no statutory provisions dictated otherwise.[42]

Unquestionably Bates based his defense on a political-constitutional argument to provide a justification for Lincoln's assumption of war powers in the absence of congressional consent. Undeniably, too, he wished to prove his loyalty to Lincoln in the face of potential opposition in Congress, much of which would come from the border states. Overshadowing this wish was his desire to see the prosecution of the war and the necessary administrative machinery placed in the President's hands. By alluding to the primacy of the executive over the judiciary on political questions, he hoped to lessen the antipathy of the Supreme Court. His appeal was based on the inviolate sovereignty of the "co-ordinate" branches of

[41] *Attorney General Opinions,* X, 75-77, 78, 80-83, 90-91; Bates to the President, July 5, 1861, R. T. Lincoln Collection; U. S., *Executive Documents, House of Representatives,* 37th Cong., 1st Sess., V, 2, 6-8, 9-12.

[42] *Attorney General Opinions,* X, 75.

government, thus subtly refuting Republican dogma, which held that the Supreme Court's decisions on legislative acts were not necessarily binding. It was a calculated attempt, he informed Gamble, to achieve a balance in the opinion. His main theme, as many perceived, grounded itself in the argument that the President, during a civil insurrection, determined the ways to suppress it. Underneath Bates's official position lay the conscience of a perplexed but determined man who, like his chief, worked to mass the power of the Republic against domestic enemies.[43]

Reflecting on the habeas corpus question four years later, Bates concluded somewhat squeamishly that the suspensions had provided little more than an opportunity for the President to learn who was imprisoned and why. The act of suspending the writ, he correctly remembered, did not grant or sanction arbitrary power to arrest or imprison masses of people. In fact, persons unlawfully jailed were able to sue their captors under a writ of trespass.[44] He reasoned that it had been the better alternative to grant discretionary power temporarily to the President than to subordinate the civil to the military. But he failed to account for the fact that the Army was the enforcement arm, and that a decade and a half earlier he had attacked a Democratic president for the use of extraordinary executive power.

Lincoln's action in suspending the writ of habeas corpus and Bates's subsequent defense of it have received both support and criticism. In 1862 Horace Binney, in his *Privilege of the Writ of Habeas Corpus Under the Constitution*, generally endorsed Bates's opinion. It came as no surprise to the Attorney General, for he knew of Lieber's efforts in urging

[43] Bates to Gamble, July 16, 1861, Hamilton R. Gamble Papers; Randall, *Constitutional Problems under Lincoln*, 48, 282; George C. Sellery, *Lincoln's Suspension of Habeas Corpus as Viewed by Congress*, 218, 222.

[44] Beale, *Bates Diary*, 513-14.

Binney to write a defense of the President's actions. Binney concluded that Congress might authorize the suspension of the writ, but the President must implement it. In 1866 the majority of the Supreme Court, in Ex parte *Milligan,* ruled that the Congress had no power to declare martial law in areas where courts normally functioned, and that military commissions operating in such cases were illegal. Martial law, the Court stated, did not become automatically implemented when the writ of habeas corpus was suspended.[45]

In his opinion Bates did ignore the fact that the privilege of the writ actually affords protection against, not justification for, arbitrary political action by the executive. He did not relate the power to suspend the privilege of the writ with the power to arrest and imprison persons arbitrarily. In fact, he and Lincoln continued to emphasize the nonmilitary aspects of executive suspension and its advantages over martial law to the country and the citizen alike. Faced with a decision, the executive had acted, but neither Bates or Lincoln forgot, in delegating to the Army authority to effect the suspension of the writ, that they were on tenuous constitutional grounds.[46]

In spite of his reservations, Bates thought his opinion reasonable and nonpartisan, since the whole question divided the Republicans instead of uniting them; throughout the war he continued to defend it. He knew that some felt that his opinion had materially weakened the Supreme Court, while

[45] J. Wallace, *Cases Argued and Adjudged in the Supreme Court, 1863-1874,* IV, 107-31; Sidney G. Fisher, "The Suspension of Habeas Corpus during the War of the Rebellion," *Political Science Quarterly,* III, 463-66, 472-74; Lieber to Bates, July 31, 1861, Lieber Collection; Frank Freidel, *Francis Lieber, Nineteenth-Century Liberal,* 309-11.

[46] Lincoln to William Crosly and Henry P. Nichols, January 16, 1864, Basler, *op. cit.,* VII, 132; Andrew C. McLaughlin, *A Constitutional History of the United States,* 620; Sherrill Halbert, "The Suspension of the Writ of Habeas Corpus by President Lincoln," *The American Journal of Legal History,* II, 103.

others looked on it as a fearful display of executive power. One frightened marshal in Portland, Maine, notified Secretary of State Seward of his extreme reluctance to take action under the provisions of the suspension until Congress had approved.[47] But elsewhere, prisoners seized by the Army or by federal law officers continued to be held in defiance of writs of habeas corpus. Presidential authority to suspend the writ appeared beyond repeal.

Bates watched apprehensively as legislators arrived in Washington in July to convene a special session of Congress. His apparent "non-Constitutional" position was designed, privately, to keep what he feared might be a radically oriented Congress from seizing control of war policies. But he steeled himself for the members' dismay or anger at the consolidation of executive powers and the suspension of habeas corpus. Too, he worried about an official opinion he had given that declared the territories to be under the Federal Judiciary Act of 1789.[48] Congress must either sanction these measures or question their constitutionality and thereby threaten all of the Administration's policies.

Unwittingly, weeks before, Bates had insulated his own office from the storm of congressional criticism. After the firing on Sumter, the disorganization in the capital, with

[47] Bates to Gamble, August 2, 1861, Gamble Papers; Washington *National Intelligencer*, August 21, 1861; Charles Clarke to Seward, September 5, 1861, Seward to Scott, September 5, 1861, *O.R.*, Ser. 2, II, 673-74.

[48] Richardson, *op. cit.*, V, 3218-19; *Attorney General Opinions*, X, 70; E. G. Chambers to Wade, June 17, 1861, Benjamin F. Wade Papers; J. J. Butterworth to Fessenden, July 13, 1861, William Pitt Fessenden Correspondence. Senator James A. Bayard of Delaware bitterly attacked Bates's opinion. Bayard maintained that Bates's reference to "probable cause" of complicity denoted only mere suspicion of a treasonous act and could not be grounds for arrest and imprisonment. "Probable cause of guilt," he argued, had to be shown. U. S., *Congressional Globe*, 37th Cong., 1st Sess., XXXI, Appendix, 15-19.

troops hurrying to and fro, nurtured rumors of spy plots and traitors at the very gates of the White House, ready to overthrow the government. Momentarily caught up in the alarm, Bates proposed an oath of allegiance for all federal employees in order to relieve apprehension over rebels in the government. On April 30, the War Department directed all officers in service before April 1 to render a new oath. Subsequently, all executive departments dutifully adopted Bates's suggestion and required their subordinates to take a loyalty oath. Thus, in early July, when Congressman John F. Potter of Wisconsin took charge of a House committee to investigate loyalty in the government, the Bates proposal stood the Administration in good stead. Bates himself had sworn his own staff and had directed Secretary of the Interior Caleb B. Smith to do the same with the metropolitan District of Columbia police, who had been placed under federal jurisdiction. By a matter of months the Attorney General's action preceded the Loyalty Oath Act passed in early August.[49]

On July 13 Congress began enacting legislation based on the assumption that a state of war had existed since April 12. After securing Lincoln's approval, a bill designed to define and punish treason against the government was introduced in Congress. This "conspiracies bill" imposed a liberal interpretation of Section 3 of Article III of the Constitution. A person convicted of attempting to overthrow the government or engaged in subverting federal law, seizing federal property, or resisting federal authority in any state or territory could be severely punished under its provisions. Fines ranging from $500 to $5,000 and prison sentences from six months to six years could be levied. A few days later the House and the Senate passed the Crittenden Resolution supporting Lincoln's view that the war was being fought to re-

[49] Bates to Potter, July 16, 1861, Attorney General Letterbooks, B, IV; *Attorney General Opinions*, X, 109; U. S., *Statutes at Large*, XII, 326; Beale, *Bates Diary*, 187.

store the Union.[50] Congress, it appeared, had little intention of blocking the Administration's war policies.

Legislative-executive harmony was suddenly shattered at midsession by the Battle of Bull Run on July 27. The war of proclamations and paper blockades, of raw recruits and brass bands ended abruptly. Confederate forces were twenty miles from the Capitol and were thought to be advancing. Congressmen who had journeyed to the battle scene at Bull Run with picnic baskets, armed with revolvers and brandy flasks, returned to Washington fully aware that they were in a war they might easily lose.

On the eve of the battle, Bates rode with Lincoln in his carriage through the streets of a sobered Washington. Midsummer heat and war tension made sleep impossible, and Lincoln had asked Bates to share with him his burdensome thoughts. Bates talked with the President about the military— he hoped the volunteer army would succeed in protecting the capital; he did not endorse General Irvin McDowell's outline of attack, which was to advance against the Confederate positions at Manassas Junction, southwest of Washington. His concern had been heightened, too, for his son Lieutenant John Coalter Bates was moving off to battle. The ride ended with Bates feeling a new closeness to the man who directed the Union's destiny.[51]

The next day, Bates, accompanied by Julia, called on the President at the White House. Although anxiously awaiting the outcome of the battle, Lincoln invited Bates to join him

[50] George W. Julian, *Political Recollections, 1840-1872*, 195; U. S., *Congressional Globe*, 37th Cong., 1st Sess., XXXI, 129-30, 134, 232-34, 276-77, 438.

[51] Beale, *Bates Diary*, 188; Mrs. Edward Bates Diary, August 15, 1861, Bates Papers. This illuminating small diary, kept by the unobtrusive Mrs. Bates, implies that her husband and Lincoln were very close during the early months of war. Whether Mrs. Bates exaggerated the relationship or recorded a factual circumstance is undeterminable.

in following its progress by telegraph. As the two men received the fateful news of McDowell's defeat, the war took on a new magnitude for them.

Now, spurred by the loss of a major battle, Congress on July 31 passed the Conspiracies Act. It provided for district or circuit court trials of persons accused of trying to overthrow the government. A week later Congress enacted the Confiscation Bill, which legalized seizure of all property. Included in the act were provisions for the loss of slaves and slave labor for the same cause. The bill provided for condemnation proceedings in district or circuit courts, under the supervision of the Attorney General or the district attorney involved.[52]

A few days before, Bates had won a more personal triumph. On August 2 Congress enacted a bill enlarging the attorney general's office and responsibilities. Soon after the session began, Bates had sent Congress a proposal to reorganize the attorney general's office. After preliminary committee work, Trumbull introduced the bill in the Senate on July 11 and Representative John A. Bingham of Ohio, who did yeoman work on the measure, in the House. Bates explained the measure to Congress as one of consolidation, giving the attorney general supervisory control over all the district courts and over the disbursements paid out to law enforcement officers by the solicitor of the Treasury. For years these functions had been under the direction of the Secretary of the Interior. As the bill was written, it gave the attorney general the much-needed "superintendence and direction" over all United States and territorial district attorneys and marshals. These officers henceforward were to report to the attorney general and act under his authority. Some congressmen, notably John A. McClernand of Illinois, objected to the proposal, but Bingham, citing Bates as the source for his arguments, managed to obtain enough support for the bill. Its passage into law raised the attorney general's office almost to departmental

[52] U. S., *Statutes at Large*, XII, 319.

level and sanctioned its augmentation by the employment of additional counselors and clerks.[53]

Congress provided additional duties for Bates's office by an act of August 6 which called for federal prosecution of persons who aided the Confederacy in soliciting recruits for its army. On August 16 the President's proclamation, interdicting commercial intercourse with the South, delegated authority to federal attorneys and marshals to begin seizure and condemnation proceedings against all Confederate vessels. In the span of three weeks Congress and the President had enlarged greatly the scope of the attorney general's activities.[54]

Bates, however, moved cautiously in wielding his new powers. On August 10 he delivered an official opinion on a minor subject—incidental fees of district attorneys—that subtly affirmed his supervisory control over federal law officers. For the most part, he attempted to set an example as the Union's chief legal officer. He directed subordinates to familiarize themselves with legislation and to adhere to a strict interpretation of each act, particularly the one concerning confiscation.[55]

By design, he also maintained an outward show of respect for the Congress that had raised his meager staff to the stature, if not the manpower, of a department. The previous

[53] U. S., House, *Miscellaneous Documents,* 37th Cong., 1st Sess., 22; U. S., Senate, *Executive Documents,* 37th Cong., 2d Sess., I, 47. Bates's appropriations report for the fiscal year 1862-1863 was for a total of $53,550, a sizable increase over 1861-1862. Arthur J. Dodge, "Origin and Development of the Office of the Attorney General," U. S., House, *Miscellaneous Documents,* 70th Cong., 2d Sess., 77; U. S., *Statutes at Large,* XII, 285-86; U. S., *Congressional Globe,* 37th Cong., 1st Sess., XXXI, 62, 134, 365-66, 426-27.

[54] U. S., *Statutes at Large,* XII, 317; "Proclamation Forbidding Intercourse with Rebel States," August 16, 1861, Basler, *op. cit.,* IV, 487-88.

[55] *Attorney General Opinions,* I, 335.

March, Congress had charged Bates to deliver an opinion concerning a petition presented by investors who had been swindled by the firm of Russell, Majors and Waddell. These contractors had taken receipted bills signed by former Secretary of War John B. Floyd, before rendering the government the appropriate services, and had used them in obtaining loans and in prying from a hapless War Department employee United States bonds that they promptly sold on the market. Sued by various victims of these transactions, the government had to decide whether or not it must make good on the Russell, Majors and Waddell commitments. Congress therefore asked Bates for an opinion on the matter.

Bates's answer was an admirable mixture of restraint and promise. He had been unable to discover any legal precedent upon which to proceed in investigating the matter and in providing an opinion for the legislative branch. He cited the Judiciary Act of 1789 and opinions of distinguished predecessors, such as William Wirt, as obstacles in the way of fulfilling the request of Congress. "It will, therefore, be seen that, however strongly my own feelings may incline me to accept the commission with which the Senate has honored me," he wrote Vice President Hannibal Hamlin, who presided over the upper chamber, "the want of power to execute it effectively compels me to decline it."[56]

Political considerations were not the only cause of Bates's attitude toward new duties. The Attorney General's administrative staff, housed inconspicuously in the Treasury Building, was greatly burdened by its new responsibilities. However, in a short time, it adapted to the new routine. John A. Rowland functioned as opinion clerk, and C. DeWitt Smith feverishly transcribed Bates's almost illegible scrawl into official notices

<hr />

[56] Bates to Hamlin, December 14, 1861, U. S., Senate, *Executive Documents,* 37th Cong., 2d Sess., IV, 1-2; *Congressional Globe,* 37th Cong., 2d Sess., XXXII, 175-76; Senate, *Executive Documents,* 37th Cong., 2d Sess., IV, 1-2.

or letters to subordinates. Matthew F. Pleasants, hired as pardon clerk, was given other tasks when there was a lull in cases involving executive clemency. John M. Vaughan, son of Bates's old Missouri acquaintance Richard Vaughan, and Richard Bates worked eagerly as assistants under the guidance of Theodore Field, the chief clerk. Completing the office staff was Henry A. Klopfer, who appeared often in other places, bearing messages from Bates or picking up return mail addressed to the Attorney General. In all, however, the staff found its tasks almost too vast to accomplish in the available time.

In spite of his cautious attitude toward Congress and the restrictions of a small staff, Bates zealously guarded his new role against encroachment by other members of the Cabinet, especially by Seward, whom he had come to dislike. In early September he rebuked Seward for a circular on confiscation that the Secretary of State had mailed to district attorneys and marshals. Bates immediately instructed that it be disregarded. Concrete proof, he asserted, was needed to prosecute under the Confiscation Acts. The mere fact that a person had engaged in revolt against the Union was insufficient evidence; a court must determine that his property had been used to further the rebellion.[57]

In other cases he carefully circumscribed the elements of proof in confiscation cases to the Cabinet or Army commanders who, he felt, were or would be guilty of invading civil jurisdictional areas. Contrary to the instructions in Seward's circular, he insisted, there must be ample proof that the property in question was being used to aid the South. In December, 1860, a Fredericksburg, Virginia, manufacturing firm had shipped woolen goods to a warehouse in Baltimore.

[57] T. J. Coffey to Jacob H. Ela, September 12, 1861, Coffey to Hiram Willey, September 12, 1861, Attorney General Letterbooks, B, IV; Bates to Seward, September 23, 1861, William H. Seward Papers.

After the war began, the firm arranged for the return of these goods, but they were seized en route by Army authorities in Alexandria. Undaunted, the Fredericksburg company transferred their title to the items as payment of a debt to a Baltimore firm. Thus, the Baltimore company claimed the goods, only to have the Army refuse to surrender them because the material was contraband. In deciding on the case in early November, Bates ruled that the loyal Baltimore firm had a legal right to the goods. His opinion noted that the transactions had taken place before the acts of July 13 and the proclamation of August 16 forbidding commercial intercourse with insurgents. To the dismay of the Army authorities, he therefore denied the government's claim to the property.[58]

Bates found that his jurisdictional authority often brought him into conflict with the two older and more established executive officers—the secretaries of State and of War, both of whom he distrusted. Particularly on matters involving the arrests of persons did he encounter frustrating administrative obstacles from these two departments. Seward directed marshals and attorneys on matters involving the suspension of the writ of habeas corpus and contraband mail, while Army commanders in the field usually assumed they were senior to civil officers in every circumstance. Even Secretary of the Interior Caleb B. Smith sporadically dispatched orders to attorneys and marshals. In addition, Secretary of War Simon Cameron ordered persons to be placed under arrest, frequently countermanding previous instructions from others.[59]

In spite of the administrative chaos, Bates grew bolder in

[58] Bates to Hiram Willey, October 17, 1861, Coffey to Robert Crozier, December 13, 1861, Attorney General Letterbooks, B, IV; *Attorney General Opinions*, X, 153-56.

[59] F. W. Seward to W. H. F. Curley, October 21, 1861, Earl Bill to Bates, November 5, 1861, Bill to Seward, November 5, 1861, Seward to K. Lothrup, November 7, 1861, *O. R.*, Ser. 2, II, 114, 130, 1042-43; George Fort Milton, *Abraham Lincoln and the Fifth Column*, 48-49.

his attempts to wield civil power in the midst of a rapidly spreading war. He tried to get larger allotments from Smith's judiciary fund to supplement his own budget, and he began to request the release of prisoners held by the State Department, if proof of guilt were lacking. On one occasion, he stopped legal proceedings against two newspapers that had criticized the Administration. Too, he found subtle uses for the patronage power, and he frequently influenced Lincoln to make appointments that strengthened his own hand.[60]

In November he challenged the Army for the first time. A military provost judge in General George B. McClellan's command ordered Southern merchants in Alexandria, Virginia, to pay their debts to Northern merchants or be imprisoned. Bates immediately issued instructions that civil, not military, courts had precedence in these matters. Next, he dispatched a memorandum to Lincoln, expressing his thoughts on the matter: "I do not see how we can defend the Executive before the people, for the assumption of the powers properly belonging to the Judicial Courts, and for the attempt (and it would only be an attempt) to administer justice between man and man, in their ordinary civil business." The settlement of the question, he advised, must be left to Congress.[61]

Much of Bates's antagonism toward the military arose because he felt no bold commander had come forward to lead the way to military victory. Rhetorically, he asked, "Are we to encounter no risk? Can war be conducted without danger?

[60] Beale, *Bates Diary*, 196; Caleb B. Smith to Bates, September 16 and 18, 1861, U. S., Department of the Interior Letterbooks, Judiciary No. 7; Bates to Seward, December 11, 1861, *O. R.*, Ser. 2, II, 351; Bates to Broadhead, October 7, 1861, Broadhead Papers; Bates to Lincoln, October 25, 1861, R. T. Lincoln Collection; T. J. Coffey to George Coffey, October 12, 1861, Attorney General Letterbooks, B, IV.

[61] Bates to McClellan, November 16, 1861, Attorney General Letterbooks, B, IV; Bates to Lincoln, November 21, 1861, R. T. Lincoln Collection.

. . . Some gallant enterprises are necessary to establish the prestige of the army and thus increase its positive strength." It bothered him to see how loosely the military structure hung together after weeks of war, and how slow the Administration had been in making necessary adjustments. He hoped Lincoln would act when doddering old Winfield Scott submitted his resignation from the Army.[62]

Bates considered the Cabinet meeting on November 1 "a memorable day," for the question of Scott's successor was settled then. Though considerate of Scott, perhaps remembering him as once a Whig presidential candidate, Bates expressed his displeasure at the inaction of the Army. After some discussion among the Cabinet members, it was decided to replace the old veteran with the mercurial McClellan. Bates, however, nervously detected a reluctance on Lincoln's part. Thinking again of possible reaction in Congress, he quickly reminded Lincoln of his historic role. He remarked to the President that "the General chief—or chief General—is only your lieutenant. You are the constitutional 'Commander in chief,' and may make any general you please, your second, or lieutenant, to command under you."[63]

Though presuming much, Bates clearly stated his position. He chafed daily under what he felt to be the Army's unwarranted assumption of civil authority while it neglected its duties in the field. It rankled him to witness the emancipation of slaves by the Army, especially on orders of such commanders as General Benjamin Butler, who treated runaway slaves or those found in occupied areas as prizes of war, taking them into Union lines and ordering their release. Some military commanders freed slaves on the grounds that the Confiscation Act had abrogated the Fugitive Slave Act. Bates regarded military emancipation as unlawful, as he con-

[62] Beale, *Bates Diary*, 194, 196-97.

[63] *Ibid.*, 200.

sidered the Fugitive Slave Act to be still in force, but worried lest Congress soon might sanction it. As for escaping slaves, he warned that they must be arrested "as fugitives from service," and he hoped that in time slavery would "lose itself in the tropics." He concentrated primarily on keeping the war machinery of the country under the direct control of the Chief Executive, who could then operate it at his discretion while preventing its excessive use by other arms of the government, in particular emancipationist-minded generals and rash Republican zealots in Congress.[64]

[64] *New York Tribune,* November 27, 1861; Bates to Cameron, December 30, 1861, *O. R.,* Ser. 2, II, 182-83; St. Louis *Missouri Republican,* August 31, 1861; Baltimore *Sun,* September 4, 1861; Washington *National Intelligencer,* September 4, 1861; Beale, *Bates Diary,* 207-11; Bates to Lieber, December 19, 1861, Lieber Collection.

CHAPTER VI

THE FALL OF TWO GENERALS

*W*ORRIED about the Army's increasing encroachments on civil jurisdiction, Bates carefully watched the activities of General John C. Frémont in Missouri and of General George B. McClellan in the eastern theater of war. The Attorney General thought that both had the potentialities of military dictators and thus were a threat to civil authority. Too, he glumly noted that both had failed on the field of battle.

Actually, Frémont had inherited a desperate situation in Missouri in the summer of 1861. In May, Frank Blair, assisted by Nathaniel Lyon, a pugnacious Army captain transferred from Fort Leavenworth, had assembled a loyal force in St. Louis to hold the city. Governor Claiborne Fox Jackson, a pro-Southern politician, defiantly had rejected Lincoln's call for volunteers. Instead, he had convened a special session of the legislature in an attempt to take Missouri out of the Union. The Governor also ordered the establishment of "Camp Jackson," a militia area outside St. Louis, to provide a headquarters for the pro-Southern elements. Alarmed by this turn of events, Blair and Lyons fortified the St. Louis arsenal and launched a successful attack on Camp Jackson. As they led their disconsolate prisoners through the streets of St. Louis, desultory firing broke out, and several people were killed. Thereafter, fighting and killing marked mass meetings and isolated mob actions in Missouri. Finally, on May 21, General William S. Harney, Commander of the Department of Missouri, met with Sterling Price, leader of the pro-Southern forces. The two agreed to halt hostilities in the state temporarily, but Blair and Lyons felt that the pact was unwise, and they determined to end the armed truce at the earliest possible moment.

Bates fully approved of the Harney-Price agreement, for it prevented further outbreaks of violence in Missouri. Early reports reaching him from old friends, including Charles Gibson, indicated the Union forces' unreadiness, particularly in St. Louis. He passed along this information to Cameron to prepare the Secretary for an appeal for federal assistance. Gibson, however, suggested a plan which appeared to be a suitable compromise. Recruit only loyal Missourians to fight secessionists in and around St. Louis, he wrote, and trust the rest of the citizenry. Bates thought over the idea and accepted it with some reluctance, for he regarded the action at Camp Jackson as tragic. He ardently desired to see the Harney-Price pact stand up.[1] Blair and Lyons, however, were demanding Harney's relief, and, ironically, the reports Bates passed on to Cameron aided their cause. Lyons was given authority to enlist volunteers in St. Louis and to declare martial law in

[1] Bates to Broadhead, May 3, 1861, James O. Broadhead Papers; "Gibson Autobiography," Charles Gibson Papers; Gibson to Bates, April 22, 1861, Bates to Cameron, April 27, 1861, in Richard Rush and others, eds., *The War of the Rebellion: A Compilation of the Official Records of the Union and Confederate Armies*, Ser. 1, I, 671, 672-73; St. Louis *Missouri Republican*, May 25, 1861; John McElroy, *The Struggle for Missouri*, 96; Edward C. Smith, *The Borderland in the Civil War*, 245-46.

the city, if necessary. On May 31 Lincoln yielded completely
to the Blair-Lyon influence and ordered the latter to replace
Harney. Informed at the last minute of the change, Bates,
with General Scott's help, managed a compromise. Lyon suc-
ceeded to the command, but Missouri was transferred to the
Department of the Ohio, under McClellan. Bates's hopes of
preventing the Army from entering political affairs in the
state were to be disappointed, however. In spite of his efforts,
Missouri was to continue to be the scene of political turmoil
as well as military conflict throughout the war.[2]

When General John C. Frémont, famous explorer and son-
in-law of Thomas Hart Benton, arrived in St. Louis in July,
1861, he found the state in turmoil. Lyon, promoted to the
rank of brigadier general, had seized the secessionist strong-
holds of Jefferson City and Boonville and was marching
southward to Springfield. As he moved, Confederate forces
organized to resist his advance. A full-scale war, now Frémont's responsibility, was impending, and the General had
few resources with which to fight it.

Gamble and the other pro-Union leaders realized that they
must take political action in order to restore order in the
state. Disruption of political parties and the break between
the legislature and the state convention had produced administrative chaos. In early summer, the moderate Unionists of
the convention hastily laid plans to form a provisional government. As Bates had hoped, this government pledged
itself to the restoration of law and order and to the end of
military rule.[3] Active in the convention's councils, Gamble
emerged as the spokesman for the numerically strong moderate group, and subsequently was elected provisional gov-

[2] "Gibson Autobiography," Gibson Papers; Scott to Lyon, April
30, 1861, O. R., Ser. 1, I, 675; Mark Howard to Welles, May 31,
1861, Gideon Welles Papers; Bates to Sol Smith, July 12, 1861,
Sol Smith Collection.

[3] Bates to Gamble, July 16 and August 2, 1861, Hamilton R.
Gamble Papers.

ernor. With the support of his brother-in-law Bates in Washington, he set out to achieve political unity and to preserve the peace with the aid of state militia instead of federal troops.[4]

Bates and Gamble both regarded the colorful Frémont as a threat to their plans. Because "the Pathfinder" was a favorite of the Blairs, they feared he had little support among border-state conservatives, who resisted action that might turn their state into a battleground. Already Bates and Gibson had formulated a plan for an *entente cordiale* between the state's Provisional Government and the federal Administration. Included in the arrangement was the control of military policy by the Provisional Government. Bates thought the state militia should have, as its primary mission, the protection of the property of loyal slaveholders in the state.[5] If, on the other hand, Frémont were to be given a large military force of Federal troops, Missouri might easily become a major theater of the war and the citizenry be subjected to military depredations.

After August 10 an entirely different situation confronted Bates in Missouri. At Wilson's Creek, outside Springfield, Missouri, Lyon impetuously led his forces into an ill-timed battle with Price's Confederate army and was mortally wounded while attempting to rally his defeated command. Bates received the news grimly, for he realized that the battle meant open conflict in Missouri. He now had to ask for more arms and troops to be sent to his war-torn state. A hurried trip to Philadelphia to talk with Gibson, who had recent news from Missouri, confirmed his worst fears. Unhappily, he wrote Chase, "The very heart of the state [Missouri] is broken. All

[4] Bates to Gamble, December 14, 1861, Gamble Papers; Marvin R. Cain, "Edward Bates and Hamilton R. Gamble: A Wartime Partnership," *Missouri Historical Review,* LVI, 146-47.

[5] M. Blair to Doolittle, April 27, 1861, James R. Doolittle Collection; Gibson to Gamble, August 2, 1861, Bates to Gamble, August 2, 1861, Bates to Gibson, August 4, 1861, Gamble Papers.

confidence is destroyed." Only immediate Federal reinforcements would keep the state in the Union.[6]

Frémont had seriously divided the loyal Missouri elements by declaring martial law in St. Louis on August 14. Two weeks later, he issued a proclamation announcing that captured armed civilians in northern Missouri would be summarily shot and warning that his forces would confiscate secessionist property, including slaves. He planned, apparently, to emancipate these slaves by military order. If his directives should be carried out, the civil authorities in Missouri would be helpless under the Army's rigid control.

Fortunately, Lincoln forced Frémont to modify his original proclamation by eliminating those sections dealing with the execution of civilians and the confiscation of property. The President took action after receiving Frank Blair's reports of corruption on a wide scale in Frémont's command. He also dispatched Quartermaster General Montgomery C. Meigs and Montgomery Blair to Missouri to investigate the situation. Heartened by Lincoln's actions, Bates looked forward to the possible disgrace of the ebullient Frémont. He now had a better chance to fulfill his promise to "demand the instant removal of Frémont."[7]

Bates still feared that Frémont would coerce the Provisional Government and virtually destroy the delicate framework of civil control. He had observed how the General's measures had already agitated an extremist minority of pro-Southern Missourians to violent action. Disregarding Frémont's fame, he strove to bolster Gamble's threatened political authority. "The Attorney General," an editor of the *New York Tribune* noted, "is unreserved in his expression of opinion concerning

[6] Bates to Eliot, August 19, 1861, William Greenleaf Eliot Collection; Bates to Gamble, September 27, 1861, Gamble Papers; Bates to Chase, September 11, 1861, Salmon P. Chase Collection.

[7] Bates to Chase, September 11, 1861, Chase Collection.

General Frémont, and does not hesitate to pronounce his retention a public crime."[8]

By late September Bates felt certain he was making headway against Frémont. However, the President moved slowly because Frémont had started his army in a southwesterly advance to engage the Confederate forces. Lincoln desired more information. In early October, he dispatched Secretary of War Cameron and The Adjutant General, Lorenzo Thomas, on separate missions to Missouri to investigate Frémont's command. Annoyed at this turn of events, Bates wrote Broadhead, recommending that he convince Cameron of the necessity to remove the famous commander. Appropriate remarks might force Lincoln to yield and might lead to the appointment of either General David Hunter, who accompanied Cameron and Thomas on their Missouri tour, or General Henry W. Halleck as successor to Frémont.[9]

Cameron and Thomas both reported corruption and administrative confusion in the Department of the West. These revelations caused Bates to believe "beyond all question that the removal [of Frémont] must be made and instantly." It dismayed him that the President doubted the wisdom of such a measure because Frémont appeared to be popular among his soldiers. He attempted to persuade Lincoln "to avoid the timorous and vacillating course that could but degrade the Adm[inistratio]n, and make it weak and helpless."[10]

A few days later, on October 24, Lincoln decided to act.

[8] Gibson to Gamble, September 27, 1861, Gamble Papers; Adam Gurowski, *Diary, March 4, 1861–November 2, 1862*, 94; Theodore C. Pease and James G. Randall, eds., *The Diary of Orville Hickman Browning, 1850-1881*, I, 502-3; *New York Tribune*, October 7, 1861. Strangely enough, Browning thought Frémont's actions justified and proper.

[9] Bates to Broadhead, September 28 and October 9, 1861, Broadhead Papers.

[10] Howard K. Beale, ed., *The Diary of Edward Bates, 1859-1866*, 198.

He sent instructions to General Samuel R. Curtis in St. Louis removing Frémont from command: Unless the General was in the process of winning a battle, he was to turn over his army to General Hunter. In addition, the President directed a reorganization of the Department of the West under General Henry W. Halleck. After some difficulty the message reached Frémont, encamped and secluded at Springfield. Reluctantly, he surrendered command of his army to Hunter.[11] Two weeks later, Halleck left for Missouri.

On learning of Halleck's appointment, Bates wrote to friends in Missouri, fulsomely praising the general. He had a long talk with Halleck before he left Washington and provided the aloof general with information concerning loyal men in Missouri. Observing that Halleck seemed attentive, Bates also urged him to cooperate closely with Gamble and the Provisional Government. He particularly emphasized the importance of restoring order and ending military operations in Missouri. If the Confederates could be driven out of Missouri, he told Halleck, the Provisional Government would be strong enough to reunite the state. Missouri could then serve as a base of operations for an expedition down the Mississippi to seize New Orleans and seal off the Confederacy from the great river.[12]

To accomplish this latter goal the Attorney General looked to his friend James B. Eads, who planned to construct an armed gunboat flotilla on the Mississippi. Eads already had collected an assorted fleet at Cairo, Illinois, in early spring

[11] Lincoln to Curtis, October 24, 1861, in Roy P. Basler, ed., *The Collected Works of Abraham Lincoln,* IV, 562-63; Allan Nevins, *Frémont, The West's Greatest Adventurer,* II, 614-16.

[12] Bates to Broadhead and Glover, November 12, 1861, Broadhead Papers; Beale, *Bates Diary,* 201. As Bates wrote, however, Hunter was retreating northwestward after deciding against a battle. The plan initially used was similar to one drawn up by obscure Colonel U. S. Grant in Ironton, Missouri. See Bruce Catton, *Grant Moves South,* 26, 29.

and, on Bates's advice, had drawn up a plan for blockading the Mississippi. Bates thought a gunboat fleet vitally important in the campaign in the West, and accordingly he planned ways to raise money for the project. After Eads received a government contract to build seven gunboats, he sought out Montgomery Meigs, the quartermaster general of the Army, Chase, and Welles to obtain their support for suitable appropriations. In spite of his exertions, however, Eads did not receive a Treasury draft until late in 1862. But he did begin construction of the boats that played a part in the western campaigns during the spring and summer of 1862.[13]

Bates realized that a strong army must be provided for Missouri's defense also. Organizing the state militia had proved extremely difficult for Gamble. Though he lacked imagination to plan far-ranging solutions, Gamble assiduously worked to arm and equip the state troops.[14] He drew up a proposal to organize state and Federal troops to serve under a unified command in the event of Confederate invasion and came to Washington to present it to Lincoln. Though the President basically agreed with the idea, he insisted that the senior general of the Department of the West be placed in command of the state militia forces also. On the eve of Halleck's planned offensive in Missouri, Gamble agreed to the selection of General John M. Schofield for this post. The shadow of distrust, however, had fallen across the ties that bound the Administration and the Provisional Government of Missouri.[15]

[13] Eads to Welles, May 8, 1861, Gideon Welles Papers; Welles to Eads, May 14, 1861, Eads to F. P. Blair, October 29, 1861, Eads to Bates, November 10, 1861, Bates to Eads, December 2, 1861, James B. Eads Papers.

[14] Gamble to Bates, September 17, 1861, Robert Todd Lincoln Collection; Bates to Gamble, October 3, 1861, Gamble Papers.

[15] James D. Richardson, ed., *A Compilation of the Messages and Papers of the Presidents, 1789-1897*, V, 3241-43; Gamble to Bates, December 7, 1861, R. T. Lincoln Collection; Gibson to Gamble, December 24, 1861, Gamble Papers.

Bates realized the war in Missouri was growing more complicated because of its Hydra-headed nature: the efforts to keep the state in the Union and the many aspects of the internal struggle to preserve moderate political control in the face of real or potential martial law. Because of the disorder in the state, Lincoln had authorized Halleck to suspend habeas corpus. Bates felt it far wiser to prevent the Confederates from making a concerted military effort in the Mississippi Valley. His plans were grounded in the hope of keeping war from spreading in Missouri.[16]

Because of events in Missouri and Price's skillful dodging of blows by the Federal troops, Bates looked askance at any more power for the military. But congressmen, now filling up vacated seats on Capitol Hill for the winter session, regarded Frémont's removal, the disasters of Bull Run and Ball's Bluff, and the immobile condition of the Union armies in both the East and West as evidence of incompetence and treachery. Soon after it convened, Congress therefore created the investigative Committee on the Conduct of the War. Composed of three senators and four representatives, the committee probed into high Army command policies and, ultimately, into Administration politics. Fearing the zealous antislavery Republicans who dominated the committee, Bates urged a bold counterstroke by the executive: Lincoln should relieve McClellan and assume full control as commander-in-chief. He believed that McClellan, the particular target of the discontented congressmen, must be sacrificed to prevent the weakening of the Chief Executive's hand.[17]

[16] Lincoln to Halleck, November 21, 1861, Abraham Lincoln Papers (Missouri Historical Society); Lincoln to Halleck, December 2, 1861, Basler, op. cit., V, 35; Beale, Bates Diary, 204.

[17] Beale, Bates Diary, 218; Captain W. Denison to Bates, January 10, 1862, R. T. Lincoln Collection; Laura Stedman and George W. Gould, The Life and Letters of Edmund Clarence Stedman, I, 254. Bates hired Stedman, poet and literary critic, as a clerk in December, 1861.

Even the normal social functions in Washington had come to have about them a military aura which Bates disliked. He attended a New Year's Day reception at the White House where he saw hosts of military officers comprising part of what he termed "a gawdy [*sic*] show." Accompanied by his daughters Matilda and Nancy and his son Richard, he nevertheless stayed long enough to witness the ostentatious parade before the "poor fatigued President."[18]

A few days later, on January 10, Bates and the other Cabinet members learned the worst about the military. General Irvin McDowell delivered startling news about the Army's inability to resume fighting immediately. Stung by what he considered military bungling, Bates took an audacious step. He recommended that all ships under orders of the War Department be restored to the Navy, that all Army generals submit regular reports to the President, and that the Chief Executive set himself up as constitutional commander-in-chief. Contemptuously he showed that inexperienced high-ranking officers of the Army were commanding large bodies of men; Lincoln, by assuming command, would not be rejecting proven leadership. The President, Bates said, must take over

> the legitimate duties of his place—His powers are all duties—He has no privileges, no powers granted to him for his own sake, and he has no more right to refuse to exercise his constitutional powers than he has to assume powers not granted. He (like us, his official inferiors) cannot evade his responsibilities. He must shew [*sic*] to the nation and to posterity how he has discharged the duties of his *stewardship,* in this crisis. And if he will only trust his own good judgment more, and defer less to the opinions of his subordinates, I have no doubt that the affairs of the war and the aspect of the whole country, will be quickly and greatly changed for the better.[19]

[18] Beale, *Bates Diary,* 221.
[19] *Ibid.,* 223-24.

No one could object to the President's assuming, as his "legal duties," the role of military commander-in-chief, he concluded. It seemed to him that no one general could possibly control the vast army and bring to bear all the resources of the Union in the successful prosecution of the war, as could the President. He suggested, too, that vigorous action on the Chief Executive's part might thwart the Committee on the Conduct of the War.[20]

Much to Bates's joy, Lincoln acted. On January 14 he named Edwin M. Stanton as successor to Cameron. The President charged the new Secretary of War with the reorganization of the Union's military structure and the revitalization of its high command. Bates looked upon this first move with mixed emotions. He thought a military shake-up necessary, and yet he distrusted Stanton. Nevertheless, he extended to the bewhiskered, excitable new Secretary of War a cordial welcome.[21]

On January 27 Lincoln took a second important step, more to Bates's liking. He issued War Order No. 1, which directed a general movement of military forces on all fronts. On January 31 he promulgated Special War Order No. 1, which ordered the Army of the Potomac to march southward toward Richmond via Manassas. The grizzled Attorney General saw this directive as a hopeful beginning of "Constitutional restoration" under the President and the beginning of a victorious military campaign.[22]

Bates intently watched the changed military strategy. In

[20] *Ibid.*, 224-26; "Memorandum of General McDowell," in Henry J. Raymond, *The Life and Public Services of Abraham Lincoln,* 773; *Chicago Tribune,* January 6, 1862; Bates to Broadhead, January 10, 1862, Broadhead Papers.

[21] Beale, *Bates Diary,* 227-28; Benjamin P. Thomas and Harold M. Hyman, *Stanton, The Life and Times of Lincoln's Secretary of War,* 149.

[22] James G. Randall and Richard N. Current, *Mr. Lincoln,* 248; James G. Randall, *Lincoln, the President,* II, 74-77.

principle, he agreed with Lincoln's plan to keep the Army of the Potomac between the Confederates and Washington, so he thought McClellan's decision to drive up the peninsula between the James and York rivers poor tactics to carry out good strategy. Also, his misgivings about the general lack of concern for the war in the West had made it difficult for him to commend any plan of advance in the East. He finally reasoned that if the Mississippi were sealed off and the Confederacy invaded from the West, the war might easily be brought to a speedy conclusion before casualty rates began to mount.[23]

Bates knew that inaction by Union generals, particularly McClellan, would result in intervention by Congress, a consequence he now wished to avoid. He heard disquieting stories from his new friend, Commissioner of Agriculture Isaac Newton, who saw conspiracy lurking behind every building and in every office. According to Newton, Stanton's close liaison with the Committee on the Conduct of the War had become dangerous. Influenced by what he had heard, Bates began to regard the War Secretary's demonic activity with some concern.[24] But, in the West, the fall of Fort Henry and Fort Donelson and Buell's advance into Nashville enlarged Stanton's reputation. All eyes now focused on McClellan's high-spirited army in the East. Upon its future, Bates thought, the political and military control of the war now depended. If it failed, he expected Congress to attack the Administration mercilessly.

On March 8, however, Lincoln divided the Army of the Potomac into four corps, established a defense force for Washington, and relieved McClellan of all but command of the Eastern Army. The President's action greatly pleased Bates, for he considered McClellan incompetent to lead a large

[23] Beale, *Bates Diary*, 228-29, 248-49; Bates to Lieber, April 5, 1862, Francis Lieber Collection.

[24] Beale, *Bates Diary*, 227-28.

Union force. Despite the glowing praise of McClellan he heard from his new pardon clerk Edmund Stedman, a part-time literary critic and poet, he took Stanton's reports in the Cabinet to be proof positive of the General's shortcomings. He was pleased that Lincoln had stripped McClellan of much of his command, and he felt a certain smugness when it appeared that the President was to direct the general movements of the Army.[25]

Bates experienced a pleasant lull in public affairs, during which his son Woodson was admitted to West Point. In early April, he accompanied his young son to Newburgh, New York, for his preparatory examination. After an enjoyable visit there, he returned to Washington. News from the West was both good and bad; Pope had taken Island No. 10, in the Mississippi opposite New Madrid, but Grant had been fought to a draw after the Confederates surprised him on the battlefield of Shiloh, near the Tennessee River. These events reinforced in Bates his earlier conviction that not enough force had been concentrated in the West. Instead of moving up the peninsula, he suggested that McClellan should block Norfolk and prepare to move across the James and attack Petersburg. This maneuver, he instructed his Cabinet colleagues, who must have grown accustomed to his discourses on military strategy, would keep the Confederates busy while a decisive victory was won in the West.[26]

Bates's inordinate interest in military affairs in the West displayed his sectional pride and sometimes proved irritating to those about him. In January he had discussed privately

[25] *Ibid.*, 239-41, 242-43, 247. Bates successfully protected Stedman from the accusations of Caleb B. Smith, who charged the pardon clerk with being aligned with radical plotters.

[26] Bates to Lincoln, February 28, 1861, R. T. Lincoln Collection; Lincoln to Joseph G. Totten, March 8, 1862, Basler, *op. cit.*, V, 152; Beale, *Bates Diary*, 245-49; Charles Gibson, "Edward Bates," *Missouri Historical Collections*, II, 56; Warren H. Hassler, Jr., *General George B. McClellan, Shield of the Union*, 67.

with Lincoln the qualifications of an old St. Louis friend and retired Army general, Ethan Allen Hitchcock. Bates had blandly recommended a supreme command for Hitchcock, but the old general, a graduate of West Point in the Class of 1817, wisely declined. He did agree to serve as an adviser on Stanton's Army Board. Bates accepted Hitchcock's decision without comment, for he felt his mere presence in Washington would help emphasize the importance of the Western theater of war.[27]

In the spring and summer of 1862 Bates also attacked the problem of completing the southwest Missouri branch of the railroad to the Pacific. If constructed, the line would run from the Union supply base of Rolla to Springfield, Missouri. Part of the road had been finished, but when the construction company defaulted on payment of interest on its bonds the state seized control of the branch line. In turn, 125 miles of track between Rolla and Springfield had to be laid by June, 1863, or the branch line would revert to federal control. As did Gamble, Bates hoped to keep the branch line in state hands. When Gibson convinced him of the urgency of the matter, Bates wrote Halleck to ask him to rush the completion of the project. He also sent Gibson to see General William T. Sherman, Commander of the Army of the Cumberland, to solicit his aid in the same enterprise.[28]

Bates called at Willard's Hotel to discuss the railroad with General John Pope, recently arrived from Missouri to take command of the newly created Army of Virginia. Having served on Halleck's staff and thus being aware of the problems in Missouri, Pope promised to help Bates. The Attorney General received a cold reception from Pope's civilian chief,

[27] Bates to Hitchcock, January 31, 1862, Abraham Lincoln Papers (Abraham Lincoln National Life Foundation, Fort Wayne, Indiana); William A. Croffut, ed., *Fifty Years in Camp and Field: Diary of Major Ethan Allen Hitchcock, U.S.A.*, 439.

[28] "Gibson Autobiography," Gibson Papers; Bates to Halleck, April 14, 1862, R. T. Lincoln Collection.

however. Resenting what he considered Bates's meddling in military matters, the volatile Secretary of War asked for a written order from Lincoln before he would take any action.[29]

Undaunted, Bates secured the executive order. Dated July 11, it directed the extension of the railroad line to Lebanon, Missouri, fifty miles from Springfield. However, the issuance of the order was delayed, in spite of reports from Missouri indicating that a Confederate invasion was imminent. Once again Bates conferred with Lincoln. He found the order had been delayed because of insufficient funds to complete the branch line. Dejected, he dropped the matter temporarily.[30]

Prior to the controversy over the railroad, Bates was given an opportunity to see the course of war in the East. McClellan had inched his way up the peninsula toward Yorktown and Williamsburg where he would, Bates thought, force the enemy into the neck between the James and Chickahominy rivers.[31] On May 13 Bates accompanied a large party that included Welles and Seward down to Norfolk and Gosport Naval Yard. The group inspected the recent Union captures and viewed the half-sunk *Merrimac*. The next day, they journeyed up the York and Pamunkey rivers and visited McClellan's camp at White House. With victory in sight, Bates was enthusiastic. He predicted the evacuation of Richmond without a fight if the demoralized Confederate troops were allowed to retreat over the Chickahominy. Except for the loss of his

[29] Halleck to Bates, May 8, 1862, Bates to Lincoln, May 22, 1862, Bates to Pope, June 28, 1862, Pope to Bates, June 28, 1862, Stanton to Bates, July 7, 1862, R. T. Lincoln Collection; Bates to Stanton, June 20, 1862, Edwin M. Stanton Papers.

[30] Order Extending the Pacific Railroad, July 11, 1862, Lincoln to Curtis, October 12, 1862, Basler, *op. cit.*, V, 314, 459; John B. Henderson to Bates, July 18, 1862, Bates to Lincoln, September 19, 1862, R. T. Lincoln Collection; Bates to Gamble, July 24, 1862, Bates Papers.

[31] Beale, *Bates Diary*, 254-56, 258; Washington *National Intelligencer*, April 21, 1862.

tie, carried off by pack rats in the night, he found the trip heartening.[32]

McClellan's subsequent success, marred only by the cruel impasse at Fair Oaks on May 31, continued to encourage Bates. It led him to believe that the war was entering its final stages. A few days later, however, McClellan's indecision and the beginning of the Battle of Seven Days left him in deep despair. The fighting, involving both the fate of the Union and John Coalter Bates's safety, again raised his doubts about McClellan's ability. As he revealed to Lieber, his hopes, recently so high, vanished just as decisive victory had come to appear likely.[33]

On July 8 the President left for Harrison's Landing to confer with McClellan. Halleck had been named general-in-chief of all eastern armies, and Pope had assumed command of Union forces in northern Virginia. McClellan indeed appeared lost. He had created more enemies in both wings of the Republican party with his letter from Harrison's Landing to Lincoln on July 7, containing indiscreet statements concerning political and constitutional matters. Halleck's action came as no surprise when, on August 3, after a series of consultations with Lincoln, he ordered the faltering McClellan to abandon his position on the peninsula and join Pope's army on the Rappahannock. The campaign had come to an inglorious conclusion and, with it, hopes for the termination of the fighting in 1862.

Bates felt that McClellan had betrayed the Administration and, therefore, thought it proper to join his Cabinet colleagues in plotting against the General. On August 29 Chase and Stanton visited Bates's home to obtain his aid in asking Lin-

[32] Beale, *Bates Diary*, 258-59; Richard S. West, Jr., *Gideon Welles, Lincoln's Navy Department*, 216-17.

[33] Bates to Lieber, June 10, 1862, Lieber to Bates, June 19, 1862, Bates to Lieber, July 3 and 8, 1862, Lieber to Bates, July 8, 1862. Lieber Collection; Beale, *Bates Diary*, 260-62.

coln to relieve McClellan. At the time Bates was working busily in his office and did not see either man. The next morning, after conferring with Chase, he agreed to endorse the anti-McClellan movement. Later in the day the scheme produced a written petition demanding McClellan's removal, which Chase received from Stanton's office. After making a few changes, the Secretary of the Treasury presented the letter to Welles. Although he thought it acceptable in principle, Welles nevertheless refused to sign, for fear of insulting Lincoln. He suggested that Chase look up Blair, who enjoyed such conspiracies, and solicit his aid. But two days later, when Welles saw the memorandum again, the Postmaster General's signature was not on it.[34]

At the time of the attempted coup by the Cabinet, Bates was engaged in raising more arms and material for Gamble, who had sent alarming news of a Confederate invasion in Missouri. Bates realized he needed the assistance of both Chase and Stanton. Although he opposed McClellan, his willingness to endorse the Chase-Stanton petition to bring about the General's relief reflected in part his anxiety over the situation in Missouri. After he read the Chase-Stanton document, he agreed to sign it, provided he was permitted to alter any of the statements. Chase consented, for he needed signatures. Bates therefore prepared his version, which was a concise and brief request for McClellan's relief in the best interests of the country.[35] He, Chase, Stanton, and Smith then signed it. When Welles saw the memorandum the second

[34] David Donald, ed., *Inside Lincoln's Cabinet: The Civil War Diaries of Salmon P. Chase*, 116; Howard K. Beale, ed., *The Diary of Gideon Welles, Secretary of the Navy under Lincoln and Johnson*, I, 93-95, 100; Thomas and Hyman, *Stanton*, 220; Burton J. Hendrick, *Lincoln's War Cabinet*, 313.

[35] Bates to Stanton, May 27, 1862, Attorney General Letterbooks, B, V; Gamble to Bates, July 27, 1862, *O. R.*, Ser. 1, XIII, 515; Lincoln to Gamble, July 28, 1862, Basler, *op. cit.*, V, 347; Donald, *op. cit.*, 117.

time, he again refused to sign and expressed surprise at Bates's action. He mistakenly concluded that Stanton and Chase had exerted great pressure on the Attorney General.[36]

On September 2 Lincoln called a Cabinet meeting amidst dramatic happenings. The day before, the Cabinet had learned that the President had summoned McClellan to the White House, but no one knew the outcome of the discussion. Their speculations proved false. The President had placed McClellan in charge of Washington's defenses and had assigned him to reorganize the demoralized Union forces. Furious, Stanton protested McClellan's new assignment, as he thought Lincoln's order foiled the attempt to relieve McClellan of his command. Bates said little, but that night he wrote Lieber, warning him to expect a prolonged, defensive war. As he had written Gamble the day before, he felt that the Administration would "sink into contempt."[37]

The failure of the Cabinet's coup against McClellan seemed to portend difficult times to come. Bates did not retreat as rapidly as did Chase and Stanton, however. At another Cabinet meeting on September 9, he handed Stedman's pro-McClellan poem, "Wanted—A Man," to Lincoln and sat back, unamused, as the President read it. He thought that the General did not merit such adulation, since Lee had advanced beyond the Potomac into Maryland and was threatening both Washington and Baltimore.[38] Once more, Union troops had to hurry from northern states to meet an inspired invader.

In mid-September McClellan's infantry sat astride the Boonesboro Road, west of Antietam in Maryland. Lee ordered a retrograde movement to Antietam, which he chose to defend.

[36] Undated memorandum, Stanton Papers; Beale, *Welles Diary*, I, 100-101; T. Harry Williams, *Lincoln and the Radicals*, 177-78.

[37] Donald, *op. cit.*, 118; Beale, *Welles Diary*, I, 104-5; Bates to Lieber, September 2, 1861, Lieber Collection; Bates to Gamble, September 1, 1862, Bates Papers.

[38] Stedman and Gould, *op. cit.*, I, 281.

However, McClellan attacked Lee on September 17 and, in a costly struggle, forced the Confederates to begin a retreat back across the Potomac. News reached Washington that the Union general had won a decisive victory, and the capital resounded with a wild burst of enthusiasm. Lincoln and his Cabinet felt no such joy, for they had additional news, not released to the public. The Confederates were not being pursued by McClellan's army. Frantically, the War Department ordered the General to destroy or capture Lee's retreating forces.

Both sides had suffered ghastly losses in the battle. For this reason, and because of a typical overestimation of enemy strength, McClellan did not comply with Stanton's orders to pursue and capture or destroy the Confederate Army. Incredulous over these events, Lincoln journeyed to the battlefield. A few days later he returned to Washington, convinced of McClellan's permanent affliction of the "slows." A great opportunity had been lost, and McClellan's army again was immobilized on the Potomac. Most of the Cabinet agreed that McClellan must advance at once.[39]

Bates was greatly aroused. He argued that McClellan should be removed immediately. His lack of aggressiveness, Bates felt, had damaged the Union's cause and exposed the Administration to congressional criticism. Although he did not speak out openly, as did Stanton and Chase, Bates rebuked Lincoln privately for vacillating. In another Cabinet meeting on November 4, Lincoln reported that McClellan had not begun a forward movement, though actually, he had moved down the east side of the Blue Ridge Mountains. Reflecting on this news, Bates reached a fever point of concern; he asked Lincoln to put Halleck in charge of the field army.[40] Lincoln

[39] Tyler Dennett, ed., *Lincoln and the Civil War in the Diaries and Letters of John Hay,* 52.

[40] Beale, *Welles Diary,* I, 180; *New York Tribune,* November 5, 1862.

hesitated, laconically calling attention to Halleck's lack of sufficient experience in commanding a large force in the field. Actually, the President had decided to relieve McClellan and to replace him with General Ambrose Burnside. As soon as Bates learned the news the next day, his anger subsided. In a matter of days his mood changed entirely; the President, he felt, had command of the situation. He wrote his friend Samuel B. Ruggles, prophesying a significant change in the course of the war.[41]

[41] Lincoln to Halleck, November 5, 1862, Basler, *op. cit.*, V, 485; Bates to Ruggles, November 20, 1862, Abraham Lincoln Collection (Brown University Library, Providence); John G. Nicolay and John Hay, *Abraham Lincoln: A History*, VI, 194-95.

CHAPTER VII

THE FIERCEST PASSIONS
OF OUR NATURE

*O*N DECEMBER 3, 1861, Bates addressed the Supreme Court
of the United States during its first wartime session. As the
first order of business he delivered a eulogy on Justice John
McLean, who had recently died. But the justices of the Court,
who sat this bleak morning in the old semicircular Senate
Chamber on the main floor of the Capitol were to hear something more than the usual first-session formalities.

For weeks Bates had thought about this confrontation of
the Court he had revered all of his life. He was apprehensive
that his opinion in the Merryman case and his acquiescence
in the Administration's punitive measures against civilians
might make unwelcome his appearance before the august
tribunal. A bit nervous, he gazed closely at the justices.
There was the tall, robust Robert C. Grier of Pennsylvania,
a contrast to the ghostly, thin, hawk-eyed Chief Justice, Roger
B. Taney. Also present was Georgia Unionist James M. Wayne,
who had abandoned both section and state to stand with

Lincoln and the North; Nathan Clifford of New Hampshire, formerly Polk's attorney general and the most recent appointee to the Court; and Samuel Nelson of New York, an authority in admiralty law and a student of international relations.

Bates appeared self-assured, but he wondered about the Court's reaction to the sudden expansion of executive power after the firing on Sumter. Having sanctioned these extraordinary executive measures, he now stood before the Court as the Government's chief legal officer to defend them. His own growing realization that a grim war lay ahead and that it would necessitate a concentration of governmental might, helped to bolster his courage. He was glad, though, that he had recently expedited the discharge from military service of minors brought before state courts on writs of habeas corpus. He also hoped his cautious directives to law enforcement officers might have been noticed and approved by the conservative Court.[1]

Shortly before this appearance before the Taney Court, Bates had been busy drafting plans to reorganize the federal court circuits. Two circuits had dissolved when the South seceded, and another was without a judge. Lincoln had hesitated to fill the vacancies on the Court that had existed since the Buchanan administration until the circuits had been established by Congress. His delay had made reorganization of the Supreme Court the center of a political storm. Several Republican leaders hoped to create additional circuits, and thus more Supreme Court vacancies, in an effort to dismantle the Jacksonian Court. Others wanted favored appointees placed on the Supreme Court bench and looked on a court reorganization bill as their opportunity. Lincoln suggested a

[1] *Opinions of the Attorneys General of the United States,* X, 146; Bates to Lincoln, June 21, 1861, Robert Todd Lincoln Collection. Bates also ruled that the President had no right to appoint United States commissioners normally named by the judges of the circuit courts.

more constructive system, along guidelines of equitable size and population, but he had to consider the wishes of his adopted party. To Bates had fallen the onerous task of drafting a reorganization plan which the Administration would sponsor. It seemed an odd job for a man who, as a young lawyer in the 1820's, had resented bitterly the State rights partisans who had attempted to reform the Marshall Court.

Since Bates did not share the general Republican ill will toward the Taney Court, he decided against a plan that would fill the bench with partisans of doubtful ability. In late November he confided to a representative of Governor H. P. Payne of Ohio that he intended to propose a moderate reorganization of the judiciary, and he expected the President to support it. He apparently felt that the discretionary power given him by Lincoln was great, and he planned to draft the bill accordingly.[2]

However, Senator John P. Hale of New Hampshire and some of his colleagues in the Congress challenged the Administration's initial recommendations solely on the grounds that only the legislature had the power to reconstitute the Court. Lincoln, in fact, had obliquely encouraged those who wished a radical revision by suggesting that Supreme Court justices either be relieved of their circuit duties or that their circuits be abolished altogether. In drawing up his plan, Bates ignored both the congressional argument and the President's proposals and added two circuits, thus increasing the number of vacancies to five. His efforts in behalf of a moderate reorganization plan, however, had not been publicized when he spoke to the Court.[3]

[2] Payne to Treat, November 27, 1861, Samuel Treat Papers.

[3] Annual Message, December 3, 1861, in Roy P. Basler, ed., *The Collected Works of Abraham Lincoln*, V, 42; Joseph Casey to Davis, December 11, 1861, David Davis Papers; David M. Silver, *Lincoln's Supreme Court*, 39-41; U. S., *Congressional Globe*, 37th Cong., 2d Sess., XXXII, 26-28.

Thus, when Bates addressed the Court, conflicting emotions tore at his thoughts. On the one hand, he was anxious that individually the justices would accept the Administration's policies, and, on the other, he felt responsibility for his power to draft the executive's plan on the reorganization of the judiciary. He decided to speak boldly.

> Your just power is diminished, and into a large portion of our country your writ does not run and your beneficent authority to administer justice according to law, is for the present, successfully denied and resisted. . . . The still, small voice of legal justice is drowned by the incessant roll of the drum, the deafening thunder of artillery. To that extent, your just and lawful power is practically annulled, for the laws are silent. . . . Now, indeed, we are over-shadowed with a dark cloud, broad and gloomy as a nation's pall; but patriotism can discern the bow of promise set in that cloud, spanning the gloom with its bright arch, to foreshow the coming of a day of sunshine and calm, and to justify our hopes of a speedy restoration of peace, and order, and law.[4]

In spite of his apprehensions, Bates was determined to justify executive action on the grounds of necessity while indicating his respect for the Court. He knew that the justices were alarmed over the attempts, reminiscent of Thomas Jefferson's assault on the Marshall Court, that were being made by Hale, John A. Bingham of Ohio, and Trumbull of Illinois to vacate their seats. If he could capitalize on their hostility toward enemies in the Congress, he might persuade the members of the Court to enter into a silent agreement with the executive branch which would, in effect, give the President the role of senior partner. His remarks concluded, he looked searchingly at the somber justices, attempting to gauge their reaction. He could determine little, however, from Taney's

[4] J. S. Black, *Reports of Cases Argued and Determined in the Supreme Court, 1861-1862*, I, 9.

brief speech prior to the adjournment of the opening session.[5]

A few days after his appearance before the Court, Bates called on Justice John Catron to raise again the possibility of an understanding between the executive and the judiciary, and to learn what he could about Catron's views on the debates in Congress. Prior to the first meeting of the Court, he had made similar visits to both Taney and Wayne. An old Jacksonian, Catron assured him of his opposition to any radical changes affecting the high bench and his resolve to state his views to the Senate Judiciary Committee. Senator Hale's irrational resolution, calling for the termination of all appointments of Supreme Court justices, indeed appeared ominous to him and his colleagues.[6]

A few weeks later, Bates felt partially relieved when a bill came out of Senate committee, providing for the establishment of nine reorganized circuits. Three circuits would be created in the North, three in the South, and three in the Middle West. The bill left the number of justices unchanged, thereby providing Lincoln with only three vacancies to fill. Seeing that the moderate proposal contained many of the features of the one he had worked on, Bates concluded that his role in the controversy over reorganization of the courts had ended.[7]

While debates on the judiciary bill now took place in the Senate, where a circuit court system based on population was supported, and in the House, where ambitious politicians championed complete reorganization, Bates advocated neutrality by the executive. He balked at Lincoln's suggestion of

[5] Charles G. Haines, *The American Doctrine of Judicial Supremacy,* 378; U. S., *Congressional Globe,* 37th Cong., 2d Sess., XXXII, 26-28, 37.

[6] Bates to Treat, December 7, 1861, Treat Papers; Howard K. Beale, ed., *The Diary of Edward Bates, 1859-1866,* 204-5.

[7] U. S., *Congressional Globe,* 37th Cong., 2d Sess., XXXII, 8-9, 187-88.

creating a new circuit court in Arkansas by abolishing two old ones, for he surmised that the Supreme Court would not look favorably on the establishment of a new judiciary system by executive decree and without congressional sanction. Also, it would be impractical to believe that a new court system could function in an area not occupied by Union forces. Bates wanted to wait and let Congress make the next move.[8]

In January a new development in the reorganization question occurred when both Taney and Catron became too ill to attend sessions of the Supreme Court. An appointment had to be made in order to ensure the high bench of a quorum. Quickly, in an act motivated largely by political considerations, Lincoln named Noah H. Swayne of Ohio to the Court. The move caught Bates by surprise, although for weeks he had contemplated possible candidates for the vacancies. Taney's dramatic departure, in such a way as to leave doubtful his return, and the activities of Caleb B. Smith's friends to place the Secretary of the Interior on the Court, prompted Bates to endorse the candidacy of Orville Browning. In late March he spent several hours with the newly appointed Swayne, talking about the possibilities of a Confederate surrender. However, Bates had on his mind the goal of getting the conservative Browning appointed to the Court. He was delighted when Swayne returned his call by coming to the Treasury Building and that night visiting his residence in "F" Street. This time, Browning and the Supreme Court vacancy was their main topic of conversation. He found Swayne an interested listener, for the Ohioan was a politician, too. From Swayne he learned of new attempts in the Congress to

[8] *Ibid.*, 173-74, 469; Bates's endorsement on a letter, James Phelps to Lincoln, December 19, 1861, R. T. Lincoln Collection; Lincoln to Bates, December 30, 1861, Basler, *op. cit.*, V, 82.

gerrymander the circuits so as to give sections or states an advantage in the selection of appointees to the Court.[9]

On July 15, 1862, Congress finally passed the Judiciary Act, reorganizing the federal court system. Under its provisions Lincoln was to make two new appointments, including one to the ninth circuit, which comprised four states west of the Mississippi River.[10] Bates, however, had little to do with the impending Court selections. Lincoln had never consulted him in the appointment of Swayne, nor did he ask him about his views on other possible choices. The President merely requested from him an opinion on whether he could make a Court appointment while Congress was not in session.

Concealing his disappointment, Bates stated that the President had the right to make temporary appointments, contingent on the approval of the Senate when it convened.[11] Two days later, Lincoln issued a Supreme Court commission to David Davis, his manager at the Chicago convention and an old Illinois colleague and friend. For the first time since 1860 the Supreme Court had its full complement of nine justices, but Browning was not among them.

The reorganization by Congress of the judiciary and Lincoln's semipersonal considerations of both Swayne and Davis turned Bates from the intrigues of policy-making back to the routine of office, where he could expect little interference.

[9] Beale, *Bates Diary*, 244; Silver, *Lincoln's Supreme Court*, 62; Willard L. King, *Lincoln's Manager: David Davis*, 194; Maurice G. Baxter, *Orville H. Browning, Lincoln's Friend and Critic*, 113. Bates and Swayne remained good friends throughout the war.

[10] U. S., *Statutes at Large*, XII, 576; U. S., *Congressional Globe*, 37th Cong., 2d Sess., XXXII, 2914, 3255, 3310, 3351; Charles N. Gregory, "Samuel Freeman Miller: Associate Justice of the Supreme Court of the United States," *Yale Law Journal*, XVII, 427.

[11] *Attorney General Opinions*, X, 356-57; Bates to Lincoln, October 15, 1862, R. T. Lincoln Collection.

Pressure from Congress for rigid enforcement of the Conspiracies Act had expanded the scope of military arrests and had resulted in the further extension of martial law. A number of Republican leaders in Congress appeared determined, ironically, to have the Administration use the power it had claimed for itself, regardless of the questionable methods involved and the resulting injustices. On the other hand, conservatives such as Browning attacked the Administration for going too far in detaining persons accused of treason against the government. Bates hoped to avoid criticism from either group and to work out a moderate policy of arrest and prosecution under his office.

Basic to the problem still was the question of conducting military operations against an unrecognized belligerent who stood liable for both armed revolt and treasonous activities against the government. Bates considered the suspension of the privilege of a writ of habeas corpus as a measure more desirable than either strict martial law or summary justice meted out by military commissions, and he hoped, privately, that it would aid in maintaining executive supremacy over the prosecution of the war. However, the very nature of the rebellion and the task of apprehending and bringing to trial those who allegedly participated in it plagued him. Though the military had, theoretically, acted under the authority of the Secretary of State, Bates was stunned by their swiftness and thoroughness in Maryland, where many persons were arrested, including George William Brown, Mayor of Baltimore, and George P. Kane, the city's noted police commissioner. Writing to William M. Addison, district attorney at Baltimore, he revealed a slight confusion regarding mass arrest ordered and used indiscriminately against a civil populace when it no longer seemed necessary. The frightening prospect of the Army being utilized to enforce the government's will, he wrote Addison, could only be countered by provisional civil courts to supplant the sword.[12]

Frustrated, Bates turned his ire on his associate Seward and on Congress. He thought that by employing secret agents and sending orders to Army authorities the Secretary of State was destroying all semblance of civil liberty and minimizing the chance of keeping the conduct of the war under the President's direction. He believed that Seward had yielded to pressure from Congress in ordering the arrests of all persons suspected of disloyal practices, especially in the areas around Washington. Alarmed by the prospects of a Seward-Congress alliance, he was no longer content to view the role of the attorney general as mere legal adviser to the President. The activities of certain congressmen, especially those of the Potter committee, which was assigned to ferret out supposed traitors or Confederate sympathizers in the government, and Seward's concomitant policy of arrests, quickly moved him toward reshaping his own ideas regarding his office. In spite of his outward show of deference, he soon was outraged by Potter's investigators who, for weeks, had been compiling a list of persons suspected of treasonous activities.

The committee had furnished names to Bates, including that of his good friend and faithful subordinate Edward C. Carrington, district attorney in Washington, obviously in the hope that he would prosecute the allegedly guilty persons for treason. Instead, he defiantly filed the lists away as statistical evidence of fanaticism in certain circles in Congress and conclusive proof that the administration of the war should not be turned over to the legislators. In early

[12] Bates to Seward, February 25, 1862, Attorney General Letterbooks, B; Bates to Addison, February 17, 1862, in Richard Rush and others, eds., *The War of the Rebellion: A Compilation of the Official Records of the Union and Confederate Armies*, Ser. 2, II, 418; Henry W. Ballantine, "Martial Law," *Columbia Law Review*, XII, 536, 538.

February, however, he decided that the situation had grown intolerable. He called on Seward to protest the growing number of persons held in federal custody and vainly to recommend that there be a general suspension of all arrests. "Almost every day," he complained, "there are new instances in which the Secretary of State carries out his supposed powers about prisoners and legal proceedings."[13] It seemed to him that Seward, along with congressmen such as Potter, served as the compliant tools of radicalism.

That same month, much to Bates's relief, a change in administrative routine occurred. Assigned to supervise political arrests, Secretary of War Edwin M. Stanton began ordering the discharge of prisoners when evidence of their alleged offenses could not be produced. Encouraged by Stanton's efforts, Bates attempted to establish a friendly understanding with the new Secretary of War, for he hoped to persuade him to hand nonmilitary prisoners over to civil officers. The detention of persons whose treasonous activities included such minor offenses as criticism of the Administration's war policies and refusal to subscribe to oaths of allegiance he thought greatly degraded a government that claimed to be constitutional. Lincoln, too, had many of the same forebodings. George Templeton Strong, the New York diarist, who called on Lincoln in late January, 1862, to secure a pardon for a prisoner, learned how much the President sympathized with the position taken by his Attorney General. As he himself, the Chief Executive informed Strong, Bates was inclined to be very "chicken-hearted."[14]

[13] U. S., *Congressional Globe*, 37th Cong., 2d Sess., XXXII, 178-80, 527, 2327; Bates to Seward, February 4, 1862, William H. Seward Papers; Beale, *Bates Diary*, 230; U. S., House, *Executive Documents*, 37th Cong., 2d Sess., III, 77-81.

[14] James D. Richardson, ed., *A Compilation of the Messages and Papers of the Presidents, 1789-1897*, V, 3303-4; Bates to Stanton, February 26, 1862, *O. R.*, Ser. 2, II, 247; Allan Nevins and M. H. Thomas, eds., *The Diary of George Templeton Strong*, II, 205.

At first, Stanton appeared disposed toward leniency. He set up a commission to screen cases involving the arrest of persons for political reasons. It greatly heartened Bates to see this apparent change of policy, which he thought would eventually bring about the release of men arrested on unfounded charges in the first frantic weeks of the war. Prosecution of treason cases must be delayed, he instructed Broadhead, as the aggressive policy against alleged traitors was being brought to a close.[15] A few days later, he further advised Broadhead and other attorneys to indict only those who openly violated the Conspiracies Act. Persons of prominence suspected of disloyalty, he directed, should be prosecuted for "ulterior purposes." In order to keep from offending Stanton, Bates also ordered his attorneys to exercise the utmost caution in prosecuting treason cases that might result in a jurisdictional dispute with the War Department.[16]

In spite of encouraging signs, the change of official responsibilities did not lessen the range of arrests. Stanton, who at first appeared to be more humane than Seward, continued to order arrests in the Chief Executive's name. He had the Army at his direct disposal and seldom hesitated to use it to override civil government if he thought conditions warranted. Military control naturally impaired normal civil processes and made the Army stronger than ever. Acting as special prosecutor for the War Department, William Whiting, at Stanton's bidding, planned a general extension of military rule that deliberately encroached on civil government. Most acutely disappointing to Bates was the fact that many persons remained in Washington's Old Capitol prison while others were being sent there in the name of

[15] Bates to Broadhead, April 10, 1862, Attorney General Letterbooks, B.

[16] *Ibid.*, April 15, 1862; Bates to William M. Addison, April 17, 1862, Bates to Benjamin H. Smith, May 7, 1862, *O. R.*, Ser. 2, II, 285-86, and III, 524.

military necessity and under the authority of the executive.[17]

Still reluctant to interfere with Stanton, Bates did not mind clashing with Seward on matters involving the detention of individuals. He acted vigorously against the Secretary of State in the case of William Gilchrist, a Canadian arrested the previous September for allegedly trading in contraband goods with the Confederacy. Aiding him was the British Ambassador Lord Lyons, who had besieged the Administration with memorandums protesting Gilchrist's arrest for treason. At first, Bates asked Seward to release Gilchrist for diplomatic reasons, but this stratagem failed. He finally resorted to his influence with Lincoln in order to get the Canadian freed, much to the consternation of Seward, who labeled him a meddler.[18]

Even as chief legal officer of the government, Bates fully realized now that he had little opportunity to intervene in the actions of either Stanton or Seward and to bring about release of prisoners or to restrain authorities who were acting on orders from the War and State departments. The Merryman case and the debacle caused by the arrests in Maryland had forced him into defending actions similar to those he considered so deplorable in Seward and Stanton. When guerrillas began terrorizing his own state, he condoned Gamble's policy of summarily prosecuting and sometimes executing irregulars who looted and pillaged. The rise of some nefarious secret societies in the Midwest, which plagued the government, also caused him to support a repressive policy against all anti-Administration groups.[19] His desire

[17] Edward S. Martin, *The Life of Joseph Hodges Choate*, I, 243; James G. Randall, *Constitutional Problems under Lincoln*, 151; *Appletons' American Annual Cyclopaedia*, II, 590; James G. Randall, *Lincoln, the President*, III, 198-99.

[18] Coffey to Seward, February 1, 1862, Bates to Seward, April 2, 9, and 17, 1862, *O.R.*, Ser. 2, II, 852, 855-57.

[19] Gamble to Bates, July 14, 1862, Bates to Gamble, July 24, 1862, Bates Papers; Frank L. Klement, *The Copperheads in the Middle West*, 17-23.

to preserve the Union left him little choice but to act in concert with his colleagues, the officers of the government, when, in less critical times, he might have inveighed against the reduction of individual rights.

Bates therefore had to assist in protecting both executive and legal officers who enforced the Administration's policies of arrest and of confiscation of property. In 1861, Pierce Butler, a wealthy Philadelphian, had caused the first major threat to federal immunity by bringing suit against Secretary of War Cameron. A Confederate sympathizer, Butler had been arrested and sent to a federal prison after visiting friends and relatives in the South. Subsequently, he charged Cameron with trespass, assault and battery, and false imprisonment. Informed of the matter, Bates quickly advised legislation by Congress to protect federal officers in similar suits. Seward supported the proposal and suggested that Bates draft a bill that would provide for immunity of federal officers. Dutifully, the Attorney General accepted the task and wrote out a proposed bill which he presented to Senator Wade for consideration by Congress.[20]

The increasing number of arrests of Confederate sympathizers who encouraged desertion from the Union Army or the evasion of militia service moved the government to adopt a stringent measure that indirectly protected military officers. In late September, Lincoln issued a proclamation suspending the privilege of the writ of habeas corpus in cases of arrest for aiding the rebellion, evading service in the state militia, or committing any offense regarded as treasonous. Under the terms of the executive proclamation, persons accused of these offenses were to be tried by military courts and, if convicted, denied the privilege of habeas

[20] Bates to Judiciary Committee, May 8, 1862, U. S., House, *Miscellaneous Documents,* 37th Cong., 2d Sess., 2, 6-7; Beale, *Bates Diary,* 252; Bates to Lieber, April 24, 1862, Francis Lieber Collection; Bates to Coffey, May 5, 1862, *O.R.,* Ser. 2, II, 508.

corpus as long as they were imprisoned. Army commanders thus might use the proclamation to take broader action without any fear of civil legal reprisals.[21]

Bates regarded the swift, remorseless action that followed Lincoln's habeas corpus proclamation as far too drastic. In instructions sent to district attorneys and marshals, he attempted to soften the effect of the proclamation by urging a policy of judicious delay in both arrest and prosecution of those charged with encouraging desertion or with other offenses deemed treasonous. While he would provide executive immunity for district attorneys faced with "unjust assaults," he would not resort to the denial of a fair hearing for those taken into custody by the Army. Instead, Bates insisted on maintaining the benevolency of the executive branch by using the presidential pardoning power. In December he suggested to the Senate Judiciary Committee that the President be authorized to abolish portions of prison sentences or of financial penalties. It did not seem, however, a strong gesture compared to the widening and protected hegemony of the Army.[22]

Bates's efforts in other directions strengthened his office for the almost inevitable clash with the military. In early 1862, he ventured beyond the substantive facts in an opinion on the California coal land cases and ruled it proper for the government to seize lands so that proceeds from mineral resources might be used to bolster the country's sagging financial condition. In March he upheld the constitutionality of the new noninterest-bearing Treasury notes, or "greenbacks," whose issuance was authorized by the Legal Tender Act of February 25, 1862. Expediency governed his decision,

[21] Proclamation Suspending the Writ of Habeas Corpus, September 24, 1862, Basler, *op. cit.*, V, 436-47.

[22] Bates to Price, January 6, 1863, *O. R.*, Ser. 2, I, 667; Bates to Chairman of the Senate Judicial Committee, December 12, 1862, Attorney General Letterbooks, B.

for the Treasury was empty and the country's taxation system inadequate. Though he did not share Taney's opposition to the issuance of legal tender on the grounds that Congress lacked the power to issue paper money, he had private reservations about the unsecured greenbacks. That same month he intervened, on the government's behalf, in a case brought before the Supreme Court by the State of New York concerning its right to tax United States stocks deposited in the Bank of the Commonwealth. The New York court had upheld the tax, but the Supreme Court, after hearing the case, reversed the decision, thus nullifying the state's action.[23]

On certain matters that appeared somewhat peripheral to his office, Bates also took an unusually strong stand. The controversies over the exchange of prisoners of war and over the President's authority to command state militias aroused him especially. On the first issue, Bates opposed a liberal exchange between Union and Confederate authorities or the paroling of Southern prisoners. In one of his more callous moments, he even supported McClellan's plan to march captured prisoners ahead of Union troops in order to explode "booby-trapped" shells left by retreating Southern forces. As to the President's right to assume command over state militias, Bates never once expressed any doubts. In both controversies, he saw the circumstances as directly related to the prosecution of war and, in both, he was motivated by human emotion as well as by official interest. John Coalter was serving in the Union Army; another son, Fleming, in one of the war's many tragic episodes, was fighting with Price's Confederates in Missouri. Above all

[23] Lieber to Bates, January 8, 1862, Lieber Collection; *Attorney General Opinions*, X, 184-87, 196-97; Bray Hammond, "The North's Empty Purse, 1861-1862," *American Historical Review*, LXVII, 3, 7, 12; Beale, *Bates Diary*, 239; 2 *Black*, 620-35; Bates to W. R. Vermilge, March 29, 1862, Attorney General Letterbooks, B.

else, Bates wished to see a quick end to the conflict. All the power of the Republic, he wrote Lieber, must be brought to bear against the Confederacy in order to end the fighting.[24]

Contrary to Stanton, however, Bates, because of his inherent conservative nature and his fondness for the Southern people, never could bring himself to pursuing a policy of total war against the civilian population of the Confederacy. He fully demonstrated on the confiscation question his unwillingness to set a precedent of ruthlessness. His interpretation of confiscation as a municipal regulation had long clarified his determination to leave the matter to civil officers and courts.[25] The "law of confiscation," he wrote one district attorney concerning the Act of 1861, was limited to civil courts which, he hopefully suggested, would soon be operating "in the rear of our armies." He was alert, though, to additional legislation Congress might pass to give the Army more authority to confiscate. Lyman Trumbull's bill, introduced in December, 1861, seemed such a measure, for it was designed to confiscate all property of officers of the Confederacy, both military and civil. Criminal intent was implanted in the bill, and provisions calling for the death penalty, fines, imprisonment, and confiscation were added. However, only in the event of treason did the death penalty apply, while lesser punishments usually were reserved for enemies of the country. Bates regarded the bill as a violation of all forms of individual rights because, in most cases, the defendant would not be present. It appeared to him that Congress meant to circumvent executive authority and to enact its own enforcement measures of the 1861 Conspiracies and Confiscation acts. He also realized that the bill would give the Army more latitude in civil affairs.

[24] *Attorney General Opinions*, X, 279-84; Beale, *Bates Diary*, 237, 240, 255; Bates to Lieber, May 9, 1862, Lieber Collection.

[25] Bates to Benjamin W. Smith, March 5, 1862, Attorney General Letterbooks, B, V.

Bates was somewhat relieved when opposition to Trumbull's bill arose from several quarters in Congress. Generally included in the resulting controversy was the question as to how much the executive power might be enlarged. Paradoxically, the demands of Benjamin F. Wade, Zachariah Chandler, Lyman Trumbull, and others to centralize more power in Washington often resulted in debates on legislative versus executive supremacy, with discussion of all the inherent questions of presidential "dictatorship." Thus, those who supported the Administration denied that Congress had the confiscatory power proposed in Trumbull's bill, while others maintained that the national legislature had no right to emancipate slaves under the measure. A few saw in the proposal a tacit recognition of the Confederacy as a belligerent and therefore opposed confiscation altogether. Arguments against the bill heartened Bates and some conservative legislators, though they knew the majority of the Congress supported the confiscatory legislation.[26]

Bates thought that most of the Republicans in Congress intended to give more discretionary authority to such men as General Benjamin F. Butler, nationally infamous because of his confiscatory policies in New Orleans. Moreover, he feared that if Trumbull's bill was passed, control of enforcement would pass from the executive branch and increase the chance of general emancipation and unjust prosecution of Southern property owners. In addition to his somewhat curious concern for the Southerners' individual property rights, Bates reasoned that the bill would ruin any chance of an easy peace and of a quick reunion of North and South

[26] U. S., *Congressional Globe*, 37th Cong., 3d Sess., XXXIII, 334, 932-46, 1049-54, 1136-41; Theodore C. Pease and James G. Randall, eds., *The Diary of Orville Hickman Browning, 1850-1881*, I, 533; James G. Randall, "Some Legal Aspects of the Confiscation Acts of the Civil War," *American Historical Review*, XVIII, 85; William D. Mallam, "Lincoln and the Conservatives," *Journal of Southern History*, XXVIII, 39-40.

at the end of hostilities. If the bill were enacted into law, the Administration would be saddled with a congressional-military confiscation policy, enforced by army commanders.[27]

By July 15 amorphous sentiment in Congress toward the bill solidified into votes, and the "act to suppress insurrection, to punish treason and rebellion, to seize and confiscate the property of rebels" passed. A vague distinction was made between those guilty of overt treasonous activities designed to cripple the Union, and those who participated in the rebellion as soldiers or aided the Confederacy in a material way. However, amendments to the bill provided for court trials of suspected persons who, if convicted of joining the Confederate cause, stood to lose their property, including slaves. The act provided also for forfeiture of property beyond the lifetime of a person. Finally, if an accused person did not appear for trial in federal court, he would be judged guilty and his property confiscated.

Lincoln examined the bill, but returned it unsigned on July 17. He objected to the forfeiture clause, which virtually amounted to a bill of attainder, the principle of congressional control of emancipation in the states, and the clause requiring an accused person to appear in a federal court or lose his property. Upon receiving this message, Congress passed a joint resolution stipulating that no forfeiture or punishment under the act extended beyond the lifetime of a person. Reluctantly, Lincoln signed the bill with the appended resolution.[28]

Many reasons may be found for the Administration's rather

[27] Pease and Randall, *op. cit.*, I, 555; Washington *National Intelligencer*, July 1, 1862; Bates to Stanton, May 23, 1862, Attorney General Letterbooks, B, V.

[28] U. S., *Congressional Globe*, 37th Cong., 2d Sess., XXXII, 3379-83. To Senate and House, July 17, 1862, Proclamation of the Act to Suppress Insurrection, July 25, 1862, Basler, *op. cit.*, V, 328-31, 341; U. S., *Statutes at Large*, 590-92, 637; Richardson, *op. cit.*, V, 3286.

easy surrender on the Confiscation bill, none of which was
more important than the lack of military success in the field.
Practical and political matters counted also. Actually, while
many Republicans voted against the bill, moderates like
Browning voted for it, thinking it would destroy Southern
morale and bring a speedier end to the war. Senator William
Pitt Fessenden of Maine, often identified as a political foe
of the Administration, declared that the measure had been
a mistake from the start because the President was to be
the implementing authority. Also, presidential amnesty for
persons affected by the act could alter a decision reached
in court. It was apparent that recognition of the President's
pardoning power in the bill and the implied authority given
the Army to liberate and enroll Negroes represented a
curious combination of extremism and moderation. The blend-
ing of views persuaded Lincoln and his Cabinet to accept
it as a fair compromise in the light of the Union's military
failures and of the renewed political opposition.[29]

Bates considered executive implementation of the Confiscation Act a major victory. Again, he thought, Congress
had enacted a repressive measure, apparently without de-
voting much thought to who would enforce it. On November
13 he received more encouraging news when Lincoln officially charged him with carrying out the provisions of
the act. Actually, he had known Lincoln's intention days
in advance, so he had prepared a rough draft of an implementing order. A few days later, he casually wrote to

---

[29] *New York Times*, July 17, 1862; U. S., *Statutes at Large*,
XII, 422-23. In June, Congress passed a bill levying a penalty tax
on lands in "insurrectionary districts." Unredeemed land was to
be sold to the highest bidder, but the President had to determine
what districts were in revolt. U. S., *Congressional Globe*, 37th
Cong., 2d Sess., XXXII, 2560.

Lincoln's secretary John Nicolay for a copy of the official directive, though he was well aware of its contents.[30]

When the Chief Executive's official notification came, Bates was at home ill, attended by an anxious Julia. He summoned Coffey, and the two held a long afternoon conference to discuss a tentative directive Bates had drawn up. Together they also went over each section of the legislative measure, noting that Congress had failed to provide for implementation or court procedures. A few more hours was all that was needed to complete the directive, which Coffey immediately relayed to attorneys located at key points. District attorneys were to assume supervisory control over United States marshals who were ordered to carry out the actual confiscation. The attorneys were to make certain that the property seized belonged to the persons arrested, prosecuted, and found guilty of specific offenses listed in the act. In litigation over prizes and revenues, legal officers were to act only after ascertaining all the facts involved. Nowhere in the directive did Bates discuss the act's constitutionality or whether it represented an enactment by one belligerent against another. He emphasized only the restricted mechanics of enforcement and carefully construed them to be of a civil, not a military, nature.[31]

A few weeks later, Ward Hill Lamon, the colorful marshal of the District of Columbia, presented Bates with his first opportunity to contest the Army's role in confiscations. Early in December Lamon complained to the Attorney General about General John H. Martindale, Military Governor of the District of Columbia. Lamon reported that Martindale

[30] Richardson, *op. cit.*, V, 3325-26; rough draft, November 13, 1862, Order about Confiscation, manuscript Bates Diary (Library of Congress).

[31] Coffey to Richard H. Dana, Jr., E. Delafield Smith, George A. Coffey, William Price, December 1, 1862, Attorney General Letterbooks, B, V.

had ignored a civil writ on the property of a Confederate
official who formerly resided in Baltimore, and had ordered
military seizure. Lamon had protested, but Martindale refused to turn the property over to him. Although Lamon
had been the object of much criticism by members of
Congress because he had imprisoned fugitive slaves in the
District of Columbia jail and had barred official visitors
from the premises, Bates decided to clarify his interpretation of the Confiscation Act and to prevent what he conceived to be military usurpation of civil authority. He wrote
the General concerning the "dangerous irregularity" of his
actions.[32] He warned Martindale that the issue of confiscation would no longer be complicated by a jurisdictional
dispute between the military and civil authorities. Civil
officers in the District of Columbia, he informed the military
commander, were not to be interfered with in the lawful
performance of their duties. After complaining to Stanton,
who did not take part in the matter, the ruffled General
agreed to restore the property.[33]

Soon after the Martindale incident, Bates prepared more
explicit instructions for all attorneys and marshals. Before
making actual seizure, marshals were required to have written authorization from the district attorney, and each attorney was required to keep a complete record of all confiscations and reasons therefor. "Hasty and improvident
seizures" were at all times to be avoided. Attorneys were

[32] Bates to Martindale, December 19, 1862, *ibid.;* Doster to
Martindale, December 19, 1862, Martindale to Bates, December
20, 1862, U. S., House, *Executive Documents,* 37th Cong., 3d
Sess., V, 6-7, 8-9; Ward Hill Lamon, *Recollections of Abraham
Lincoln, 1847-1865,* 251-55.

[33] Bates to Lamon, December 22, 1862, Abraham Lincoln Collection (Huntington Library); Bates to Martindale, December 22,
1862, Attorney General Letterbooks, B, V; Bates to Martindale,
December 26, 1862, U. S., House, *Executive Documents,* 37th
Cong., 3d Sess., V, 10.

to request return of confiscated property seized by the Army and to institute condemnation suits immediately after taking custody of any property. Finally, Bates declared that his instructions covered proceedings initiated under the Confiscation Act of July 6, 1861, which the President had authorized him to oversee.[34]

By the time his newest orders were dispatched on January 8, 1863, Bates was encountering vocal opposition to his policy. Speaker of the House of Representatives Galusha A. Grow did not like the Administration's lenient confiscation policy and singled out Bates's circular as an especially grave error in point. Sensing an opportunity for an investigation, he submitted questions to Bates on confiscation proceedings in the District of Columbia, where several congressmen thought enforcement had been lax. Bates defiantly answered Grow by calling his attention to recent orders issued to District Attorney Carrington concerning the recovery of property seized by the Army, which, in effect, meant that Southerners would have a fairer hearing in civil court. Such, he explained to the Speaker, was his policy on confiscation which, he sarcastically concluded, was not based on newspaper reports or unfounded rumors. Guilt must be proven clearly before the government would undertake prosecution of an accused person.[35]

Actually, Bates hoped to escape legislative wrath by capitalizing on the lack of agreement in Congress concerning military confiscation. After notifying his own legal officers, he sent the Secretary of War a memorandum, reminding him that property seized by the Army could be condemned only after proper judicial proceedings. Endorsement of this

[34] Bates to District Attorneys and Marshals, January 8, 1863, Attorney General Letterbooks, B, V; Order to Bates, January 8, 1863, Basler, *op. cit.*, VI, 45-46.

[35] Bates to Galusha A. Grow, January 14, 1863, Attorney General Letterbooks, B, V.

view would make military confiscation merely an inter-
mediary step that would lessen, Bates hoped, the general
effects of seizures of property by the government. In a
forceful letter he asked the volatile Stanton for a general
order directing military commanders to turn over confiscated
property to civil officers. Stanton did not easily take the
bait; he would give no general order affecting military
confiscation. In February, however, he did reluctantly make
General William S. Rosecrans deliver up property that had
been taken illegally by the Army in Nashville, Tennessee.
Bates at once relayed instructions to the United States
marshal in Nashville, directing him to stand firm against
any more attempts by the Army to confiscate property.[36]

Gradually, however, Bates's attempt to simplify confiscation procedures failed. First to complicate matters were the
unresolved judicial questions over the duration of forfeitures
and whether or not real estate was included in the provisions
of the Confiscation Acts. In 1864, Judge Catron, in *United
States v. Republican Banner Officers,* was to decide that
real estate did fall under the confiscation measures. In early
1863, however, Bates avoided such technical questions by
emphasizing the need for proper administrative procedures
and for sufficient proof of the owner's guilt before a writ
on property was issued. However, in March, Congress again
moved ahead of him by passing the Abandoned Property
Act. The bill provided for the seizure of movable property
left behind by Confederate forces and civilians, and included
crops and lands. Further removing matters from the Attorney
General's hands was the stipulation that Treasury agents
were to take charge of the confiscated property and arrange
for its sale. Lastly, Congress omitted any mention of the

[36] Bates to Stanton, January 21, 1863, Bates to E. R. Glascock,
February 27, 1863, *ibid.;* Stanton to Rosecrans, February 27, 1863,
O. R., Ser. 3, III, 57-58.

duration of the original forfeiture or the extent of military control.[37]

In spite of his carefully laid plans, Bates, by mid-1863, appeared to be thwarted again. Occasionally, he spoke up to obtain Lincoln's approval for redressing alleged injustices when he discovered military confiscation to be "needless, groundless and wanton interference . . . as if the other object were to contemn and degrade the civil power."[38] Doggedly he continued to protest Stanton's bellicose attitude, but to little avail. As before, he had to face the realization that the Army was the government's strongest enforcement arm in wartime and, consequently, the bulwark of the Union. But he continued to maintain that the Chief Executive was the symbol of civil stability. In spite of the President's suspension of the writ of habeas corpus, Bates

[37] 27 *Federal Cases*, 781-82; Bates to James T. Close, September 16, 1863, Attorney General Letterbooks, C. In cases involving confiscation after the war, several interesting decisions were reached. In *Semple v. U. S.* (1868), the Court reached a verdict confirming the constitutionality of confiscation, 21 *Federal Cases*, 1072-73. In *McVeigh v. U. S.* (1870), it was decided that an owner of property that had been confiscated had the right to appear before the Court in his own behalf, 11 *Wallace*, 259-68. In *Miller v. U. S.* (1870), both Confiscation Acts were declared constitutional by the Court. In the same decision, Bates's policy of enforcing the Confiscation Acts was upheld also, 11 *Wallace*, 259-68, 268-331. In the *Confiscation Cases* (1872), the decision reached allowed the Government to exercise the belligerent right of confiscation and held that proceedings under the 1862 act did not attach criminality. The *Confiscation Cases* of the following years (1873) produced a decision that the attorney involved had no authority to order seizure of John Slidell's lands in Louisiana, 20 *Wallace*, 92-114; U. S., *Statutes at Large*, 820; *Attorney General Opinions*, XI, 80-82.

[38] Baltimore *Sun*, May 16, 1863; Bates to J. G. Knapp, September 16, 1863, Attorney General Letterbooks, C; James G. Randall, *Lincoln and the South*, 127-28; Beale, *Bates Diary*, 350.

thought that Lincoln must fulfill his "statutory trust" of protecting civil institutions.[39]

Obscuring Bates's half-vision of an Olympian executive that prosecuted a civil war while he zealously guarded individual and property rights, was the spectre of ever-rising opposition in Congress and the cloud of disunity within the Cabinet. Political and constitutional arguments against the actions of the executive branch were more frequently brought up in Congress. Ofttimes the legislators attacked Lincoln and his advisers on the one hand for waging war in a dilatory fashion and on the other for consolidating "unconstitutional" power in the executive. Added to these imposing burdens was a steady erosion of morale, beginning with Pope's defeat at the Second Battle of Bull Run, among Cabinet members who clashed tensely over jurisdictional limits. Bates noted, too, how frequently Republican leaders in Congress praised military commanders who freed slaves and confiscated civilian property, thereby whittling away at the already frail unity within the Cabinet. Many, such as Senator Hale, who disliked Bates, plotted tirelessly to strip the executive branch of its power and prestige and to give Congress the upper hand in prosecuting the war. Events, such as McClellan's failure to pursue the enemy after Antietam and Republican losses at the polls in the fall of 1862, provided additional ammunition for those who opposed Lincoln.[40]

In order for the President to restore unity in the executive

[39] Stedman to Charles Stedman, November 8, 1862, in Laura Stedman and George W. Gould, *The Life and Letters of Edmund Clarence Stedman*, I, 292; Bates to Lieber, October 10, 1862, Lieber Collection.

[40] Bates to Gamble, September 21, 1862, Bates Papers; Bates to Lincoln, October 16, 1862, R. T. Lincoln Collection; Howard K. Beale, ed., *The Diary of Gideon Welles, Secretary of the Navy under Lincoln and Johnson*, I, 146-47; U. S., *Congressional Globe*, 37th Cong., 2d Sess., XXXII, 1390, 1464, 1772.

branch and to still the severe criticism in Congress, Bates realized, victory in the field had to be won. All through December, he and the rest of the Cabinet anxiously awaited news from General Ambrose E. Burnside, in command of the forces that had left the staging area at Mount Falmouth and had moved to strike the Confederate forces on the Rappahannock. Reports of a great battle soon reached Washington, but they were followed by grim news of another Union disaster. At Fredericksburg, on December 13, Burnside had hurled his troops against the entrenched Confederate Army and had suffered a terrible defeat.

The defeat at Fredericksburg sent several congressmen into a fury over the Administration's war policies. Many began discussing the merits of individual Cabinet members, especially those of the greatly disliked Secretary of State. By Christmas week, anti-Administration men in Congress, including a surprising number of conservatives, were demanding a reorganization of the Cabinet and a drastic revision of the Administration's war plans. The main target of the opposition in Congress was Seward. Bates learned, too, that the congressional cabal had called for his and Blair's resignations as well. A special Senate committee was established to investigate the need for wide-sweeping constitutional changes, with possible control of military and civil affairs by the legislative branch. Bates discovered that the committee planned first to force Seward out of the Cabinet and that their censure of Stanton was only a ruse to drive moderates, like himself and Blair, from the Government. Characteristically, he regarded the embittered senators as a small minority and, at the Cabinet's session on December 19, voted against inviting them to discuss any matter relating to the President's advisers. After the meeting adjourned, however, he learned that the President had agreed to meet with a special delegation of the committee that very night.[41]

When the Cabinet and the committee met that evening, Bates began to comprehend the full extent of the crisis. As a result of the pressure from Congress, Seward had submitted his resignation two days before, but Lincoln had refused to accept it. Led by Senator Jacob Collamer of Vermont, the Republican delegation, composed of Charles Sumner of Massachusetts, William Pitt Fessenden of Maine, Lyman Trumbull of Illinois, Samuel C. Pomeroy of Kansas, Benjamin F. Wade of Ohio, Jacob M. Howard of Michigan, Ira Harris of New York, and James W. Grimes of Iowa, moved to reverse the President's decision and to force other changes on the beleaguered Administration.

Throughout the four-hour conference Bates watched Lincoln anxiously, hoping all the time for his denunciation of the unwelcome committee. Not once did the watchful Bates detect loss of composure on the part of the President, but noted, instead, how Lincoln "commented, with some mild severity" on statements made by the senators. The delegation had hoped to coerce Lincoln into accepting the principle of requiring unanimity from the Cabinet on every question. If a member should dissent on any issue, he must be, according to the senators, dismissed from the Cabinet! Bates, realizing how revolutionary these proposals were, joined his colleagues in protecting Seward and the President. He vigorously seconded Blair's statement that there was general unity in the Cabinet and that it supported the President's main policies. Even Chase, who secretly had

[41] Bates to Onward Bates, December 13, 1862, Bates Papers; *New York Tribune,* December 22, 1862; Beale, *Welles Diary,* I, 196; Benjamin P. Thomas and Harold M. Hyman, *Stanton, The Life and Times of Lincoln's Secretary of War,* 254; U. S., *Congressional Globe,* 37th Cong., 3d Sess., XXXIII, 13-14, 26-37, 130-31, 260-69. Interestingly, most congressmen concealed their opposition to the Administration's policies in the official debates.

conspired with the committee, joined in the chorus that declared Cabinet harmony. Bates was inspired by the scene because he had little hope of seeing the Cabinet, as a group, standing up to the senators. At the end of the meeting, he confidently predicted that the executive branch would continue as the guiding hand of government.[42]

The next day, however, Bates heard rumors of sweeping changes, brought to him by his military informant, Brigadier General James H. Van Alen, the man who had served as Greeley's campaign agent in 1860. According to one disturbing report, McClellan had been restored to command; another brought news of Seward's and Chase's resignations. Bates paid little heed, in spite of the persistency of the stories, but some of the rumors were true. In a master stroke Lincoln had forced Chase, who had allied himself with anti-Administration congressmen, to submit his resignation; if Congress forced Seward out of the Cabinet, Chase, the favorite of the antislavery men, had to resign also. Several congressmen reflected long on the possibility of Seward and Chase leaving the Cabinet and on the persons Lincoln might select to fill the resulting vacancies. Bates, with Blair and Welles, would still be official advisers, wielding considerable influence. No changes were made, however; Seward and Chase continued at the head of their departments. Another impasse between the President and Congress had been resolved.[43]

Though reassured by the Cabinet's weathering this most recent crisis, Bates was shaken by the suddenness of the congressmen's move. He privately felt that there had been a conspiracy between extremists in Congress and members of the Cabinet. Because of his convictions, he oversimplified

[42] Beale, *Bates Diary*, 269-70; Pease and Randall, *op. cit.*, I, 602-3; Beale, *Welles Diary*, I, 196-98; Hans L. Trefousse, *Benjamin Franklin Wade: Radical Republican from Ohio*, 190-96.

[43] Beale, *Bates Diary*, 270-71; Randall, *Lincoln the President*, II, 248-49; Albert B. Hart, *Salmon Portland Chase*, 302-3.

the issue, drawing the battle lines sharply between conspirators in Congress and the executive. He overlooked Browning's role in creating the Senate committee, Trumbull's defense of Lincoln, and the latter's close personal relationship with Sumner. Introspectively he reversed himself and decided that Seward, Stanton, and Chase had not really measured up to the test. Only he, Blair, and Lincoln had taken firm stands against the Senate committee and had opposed its apparent intention to overthrow the Government. "The thing dribbled out," he wrote. "The only effect which I see properly attributable to the movement, is a closer connection than before, between extreme Senators and the assailed Secretaries Seward and Stanton—they keep their places, but come up manfully to the extreme measures of their assailants."[44]

To Bates, the Cabinet crisis brought clearly into focus the heretofore shadowy alliance he visualized between the Army and radical Republicans in Congress who intended to prosecute a ruthless war against the South. He had now ceased to be the resolute partisan who had addressed the Supreme Court a year before. Then, he had not objected so strenuously to the unconstitutional measures adopted or contemplated as long as they were under the control of reasonable men like himself and Lincoln. But the indulgence of the Army by the Administration, the acquiescence in extraordinary powers for Stanton and Seward, and the rise of what he believed to be an extremist group in Congress that seemed bent on imprisoning every dissenting civilian or on confiscating all Southern-owned property, gradually unnerved him. And now before him loomed the shadow of a larger and more unsettling issue—emancipation. For months he had

[44] Beale, *Bates Diary*, 271; Charles A. Jellison, *Fessenden of Maine: Civil War Senator*, 159. The author correctly points out that the creation of the committee was not the work of "extreme" senators.

regarded its coming with silent trepidation. Soon a decision had to be reached concerning the freed slaves, and he could only speculate as to how far Lincoln might go toward supporting a compensation-colonization plan. Orville Browning had guessed the answer to both questions. Lincoln's policy now was fixed on emancipation, Browning insisted, and he would not long tolerate those who might "be in his way on the Negro question."[45]

[45] Pease and Randall, *Browning Diary*, I, 603.

CHAPTER VIII

THE ATTORNEY GENERAL
AND SLAVERY

*B*ATES's views on slavery were rooted in his Virginia background and his long residence in Missouri. The idea of making the Negro the equal of the white appalled him, though he grew increasingly aware of the war psychology of antislavery. His sympathy for Southern property owners sometimes clouded a personal sense of human justice and caused his compassion for the unfortunate Negroes to fail before a legalistic approach to slavery. Therefore, emancipation of slaves by the military under the Confiscation Acts appeared to him the wildest form of folly and should be prevented by executive authority. Even the President's program of emancipation he viewed skeptically as an alternative to the universal liberation of slaves by the Army, for he believed that great social changes could not be quickly brought about.

After Sumter, Bates had grudgingly altered his views on emancipation. Butler's treatment of fugitive slaves as contraband and Frémont's emancipation proclamation had alerted him to what he considered a fearful consequence of war. The Crittenden Resolution to preserve the Union could not remain the sole objective of the war as the freeing of slaves rose to equal it in importance. In December, 1861, Bates agreed to support Lincoln's proposed compensation-emancipation plan.

Bates favored the speedy deportation of freed slaves as a necessary component of the Administration's emancipation program. He had long adhered to Henry Clay's colonization plan, including the granting of appropriate federal funds for a gradual resettlement of ex-slaves in other areas of the world. Now, he also advocated a strictly regulated system to be administered by the executive. Once Congress took over the matter, he believed, it would legislate measures that would damage the American social structure even more drastically. For this reason, he opposed enlistment of Negroes into the Army; a nagging sense of justice told him that if they fought for the Union the ex-slaves would merit a better fate than to be transported to a strange land. Only by the implementation of a compensation-emancipation-deportation plan, he decided, could the Administration avoid the embarrassment of providing for the freed slaves.[1]

Bates therefore publicly approved of Lincoln's recommendations, presented to Congress in early March, 1862, calling for the compensation of loyal slaveholders and promising federal assistance to any state that provided for gradual emancipation. Privately, he hoped for a congressional measure that would authorize the states to initiate and administer compensated emancipation. Lincoln had the same idea when he summoned representatives of the border states to a conference on his proposed emancipation program. Already

[1] Gideon Welles, "Administration of Abraham Lincoln," *The Galaxy*, XXIV, 439; Warren A. Beck, "Lincoln and Negro Colonization in Central America," *The Abraham Lincoln Quarterly*, VI, 165; Bates to Lieber, December 19, 1861, Francis Lieber Collection.

plans had been drafted for the colonization of freed slaves, a fact which should have appealed to the border states because thereby the property rights of loyal slaveholders were to be protected and freed slaves colonized. If adopted, the Administration's proposals would eliminate debates on constitutionality in Congress and prevent widespread emancipation by the military.[2]

Bates, therefore, was alarmed when Congress took the initiative. On March 13, the legislative branch obliquely approved a part of the President's plan by acting on an earlier resolution proposed by Senator Sumner. Congress passed an article of war that forbade the return of slaves to their owners by the Army. Congressmen then turned to debating the proposed District of Columbia Emancipation bill. Passed on April 11, the act abolished slavery in the District of Columbia, with compensation for loyal owners. Bates, uncertain of the outcome of the deliberations in Congress, implored Lincoln to stand firm and "not yield to the Northern abolitionists or to the timid doubters of the border slave states." As his friend Senator James R. Doolittle of Wisconsin, he felt that any emancipation must be followed immediately by colonization. He considered it a partial victory when Lincoln hesitated to sign the bill abolishing slavery in the District of Columbia until Congress should add a $100,000 appropriation to aid colonization.[3]

[2] Allan Nevins, *The War for the Union: War Becomes Revolution*, 31-32; Message to Congress, March 6, 1862, in Roy P. Basler, ed., *The Collected Works of Abraham Lincoln*, V, 144-46; Howard K. Beale, ed., *The Diary of Edward Bates, 1859-1866*, 241; U. S., *Congressional Globe*, 37th Cong., 2d Sess., XXXII, 1102, 1103, 1112.

[3] Lincoln to Greeley, March 24, 1862, Message to Congress, April 16, 1862, Basler, *op. cit.*, V, 169, 192; U. S., *Statutes at Large*, XII, 376-78; U. S., *Congressional Globe*, 37th Cong., 2d Sess., XXXII, 130, 1048, 1142, 1180, 1246, 1614-23, 1637-49, 1650-52, 1893. Wilson and Sumner worried about the enforcement of the articles of war and kept up a running debate on it.

Bates closely watched the effects of emancipation by presidential action on the role of the Army. In May, General David Hunter, commanding the Southern Department, issued an order which freed the slaves under his jurisdiction. Hunter assumed that martial law permitted him to emancipate Negroes and to muster them into the Army, but Lincoln revoked his edict. The General's action reopened the questions of direct emancipation by the military and of Negro enlistments. To Bates the new turn of events meant another obstacle in the way of the Administration's policy of liberating slaves gradually and sending them off to colonies.[4] Knowing that military commanders had been encouraged by the Secretary of War to use ex-slaves as troops, he realized the time for compromise was at hand. He instructed his subordinates to relax enforcement of the Fugitive Slave Act. Yet, in answer to a query from Maryland's Governor Augustus W. Bradford he denied obliquely that the law returning slaves to their masters had been suspended. Actually, he hoped to eliminate civil "slave-catching," which had been a source of embarrassment and irritation to the Army and to Congress since the beginning of the war.[5]

The changing situation in Missouri also caused Bates to alter his thoughts on emancipation during the first half of 1862. In his state, both abolitionists and conservatives were

[4] Chase to Butler, July 31, 1863, Chase to Robert Dale Owen, September 10, 1862, in Jacob W. Shuckers, *The Life and Public Services of Salmon Portland Chase*, 376-79; Benjamin P. Thomas and Harold M. Hyman, *Stanton, The Life and Times of Lincoln's Secretary of War*, 233; Howard K. Beale, ed., *The Diary of Gideon Welles, Secretary of the Navy under Lincoln and Johnson*, I, 158.

[5] Bates to Broadhead, April 15, 1862, Bates to John J. Jackson, May 7, 1862, Bates to Benjamin Smith, May 7, 1862, Attorney General Letterbooks, B, V; Bates to A. W. Bradford, May 10, 1862, in Richard Rush and others, eds., *The War of the Rebellion: A Compilation of the Official Records of the Union and Confederate Armies*, Ser. 2, I, 817; James G. Randall, *Lincoln the President*, II, 134-35; Lieber to Bates, June 8, 1862, Lieber Collection.

preparing for a bitter struggle over slavery. Bates, as did Missouri's chief representatives in Congress, Frank Blair in the House and John B. Henderson in the Senate, knew that an ultraconservative policy on slavery might easily result in political disaster. As did Blair and Henderson, Bates reflected the views of St. Louis County rather than those of rural Missouri, where slavery was regarded as a social and economic necessity. This division of opinion rendered inevitable a political split over slavery in Missouri when Lincoln appealed for cooperation by the border states. The Missouri State Convention, meeting to discuss the President's proposal, revealed in its debates the extent of the breach. Few delegates could agree on anything, and the German element of Missouri refused altogether to accept a plan for colonization. Gamble, exhibiting characteristic stubbornness, also opposed the Administration's proposals.[6]

Intransigence on emancipation in other border states left Bates without a star to follow as the early summer debates in Congress on a second Confiscation bill dragged on. On July 12 Lincoln acknowledged his own dilemma by making another appeal to the border states. This time, the President asked for cooperation in a federal-state emancipation program which included colonization. He, too, had become concerned over emancipation by the military and feared a legislative alternative which might result in an attempt by Congress to effect emancipation through the Army. Therefore, it was with great urgency that Lincoln asked Congress on July 14 to authorize the issuance of governmental bonds

---

[6] U. S., *Congressional Globe,* 37th Cong., 2d Sess., XXXII, 58-59, 1631-34; Harrison A. Trexler, *Slavery in Missouri, 1804-1865,* 224, 233-34; William B. Hesseltine, *Lincoln and the War Governors,* 244.

to states which adopted a compensation-emancipation program.[7]

In a sense, emancipation was a kind of punitive confiscatory policy. The appropriation of $100,000 provided for in the District of Columbia act to colonize ex-slaves was to be taken out of monies received from the seizure and sale of Confederates' property. In addition, an appropriation bill of $500,000 was passed to implement a colonization program for Negroes freed by the states. Appraising the confiscation-emancipation-colonization principle as a way to attract votes, many congressmen voted affirmatively for the proposed bill. In addition to punishment for treason and other insurrectionary offenses, Southern property owners were subject to confiscation of their property, including slaves. Negroes freed under the act were to be regarded as "captives of war," liberated by executive decree and to be colonized at the pleasure of the Administration. No compensation for their former owners was provided, thus making the act truly confiscatory.[8]

The Second Confiscation Act reflected the views of factions in Congress which disagreed on both gradual and immediate emancipation and on the purpose behind seizing the property of civil enemies. Antislavery men stressed the sections of the act that called for the manumission of slaves belonging to those charged with rebellious activities, while others looked on confiscation as a punitive measure designed to weaken the strength and morale of the Confederacy. As to the colonization of slaves, however, the act left much to be desired. The provisions of the act did not relate to the welfare of the Negroes themselves, and no military or civil officer was

[7] Appeal to Border State Representatives to Favor Compensated Emancipation, July 12, 1862, Basler, *op. cit.*, V, 317-18, 324; Benjamin Quarles, *Lincoln and the Negro*, 107-10; U. S., *Congressional Globe*, 37th Cong., 2d Sess., XXXII, 3322-23, 3340.

[8] U. S., *Statutes at Large*, XII, 582, 589-92.

charged with its enforcement.

Bates viewed the new legislation as another effort to strip the executive branch of its control over emancipation and to turn the Union in the direction of revolutionary social change. He therefore thought it vital that the Administration accelerate its plans for emancipation and colonization. On July 22, in the Cabinet, he joined Stanton in approving of the President's momentous decision to issue a general proclamation of emancipation. By an executive emancipation proclamation, a march could be stolen on the Administration's foes in Congress. Also, the executive would be free to proceed with colonization plans, once the slaves had been freed. Since the compensation-emancipation proposals had suffered setbacks, Bates looked on Lincoln's historic decision as a change in tactics to gain the same ends. He carefully examined the document, in which Lincoln prescribed emancipation in seceded areas by January 1, 1863, unless the states involved had returned to the Union. Bates approved the document, but he agreed with Seward that issuance of the proclamation should be delayed until Union armies had won a decisive victory.[9]

Lincoln continued to explore possible solutions to the Negro problem. Early in August he conferred with a delegation of free Negroes and candidly presented a colonization plan, but reflected some doubts as to its success. Bates thought Lincoln's speech proper, but he nevertheless detected a note of vacillation. Lincoln made no specific statement on the implementation of colonization although Bates knew negotiations concerning the founding of a colony at Chiriqui in northern Panama had begun. Along with the rest of the Cabinet he had heard of plans to send ex-slaves to the

[9] David Donald, ed., *Inside Lincoln's Cabinet: The Civil War Diaries of Salmon P. Chase*, 95-96, 99; John G. Nicolay and John Hay, *Abraham Lincoln: A History*, VI, 127; John Hope Franklin, *The Emancipation Proclamation*, 33-37, 39-44.

Central American region to mine coal for Welles's Navy.
While it was true that Lincoln was dealing with Ambrose
W. Thompson of the speculative Chiriqui Improvement Company, an enterprise formed to buy up lands which could
be used for colonization, Chase and Welles opposed the
move on the grounds that the title to Chiriqui had not
been cleared.[10]

Bates, on the other hand, was enthusiastic over the news of
colonization in spite of adverse reports about the coal de-
posits at Chiriqui and of diplomatic difficulties caused by the
dispute between Colombia and Costa Rica over the Chiriqui
grant. In addition, some Latin American countries opposed
Negro immigration from the United States. Bates felt much
relieved when he learned that Lincoln intended to sign a
contract with Thompson's Chiriqui Improvement Company
and to dispatch Senator Samuel C. Pomeroy of Kansas as
a special presidential agent to arrange for the establishment
of the colony.[11] On September 22, following the battle at
Antietam, he felt optimistic enough to join his colleagues in
fully approving Lincoln's promulgation of the Emancipation
Proclamation.

Nine days later, at Lincoln's request, he and the other
members of the Cabinet presented their views on the whole
question of emancipation and colonization. Characteristically,
Bates had gone to the trouble of preparing a lengthy memorandum concerning treaty involvements and the conduct
of colonization, which he read to his colleagues:

> I am clearly of opinion that it is wise and humane to
> form such treaties with all of these Powers, or as many
> of them as will agree to our terms. The more the better,
> both for the Government and the individual emigrants,

[10] Remarks to Deputation of Western Gentlemen, August 4,
1862, Basler, *op. cit.*, V, 256-57; *New York Times*, August 26,
1862; Ben Perley Poore, *Perley's Reminiscences of Sixty Years in
the National Metropolis*, II, 107; Beale, *Welles Diary*, I, 150-51.

[11] Beale, *Welles Diary*, I, 151-52.

because it enlarges the range of choice, and the inducements and opportunities for both.

Second. I think that such treaties ought to be single,
confined to that one object, so as to avoid, if possible,
all other debatable questions, and all disturbing elements.
And I think it would be desirable, to have inserted a
clause (if that may be) to preserve the treaty from
abrogation, in case of a future war.

Third. Such treaties ought, of course, to be mutually
beneficial to the contracting parties—i.e. to the foreign
Governments, by offering a supply of population and
labor, such as they desire; and to us, by mitigating our
embarrassment on account of that same population—
drawing off at once, a portion of that population, and
enlarging and multiplying the channels of trade and
friendly intercourse, so as greatly to accelerate that
drainage in the future.

But besides that, and to secure that end, such treaties
ought, carefully, to provide for the just and humane
treatment of the emigrants—e.g. ensuring an honest liveli-
hood by their own industry, either in the voluntary
service of others, or upon their own land, or both; and
guaranteeing to them their liberty, property and the
religion which they profess.

Fourth. We ought, I think, to open as many channels,
and offer as many inducements for the egress of that
population, as possible, to the end of satisfying the
judgement, and gratifying the wishes, and even the
whims, of the various classes of emigrants, and of all
the diversities of our own people, who are disposed, in
any manner, to advance the great enterprise.

Fifth. Simple emigration is free; for I do not know
of any foreign State whose laws prohibit men, only
because they are negroes, from coming in, acquiring a
domicile among the people, owning property, and estab-
lishing a civil and social status. Among our colored
people who have been long free, there are many who
are intelligent and well advanced in arts and knowledge
and a few, who are educated and able men. These are
free to go where they please, in foreign countries (though
it has been guessed by some of our politicians, who

are wiser than the constitution, that this government has no power to grant them passports for their protection, in foreign parts).

This class is excellently qualified and might be efficiently used for guides, instructors, and protectors of those of their race who are fresh from the plantations of the South, where they have been long degraded by the total abolition of the family relation, shrouded in artificial darkness, and studiously kept in ignorance, by state policy and statute law.

Sixth. I think that those of our blacks who go forth under our present efforts, should go as emigrants, not colonists. A colony in modern political law, means a dependency of the mother country, entitled to its protection and subject to its sovereign power. Emigrants, on the contrary, are incorporated, as individuals, into the body politic which they enter and are no longer subjects of their former sovereigns. They may still have the sympathies of their former country, but have no right to appeal to its power for protection, except upon grounds of international comity, and of treaty stipulations, made in their favor.[12]

Naïvely Bates at first assumed there existed a consensus in the Cabinet on the emancipation and colonization questions. On the contrary, Chase, backed by abolitionist congressmen, favored immediate and full freedom for the slaves; Stanton relied on emancipation as a supplement to conscription and therefore did not endorse immediate colonization; Welles thought little of either universal emancipation or resettlement of the Negroes in other parts of the Western Hemisphere. Only Blair joined Bates in advocating forcible deportation of the slaves freed under the proclamation. Lincoln rebuffed them both by rejecting any involuntary deportation, a position

[12] Beale, *Bates Diary*, 262-64; Andrew N. Cleven, "Some Plans for Colonizing Liberated Negro Slaves in Hispanic America," *The Journal of Negro History*, XI, 35-49; P. J. Staudenraus, *The African Colonization Movement, 1816-1865*, 246-48; Nicolay and Hay, *Lincoln*, VI, 357.

consistent with his views ten years earlier. All in all, the Cabinet and the President were divided on the present and future status of the Negro, with no certainty as to who should supervise the process of emancipation. To Bates this sudden disunity on the vital question of freed slaves was disastrous.[13]

Bates emerged from the deliberations determined to implement control of emancipation and colonization by the executive branch. He felt committed to what he believed to be Lincoln's original program, as opposed to one instituted by Congress, shunning anyway a radical party position on the future status of the Negro. If centralized in Congress, the grand design for the Negro might subvert the rights of states and of slaveholders who often were the local political leaders and the stalwarts of another, and what Bates considered a more stable, society. Under Lincoln's direction, he believed, there would be no holy struggle against slavery and no amalgamation of the two races after emancipation. Lincoln must have a free hand, he confided to Gamble, in supervising the manumission and future resettlement of the Negroes, for he would follow a conservative policy.[14]

Because of his single-mindedness, Bates had difficulty foreseeing many of the changes which were to be wrought by the struggle against slavery and failed to detect the subtle changes in Lincoln's outlook on the Negro problem. Even while the Administration prepared to liberate portions of the slave population, events that would alter his own course were occurring. In September, 1862, the schooner *Elizabeth and Margaret* was stopped by a Treasury revenue cutter because the vessel's captain was a Negro man. Chase, hoping to commit the Administration to an antislavery policy altogether, called on Bates for an opinion concerning the captain's citizenship.

[13] Beale, *Welles Diary*, I, 152-53.

[14] Bates to Gamble, September 19, 1862, Bates Papers. Bates had brought a colored servant, Tom Hare, with him from Missouri.

Carefully Bates examined Chase's inquiry. In preparing his reply, he restudied Greek and Roman definitions of citizenship as well as those to be found in modern legal decisions. He looked over several modern treatises on the subject, including an interesting one read the previous summer by George Livermore before the Massachusetts Historical Society. Finally, he asked Lieber for his opinion. As he organized his thoughts, the significance of the decision began to press in on him. He felt it a great consolation that the case before him involved a free Negro, so that his claim to citizenship would not be a question of a slave's status under the Constitution.[15]

In his opinion, rendered on November 29, Bates noted that there was no standard for citizenship, least of all for the right of suffrage. American citizenship, he argued, "does not necessarily depend upon nor coexist with the legal capacity to hold office and the right of suffrage."[16] A citizen, therefore, had only to be a member of a political community, whether he was born white or black. Even a slave might be accorded the status of citizenship, since such recognition did not mean that a person had "all the rights, privileges and immunities" normally granted a voter. It could be, Bates concluded, that "a child in a cradle, viewed as a citizen merely, is the equal of his father in the Senate."[17] He decided, therefore, that the Negro commanding the vessel possessed the privileges of citizenship.

Bates's opinion did not reflect an antislavery view, though his involved discussion to demonstrate that "men of color" could be citizens led many people to believe it did. Several

[15] Beale, *Bates Diary,* 522; William R. Livermore, "The Emancipation Pen," *Proceedings of the Massachusetts Historical Society,* XLIV, 595.

[16] U. S., *Opinions of the Attorneys General of the United States,* X, 387.

[17] *Ibid.,* 388-99; Bates to Lieber, December 1, 1862, Lieber Collection.

statements of conjecture, superfluous to the opinion, obscured
the main fact that the case involved a free Negro. Also, many
ignored Bates's vigorous reaffirmation of social control through
the Constitution. Since Bates had placed the status of citizenship above the power of states to destroy and had repudiated
Taney's pronouncement in the Dred Scott verdict that Scott
was not a citizen because he was a Negro, several thought
that the Attorney General had been converted into an antislavery zealot. Indeed, some of his remarks had a peculiar
admonitory ring about them as he refuted legal authorities
and opinions of his predecessors.[18] Few knew, however, that
his opinion did not reflect his private convictions regarding
the constitutional sanctity of property or the right of states
to regulate suffrage qualifications for all persons residing
within their boundaries. Nor did many note that his interpretation of the Dred Scott decision included no consideration
of Negroes held in bondage. Several adherents of the antislavery view interpreted the Attorney General's opinion as a
declaration of the Negroes' rights to privileges and immunities
already enjoyed by their white brethren. It gave, editorialized
the *New York Times,* free Negroes the unprecedented rights
to command vessels, to sue in federal courts, and to receive
passports.[19]

As soon as he learned the manner in which his opinion
had been misinterpreted, Bates belatedly attempted to qualify
it. He had not meant to establish the constitutional status of
emancipated slaves, he wrote Robert C. Winthrop; instead,
he had aimed only at resolving the question of whether or
not a "free-born American man of color was a citizen."[20] His

[18] *Attorney General Opinions,* X, 400-409, 413.

[19] *Ibid.,* 409-13; Beale, *Bates Diary,* 536; Lieber to Bates, October 25, 1862, Lieber Collection; *New York Times,* December 17
and 27, 1862.

[20] Bates to Winthrop, January 12, 1863, Abraham Lincoln Collection (Massachusetts Historical Society).

reasoning was based on the constitutional stipulation which provided that if a slave were freed by legislative action he "would be counted by the head," thus implying a bestowal of citizenship. No legislature or government could separate a person, born within its geographical limits, from its body politic, Bates insisted, in view of the provision by the Constitution, but it was a plain truth that touched neither on the question of slaves soon to be, or already, free.[21]

Embarrassed by the reaction to his loosely worded opinion on citizenship, Bates spoke more precisely in commenting on the Emancipation Proclamation, to take effect on New Year's Day. He was annoyed at the time by Greeley's inference in an editorial in the *Tribune* that the Attorney General was among those opposed to the issuance of the proclamation. Above all, he did not want to appear disloyal to Lincoln's apparent policy. Therefore, he vigorously recommended that the emancipation message be plainly labeled a war measure and presented to the public as a move against the "bold and active enemies" of the government. To underscore the proclamation's purpose as a political weapon of war, he also suggested the restriction of emancipation measures to areas physically occupied by the Union Army. In spite of Bates's aggressive posture, however, Lincoln's appeal to Congress for compensation to loyal slaveowners and to states that abolished slavery before 1900 was much more to his liking.[22]

By the time of the official announcement of the proclamation, however, Burnside's disaster at Fredericksburg and the Cabinet crisis severely threatened the Administration's emancipation policy. Bates was doubly disturbed because a bill proposing statehood for West Virginia, which he regarded

[21] Bates to Winthrop, January 5, 1863, *ibid.*

[22] *New York Tribune*, September 26, 1862; preliminary draft of final Emancipation Proclamation, December 30, 1862, Basler, *op. cit.*, VI, 25. The written recommendations of the Cabinet were presented on December 31.

as an uncalled-for emancipation move, had been pushed to
the fore in the war-wracked Congress. He had opposed statehood for West Virginia since 1861 when a convention of
delegates from the northwestern counties of Virginia had
met in Wheeling to form a temporary government of Vir-
ginians loyal to the Union and to discuss the creation of a
new state. Under the leadership of the "restored" governor
of Virginia, Francis H. Pierpont, the convention at Wheeling
had drafted a constitution for a proposed new state, West
Virginia, to be carved out of the northwestern counties of the
Old Dominion. Bates looked on the plan as an unconstitutional threat to the restoration of the Union and another
unorthodox solution to the controversy over emancipation. He
objected specifically to the terms of the congressional admission bill, which provided for gradual abolition of slavery in
West Virginia.[23]

Bates was convinced that a scheme had been hatched by
the forces that supported statehood for West Virginia and
the radical abolitionists in Congress who had conspired
to bring about the Cabinet crisis in December. He attacked
proponents of the admission bill for forcing through "rapidly
and secretly" a measure aimed at thwarting the Administration's emancipation and reconstruction plans.[24] Alarmed, he
called on Lincoln at the White House to warn him that the
bill was "unconstitutional, anti-traditional and impolitic." He
suggested that the legislation be put to a test vote in the
Cabinet in order to determine the Administration's position
on the constitutionality and political expediency of admitting
West Virginia to the Union. Lincoln, perceiving his agitated

[23] Beale, *Bates Diary*, 271; Charles H. Ambler, *Francis H.
Pierpont, Union War Governor of Virginia and Father of West
Virginia*, 134-36; U. S., *Congressional Globe*, 37th Cong., 3d Sess.,
XXXIII, 37-39, 41-51, 53-59.

[24] Bates to John J. Jackson, May 7, 1862, Attorney General Letterbooks, B, V; Franklin, *Emancipation Proclamation*, 82-93.

state of mind, agreed. On December 23, the President requested written statements from his advisers on these precise
points. Bates spent Christmas Day preparing his answer
repudiating West Virginia statehood as "a perversion of the
Constitution and political morals." Two days later, he submitted it to Lincoln.[25]

Much to his dismay, Bates found himself in a minority in
the Cabinet and opposite Lincoln, who supported the West
Virginia bill on the grounds that it was not only constitutional
but also a wise political move. To compound Bates's frustration, the Chief Executive connected the statehood bill with
emancipation: "The admission of a new state," he declared,
"turns that much slave soil to free." On the contrary, Bates
felt that West Virginia's proposed constitution, which abolished slavery by granting freedom to children of slaves born
after July 4, 1863, was part of the folly of admitting the new
state. Allowing a newly created border state to establish its
own emancipation policy, he thought, set a poor example.
On December 30, the day before Lincoln publicly endorsed
West Virginia's admission, Bates had presented his views
on both the admission of the new state and on the Emancipation Proclamation in a Cabinet meeting. His thoughts on the
admission of West Virginia were more pronounced. He feared
that the act was the first step taken by Congress toward
dividing the country into new states in order to legislate a
piecemeal emancipation program. His arguments, however,
failed before Lincoln's support of West Virginia's admission

[25] Beale, *Bates Diary*, 271; Bates to Lincoln, December 27, 1862,
R. T. Lincoln Collection; Beale, *Welles Diary*, I, 205; To Members
of the Cabinet, December 23, 1862, Basler, *op. cit.*, VI, 17; *Attorney General Opinions*, X, 427-35; U. S., *Statutes at Large*, XII,
633-34.

as a way to guarantee state control over the abolition of slavery.[26]

Besides the problems attendant on statehood for West Virginia, the political consequences of emancipation in his own state also bedeviled Bates. Emancipationists led by Charles D. Drake, a Democrat-turned-Republican lawyer, were demanding immediate freedom for the Negro in Missouri.[27] Bates attempted to persuade Gamble to adopt a plan of emancipation, knowing that Stanton and Halleck had begun to criticize openly the Missouri governor's conduct in both civil and military affairs. The Governor, however, insisted on gradual and compensated emancipation. When the state legislature, which sat from December, 1862, until March, 1863, failed to reach a consensus on the question, Gamble felt justified in waiting for passage of a congressional appropriation of $10,000,000 to compensate Missouri slaveholders.[28] Months before, Bates would have approved, but now it appeared that Gamble had refused to cooperate with the Administration.

Failure of the federal government to appropriate the money for Missouri prevented any easy or quick settlement on emancipation when Gamble, according to plan, summoned the State Convention in April, 1863. The Governor presented a resolution to the convention interdicting any action on eman-

[26] Opinion on the admission of West Virginia into the Union, December 31, 1862, Basler, *op. cit.*, VI, 25, 27-28; Bates to S. Ferguson, April 17, 1863, Attorney General Letterbooks, C; Beale, *Welles Diary*, I, 206-7; Bates Memo, December 31 [?], 1862, R. T. Lincoln Collection; Nicolay and Hay, *Lincoln*, VI, 419-20; Richard O. Curry, "A Reappraisal of Statehood Politics in West Virginia," *Journal of Southern History*, XXVII, 403-7. Only one-half of the counties and 60 per cent of the population in the new state were Unionist.

[27] Gibson to Bates, December 9, 1862, R. T. Lincoln Collection.

[28] Barton Bates to Gamble, January 21, 1863, Hamilton R. Gamble Papers; Samuel B. Harding, "Missouri Party Struggles in the Civil War Period," *The Annual Report of the American Historical Association*, I, 99; U. S., *Congressional Globe*, 37th Cong., 3d Sess., XXXVII, 91, 207, 1545.

cipation until 1866 and providing for a "training period" for slaves under forty years of age until 1874. His proposal touched off a fierce debate in the convention between the conservatives and the Drake emancipationists. Its reverberations were felt in Washington, and its implications threatened the already strained relationship between Lincoln and Gamble.[29]

Ill and exhausted, Bates decided to go back to his home state for a short vacation. Leaving official matters in Coffey's hands, he departed from Washington. He arrived in St. Louis with Julia, Richard, and Matilda on June 25 and immediately proceeded to Grape Hill.[30] Once settled and rested, he began following the activities of the convention, then in its last adopted a compromise resolution legalizing slavery in the days. He learned that the convention delegates finally had state until 1870, while providing for the freeing of all Negroes brought into Missouri before that time.

Fully aware of the changing mood of the President and Congress toward slavery, Bates realized that the Missouri ordinance was too conservative. He reasoned that a gradual-emancipation bill might serve better to avert a clash between the Provisional Government and the Administration; he also understood the complexities of sentiment within a border state. As Attorney General, however, he had to look at the question from a national point of view. He did feel somewhat satisfied over Missouri's partial fulfillment of the President's program even at the sacrifice of local prejudices and interests.[31]

Despite his mixed emotions, the outcome of the debate on

[29] Message to the Convention, June, 1863, Gamble Papers; Glover to Bates, May 15, 1863, R. T. Lincoln Collection.

[30] Beale, *Bates Diary*, 299; Baron de Gerolt to Eads, June 12, 1863, James B. Eads Papers.

[31] St. Louis *Missouri Republican*, July 2, 1863; St. Louis *Missouri Democrat*, July 10, 1863.

emancipation in his own state left Bates almost totally disillusioned over the Administration's position on slavery. He
believed that Chase, Seward, and Stanton were gravitating
into the orbit of abolitionist-minded senators and representatives who used the Negro issue as a political cudgel. It seemed
to him, also, that Army commanders everywhere were encouraged to enlist ex-slaves into their ranks, a step he considered tantamount to recognition of Negroes as equals.[32]
Also, he knew that the pressures from antislavery groups,
which had burst the tight container of Administration policy,
had a significant effect on Lincoln. Bates realized that Lincoln
now was planning to use colored troops in the fighting.[33]
Much more than he dared to admit, the Chief Executive had
lent his voice to a new cause of war. To Bates's dismay, he
had fallen in line with the emancipationists, who believed they
were fighting for "the holy cause of civilization and Christianity." In truth, the President at least was considering what
Bates long had opposed—the "civil and political equality" of
whites and Negroes.[34]

For the time being, however, Lincoln decided to support
the conservative measures of the Missouri State Convention.
He ordered General John M. Schofield, newly appointed
commander of the Missouri Department, to protect the rights
of loyal slaveowners at all costs. To complicate matters, a
bitter foe of the Administration, William McKee, editor of
the *Missouri Democrat,* obtained a copy of Lincoln's directive

[32] Beale, *Bates Diary,* 292; *Chicago Tribune,* July 3, 1863; Lin-
coln to Stephen A. Hurlbut, July 31, 1863, Lincoln to N. P. Banks,
August 5, 1863, Lincoln to James C. Conklin, August 26, 1863,
Basler, *op. cit.,* VI, 358, 365, 409.

[33] Lincoln to Andrew Johnson, September 11, 1863, Annual Message to Congress, December 8, 1863, Basler, *op. cit.,* VI, 440, and
VII, 49-50.

[34] Lincoln to Montgomery Blair, November 2, 1863, Lincoln to
General James S. Wadsworth, January, 1864 [?], Basler, *op. cit.,*
VI, 555, and VII, 101-2; Beale, *Bates Diary,* 309.

and published it. Schofield directed McKee's arrest, but Lincoln countermanded the order as soon as the news reached the White House. Under heavy attack by the emancipationist faction known as "Charcoals," Gamble interpreted the President's original letter to Schofield as a personal insult, and refused to cooperate further with the Administration.[35]

By the time the new Gamble-Lincoln rift had come to light, Bates already had left St. Louis for Washington. With Julia and three grandchildren he visited Chicago, Milwaukee, Mackinac Island, Detroit, and Niagara Falls. In Chicago, Browning detained him long enough to ask about the Administration's reconstruction plans, made in the face of opposition from Congress. Although Bates confidently reassured Browning, he inwardly felt the same apprehension over the situation in Missouri and the changing character of the war as did the ex-Senator. He suspected that the widening philosophical split over slavery between the conservative Gamble and the increasingly liberal Lincoln epitomized the change.[36]

Seizing upon the breach between the Administration and the Provisional Government, the Drake men acted in September, 1863. A delegation was chosen to call on Lincoln in Washington and to present demands for the removal of conservative military and civil authorities in Missouri and for the implementation of a plan for immediate emancipation. On learning of their designs from his Missouri correspondents, Bates hurriedly conferred with Lincoln. He insisted that the awaited delegation, composed of Republicans from both Missouri and Kansas, was a political minority group antagonistic

[35] Lincoln to Schofield, May 27, 1863, Lincoln to Schofield, July 13, 1863, Lincoln to Schofield, July 20, 1863, Lincoln to Gamble, July 23, 1863, Basler, *op. cit.*, VI, 234, 326, 338, 344.

[36] Beale, *Bates Diary*, 300-302; Gamble to Bates, August 10, 1863, Bates Papers; Bates to Union Meeting of St. Louis, in *New York Times*, August 3, 1863; William E. Smith, *The Francis Preston Blair Family in Politics*, II, 219-23.

to the Provisional Government of Missouri. The Drake extremists, he said, came to dictate terms rather than to present their views. Privately, he worried about their capability of damaging more seriously the delicate strand of loyalty holding the Administration and the Gamble government together.[37]

On September 30 the Drake men assembled in the White House for their meeting with Lincoln. Tersely, the group outlined its desires for immediate emancipation in Missouri and for the purging of Gamble's administration, including the removal of Schofield. For nearly four hours the discussion continued. Lincoln informed them that the Administration had no intention of withdrawing its support from the Gamble government; the delegates trooped out, disappointed at their apparent failure.[38] Jubilant, Bates gloated over their defeat. In a burst of vanity, he took much personal credit for Lincoln's statements and for his resolution to uphold Gamble and leave the direction of Missouri's policy in the Governor's hands. After his exultation, however, Bates realized that Gamble could not ask for more from the President, who had gone to the limit for the Provisional Government.[39]

The confrontation of the Drake group caused Bates to conclude that it was "high time that all honest conservative men should lay their heads together and contrive the best schemes they can to save something from the wreck which the unscrupulous radicals are conspiring to bring upon the coun-

[37] Beale, *Bates Diary*, 308; Rollins to Bates, September 13, 1863, Broadhead to Bates, September 26, 1863, R. T. Lincoln Collection; Bates to Broadhead, September 26, 1863, James O. Broadhead Papers; Tyler Dennett, ed., *Lincoln and the Civil War in the Diaries and Letters of John Hay*, 94-95; Charles D. Drake Autobiography, XXXIII, 915, 917.

[38] Drake Autobiography, XXXIII, 918, 923, 926; Dennett, *Hay Diaries and Letters*, 97; Bates to Gamble, October 10, 1863, Bates Papers.

[39] Lincoln to Gamble, October 19, 1863, Bates to Lincoln, October 22, 1863, R. T. Lincoln Collection; Bates to Gamble, October 24, 1863, Bates Papers.

try."[40] Unless the conservatives united, he predicted, the German Republicans would conspire "to control, if possible, the Government of the Country, as foreigners. . . . They ostentatiously proclaim that they stand aloof from all American parties, having for their only object the concentration of the entire radical German strength, so as to enable them to wield this avowedly foreign power, to turn the scale, in all doubtful elections among Americans." Recklessly he depicted a gigantic anti-American plot of malignant abolitionism, led by those who "refuse to be Americans and insist upon being Germans."[41]

At the end of the year, however, Bates endorsed the Emancipation Proclamation. He accepted the decision to liberate the slaves as a necessary step in the preservation of the Union. Subordinating his prejudices in deference to the changing attitude of the man he served, he nevertheless privately regarded general emancipation as a plaything of scheming politicians and a threat to the restoration of the constitutional *status quo* at the end of the war. Never once had he questioned the President's power to emancipate the slaves, but he expressed doubts constantly about the exercise of this authority by Congress and the Army. Knowing, however, that Lincoln was determined to have his way on emancipation and, perplexed as to his own position, he officially adopted a lenient attitude toward the enforcement of the Fugitive Slave Act.[42]

But the great changes following the Emancipation Proclamation sent Bates into despair. Lincoln used a provision of the proclamation as the basis for enlisting Negroes in the Union armies. Within a few short months, Negroes had been organized into regiments and the Bureau of Colored Troops

[40] Beale, *Bates Diary,* 312.

[41] *Ibid.,* 313.

[42] John P. Usher, in A. T. Pike, ed., *Reminiscences of Lincoln,* 90; James G. Randall, *Lincoln and the South,* 98-112.

created by the War Department. The Negro troops so enlisted were not given a bounty, but instead received only laborer's pay, thus serving for $6 a month less than white soldiers. Angered by this discrimination, Governor John Albion Andrew of Massachusetts, who was enthusiastically raising Negro regiments, initiated a test case involving Samuel Harrison, a colored chaplain in the 54th Massachusetts Infantry. Harrison, upon Andrew's urging, applied for equal pay and allowances, retroactive to the date he entered the Army. In March, 1864, Senator Sumner delivered Harrison's petition, along with a letter from Andrew, to Lincoln who, in turn, presented the papers to Bates. Torn by conflicting emotions, Bates came to the only conclusion he could, since the Negroes were in the field, fighting for the Union. Negroes mustered into service under the provisions of the Militia Act of July 17, 1862, or those freed before April 19, 1864, he declared, were entitled to equal pay and allowances. Lincoln, however, held up the decision while Congress debated the matter. On June 15, 1864, a bill was passed, providing for equal pay for Negro soldiers included in the categories Bates had specified, retroactive to January 1, 1864.[43]

The opinion did not, of course, reflect Bates's true feelings. He was more dismayed than ever by the events in the new session of Congress and the daily debates there on the future of freed Negroes. By mid-February, the ultraism of Sumner, who was sponsoring legislation repealing the Fugitive Slave Law and giving the franchise to freed Negroes, prompted him to call on Lincoln to find out how much the President had

[43] *Attorney General Opinions,* X, 54-58; Bates to Stanton, June 20, 1864, R. T. Lincoln Collection; Lincoln to the Senate, May 7, 1864, Basler, *op. cit.,* VII, 332; Quarles, *Lincoln and the Negro,* 171-72; U. S., *Statutes at Large,* XIII, 129-30. Sumner reported Bates as saying that there was nothing in the Constitution to prevent a Negro from being President. For the interesting ways he, Wilson, and others used Bates's opinion, see U. S., *Congressional Globe,* 38th Cong., 1st Sess., XXXIV, 2851-54.

bargained with the extreme antislavery men and how much the man he once considered almost as conservative as himself had changed. He confided to Lincoln that he thought the proposed Thirteenth Amendment, which called for abolition of slavery, the repeal of the Fugitive Slave Law, and Senator Henderson's plan to free the families of Negroes who had served in the Union military forces, all were the work of enemies determined on the destruction of the Administration's policies and on the revamping of the American political system. His deep-seated conviction that the Negro was socially and politically inferior caused him to scoff at attempts to legislate equality. "Surely Cicero was right," he observed, "when he said that 'in every civil war, success is dangerous, because it is sure to beget arrogance and disregard of the laws of the Government—(i.e., the Constitution).' These men, flattered with a little success, have opened up to themselves a boundless sourse [*sic*] of power. When the Constitution fails them they have only to say 'this is a time of war—and war gives all needed powers'! I am afraid that this Congress is becoming perfectly Radical and revolutionary."[44]

To emphasize his point, Bates kept up a barrage of warnings designed to convince Lincoln of the connection between the proposed antislavery measures in Congress and radical Republican strategy in the approaching presidential election. It was a political conspiracy, he told his chief, designed to thwart the Administration's policies and to send Lincoln down to defeat. The anti-Lincoln movement was directed by congressmen who, while advocating equality for the Negro, were not concerned at all with the welfare of the freed slaves. Stirred by the passion of his conviction, Bates virtually repudiated his previous position and began denying that Congress, during a civil war, had the power to act on matters constitutionally related to the internal affairs of states. He was intent,

[44] Beale, *Bates Diary*, 331, 333; U. S., *Congressional Globe*, 38th Cong., 1st Sess., XXXIV, 14, 145, 521-23, 700-713, 744, 864.

though, on stopping foes in Congress who would emasculate the executive's efforts for reconstruction while ostensibly championing the rights of ex-slaves.[45]

Obviously, Bates regarded nearly all clamorings for rights for the Negro as political maneuverings. The manipulations of the Virginia Constitutional Convention at Alexandria, designed to produce an antislavery constitution and government for a state still in the Confederacy, the legislative provision obliquely endorsing Negro suffrage in the Montana territory, and the debate in Congress over the Freedmen's Bureau, a Negro welfare agency run by the Army, all appeared to him schemes of the "Les Amis des Noirs" who had discovered a bogus but indispensable political issue. He sincerely believed, as he pointed out to Sumner, that the Negroes' rights had and would continue to be gained through court decisions and not through legislation drawn up by opportunistic politicians.[46]

Bates's apprehensions all appeared to be borne out by the Fort Pillow incident. On April 26, 1864, he heard unofficially of the capture, by Confederate General Nathan B. Forrest, of Fort Pillow, near Columbus, Kentucky. Included in the reports were rumors that a number of Negro troops had been executed in the confusion following the fort's capitulation. At first, Bates did not believe it true, but he heard conclusively, in Cabinet session, of how Negro soldiers had been shot, presumably after the battle was over. Although he pointed out that the employment of Negroes in the Army had led to the incident, he recommended punishment for the Confederate officers involved in the incident, provided they were ever captured. He sincerely denounced their actions as a callous

[45] Beale, *Bates Diary*, 347-48, 355; Lincoln's note to Bates, May 3, 1864, Attorney General Papers; John G. Sproat, "Blueprint for Radical Reconstruction," *Journal of Southern History*, XXIII, 38-39.

[46] Beale, *Bates Diary*, 334-35, 353, 371, 383.

violation of the rules of war; the Negroes should have been treated as prisoners and not executed as criminals.[47]

In spite of a strong sense of justice, Bates felt he stood in the midst of a social revolution that he thought deplorable. Although he judiciously accepted Lincoln's emancipation program without comment, he had moved little from his original position opposing any plan to keep the white and Negro races together in the same country. He believed that the sacrifices by the Union had not been made for such a purpose. He wrote,

> The Blacks rejoice exceedingly, over the results of the war, already accomplished in their favor, and exult in the hope of the continuance of the war, in all its desolations. And this is reasonable in them; for they are taught by those at the North, who, ostentatiously claim to be their only friends, that the war is waged solely for their emancipation, and for wiping out the blot of negro slavery, from this continent. I do not believe that the negro[e]s desire that the Whites shall be reduced to slavery; but if, by the destructive processes of the war, their own personal freedom can be accomplished, we cannot expect them to reject that consummation, because, by the same processes, all the civil, social and political rights of white men may be destroyed.[48]

In commenting on the Missouri State Convention, assembled months later to abolish slavery by an ordinance of emancipation, he deplored again the course of "the Radical Party," bent on legislating the future conditions of Negroes within the states. By this time he realized that colonization had been abandoned and that the war was ending with universal emancipation of all the slaves—a political triumph, he thought, for the antislavery extremists who had overwhelmed the be-

[47] Bates to Lincoln, April 23 and May 4, 1864, Bates to Stanton, June 20, 1864, R. T. Lincoln Collection; Beale, *Bates Diary*, 365, 379; *Attorney General Opinions*, XI, 43-44.

[48] Beale, *Bates Diary*, 395.

nevolent Lincoln. His own views on the magnitude of the
Negro problem had not outgrown his earlier attitudes toward
slavery extension and the political necessity of wartime emancipation. At the beginning of the struggle between North and
South he had insisted on the property rights of loyal slaveowners and the patient consideration of sentiment in the
border states toward the domestic institution that bound
black men to white men. As the war progressed, he maintained
emancipation by the executive as only a temporary expedient
until the Union should be restored and the states allowed to
decide the matter for themselves. As the Negro question came
more sharply into focus, he fell back on a constitutional neutrality which he believed had been the traditional position
of the West in the days before Sumter. His unwillingness to
sanction wartime legislative settlement of slavery or to act
positively in an official capacity on the question of emancipation isolated him first from the Cabinet and then from Lincoln. More important, he lost his remaining chance to influence the councils of government at a time when the restoration of the country's unity appeared imminent.

CHAPTER IX

THE LEGAL QUESTIONS OF WAR

*A*LTHOUGH the Emancipation Proclamation of January 1, 1863, overshadowed other events, two constitutional decisions in the same year proved equally momentous. In 1863 the Supreme Court dealt with the issues of blockade and belligerency in the prize cases. In addition, the revival of the issue concerning habeas corpus created a major constitutional controversy equal to the Merryman case. Both questions challenged the powers of the executive and involved the office of the Attorney General.

Bates had long seen the question of the Confederates' belligerency as a serious consideration in the Union's prosecution of the war. He realized the gravity of questions that were raised continuously from the time blockade was proclaimed in April, 1861. If the conflict was to be regarded as a civil insurrection instead of a declared war, it would be impossible to cite international law as the basis of blockade. Too, the question of effectiveness, outlined in the 1856 Declaration of

Paris as a necessary criterion for blockade, caused serious
doubts about the Union's efforts. As did Welles, Bates therefore advocated closing the ports, thus making the government's action a domestic measure designed to avoid the question of belligerency. For this reason, he had been ambivalent
on the President's early decrees concerning blockade. He
wrote,

> I am afraid of the effects of these anomalous measures
> upon the very complicated subject of our blockade. If
> we begin to make exceptions in favor of particular ar-
> ticles and particular nations, we do, unavoidably, draw
> into question the existence of the Blockade itself. And
> that question is cognizable, not by our courts alone,
> but also by the courts of all maritime nations; for the
> subject of Blockade belongs to the Law of Nations. Now,
> a Blockade, to be lawful and honest, and therefore to
> be respected by neutral nations, must be enforced,
> uniformly and strictly. We cannot play the loose game
> of open and shut, just as may suit our varying policy of
> the passing time—for other nations will judge of it,
> as well as we.[1]

Bates felt, too, that his inexperience in matters relating to
international law placed him at a disadvantage in dealing
with the blockade. Partly because of his insecurity and partly
because he truly believed the conflict did not involve two
recognized sovereignties, he remained conspicuously silent
on the blockade issue. By regarding the blockade as the closing
of ports, not warranting a grant of belligerency, he avoided
giving an official opinion on it. Privately, he believed that if
a people were recognized as having the right to wage war,
they eventually could claim their separate sovereignty. Accordingly, he took great care to refer to the blockade as an emer-

---

[1] Howard K. Beale, ed., *The Diary of Edward Bates, 1859-1866*,
265.

gency measure, taken against armed insurrectionists who possessed no rights of belligerency.[2]

In late 1861 Bates had faced a formidable problem that could have been related to the blockade. On November 30, 1861, Nathaniel Gordon, captain of the ship *Erie*, which had been brought into port by the Union Navy, was convicted in the Southern District of New York for engaging in the outlawed slave trade. Lincoln, in his proclamation of the blockade on April 19, had declared that anyone sailing under Confederate letters of marque or anyone who "shall molest a vessel of the United States, or the persons or cargo on board of her . . . will be held amenable to the laws of the United States for the prevention and punishment of piracy." The Gordon case, however, involved the different circumstance of slave running, which carried the death penalty if the accused was convicted. Bates was certain Gordon was guilty as charged, but the incident could shed a revealing light on both the effectiveness and the nature of the Union blockade.[3]

In reviewing the case, Bates laid down a principle he was to follow consistently. He decided to avoid any discussion on the question of the blockade while the case took its normal course in court. Accordingly, Gordon was convicted, and the conviction was upheld by the Supreme Court. Bates, however, received a request for an opinion from Lincoln, who was unsure of the proceedings. Bates was concerned over the President's uncertainty, but he granted that Gordon might be given a reprieve. Privately he advised Lincoln to carry out the prescribed death penalty against the unfortunate slaver. He was greatly upset when Lincoln, worried over the serious illness of his son Willie, delayed Gordon's execution. The

[2] *Ibid.*, 266; Bates to Lieber, March 2, 1862, Francis Lieber Collection.

[3] Proclamation of a Blockade, April 19, 1861, in Roy P. Basler, ed., *The Collected Works of Abraham Lincoln*, IV, 338-39; Bates to J. Hubley Ashton, October 5, 1861, Attorney General Letterbooks, B.

point of the law involved was whether or not the President had the right to lessen the severity of the sentence, and Bates ruled that he did not, because of Gordon's conviction as a slave runner. Taney, too, had decided against any interference in the case by the Supreme Court. Again Bates urged that Gordon be executed as scheduled, for he thought that any more delay in the case might lead to both a public and an international examination of the blockade and its effectiveness.[4]

Underlying Bates's recommendations was his belief that the initial proclamations of blockade were both illegal and impolitic. He opposed the statements and not the practice, since he regarded the closing of the ports as the same as a blockade but without the risk of violating international law. The congressional acts of July 13 and August 6, 1861, granting to the executive the power to close Confederate ports where the federal revenue could not be collected, indirectly had validated Lincoln's action after March 4, 1861. The strict enforcement of a blockade from April 19 to July 13 and the implementation by the Union of the doctrine of continuous voyage, by which vessels carrying contraband cargo thought to be destined for a Southern port could be seized, however, had raised serious questions. Bates feared that their solutions might lead eventually to recognition of the Confederate States by other nations.

Only three weeks before Gordon's conviction, Captain Charles Wilkes of the Union Navy unwittingly took the first step leading to the first great crisis over blockade. Commanding the Union vessel *San Jacinto*, Wilkes intercepted the British mail steamer *Trent* and discovered on board two Confederate envoys, John Slidell and James Mason, bound for

[4] Beale, *Bates Diary*, 229-30, 233-34; Bates to Lincoln, February 19, 1862, R. T. Lincoln Collection; 1 *Black*, 503-6; David M. Silver, *Lincoln's Supreme Court*, 157-58. Gordon was subsequently hanged.

France and England. Wilkes impetuously placed both men in custody and conveyed them to a Federal prison cell in Boston. Immediately the British government condemned the American naval commander's action as a serious breach of their sovereignty and demanded the release of both men. Now the Lincoln administration confronted the world's greatest maritime power over a vital point of international law.

Ironically, Bates at first regarded the capture of Mason and Slidell as a Union coup rather than as a violation of international law. Elated over Wilkes's action, he recommended that the two Confederate emissaries be indicted and tried for crimes against the United States. In his enthusiasm he overlooked the fact that Wilkes had failed to bring the *Trent* into port as a prize of war; he staunchly maintained that the removal of Mason and Slidell as contraband of war had not violated the law of nations. He had a hazy notion of some of the more important cases during America's early nineteenth-century struggle for neutral rights and believed that they had established the necessary precedents for Wilkes's conduct. Searching determinedly for these required precedents, he scoffed at those "timid persons . . . alarmed, lest Great Britain should take offence at the violation of her flag."[5]

A few weeks later, Bates completely reversed himself and, along with the rest of the Cabinet, admitted the rashness of Wilkes's act. He advised compliance with the British demands that the Confederate representatives be freed and that an official apology be rendered by the United States Government. In the days following the capture at sea he had learned much about international conduct. The repeated warnings of Seward, who from the first understood the diplomatic involvements, and the admonishments of Senator Charles Sumner, Chairman of the Senate Foreign Relations Committee, who knew much about the reaction of British leaders, had con-

[5] Bates to E. M. Norton, November 16, 1861, Attorney General Letterbooks, B, IV; Beale, *Bates Diary*, 202.

vinced him that it was highly inadvisable to imprison the Confederate agents. He remembered his youth, when he had acquired a healthy respect for the Mistress of the Seas after the devastation wrought by the British Navy along the Atlantic Coast and the sack of Washington by British troops during the War of 1812. Also, in the present situation, the hostility of European sentiment raised the specter of international recognition of the Confederate states and foreign intervention. As did his colleagues, Bates appreciated the manner in which the British, after their proclamation of neutrality the previous May, had remained uncommitted to either side, recognizing only the existence of a conflict. Finally, his new friend, Count Adam Gurowski, the fanatical Polish revolutionist, brought word of the dissatisfaction among the European diplomatic corps over the *Trent* affair. Now, it appeared to him, the seizure of Mason and Slidell might set Britain and the whole of Europe against the Union's cause.[6]

On Christmas Day, despite a bad cold, he attended a tense Cabinet meeting called to discuss the British demand for the release of Mason and Slidell. He voiced his credence in a rumor that Wilkes and the Confederate ministers had planned the whole episode to embarrass the Lincoln administration, but no one present agreed with him. Impassively he listened to Seward and Sumner as they read letters from English leaders John Bright and Richard Cobden. A general discussion followed. When it was his turn to speak, Bates again somberly depicted an international conspiracy designed to break the blockade, establish European trade relations with the Confederacy, and bring Britain into the war against the Union. Blockade of the North itself, he speculated,

[6] Beale, *Bates Diary*, 205-6, 208-9; Titian J. Coffey, in Allen Thorndike Pike, ed., *Reminiscences of Abraham Lincoln*, 245; Benjamin P. Thomas, *Abraham Lincoln: A Biography*, 282-83. Gurowski, never a close friend, described Bates as an "old cunning whig." Adam Gurowski, *Diary, March 4, 1861—November 2, 1862*, 16.

would be certain. To prevent any of these eventualities he advised the release of Mason and Slidell. "In such a crisis," he said, "we cannot hope for success in a super added war with England, backed by the assent and countenance of France. We must evade it—with as little damage to our own honor and pride as possible." Thus he dropped the "question of legal right" and suggested to the reluctant Cabinet that Mason and Slidell be given their freedom.[7]

In addition to the danger of recognition of the Confederacy by European nations and intervention by them, Bates worried over the Supreme Court's possible invalidation of the "Presidential war," that period between April and July, 1861, during which Lincoln had acted without the sanction of Congress. He realized that it was best to avoid a decision from the high court on the constitutionality of the blockade against a people whom the Administration refused to recognize. If the settlement of the Mason-Slidell case should be prolonged, he reasoned, the whole question might go to the Supreme Court, where it would explode like a bombshell. He realized that the United States, in order to compel European respect, had to maintain an effective blockade as if against an armed belligerent and yet adhere to the fiction that the sealing off of Southern ports was merely enforcement of municipal regulations. So chastened did he become after Mason and Slidell were given their freedom that he declined to make any official comment on the breach of the blockade by neutral nations and heartily approved of a court decision in Key West order-

---

[7] Beale, *Bates Diary*, 213-17; Martin P. Claussen, "Peace Factors in Anglo-American Relations, 1861-1865," *Mississippi Valley Historical Review*, XXVI, 513; Ephraim D. Adams, *Great Britain and the American Civil War*, II, 94-95.

ing the release of the Spanish ship *Teresita,* seized as a prize
of war.[8]

By no means had Bates seen the end of the questions
aroused by the blockade. He was charged with over-all supervision of litigation concerning the blockade because district
attorneys prepared and argued prize cases in the lower courts.
Lack of legal precedents and of lawyers trained in admiralty
law made the burden doubly vexsome. Unfortunately, few
of Bates's subordinates could match the skill and experience
of William M. Evarts, a noted admiralty lawyer in New York
who often represented the captors in prize cases. Too, district
attorneys and marshals, charged with safeguarding vessels
and cargoes, frequently received communications from Seward and Welles that contradicted Bates's instructions. As a
final complication, district attorneys fulfilled dual roles as
prosecutors for the government and as representatives of the
captors who claimed their share of the prize money. Several
district attorneys realized lucrative profits from fees thus
obtained, and justice sometimes was secondary to prize
monies as a consideration in the cases. Congressional legislation, enacted on March 25 and on July 17, 1862, made the
settlement of fees and the disposition of seized cargoes the
responsibility of a board of prize commissioners, but cases
were still tried in court and ships and cargoes sold after
condemnation.[9]

Most pressing were the economic consequences of the
blockade. Seward and Chase wanted to continue a discreet
trade in cotton with Southern states in order to provide a

[8] U. S., *Opinions of the Attorneys General of the United States,*
X, 347-48; Bates to Lieber, November 2, 1862, Lieber Collection;
Charles F. Adams, *Richard Henry Dana, Jr.,* 268; Chester L. Barrows, *William Maxwell Evarts: Lawyer, Diplomat, Statesman,* 103-
4, 106.

[9] Evarts to E. Delafield Smith, November 26, 1861, William
M. Evarts Correspondence; U. S., *Statutes at Large,* XII, 374-75,
608; Samuel Shapiro, *Richard Henry Dana, Jr., 1815-1882,* 118.

supply for Britain and France. Both used the long-debated argument that interruption of cotton shipments might result in recognition of the Confederacy by foreign governments. Bates argued to the contrary; a commercial blockade, impeding the flow of cotton and other Southern commodities, might result in European intervention, but he did not think that the Union should degrade herself by engaging in secret trade with the Confederacy. "War and trade," he said, "do not naturally work together . . . and to compel them to do this unnatural co-action, is to disregard a great principle, and break fundamental law."[10]

Bates maintained that the Southern ports eventually would be seized, the blockade lifted, and the Southern cotton trade with Europe resumed. Stanton had the same idea, but Seward questioned whether or not the capture of the ports might terminate the blockade. Bates felt that Seward misconstrued the whole question, and he replied heatedly that since the act of blockade was a hostile one, it must be ended as soon as the ports were in the hands of Union authorities. His argument had little effect on Seward, however, because the latter held that the military opening of the ports did not automatically signal the resumption of normal commerce.[11]

The Administration's failure to agree even among themselves on a blockade policy complicated the settlement of cases involving foreign and American shipowners who fiercely contested the interruption of commerce. Bates witnessed the growing seriousness of this litigation and realized that he

[10] Beale, *Bates Diary*, 264-66. In September, 1863, Bates modified his position and argued for unrestricted trade along the Mississippi River. David Donald, ed., *Inside Lincoln's Cabinet: The Civil War Diaries of Salmon P. Chase*, 187.

[11] *Ibid.*, 266; Bates to Henry W. David, February 20, 1863, Attorney General Letterbooks, B, V; Howard K. Beale, ed., *The Diary of Gideon Welles, Secretary of the Navy under Lincoln and Johnson*, I, 165-66; Thomas H. O'Connor, "Lincoln and the Cotton Trade," *Civil War History*, VII, 26-27.

might have to take an official stand. Most claimants contended that no state of war existed between April and July,
1861, and therefore the blockade had been illegal. Others
were suing the government for unlawfully confiscating private
property. It became all too evident that the Supreme Court
would be called upon to settle the issue. Evarts, who represented the government in New York courts, had been urging
Bates for months to take the prize cases to the Supreme
Court. Actually, Evarts was concerned over the disposition
of the case involving the *Savannah*, whose captors he represented. Convinced of the growing magnitude of the issues involved and ignorant of Evarts' motivation of personal gain,
Bates heeded his advice. He began preparing the government's
case for the fateful presentation before the Court.[12]

At first, Bates planned to ask for a special session of the
Court to try the prize cases. Later he decided to wait until
the three new Lincoln appointees took their places on the
bench. He therefore devoted his time to the selection of a staff
to assist him. After some consultations, he requested Evarts
and Charles Eames, a legal adviser in Welles's department,
to serve as counsels for the government. Fortuitously, Richard
H. Dana, Jr., the noted author, who served as United States
attorney for the District of Massachusetts, volunteered to aid
the government prosecutors without fee. Dana was interested
in a case that he had argued in the lower court concerning
the *Amy Warwick*, a vessel that had been condemned in
Boston as a prize of war. Bates eagerly welcomed the Massachusetts lawyer, for he decided the addition of Dana to his
staff permitted him to withdraw from active participation in
the trial. He soon began making final arrangements for the

---

[12] Evarts to Bates, November 23, 1861, Evarts to Seward, November 23, 1861, Seward to Evarts, November 26, 1861, William M.
Evarts Correspondence; Bates to Evarts, January 22, 1861, Attorney General Letterbooks, B, IV; Barrows, *Evarts*, 111-12. Evarts
had pressed for charges of piracy against the blockade runners in
the *Savannah* case, holding that the offenders were not belligerents!

cases to be tried en bloc, beginning on February 10, 1863. He knew that a verdict against the government could mean political disaster for the Administration, but he counted on the competence of his staff and on the partisanship of the three new Republican justices, Davis, Miller, and Swayne.[13]

In his various dealings with the Supreme Court Bates had come to have many misgivings about individual justices. Much of his lack of respect for the high tribunal resulted from frustrations of the months past when he thought the Court had failed to exert a needed conservative influence. Feeling it his duty, however, he forced himself to maintain amicable relations with members of the Court, usually at the various social functions at which dignitaries gathered.[14] As he had a year before, on the eve of its session dealing with the prize cases he again delivered an official opinion to the Court which was intended to please the justices. On February 9, 1863, he declared that the pardoning power of the Chief Executive, relating to the release of vessels and cargoes condemned in prize courts, was limited. Even granting to the President the most extraordinary war powers, Bates was denying the President's right to restore property lawfully condemned in a prize court. His well-timed opinion upheld the accepted judicial interpretation, based on principles of common law, that condemnation of property in a prize court did not involve a criminal offense.[15]

Bates expected much from his distinguished team of Dana, Eames, and Evarts, but he carefully observed the Court's

[13] Bates to Evarts, March 11, 1862, Coffey to Dana, November 26, 1862, Coffey to Evarts, January 15, 1863, Attorney General Letterbooks, B, V; Shapiro, *Dana,* 121; Silver, *Lincoln's Supreme Court,* 107-8.

[14] Davis to Mrs. Davis, January 1, 1863, David Davis Papers.

[15] Lincoln to Bates, January 23, 1863, Basler, *op. cit.,* VI, 74; *Attorney General Opinions,* X, 453-55. On that same day, Bates was in court appealing a decision of the Florida district court, which had released a vessel charged with running the blockade because a portion of its cargo belonged to Northern owners.

reaction to the presentation of the government's case. In the early evening of February 25, six days after the opening of the session on the prize cases, he received Justice Swayne, who came with confidential information. According to Swayne, Eames already had alienated the Court and had jeopardized the government's case. The Attorney General was disturbed. He wrote in his diary,

> I am sure that they [the Court] did him a great injustice, for they said that his speech was not argument at all—did no good, but harm. . . . That he had never argued a case before—and did not know how. . . . That the other counsel, Evarts and Dana, shared the feelings of the Court. This is all very unjust, not to say c[r]uel, and shows a degree of passion and prejudice not very creditable to that high Court—I am afraid that the feeling may endanger the Prize Cases.

He assured Swayne that he would take the matter under consideration, but he had no intention of removing Eames.[16]

Confronting the three government lawyers were cases involving four vessels, the *Amy Warwick*, the schooner *Crenshaw*, the barque *Hiawatha*, and the schooner *Brilliante*. The first two vessels, owned by persons residing in Confederate states, had been seized before the July, 1861, session of Congress. The *Hiawatha* was a British ship, captured on its way to Liverpool after leaving a Virginia port. Its owners claimed that the posting of the blockade proclamation in April, 1861, had not allowed sufficient time for notice of the blockade to reach the vessel, thus making its seizure illegal. The *Brilliante* was a ship of Mexican registry that had completed a voyage to New Orleans when it was boarded in Biloxi Bay by Union cruisers. Although each case had individual peculiarities, all had one point in common: The claimants argued that an

---

[16] Beale, *Bates Diary*, 281-82. Eames was counsel for the Government in two of the four cases argued before the Court. Evarts and Dana appeared as chief counsel in the other two.

insurrection, not a state of war, had existed when their vessels were seized, and therefore, the blockade was an unlawful, unprecedented interruption of normal commercial intercourse.[17]

To refute this contention, Dana and Evarts contrived an argument built on the discretionary powers of the executive during a domestic insurrection. The authority of the Government of the United States, they maintained, had been constituted in such a way that it could be employed against rebellious areas of the country without granting them belligerency status. The chief executive of a sovereign country could define rebellion as action taken by a domestic enemy who had no claim to sovereignty. Therefore, the President of the United States might proclaim a blockade and establish prize proceedings against insurgents whose disloyalty had made them public enemies.[18] The government prosecutors argued that an emergency such as civil insurrection "is a state of things, and not an act of legislative will." Furthermore, they pointed out, Congress had approved the President's proclamations and orders when it had convened. Legislative endorsement of executive acts had to be assumed after the firing on Fort Sumter, in spite of the fact that Congress was not in session. The government did not have to plead a case for its own survival, Evarts concluded; the Court had no choice but to endorse the executive's forceful action in preserving the Union.[19]

After several days of argument and counterargument, the Court announced its decision; Justice Grier delivered the majority opinion on March 10. In it he sustained the President's proclamation of the blockade as a constitutional meas-

[17] 2 *Black*, 635-50; Silver, *Lincoln's Supreme Court*, 111-13.

[18] 2 *Black*, 650, 655, 661; Sherman Evarts, ed., *Arguments and Speeches of William Maxwell Evarts*, I, 222-24.

[19] 2 *Black*, 659-60, 662, 664-65; John B. Moore, *A Digest of International Law*, I, 191.

ure taken against a rebellious element in the national community. The Chief Executive had met the crisis of secession and conflict by acting as head of a belligerent government, but not against a recognized nation. Nor had he violated the Constitution by declaring war against the states. An armed insurrection had occurred, and the President, Grier ruled, had used the statutory power, given him in the Militia Acts of 1795 and 1807, to suppress it. Grier also rejected the theory that the exercise of sovereignty did not allow for the seizure on the high seas of an individual's goods. Since the Confederacy had banded itself together, any produce coming to or leaving its shores was the property of a power hostile to the United States. Grier, therefore, concluded that prize law applied to those vessels trading in contraband of war or belonging to persons residing in areas in revolt against the federal government. All prize ships captured after April 19, 1861, were to be regarded as lawful seizures by the government acting against insurgents. Accordingly, "enemies" in rebellion had no claim to the constitutional protection of rights accorded a belligerent; nor were they to be regarded as victims of unconstitutional power.[20]

Four justices, including Chief Justice Taney, dissented. The minority opinion held that the war had begun technically on July 13, 1861, with the passage of a Nonintercourse Act similar to the legislation of 1833 that gave President Andrew Jackson the authority to collect federal revenues in South Carolina. In spite of the soundness of the arguments presented by the dissenting justices, the assumption of extraordinary executive power and the war measures carried out by the Administration were declared constitutional.

For a brief time Bates felt satisfied with the Court's decision, but he soon discovered in how many ways the tenuous questions of blockade, prizes, and neutral rights still remained

[20] 2 *Black*, 665-82; Washington *National Intelligencer*, March 11, 1863; *Appletons' American Annual Cyclopaedia*, III, 765-66.

unsettled. Three days after the announcement of the decision in the prize cases, Senator Sumner came to him with a proposal. He desired Bates's aid in delaying the implementation of a privateering bill passed by Congress the week before. Under the provisions of the act, which Sumner had denounced in the Senate, the President had authority to issue letters of marque to private vessels which would be sent to prey on blockade runners and seek out other Confederate vessels. Bates disapproved of the law himself and thus mildly surprised the Massachusetts abolitionist by agreeing to oppose its execution. He thought it highly irregular, he told Sumner, to commission vessels with letters of marque and to encourage them to intercept shipping. When the matter came up in the Cabinet, he would speak against it.[21]

After a consultation with Welles, who also disliked the act, Bates marshaled his arguments against the privateering measure. In the Cabinet session on March 17 he mentioned the possibility of British economic retaliation if privateering were adopted by the Administration. Chase and Seward argued that the letters of marque would have a salutary effect because Britain would be forced to cease the construction of ships for the Confederacy. Having anticipated this line of reasoning, Bates had a counterargument ready. Letters of marque issued by the government, he said, identified the Union war cause with profit-making, while no real aid was provided the Navy in maintaining the blockade. "The objective of the privateers," he explained, "is not to fight but to capture."[22] He concluded that privateering presented too many disadvantages to be an effective tool of the government, pointing out how defenseless most privateers would be against Confederate raiders. He therefore recommended a reconsideration of the issuing of letters of marque. Seward, however, was not ready to surrender. The Secretary of State

[21] Beale, *Bates Diary*, 284; U. S., *Statutes at Large*, XII, 758.
[22] Beale, *Bates Diary*, 284; Beale, *Welles Diary*, I, 247-48.

presented to the Cabinet a complete set of regulations concerning government licensing of privateers. Observing how
determined Seward appeared, Bates decided to compromise.
He suggested the commissioning of private vessels in the Navy
instead of granting letters of marque. Much to his relief,
Seward and the Cabinet assented.[23]

The privateering bill was not the only congressional enactment to complicate the question of neutral shipping. Congress
also approved the practice of civil officers appropriating
property, neutral and otherwise, before its condemnation in
a prize court. In such cases, the estimated value of the seized
vessel's cargo was deposited in the Treasury prior to its condemnation, and the property itself was then turned over to
the district attorney or federal marshal. Bates regarded the
measure as a proper one, for he acknowledged that Congress
had the right to regulate the disposition of captured property.
However, as he had in recent instructions charging federal
officers with the unenviable responsibility of determining
which of the Confiscation Acts was applicable to prizes taken
by the Potomac blockading squadron, he cautioned district
attorneys to proceed cautiously. In both instances, he instructed legal officers to determine whether or not such property had been appropriated unlawfully or by loose construction
of the legislative enactments. If the property had been seized
on doubtful grounds, the district attorney concerned must
restore it to the rightful owners until the case had been tried
in prize court.[24]

By early April the difficulties of the past weeks, especially
the time he had spent on the questions of blockade and
prize, had exhausted Bates. He therefore willingly accepted

[23] Beale, *Bates Diary*, 284-86; Beale, *Welles Diary*, I, 248-49;
Frederick Bancroft, *The Life of William H. Seward*, 391-92; William M. Robinson, Jr., *The Confederate Privateers*, 316.

[24] *Attorney General Opinions*, X, 467-68, 519-22; U. S., *Statutes
at Large*, XII, 759-60; David R. Deener, *The United States Attorneys General and International Law*, 367-69.

Lincoln's invitation to accompany the President's large party to Acquia Creek, site of Major General Joseph ("Fighting Joe") Hooker's headquarters. As Lieutenant John Coalter Bates was in the Army of the Potomac under Hooker's command, Bates welcomed an opportunity to see the son of whom he was quite proud. When the party arrived at "Hooker's Camp," after encountering an unseasonal snowstorm, he learned that Coalter had received a temporary leave of absence from his regiment and had gone up to Washington, probably passing the President's party somewhere en route. Disappointed, Bates nevertheless attended a grand review which Hooker staged for his visitors. He thrilled at the show of military pomp and strength. It was, he wrote, "the grandest sight I ever saw." Stirred by what he witnessed, he concluded that Hooker had his army ready for a general movement across the Rappahannock and a decisive military stroke.[25]

Bates returned to Washington in high hopes, but in a short while the Union Army met defeat again. Crossing the Rappahannock on the morning of April 27, the Army of the Potomac bypassed Lee's left flank in preparation for an attack on the Confederate rear at Chancellorsville. Before the plan materialized, however, General Stonewall Jackson broke through the Union's blocking position on the right flank, split Hooker's force, and turned a promising advance into a disaster for the North. After inflicting heavy losses on the Confederates, the Union Army was forced to retreat once more.

To Bates and to official Washington generally, the defeat at Chancellorsville was both a stunning psychological as well as military reverse. Alarming rumors were rampant in the capital. The gossipy Isaac Newton reported to Bates that Halleck was to be dismissed, McClellan to be called back as commander, and the Cabinet, with the exception of Chase

[25] Beale, *Bates Diary*, 287-89; Bates to Reverend E. C. Wines, April 11, 1863, Salmon P. Chase Collection.

and Welles, to be replaced immediately by choices of the
Congress. The tales created distrust among the members of
the Cabinet, making an internal split imminent. Montgomery
Blair levied charges of deceit against Seward, Stanton, and
Chase. But Bates suspected Blair's motives, for he still distrusted all members of the famous political family. "True,"
he reflected, "I have no confidence in Seward, and very little
in Stanton; but that does not make me confide in tricky politicians who have not the first conception of statesmanship."[26]
He feared that all semblance of Cabinet unity had disappeared
and that hope of military victory in 1863 was gone. The
Union cause, which had shone so brightly only a few short
weeks before, now faded into twilight.

Bates nevertheless had to put aside his fears and return to
judicial problems concerning the blockade and prize proceedings. Two cases, involving the vessels *Labuan* and *Peterhoff,* and pending for some time in the New York District
Court, had grown more troublesome and again involved Great
Britain in American policy. The *Labuan,* an English steamer,
was seized as it was taking on a load of cotton at a Southern
port, and the *Peterhoff,* an English mail packet, was carrying
contraband of war when it was captured in the Caribbean.
The owners of both vessels claimed that their ships were not
bound for a blockaded area, but the *Peterhoff* was carrying
munitions that were to be transported across the Rio Grande
to Confederates at Brownsville, Texas. Bates ordered a delay
in the proceedings until he should have time to examine the
two cases, which he considered to be of a "very grave national character." The cases undoubtedly would test the
Union's doctrine of continuous voyage applied against neutral
ships that were sailing for neutral ports but carrying goods
intended for overland transshipment to blockaded areas. The

[26] Beale, *Bates Diary*, 291.

Peterhoff, sailing between London and Matamoras, Mexico, carried cargo bound for the Confederacy.[27]

Tried before Judge Samuel Betts in the New York District Court, the *Peterhoff* case caused a major clash between Welles and Seward over the disposition of the vessel's mail. Seward insisted that the seized mail be forwarded, unopened, to the British consul in New York, and he instructed E. Delafield Smith, district attorney in New York, to do so. In spite of the fact that British reaction to the seizure of the *Peterhoff* had created an international incident, Welles disagreed with Seward and objected to his action. Welles believed that the mail should be retained to be used in court as evidence of the vessel's complicity in violating the blockade. Without hesitation Bates sided with the Secretary of the Navy, partially because he was angry at Seward for sending instructions to Smith—instructions that he duly countermanded.[28] Deciding that it was time to confront the Secretary of State on ground of his own choosing, Bates supported Welles on the basis of both international law and congressional enactment; he insisted on the mail being forwarded to the appropriate court for proper disposition. His open defiance of the Secretary of State was short-lived, however. Lincoln supported Seward against Welles and Bates. While the *Peterhoff* was

---

[27] 14 *Federal Cases,* 906; Bates to E. Delafield Smith, May 1, 1863, Attorney General Letterbooks, C; Ludwell H. Johnson, *Red River Campaign: Politics and Cotton in the Civil War,* 16-17. At the time of the *Trent* affair, Bates realized the Union had reversed the traditional American position on neutral rights; Beale, *Bates Diary,* 215.

[28] 19 *Federal Cases,* 316-58; Beale, *Welles Diary,* I, 266-67, 278-83; Beale, *Bates Diary,* 293; Bates to Smith, May 4, 1863, Attorney General Letterbooks, C; *New York Times,* May 5, 1863.

condemned as a prize of war because of the ultimate destination of its cargo, its mails were released.[29]

Bates's action in the *Peterhoff* case conformed to his view
of the strict legal enforcement of blockade as a municipal
regulation and his observance of neutral rights. As with the
Peterhoff's mails, he insisted on bringing vessels in as prizes
and keeping them under the control of civil authorities until
adjudication took place in the courts. Thus, he placed statutory
enforcement above considerations of international law. In
essence, he agreed with Seward that any vessels with cargo
ostensibly bound for a neutral port, but actually on its way
to a blockaded port, was liable to seizure and condemnation
because of its intended purpose. Unlike the Secretary of
State, though, he did not acknowledge the doctrine of "continuous voyage" in his deliberations.[30]

Also contrary to Seward, Bates felt his interpretation of the
blockade as an enforceable municipal regulation allowed the
government to detain vessels and their cargoes and crews
with impunity. Interestingly enough, Seward, while disagree-
ing with Bates's view on the blockade, did not often interfere
with his administration of prize matters and occasionally endorsed the Attorney General's actions. In August, 1864, Seward fully approved of Bates's advice to the district attorney
in San Francisco to seize the French vessel *Rhine*, which was

[29] James B. Scott, ed., *Prize Cases Decided in the United States
Supreme Court, 1789-1918*, III, 1629-53; Beale, *Welles Diary*, I,
290, 301; Alexander Holtzoff, "Some Phases of the Law of
Blockade," *The American Journal of International Law*, X, 63-64.
Though a portion of the cargo was restored to its owners, the
government ultimately lost its case (1866) and had to render
compensation also.

[30] Bates to Welles, May 23, 1863, Attorney General Letterbooks, C; Lincoln to Welles, July 25, 1863, in James D. Richardson,
ed., *A Compilation of the Messages and Papers of the Presidents,
1789-1897*, V, 3377-78; *Attorney General Opinions*, X, 513.

taking on a cargo destined for a Confederate port.[31] A few weeks later, Bates, in an opinion given in answer to the protests of Lord Lyons, the British minister, over the condemnation of his country's vessels in a New Orleans district court, had the complete support of the Secretary of State. "Strictly speaking," Bates contended, "we have no prize courts." However strongly Seward may have disagreed with the deeper meaning behind this legal justification, he did not dispute the Attorney General's goal of bringing vessels into port for search and possible condemnation.[32]

Nor did Bates meet with much opposition in his attempts to extend national jurisdiction to the high seas and territorial waters. When the case of the Lake Erie pirates came before him in late 1864, he decided that the marauders, who had plundered vessels on the Great Lakes and fled to Canada, were guilty of piracy. After carefully studying the case, however, he recommended extradition of the guilty men on the charge of robbery because the British did not consider the Great Lakes international waters. Once the offenders were in American hands, he craftily concluded, there was nothing to prevent their being tried for the crime of piracy.[33]

In late 1864 the Supreme Court partially endorsed Bates's position on the blockade and prizes. The case involved the *Circassian,* a British vessel that had been seized on May 4, 1862, off the northern coast of Cuba. No contraband cargo had been found on board, but the ship's papers indicated that the vessel was sailing for a blockaded port after leaving Havana. Aided by Eames, Bates prepared the government's

[31] Bates to Dana, December 28, 1863, Abraham Lincoln Collection (Massachusetts Historical Society); Bates to Seward, January 13, 1864, Bates to Seward, August 5, 1864, Bates to William Sharp, August 5, 1864, Attorney General Letterbooks, C; Beale, *Welles Diary,* II, 106.

[32] *Attorney General Opinions,* XI, 117-19.

[33] *Ibid.,* 114-15; Beale, *Bates Diary,* 417.

case against the alleged blockade runner, charging that its ultimate destination was a Confederate port. The ship's log indicated that it was bound for New Orleans, then considered a blockaded port despite the fact that the city had fallen into Union hands in late April. In presenting the government's case, Bates agreed that once a port came under Union control the blockade was suspended, but that the *Circassian* nevertheless had intended to run the blockade, as its manifest proved. In reaching its decision in December, 1864, the majority of the Supreme Court decided that the occupation of a port did not necessarily terminate its blockaded status, but it upheld the views of the Administration, sustained by the Attorney General, regarding the seizure of a vessel sailing from a neutral port to a blockaded one. The Court concluded also that the ship's papers could be held as evidence of intent until the case had been settled.[34]

The decision on the *Circassian* followed Bates's argument on the power of the executive to lift the blockade or, in his own terminology, to open the ports, as he thought that "Blockade is an act of war, which a nation cannot commit ag[ain]st itself." In a session of the Cabinet that he attended late in 1864, he endorsed the President's

> power by law to close the ports. In that case, the party attempting to bring in goods, can be punished only as a smuggler. But the attempt to break blockade, works a forfeiture of ship and cargo—must be adjudged under the law of nations, and constantly imperils our relations with neutrals.[35]

The *Circassian* decision also reinforced his views on neutral shipping that had, or presumed to, violate the blockade and even sustained his arguments in the *Peterhoff* case regarding neutral mails.

However satisfying the decision in the *Circassian* case may

[34] 2 *Wallace*, 135-60.
[35] *Ibid.;* Beale, *Bates Diary*, 427.

have been to Bates in later months, he meanwhile faced the contumacious questions of habeas corpus and arbitrary arrest in 1863. Over some months, many persons, including newspaper editors, ministers, and political opponents of the Administration, had been arrested and sometimes imprisoned on the flimsiest of charges. On September 24, 1862, in a fit of pique Lincoln had suspended the writ of habeas corpus for citizens arrested for treasonous activities, including aid to deserters and resisting conscription. The executive proclamation, Bates soon found to his dismay, extended the Army's control over a larger area and made arbitrary arrest more widespread. By mid-1863 indiscriminate arrests and detentions by both military and civil authorities threatened individual liberties under the Constitution.[36]

Bates had feared that the Army would assume wide discretionary power in civil arrests on the basis of Lincoln's proclamation and Stanton's aggressive directives to field commanders. From week to week he found his predictions coming true as the prison lists lengthened. He concluded that the imperious Secretary of War was bent on defying civil authority in order to make his office and the Army omnipotent. No longer did Bates regard Stanton as a better-than-average military administrator, but instead, he saw the bewhiskered Secretary as a ruthless and irresponsible power-seeker who had disrupted the harmony of the Cabinet. Fearing that Stanton's conduct would bring retaliation against the Government by the Congress or the Court, he began subtly warning his cabinet associate. In early 1863 he advised Stanton that his attempt to test the suspension of the writ of habeas corpus before the Supreme Court of Missouri was a mistake. An adverse decision from the state court, he maintained, would

---

[36] Bates to Chairman of the Senate Judicial Committee, December 12, 1862, Attorney General Letterbooks, B, V; Proclamation Suspending the Writ of Habeas Corpus, September 24, 1862, Basler, *op. cit.*, V, 436-37.

damage the prestige of the executive branch in the eyes of both Congress and the public. A few weeks later, in Lincoln's presence, he objected to Stanton's appointment of a draft commissioner in Wisconsin, where demonstrations over the Conscription Act were occurring. Under customary procedures and existing statutes, he informed the irate Secretary, the President normally appointed such officials. Stanton sullenly resented what he thought were the remarks of an intruder, but promised to reconsider his decision.[37]

The War Department, however, had far more resources than the loose network of district attorneys and marshals under Bates's control. Under the Conscription Act of March 3, 1863, the Army supervised, through a system of enrollment officers and provost marshals, the enforcement of draft legislation. Stanton was given administrative control over the conscription of each person, including the furnishing of a substitute or the payment of $300 as commutation. He created an entirely new, labyrinthine administration made up of military provost marshals who took orders only from Stanton, thereby further extending the Army's hegemony over civil affairs.

Bates looked to Congress for redress of what he thought to be unlawful procedures on the part of the military, but he was disappointed repeatedly. Conservative congressmen, such as Crittenden and Senator James R. Doolittle of Wisconsin, did use the Attorney General's statements in proposing legislation aimed at the restoration of rule to civilian officials, but lawmakers friendly to the Army quoted Bates's opinion on habeas corpus to defend their stand against his arguments.[38] The Administration's foes realized Lincoln's dilemma

[37] Bates to Stanton, January 31, 1863, Edwin M. Stanton Papers; Benjamin P. Thomas and Harold M. Hyman, *Stanton, The Life and Times of Lincoln's Secretary of War*, 247-49; Beale, *Bates Diary*, 280.

[38] U. S., *Congressional Globe*, 37th Cong., 2d Sess., XXXII, 1083; *New York Times*, February 24, 1863.

—to declare a moderate policy now was in part a repudiation of the earlier suspension of the writ and the reasons for it, as well as being an unwise political move. Accordingly, Thaddeus Stevens of Pennsylvania introduced an indemnity proposal, designed ostensibly to protect the President and his officers against civil action, but calculated in part to stir up controversy over the executive's suspending power. Another feature of the legislation gave the executive the right to suspend the habeas corpus privilege. Bates realized that while the completed bill afforded necessary protection for civil officers, it also obliquely raised the question of the suspension of habeas corpus that his opinion of July, 1861, supposedly had settled. Amid these conflicting views on habeas corpus, Congress passed the Indemnity Bill on March 3, 1863.[39] Some thought it an unconstitutional delegation of legislative power to the executive; others feared it afforded more latitude in civil matters to the executive. Some approved of its indemnity measures, but opposed the sections that gave the President authority to suspend the writ of habeas corpus. Actually, its provisions left much to individual interpretation. Federal judges were to be furnished lists of persons held by military authorities or of those arrested and indicted by a grand jury, within twenty days after they had been apprehended; persons who had been confined without charge for twenty days were to be released. Nowhere in the language of the act was there a clear settlement of the dispute between Congress and the executive, yet the indemnity extended to federal

[39] U. S., *Congressional Globe*, 37th Cong., 3d Sess., XXXIII, 20; U. S., *Statutes at Large*, XII, 756; James G. Randall, "The Indemnity Act of 1863: A Study in the War-Time Immunity of Governmental Officers," *Michigan Law Review*, XX, 596.

officers and the power to suspend habeas corpus appeared to be potent weapons in the hands of the President.[40]

Shortly after the passage of the Indemnity or Habeas Corpus Act, as it was called, an incident resulted in its use. On May 1, 1863, Clement L. Vallandigham, a former congressman from Ohio, delivered a fiery anti-Administration speech at Mount Vernon, Ohio. By delivering the speech, Vallandigham acted in defiance of an order issued by General Ambrose E. Burnside, military commander of the district. Subsequently, the Democratic leader was arrested, charged with treason, and given a prison sentence by a military court. George E. Pugh, Vallandigham's counsel, applied for a writ of habeas corpus, but District Judge Humphrey H. Leavitt refused to issue it. Although the convicted man was banished by Lincoln to the Confederacy, his case eventually reached the Supreme Court on a writ of certiorari. Bates detested Vallandigham and had little sympathy for the loyal, if unfriendly, "War Democrats," or "Copperheads," as he and others called them. He treated the Vallandigham affair as a treasonous plot of the Democratic party to embarrass the Administration.[41] The Ohioan, he reflected two years later, had been "a democratic apostle, wicked enough to plot treason but too timid to execute it." In this case political considerations outweighed his concern for justice by military commission, and he deemed it imprudent to contest Lincoln's judgment.[42]

[40] James G. Randall, *Constitutional Problems under Lincoln,* 130-31, 166, 192; James G. Randall, "Civil and Military Relationships under Lincoln," *The Pennsylvania Magazine of History and Biography,* LXIX, 202; George C. Sellery, *Lincoln's Suspension of Habeas Corpus as Viewed by Congress,* 39-40; Willard L. King, *Lincoln's Manager: David Davis,* 248; Silver, *Lincoln's Supreme Court,* 131-32.

[41] Bates to W. H. F. Gurley, April 20, 1863, Attorney General Letterbooks, C; Bates to Stanton, January 19, 1864, Stanton Papers.

[42] Beale, *Bates Diary,* 469; Alexander McClure, *Recollections,* 228-29; 1 *Wallace,* 243-54.

A few weeks after Vallandigham had passed through Southern lines, Bates learned of the harsh actions of the military commander in Kansas who allegedly had delivered civil prisoners to a lynch mob. This time Bates did not condone the Army's action. To prosecute men before a military court was bad enough, he wrote Lincoln, but to allow a mob to carry out a sentence against them was even less tolerable. Such incidents, over which he had little control, made him fear similar actions by military commanders in New York and in other areas where draft riots were occurring. With the civil authority impotent, the Army might resort to any measures under the guise of military necessity.[43] However, ineffectual his protest might be, Bates felt he must state his objections to Lincoln.

Naturally, Bates faced a dilemma. In the first year of the war he had staunchly upheld the President's right to suspend the writ of habeas corpus and had endorsed the use of extraordinary powers by the executive. As problems arose and increased in complexity, he had observed that the President relied more and more on the Army. Left undefined always was the dividing line between military dictatorship and the powers necessary to prosecute the war. Bates knew that in time of war it was almost impossible to make such a distinction; Lincoln had to strengthen the Army, sanction its increasing authority, and count on it to fight and temporarily rule the South. To Bates the doctrine of "military necessity" had been abused and now posed a serious threat to the restoration of civil control in segmented areas where major generals or provost marshals held the upper hand.

Bates could readily sympathize with those who opposed the Administration's policies. He fully understood the defiance by state courts that Lincoln angrily described in a Cabinet

[43] Bates to Lincoln, June 5, 1863, John Nicolay Correspondence.

meeting on September 14. Draft evaders and deserters were being set free by state judges, who issued writs of habeas corpus ordering their release. These cases, Lincoln heatedly declared, were plots hatched by Democratic Copperheads, necessitating a general suspension of habeas corpus as provided in the act passed in the previous March.[44] Much to Bates's surprise, Chase spoke sympathetically of the problems of the state judges. Welles and Blair, however, supported Lincoln, the latter recommending that a test case be devised whereby a federal prisoner, released on a writ by a state judge, might be apprehended again and brought to trial in a federal court.[45] While waiting his turn to speak, Bates agonizingly made up his mind. He would support Lincoln on a compromise basis. He denounced the right of subordinates to contest the President's constitutional or statutory authority or to interfere with the Executive acting in his capacity as Commander-in-chief of the military forces. But he opposed any retaliatory measures against the state judges. "I objected," he later wrote, "that no judicial officer had power to take a prisoner or soldier, out of the hand[s] of the Pres[iden]t, by Hab[eas]: Corp[us]: and proposed that we act purely upon the defensive—i.e. inform the judge who issued the writ, of the cause of imprisonment, refuse to deliver the body, and retain possession by force, if need be."[46] His sanction of the President's power bore evidence of his doubts, but his words lent themselves to a broader enforcement and interpretation of the Habeas Corpus Act.

Stanton, Bates suspected, planned to use the President's proclamation as an order directing the Army to enforce suspension of the habeas corpus.[47] Chase, militant again,

[44] Beale, *Bates Diary,* 306.

[45] *Ibid.;* Donald, *Chase Diaries,* 192-93; Beale, *Welles Diary,* I, 432-33.

[46] Beale, *Bates Diary,* 306.

[47] Donald, *Chase Diaries,* 194.

appeared to favor the Secretary of War's idea and suggested that the proclamation be promulgated in the name of military necessity. In this way, protection might be afforded federal officers who refused to comply with writs of habeas corpus issued by state judges. Here was a suggested compromise upon what all of the Cabinet realized was an enlargement of executive power. Chase was proposing an exchange between the Administration and Congress that would acknowledge the right of Congress to delegate suspending authority under the provisions of the Habeas Corpus Act and would strengthen the President's hand. Therefore, if by issuing the proclamation the Administration admitted that the suspension of habeas corpus was a legislative power, the executive had no choice but to enforce it as an act of military necessity. Bates understood the predicament and agreed, with the rest of the Cabinet, to adjourn in order to allow Seward time to prepare a suitable draft of the proclamation. On returning to the White House in the evening he examined Seward's statements and reluctantly approved them.[48]

Bates regarded the proclamation mainly as a means to indemnify military officers in areas where habeas corpus had been suspended. He granted that such protection was necessary for officers involved in arresting those accused of spying, plotting treason, or evading the draft, but, at the same time, he refused to treat the proclamation as being general in nature. To do so would accede to what he regarded as "a general and growing disposition of the military, whenever stationed, to engross all power."[49] He had his official responsibilities to fulfill in disbursing to district at-

[48] *Ibid.*, 195-96; Beale, *Welles Diary*, I, 433-34; Beale, *Bates Diary*, 307.

[49] Proclamation Suspending Writ of Habeas Corpus, September 15, 1863, Basler, *op. cit.*, VI, 451-52; Bates to J. G. Knapp, September 16, 1863, Attorney General Letterbooks, C.

torneys the $100,000 appropriated by Congress for the defense
of military and civil officers. He now had cause to reflect
bitterly upon a key phrase in Lincoln's annual address to
Congress: "In the midst of other cares, however important,
we must not lose sight of the fact that the war power is still
our main reliance."[50]

[50] Annual Message to Congress, December 8, 1863, Basler, *op.
cit.*, VII, 52.

CHAPTER X

AFFAIRS IN MISSOURI

$\mathcal{B}$ATES did not permit even the prize cases and the questions concerning habeas corpus to divert him for long from consideration of Missouri's changing problems. Gamble, Broadhead, and Eads continued to supply him with information on local affairs, as did Gibson, who often journeyed between Washington and St. Louis. From Barton Bates he received confidential and objective appraisals of civil and political developments, especially of the problems of the Provisional Government.

All through 1862 Bates looked upon the situation in Missouri as a scale-model war, with all the attendant problems of confiscation, emancipation, military rule, and disruption of civil authority. He visualized the centrifugal force of war swirling up the Mississippi Valley, where great decisions were soon to be made. So great was his fondness for his home state that, combined with his inveterate western sectionalism and his vision of a great western empire, it influenced his judgment on how the war should be waged in Missouri.

Bates's efforts to build up Eads's gunboat fleet as well as his intervention in the past to ensure a moderate military command in Missouri tied him closely to affairs in his state. He worried as actively as Gamble about the constant turmoil caused by the guerrilla warfare, realizing that control by the Federal forces and martial law would have to continue in the state as long as bushwhacking, raiding, and looting were common occurrences. Also, he knew Missouri's internal problems prevented the full concentration of military forces necessary to remove the Confederates from the Mississippi Valley and, subsequently, to invade the South.

From the beginning, Bates had endorsed Gamble's command over both the Missouri State Militia, a regular state militia called into service to aid the Union Army, and the Enrolled Missouri Militia, which served as a local volunteer force to fight guerrillas. He fully approved of the appointment of General John M. Schofield to command the entire militia force, considering him both moderate in judgment and cautious in action. Unlike Gamble, he did not deem it vital to determine whether the Governor or the President had ultimate authority over the state militia. He did think it sound for Gamble to appoint and remove officers of the Enrolled Missouri Militia, since it was local in nature. Schofield nominally sanctioned a federal-state plan of cooperation, including an agreement for all enrolled and Missouri militia—the latter composed of ten regiments—to remain under Gamble's jurisdiction. However, other federal military commanders, in particular Major General Samuel R. Curtis, head of the Department of Missouri and Schofield's immediate superior, regarded the state troops as an undisciplined mob of doubtful loyalty and ability.[1]

As the fighting in Missouri increased in ferocity it became necessary to pour more Federal troops and money into the war-torn state. Gamble received a Treasury draft of $225,000 to pay for supplies and equipment, and during the fall an additional $300,000 was given him after he promised to limit the state militia to ten thousand men. Bates constantly urged more aid for his state, frequently seeking out Lincoln and Stanton to persuade them of the grave conditions in Missouri. Paradoxically, he disliked the idea of sending more Federal troops into an already turbulent area. But the reality of invasion by the Confederates posed a greater threat momentarily than the potential disruption of the Provisional Government's moderate policies.[2]

The course of the fighting in Missouri resulted inevitably in the expansion of federal authority under General Curtis. A dedicated and dogmatic soldier who had resigned from Congress to accept a commission, Curtis had earned a reputation for ability as a military commander at the Battle of Pea Ridge. Soon after his appointment to the Department of Missouri he assumed that he had the right to command state troops and to enter into the political councils of the Provisional Government. Harassed by guerrilla action at widespread points, he displayed great impatience with less than drastic measures. Most of his political friends were in the Drake faction and looked with favor on his wide-sweeping

[1] Gamble to Halleck, October 10, 1862, Gamble to Lincoln, November 17, 1862, Hamilton R. Gamble Papers; Lincoln to Bates, November 29, 1862, in Roy P. Basler, ed., *The Collected Works of Abraham Lincoln*, V, 515-16; Bates to Gamble, December 2, 1862, Bates Papers; William E. Parrish, *Turbulent Partnership: Missouri and the Union, 1861-1865*, 80-84.

[2] Bates to Stanton, May 27, 1862, Attorney General Letterbooks, B, V; Bates to Gamble, September 1 and 11, 1862, Bates Papers; Bates to Lincoln, September 19, 1862, R. T. Lincoln Collection.

directives for confiscation and on his assessment system
that indiscriminately taxed Confederate sympathizers. Many
of his aggressive actions were based on his General Order
No. 35, issued in December, 1862, which allowed military
provost marshals to arrest and try "pretended Union men"
allegedly bent on sabotaging the Federal command. The
order contained strict prohibitions against public gatherings,
particularly religious ones, and gave provost marshals authority to require loyalty oaths and to protect fugitive slaves.
This Frémont-like posture, as well as other disturbing reports
about Curtis, alarmed Bates. Thomas Ewing, formerly Secretary of the Treasury and of the Department of the Interior, insisted that Curtis had been engaging in illegal
speculation in cotton. Senator Henderson of Missouri informed Bates of the General's involvement in state politics
to the extent that he, Henderson, had to secure Curtis'
removal in order to be re-elected. Even Missouri's Congressman John S. Phelps called on the Attorney General to express
his views on Curtis' shortcomings and his alleged illegal
participation in cotton trading.[3]

While Bates was pondering the desirability of arranging
a conference between Gamble and Curtis to settle matters
temporarily, he was brought directly into the affair. Curtis
and Gamble had been in dispute over the maintenance of
order north of the Missouri River by the enrolled militia.
Curtis contended that these troops were sympathetic toward
slaveowners and helped them to retain their human property.
Gamble, supported by Bates, Rollins, and others, counter-
charged that Curtis was attempting to establish a military

[3] Howard K. Beale, ed., *The Diary of Edward Bates, 1859-
1866,* 276, 279; General Order No. 35, Department of Missouri,
December 24, 1862, in Richard Rush and others, eds., *The War of
the Rebellion: A Compilation of the Official Records of the Union
and Confederate Armies,* Ser. 1, XXII, 868-70. As Bates realized,
Henderson wished to become known as the person responsible for
Curtis' removal, in order to advance his own political fortunes.

dictatorship in Missouri with his confiscation and assessment system. Lincoln decided to intervene by ordering a suspension of confiscation and assessment in the state. Bates immediately suggested that, in addition, negotiations between the civil and military authorities in Missouri be arranged.

Lincoln directed Curtis to hold the conference, but it yielded little. Neither Gamble nor Curtis would agree either on the limits of the Army's authority or on who specifically commanded the Enrolled Missouri Militia, a point on which the latter's attitude greatly agitated Bates. Especially irritating to him was the General's approval of Franklin A. Dick, the provost marshal in St. Louis and Bates's rival in the 1853 land court election, who ordered the Reverend Mr. Samuel B. McPheeters out of the state because of alleged sympathies for the Confederacy. Immediately, Bates came to the defense of his friend and former minister. He invited McPheeters to Washington and took him to see Lincoln. The churchman produced an oath he had taken in Missouri, confirming his loyalty to the Union. Satisfied, Lincoln directed that Mc-Pheeters be permitted to reside, unmolested, in Missouri. Also, he again requested the civil and military leaders to mediate the explosive political situation in the state. Curtis, however, angrily attacked Bates, charging that he was the main conspirator in a plot against Union authority. He implied that Bates was dangerously close to treason because of his indulgent attitude toward Confederate sympathizers. As soon as he heard of this reckless charge, Bates concluded it was time to force Curtis out of the Missouri command.[4]

After brief re-examination of the situation, Bates decided that it was best to support a Gamble-Schofield coalition in Missouri that would work harmoniously on both civil and military levels. He understood Lincoln's view of Missouri

[4] Lincoln to Curtis, December 10, 17, and 19, 1862, and January 2 and 5, 1863, Basler, *op. cit.*, VI, 8, 10, 20, 33, 36-37; Beale, *Bates Diary*, 279.

affairs as a power struggle between rival political factions
and thus planned to approach the President indirectly on
the subject rather than as a prejudiced participant. Accordingly, he turned to Senator Henderson and Congressman
Rollins. The latter, an old Whig friend of the President,
had easy access to the White House. Bates also suggested
that Gamble register a formal protest against Curtis on
behalf of the Provisional Government. It was the Frémont
affair being staged all over again, except that Bates had
resolved to play a more active role. He regarded Curtis as
dangerous because of his interference with the Provisional
Government and his retention of large Federal forces in
Missouri instead of releasing them for what Bates considered
more valuable service in the Mississippi campaign.[5]

By mid-March, after new intrigues involving Curtis, Gamble, and Schofield, Bates had persuaded Lincoln to act.
The President well realized Missouri's importance in the
structure of the Union and the importance of supporting
Gamble's government. On March 9, 1863, Lincoln directed
Stanton to appoint General E. V. Sumner, veteran commander
of the Second Corps in the Army of the Potomac, as the
new military commander in Missouri. Delighted, Bates arranged to talk with Sumner before the latter left Washington.
During their discussion he emphasized the necessity of a
cordial relationship between the Gamble government and
the Federal command.[6]

Suddenly fate intervened. Worn out by the rigors of
campaigning and suffering from old wounds, Sumner died.
Immediately, Bates detected a change of heart in Lincoln,

[5] Gibson to Gamble, January 4, 1863, Schofield to Gamble,
February 2, 1863, H. M. Gamble to H. R. Gamble, March 6,
1863, Gamble Papers; Curtis to Lincoln, December 27, 1862, *O. R.*,
Ser. 1, XXII, 877-78.

[6] Bates to Sumner, March 14, 1863, Bates to Gamble, March
19, 1863, Bates Papers; Parrish, *op. cit.*, 117-22.

who had been half-convinced that Curtis' harsh rule in Missouri was necessary and that Gamble's protestations were those of a self-seeking politician. Bates called at the White House, hoping to change Lincoln's mind and persuade him to appoint Sumner's successor at once. Curtis had to be replaced, he advised, or the Missouri situation would grow worse. He dramatically described these conferences and his apprehensions to Gamble. "Sometimes he [Lincoln] almost yields to my remonstrances, and resolves to play the man to serve the state; and then seemed to get the better of him the influence of extreme politicians and the fear of offending certain Major Generals."[7]

Bates realized that he took a calculated risk in opposing Curtis. He endangered his friendship with Lincoln as well as incurred the hostility of both the Drake faction in Missouri and the powerful Blair family which had so little regard for Gamble's administration. Meshed with the struggle over Federal commanders was an internal fight among Missouri's politically conservative, moderate, and radical elements over patronage, property, and the condition of the Negro. Bates hoped Lincoln would not alienate Gamble or intentionally damage the partnership between the Attorney General and the Governor of Missouri.[8] By carrying the matter as far as he had, he virtually staked his reputation on Lincoln's acceptance of his position, which, in many ways, was no longer strong in his own state.

[7] Bates to Gamble, April 23, 1863, Bates Papers; Curtis to David Davis, April 2, 1863, David Davis Papers; Curtis to Brigadier General Benjamin Loan, April 3, 1863, *O. R.*, Ser. 1, XXII, 194-95. Curtis informed Davis of Lincoln's reluctance to relieve him, but wrote Loan that if the President continued to support the Gamble-Bates coalition he would have "to change the commander."

[8] Gamble to Lincoln, May 2, 1863, Gamble Papers; Gantt to Blair, May 12, 1863, Blair Family Papers; Glover to Bates, May 15, 1863, R. T. Lincoln Collection; Lincoln to Henry T. Blow, Charles D. Drake, and others, May 15, 1863, Basler, *op. cit.*, VI, 218.

On April 22 Curtis settled the question as had Frémont before him. He issued General Order No. 30 of 1863, a set of instructions for judge advocates and military courts in Missouri. In it he ordered the military courts to issue death sentences for captured brigands or for those suspected of treasonous activities. The order made it apparent that Curtis meant to proscribe civil authority in the state. His defiance invited the full wrath of Gamble's government and its supporters and forced Lincoln to make a choice. After repeated urgings from Bates, Henderson, and former Governor Austin A. King, the President named Schofield commander of the Missouri department and directed that Curtis be transferred to a command in Kansas.[9]

Bates took much credit for bringing about the relief of Curtis. Openly he boasted of a personal victory over the Drake men and of a reaffirmation of Lincoln's personal esteem. The removal of Curtis, he said, "was the only course that could save Mo. [Missouri] from social war and utter anarchy." Moreover, he regarded Lincoln's moves as a vindication of his views on the problems in Missouri. To Eads he confided, "I had to fight hard for that [Curtis] removal and expect to be richly paid, in the reestablishment of law and order and productive labor in the state." In his diary he set down a greater anticipation: "The capture of Vicksburg and the Opening of the Missi[ssippi] will secure the peaceful result."[10]

Bates hoped for a gigantic military operation to sweep the Mississippi Valley of Confederate forces. Anxiously he waited for news from Vicksburg, under siege by a determined

[9] Beale, *Bates Diary,* 292; Lincoln to Schofield, May 27, 1863, Basler, *op. cit.,* VI, 234; William E. Smith, *The Francis Preston Blair Family in Politics,* II, 221; General Order No. 30, April 22, 1863, *O. R.,* Ser. 1, XXII, 237-44.

[10] Beale, *Bates Diary,* 294; Bates to Eads, May 28, 1863, James B. Eads Papers.

Union army commanded by Grant. Once Vicksburg was captured, Bates predicted,

> the Miss[issippi] will be open to our arms and our commerce—and that will break the heart of the Rebellion. That [capture of Vicksburg] done, surely the Govt. will at last perceive the propriety of occupying the lower Rio Grande, with a force strong enough to protect itself, and to prevent all contraband com[m]erce in that quarter. . . . From the very first, I always told the Govt., that the Rebellion would triumph or be crushed on the Mississippi, and that opinion is stronger in me now, than ever. If, at the beginning, we had seized the great River, where there was nothing to prevent it—fortified a few strong ports, and with armed boats, patrolled the whole length, we might have restored the Union without destroying the country—we might have been spared rivers of blood, and great heaps of ashes.[11]

In June, while Bates was in Missouri on a visit, news arrived of Union successes in the West. He concluded that it was the time for decision in the Mississippi Valley. In St. Louis he attended a public reception on July 4, celebrating the launching of one of Eads's gunboats, and heard the inventor-promoter describe to the large crowd how the Attorney General of the United States had envisioned and worked for the building of the western gunboat flotilla.[12] Shortly afterward, the honor became doubly important as reports were received of the capitulation of Vicksburg. Bates felt he had a hand in this victory, which he termed "the crowning act

[11] Beale, *Bates Diary*, 296; Lieber to Bates, April 8, 1862, in Thomas S. Perry, *The Life and Letters of Francis Lieber*, 326-27; Henderson to Lincoln, July 21, 1862, in Washington *National Intelligencer*, August 20, 1862.

[12] Bates to Welles, June 6, 1863, Abraham Lincoln Collection (Yale University Library); Welles to Eads, April 16, 1864, Eads Papers; Bates Diary, 1859-1866 (manuscript), July 4, 1863 (Library of Congress); Eads's speech, July 5, 1863, quoted in J. Thomas Scharf, *History of St. Louis, City and County*, I, 536; St. Louis *Missouri Republican*, July 11, 1863.

of the War." He also believed that the fall of Vicksburg made
it possible for western commerce to flow unimpeded and
economic prosperity and political solidarity in the West to
be settled without more fighting. His state and section,
he felt, now might be in a position to lead the nation through
reconstruction.[13]

Soon after returning to Washington, Bates again saw his
hopes frustrated. The Army regulated river trade strictly
on the Mississippi, and internal affairs in Missouri worsened.
By late summer the Drake delegation was preparing for its
journey to Washington to present demands for emancipation
in Missouri and for the immediate dismissal of Schofield.
Matters were at the low ebb for the Provisional Government.
Gamble and Schofield, at odds, ironically enough, over the
McKee incident, now were engaged in a running debate
over military courts and the enlistment of Negroes into the
Union Army. Montgomery and Frank Blair had organized
their followers to oppose both the Drake and Gamble men
and thereby had created a third political force in the state.
Renewed guerrilla activity in Missouri was yet another ob-
stacle in the way of Bates's plans to end the fighting in
Missouri and to consolidate political control in the Gamble
government.[14]

As did the ailing Gamble, Bates deplored the turn of events.
He vowed eternal hostility toward the Missouri radicals, but
he knew that more constructive efforts were needed to mend
the frayed relationship between Gamble and Lincoln. Cautiously he arranged for a conference in Washington at which
the two men might discuss questions that he considered vital
to both. He realized he ran a risk in arranging for a personal

[13] Bates to Chase, July 19, 1863, Salmon P. Chase Collection;
Bates to Lieber, October 8, 1863, Francis Lieber Collection.

[14] Rollins to Bates, September 13, 1863, R. T. Lincoln Collection;
David Donald, ed., *Inside Lincoln's Cabinet: The Civil War Diaries
of Salmon P. Chase*, 187.

confrontation of the President and his brother-in-law, but he was determined to have Gamble present his views to the President. During the ensuing discussion both he and Gamble tried to convince Lincoln that civil control in Missouri must not be sacrificed in the name of military necessity. The Governor of Missouri asked the President for a gradual withdrawal of Federal troops from his state, leaving the maintenance of internal order to his government and the local militia. Bates supported this plan as much as he possibly could, though he realized the presence of Confederate forces in Missouri made it difficult to consider ordering Union troops from the state in the hope that the militia could handle the situation.[15]

The conference yielded no basic understanding between Lincoln and Gamble. In fact, the haggard Governor returned to Missouri, after recuperating in Philadelphia from a freak accident that damaged his arm, extremely angry. Because of the visit of the Drake radicals to the President, Gamble grew even more restive and accused Lincoln of perfidy in his dealings with the Provisional Government. He issued a defensive proclamation indicating that critics of his administration were traitors. In an amazing reversal of position, he also demanded more Federal troops in order to repel the Confederate forces and to suppress his own political foes.[16] Lincoln attempted to placate the distraught Governor, but he was almost at the end of his patience. He assured Gamble of the Administration's support and its intention to sustain the policies of Missouri's wartime government. Bates, understanding the situation from Lincoln's viewpoint, asked him to be as friendly toward Gamble as he could, since the

[15] Bates to Gamble, August 3, 1863, Gamble Papers; Gamble to Bates, August 10, 1863, Bates Papers.

[16] Gamble to Lincoln, October 1, 1863, Gamble Papers; Lincoln to Gamble, October 19, 1863, Basler, *op. cit.*, VI, 526-27; Parrish, *op. cit.*, 160-61, 168-69.

Governor had labored to keep Missouri Unionists together. He knew he could not ask Lincoln to do more.[17]

In the fall, the Missouri elections produced a political impasse. Radical B. Gratz Brown, editor of the *Missouri Democrat* and emancipationist senator, was re-elected along with the conservative Henderson, who had been appointed to the Senate by Gamble in 1862. Brown gained his victory over Bates's close friend, James O. Broadhead. However, Barton Bates, elected to the state supreme court after serving on the high bench since 1862 as an appointee, helped to ensure a conservative character for that body. Nevertheless, the Drake men won several key state offices, a sign that they had promoted their cause effectively. A real setback was dealt the Gamble conservatives in December when Lincoln decided to relieve Schofield, who had re-established friendly relations with the Provisional Government. Schofield had been accused of meddling in state politics, a charge that was compounded by Drake's denunciations of the General as a Southern sympathizer who protected disloyal insurrectionists and restored property to Confederate owners. Because of their determined opposition, bolstered by encouragement from the Blairs, the Drake-Brown faction had managed to force the Provisional Government into ignominious retreat. In January of the new year, General William S. Rosecrans replaced Schofield, who received a promotion and a field command under Grant.[18]

Helpless, Bates watched the surge of his political foes in Missouri. He had tried desperately to use patronage to hold disheartened conservatives together, but his influence had

[17] Bates to Gamble, October 10, 1863, Gamble to Bates, October 17, 1863, Bates to Gamble, October 24, 1863, Bates Papers; Lincoln to Gamble, October 19, 1863, Gamble Papers; Bates to Lincoln, October 22, 1863, R. T. Lincoln Collection.

[18] Tyler Dennett, ed., *Lincoln and the Civil War in the Diaries and Letters of John Hay*, 137; Lincoln to Stanton, December 18, 1863, Basler, *op. cit.*, VII, 78-79.

been reduced by the radicals' successes. In one instance Broadhead, who had replaced the unpopular Franklin A. Dick as provost marshal general of St. Louis, warned Bates of the activities of William W. Edwards, pro-Drake district attorney in western Missouri. Bates managed to dismiss Edwards, though the Drake men sent anguished protests to Washington. Much to Bates's disgust, however, Lincoln continued to dispense favors to the antislavery elements of the party in Missouri, many of whom had joined the radical Union League of America. These politicians, he complained, "are making great efforts to create the belief that they are the Union men, and all others are against the Union."[19]

On January 31, 1864, Bates fell into deep despair when he learned of Gamble's death. Numbed by the news, he deserted partisan considerations to mourn the man he "loved and admired." At the tragic end of this lifelong partnership, Bates prophesied that Gamble would occupy an enviable place in history. "Death has fixed a seal," he wrote, "not only upon the man but his acts and policies also; and so desperate factionists, seeing small hope of success in their schemes, will, I hope, in good degree, cease from troubling."[20] He predicted the eventual survival of the conservative legacy Gamble had left, in spite of the violence and chaos it was forced to endure.

After Gamble's death, Bates lost close contact with Missouri affairs except for reports received from Barton and his other sons. Although he avidly read the St. Louis newspapers, he failed to see that the conservative strength of former Lieutenant-Governor Willard P. Hall, who had pledged

[19] Bates to W. W. Edwards, November 2, 1863, Bates to William N. Grover, January 6, 1864, Attorney General Letterbooks, C; Dennett, *Hay Diaries and Letters,* 133; Beale, *Bates Diary,* 311, 321-22, 324-26.

[20] Beale, *Bates Diary,* 329.

himself to continue Gamble's policies, was not enough to maintain the "Presidential party" in Missouri. His underestimation of radical strength was frequent, since he received only scattered pieces of information on the rapid shifting of political coalitions and factions in his state from Missouri visitors who were not reliable observers. He did not fully realize that the prestige and unity of the Gamble men was crumbling greatly, and at what proved to be a critical time, he felt confident about Missouri affairs in the hands of Hall's weakened administration.[21]

Bates continued his fight against military rule in Missouri as a matter of principle. General William S. Rosecrans was a particular object of his interest because he thought the General a worthy antagonist in the tradition of Frémont and Curtis. In March Rosecrans issued a special order directed against religious gatherings where political issues often were discussed. Previously he had attempted to impose a strict system of administering oaths of allegiance to ministers. Bates indignantly demanded that Lincoln countermand these high-handed orders. He bluntly reminded the President, as he usually did when discussing Missouri affairs, that he needed the state's support in the 1864 election.[22]

The approach of the 1864 Republican convention in Baltimore revealed much about Missouri's internal discord. Both a conservative and a radical delegation arrived from the state to attend the convention. Led by Hall, Broadhead, and Eads, the conservative group supported Lincoln, while the

[21] Bates to Lincoln, May 20, 1863, R. T. Lincoln Collection; Beale, *Bates Diary*, 334, 343. Bates's Missouri intelligence was good throughout most of the war. After Gamble's death, however, his sources appeared to be less informed and his own analysis of the Missouri situation less sharp.

[22] Broadhead to Bates, July 24, 1864, James O. Broadhead Papers; Reverend A. P. Forman to Bates, March 15, 1864, R. T. Lincoln Collection; Beale, *Bates Diary*, 357; Memorandum about Churches, March 4, 1864, Lincoln to Rosecrans, April 4, 1864, Basler, *op. cit.*, VII, 223, 283-84.

Drake-directed radicals fiercely endorsed John C. Frémont.
Much to Bates's dismay, both groups were recognized and
seated.[23] Coincidently the opening of the convention marked
the beginning of weeks of bloody fighting in Missouri and
the reappearance of civil disorder. Bates blamed the military
in general and Rosecrans in particular for the chaos. He
wrote,

> The news from Mo. is still very bad. . . . What a saga-
> cious, provident Genl. Rosecrans must be! For many
> months past, there was no embodied enemy in or near
> the state . . . and now the enemy comes upon him un-
> aware, and strikes the state . . . while he [Rosecrans],
> ignorant of their coming, and wholly unprepared, is in
> no condition to attack the foe, but is everywhere, on
> the run or on the defense.[24]

His concern grew as more discouraging reports arrived
from the West. He asked General Hitchcock to assist him
in preparing a statement on Missouri affairs which, in turn,
would be presented to Lincoln. He suggested to Hitchcock
that they survey events in Missouri since 1861 and emphasized
to the General how continuously the lack of understanding
about the state's internal politics had hampered the efforts
of the Gamble government in its valiant struggles to keep
Missouri in the Union. The main point of the survey was
to show that Missouri, in spite of its constant turmoil, had
raised a loyal volunteer group and contributed both men
and money to the Union cause.[25] Federal military commanders were to be portrayed as incompetent and dictatorial,
anxious to enforce martial law, but unsuccessful in capturing
guerrilla bands or stopping the raids of Confederate forces

[23] Beale, *Bates Diary*, 373, 374-75; John G. Nicolay and John
Hay, *Abraham Lincoln: A History*, VIII, 476-78.

[24] Beale, *Bates Diary*, 415, 416, 420-21.

[25] Bates to Hitchcock, October 24, 1863, Ethan Allen Hitchcock
Papers.

under Sterling Price. Finally, Bates suggested that he and
the aged Hitchcock draw up a petition calling for cessation
of the draft in Missouri and the removal of Rosecrans from
his command.[26] Clearly, Bates thought that Missouri had
seen enough of war.

[26] *Ibid.*

CHAPTER XI

AT THE BOTTOM OF THE CUP

For, I take it to be the highest point of human wisdom (not yet attained) to extract from the concrete of the world, all that is good, and leave all the bad untouched—to drink freely from "the poisoned chalice" of life, all that is healthful and nourishing and good, and yet leave all the obnoxious and bitter deep, in harmless impotence, at the bottom of the cup.

—BATES TO ANNA ELLA CARROLL
September 23, 1864

*B*ATES contemplated, without enthusiasm, the reconstruction of the Union. His concern centered on the procedure by which the states of the Southern Confederacy would be restored to their former status. He thought it all-important to re-establish at once political and constitutional relations between North and South, thus permitting a reconstruction of the Union. If peacetime reunion should be subject to debilitating restrictions placed on the defeated Confederates, he wrote Lieber, conflict would break out again. He firmly believed that the embittered views of the anti-Administration

men in Congress regarding confiscation and punitive measures against Confederate leaders made this grim alternative
possible. It seemed vital to him to place reconstruction under
the aegis of the executive branch of the government.[1]

As a first step, Bates considered a system of universal
amnesty essential. Under the executive branch, amnesty might
be an expedient way of returning full property and political
rights to former Confederates, permitting "qualified voters"
to regain their status in the Union without the ignominy of
being treated as a conquered people. Lincoln's plan, announced in his annual address to Congress on December 8,
1863, fulfilled most of Bates's hopes. Basically, the President
asked for the reconstruction of Southern states around a
tested minority group composed of one tenth of the voters
of 1860 who would swear an oath of allegiance in return
for an executive pardon.[2] These voters then could assemble
a state convention and establish a new state government.
Most agreeable to Bates was the part of the proclamation that
provided for full restoration of property rights to those who
signed the oath and received the pardon. Least agreeable
to him was a statement proposing control by Congress over
emancipation. However, he was willing to settle for the
executive-administered program that Lincoln outlined.[3]

Overburdened with official business of the new year and

[1] Bates to Lieber, October 8, 1863, Francis Lieber Collection;
James G. Randall and Richard N. Current, *Lincoln, the President:
Last Full Measure*, IV, 3-5; Jonathan T. Dorris, *Pardon and
Amnesty under Lincoln and Johnson: The Restoration of the Con-
federates to their Rights and Privileges, 1861-1898*, 32.

[2] Annual Message to Congress, December 8, 1863, Proclamation of Amnesty and Reconstruction, December 8, 1863, in Roy P.
Basler, ed., *The Collected Works of Abraham Lincoln*, VII, 50-52,
53-56.

[3] Bates to William N. Grover, January 6, 1864, Attorney General Letterbooks, C; Ward Hill Lamon, *Recollections of Abraham
Lincoln, 1847-1865*, 236-37; Charles H. McCarthy, *Lincoln's
Plan of Reconstruction*, 190, 194; Eben G. Scott, *Reconstruction
during the Civil War in the United States of America*, 281-82.

anxious over reconstruction plans, Bates, although confined
for a few days to his home on "F" Street, continued to direct
his office toward the goal of executive amnesty. He decided
on a bold step. After summoning Coffey, he dictated a strong
memorandum for immediate dispatch to district attorneys.
He intended to make clear to them his interpretation of the
Amnesty Proclamation. First, he stressed that many persons
charged with treasonous offenses might be pardoned. "The
President's pardon of a person guilty of acts of rebellion
will, of course, relieve that person from the penalties incurred by his crime [rebellion]." In such cases, Bates stated,
the *"bona fide* acceptance of the terms of the President's
Proclamation by persons guilty of acts of rebellion, and not
of the excepted class, will secure to such persons restoration
of all the rights of property except as to slaves." Next, he
specifically referred to the thirteenth section of the Confiscation Act of July 17, 1862, which had authorized the President's pardoning power. "It will hardly be questioned, I
suppose," he hopefully wrote, "that the purpose of this
section; inserted in a law mainly intended to reach the
property of persons engaged in the rebellion, was to invest
the President with full power to relieve such persons or
such conditions as he should prescribe from the penalty of
loss of their property by confiscation." Finally, the Attorney
General directed that all court proceedings against seized
property be terminated without awaiting for an executive
"deed of pardon." Property confiscated among those classes
excepted from executive amnesty would be sufficient to dis-
cipline defiant Confederates, while, conversely, those who
subscribed to an oath of allegiance might have their rights
fully restored.[4]

[4] *New York Times,* February 22, 1864; U. S., *Statutes at
Large,* XII, 592. Bates was careful to point out that the circular
did not involve the 1861 Act for the Collection of Import Duties,
which provided for forfeiture of commercial goods coming from
the Confederacy.

Key phrases in the Attorney General's circular clearly indicated that he planned to give the implementing power of amnesty to district attorneys and that he had expanded on Lincoln's original proclamation. Individual guilt of persons participating in the rebellion had been the basis for condemning property in a punitive manner; now the remission of that guilt by government attorneys who wielded the pardoning power of a benevolent President might restore property confiscated under such circumstances. In each separate case district attorneys might determine whether or not presidential amnesty applied. Actually, Bates hoped to end the practice of treating property of all persons residing in Confederate states as confiscable. However, in the past he had dutifully directed his subordinates to take cognizance of persons who subscribed to the oath only to recover their goods or their land. No change in this procedure would be made. United States attorneys were to act solely in the government's interest. Now, however, the local attorney was empowered to make the immediate decision, whatever the case.[5]

Another important provision in the circular touched on the restoration of plantations in Mississippi and Louisiana to their original owners. Often these lands had been confiscated under the Captured Property Act of 1863, by which more seizures occurred as the Union armies advanced. Subsequently, with the cooperation of accommodating Army officers, these lands were leased to cotton speculators who regarded their ventures and profits derived thereon as a special monopoly granted and protected by the government.

[5] Bates to Broadhead, February 26 and April 10, 1862, Bates to Stanton, February 26, 1862, Bates to William N. Addison, April 17, 1862, in Richard Rush and others, eds., *The War of the Rebellion: A Compilation of the Official Records of the Union and Confederate Armies,* Ser. 3, I, 168-69, 277; II, 247, 285-87; Bates to John Underwood, April 26, 1864, Bates to William Price, July 16, 1864, Attorney General Letterbooks, C.

Bates, opposed to this practice, instructed federal attorneys to assume control of the property whenever possible and place it in trust for the government until the end of hostilities. He did not regard these lands as having been appropriated by the government but as being occupied to prevent their use by the Confederacy. His casual deliberateness quickly stirred up opposition. A "very innocent order on its face," mourned the anti-Administration *New York Tribune,* but one that gave district attorneys control of both confiscation proceedings and legal restoration of property. However partisan its nature, the journalistic aphorism could not have been denied by the Attorney General.[6]

Bates purposely struck a bold note in the circular because of the ominous speeches in Congress concerning legislative reconstruction and the very nature of the war itself. Many congressmen maintained that condemned property had been forfeited for the lifetime of the owner, thus necessitating legislation for restoration. Such views led to reconsideration of the joint resolution amending the Treason Act, or as it was more popularly known, the Second Confiscation Act of 1862. Ensuing debates revealed that while some congressmen were content to let the question concerning duration of forfeiture be settled in courts, others, such as Stevens, insisted that property seized according to provisions of the 1861 and 1862 acts could not be restored by normal judicial process. Maintaining that property seizures broke up the plantation system and thus the basis of Southern political power, Senator Henry Wilson of Massachusetts and Congressman George W. Julian of Indiana made proposals to

[6] *New York Tribune,* February 24, 1864; Bates to Benjamin H. Smith, April 19, 1864, Attorney General Letterbooks, C; Dorris, *op. cit.,* 54-55; *Appletons' American Annual Cyclopaedia,* IV, 204.

parcel out confiscated estates as homesteads to Union soldiers and sailors.[7]

Bates regarded the vindictive plans of the congressmen as potentially disastrous to the rebuilding of the Union. If Southerners could be lured back into the national fold by a promise to restore their property, the war might come to a quick end and reconstruction sped. But if Confederate property remained in the government's hands to be disposed of by a divided and partisan Congress, the South probably would fight on and resist all overtures of peace. Also, he believed that condemned property must not be considered as forfeit for the owner's lifetime because of the variety of circumstances, both civil and military, under which confiscation had been accomplished.[8]

Although his views were conservative, Bates was not pro-Southern, as were several conservatives in Congress. With his state torn apart by the war and two sons enlisted in opposing armies, he did not feel kindly disposed to the secessionists, whom he blamed chiefly for the nation's tragedy. If Confederates were to surrender and return to the Union, he thought that an oath of allegiance must precede the restoration of property and individual rights. Throughout the war he advocated loyalty oaths for all in spite of the undesirable consequences of misguided patriotism. He knew Lincoln's proclamation of amnesty would have little effect on many army officers who refused to administer oaths to certain persons eligible for pardon or who cynically substituted the test oath for federal officeholders. Largely as

[7] U. S., *Congressional Globe*, 38th Cong., 1st Sess., XXXIV, 19, 127, 145, 184-88, 343, 521, 693, 1887; *Appletons' American Annual Cyclopaedia*, IV, 275-76, 279; James G. Randall, *Constitutional Problems under Lincoln*, 276-85.

[8] Howard K. Beale, ed., *The Diary of Edward Bates, 1859-1866*, 411; E. D. Townsend, *Anecdotes of the Civil War in the United States*, 120; Dorris, *op. cit.*, 54-57. The effect of the Amnesty Proclamation on Confederate desertions is dubious.

a result of pressure from Congress, Lincoln further proscribed oath-taking by issuing a proclamation on March 26, 1864, which denied amnesty to prisoners of war and paroled Confederates. Bates was dismayed because he reasoned that the President had been forced to compromise with radical congressmen. However, he instructed his subordinates to obey the new directives on oath-taking even though it conflicted with the instructions in his own circular. He did approve of ex-Confederates being made to prove their loyalty.[9]

Even before Lincoln's December proclamation Bates had encountered difficulty with the proceedings on amnesty. In September, Judge J. G. Knapp, a justice of the state supreme court of New Mexico, refused to swear to a restrictive military oath and was arrested by Army authorities. Upon learning of the Judge's plight Bates asked Lincoln to order his release. He denounced the Army for substituting one oath for another and for its insistence that even loyal ministers, teachers, and judges take it. If the Administration permitted this arbitrary and unlawful exercise of power, he argued, it would lose popular support in the struggle over reconstruction.[10]

The Army's actions motivated Bates to work for more liberalization of the Administration's policy by restricting the Army's jurisdiction. By early 1864, more persons were allowed to take the oath in spite of the previous practices of military authorities. The Attorney General hoped to capitalize on these desired changes. On one occasion, he persuaded Lincoln to countermand an order issued by General Rosecrans that required ministers in Missouri to submit to a military oath

[9] Bates to William N. Grover, April 13, 1864, Attorney General Letterbooks, C; Proclamation about Amnesty, March 26, 1864, Basler, *op. cit.*, VII, 269-70.

[10] Bates to Knapp, September 16, 1863, Attorney General Letterbooks, C.

of allegiance. In this instance Lincoln complied, but Bates thought that the President surrendered too easily to the will of Stanton and the Army. Many times, Bates concluded, the military was given a free hand. To force generals in the field to show mercy proved increasingly difficult and required all the tact and authority Bates could muster.[11]

Too often, Bates thought, the executive will was thwarted by aggressive military commanders who had been encouraged indirectly by Lincoln to be insubordinate. He looked on the President's proclamation of March 26, 1864, as such a mistake, for it delegated much civil power to the Army. Without hesitation, the Army used the new authority in setting up military tribunals to try civilians who had committed civil offenses. Bates watched in dismay as army generals interpreted the proclamation as they saw fit.[12] One of the most notorious was Ben Butler who, as commander of the Department of Virginia and North Carolina, increased the number of arrests and property confiscations. At first, Bates attempted to maintain a friendly relationship with the General, cleverly praising him for allowing unarmed civilians to cross over into Confederate lines, but his overtures yielded little. In June the ebullient Butler ordered a general election in Norfolk, ostensibly to give voters certified by the Army a choice between civil and martial law. Since military provost

[11] Reverend A. P. Forman to Bates, March 15, 1864, Robert Todd Lincoln Collection; Bates to Lincoln, March 21, 1864, William H. Seward Papers; Lincoln to Bates, December 14, 1863, and February 17, 1864, Lincoln to Major General Frederick Steele, March 3, 1864, Lincoln to Rosecrans, April 4, 1864, Basler, *op. cit.*, VII, 62, 189, 221-22, 283-84; Beale, *Bates Diary*, 357; Francis B. Carpenter, *Six Months at the White House with Abraham Lincoln*, 250.

[12] A. H. Carpenter, "Military Government of Southern Territory, 1861-1865," *The Annual Report of the American Historical Association for the Year 1900*, I, 470-74, 481-83, 494-95; Bates to Seward, March 24, 1864, R. T. Lincoln Collection.

marshals counted the ballots, Butler had little doubt of the outcome.[13]

Butler's actions enraged Bates on two points. First, as he told Lincoln, the General assumed that the "restored" Unionist government of Virginia had no constitutional status. Butler had "been misled by a false doctrine newly discovered as put forth by some extreme politicians to the effect that a state in insurrection is out of the Union," Bates concluded.[14] Butler's measures, he heatedly charged, represented illegal implementation of military authority by a commander interested in a political future. The Attorney General had firsthand reports from Governor Francis H. Pierpont and Judge Edward Snead of Norfolk, who opposed the General's high-handed conduct in usurping the jurisdiction of the civil government and courts. Though he righteously blamed Pierpont's difficulty on the West Virginia Governor's previous flirtation with antislavery leaders, Bates agreed to aid him. He talked with Stanton, who agreed that Butler had interfered in civil affairs. Reluctantly, the Secretary of War sent Butler a mild rebuke, but Bates wanted more; he impatiently waited for Lincoln to censure the arrogant commander. "I told the pres[iden]t," he said, "that . . . it was a simple question of jurisdiction—whether the military should put down the civil law."[15]

Bates continued to press Lincoln for action against Butler. Finally, he persuaded the President to send countermanding instructions to the General. In his communication, Lincoln cited Bates as a true patriot, "constantly restraining . . . my tendency to clemency for rebels and rebel sympathizers. But he is the law-officer of the government, and a believer

[13] Beale, *Bates Diary*, 359; Charles H. Ambler, ed., *Recollections of War and Peace, 1861-1868*, 122.

[14] Bates to Lincoln, July 11, 1864, R. T. Lincoln Collection.

[15] Beale, *Bates Diary*, 378-79, 387.

in the virtue of adhering to the law." So saying, the President
dictated the argument of his Attorney General. He informed
Butler:

> Nothing justifies the suspending of the civil by the
> military authority, but military necessity, and of the
> existence of that necessity the military commander, and
> not a popular vote, is to decide. And whatever is not
> within such necessity should be left undisturbed. . . .
> I now think you would better place whatever you feel
> is necessary to be done, on this distinct ground of
> military necessity.

The letter was a subtle warning to Butler, yet it disappointed
Bates and seemed to have little effect on the Army, which
continued to interfere with civil processes in Norfolk.[16]

Unfortunately, Butler was not the only military officer who
usurped civil control. General Lew Wallace, commanding
the Middle Department with headquarters in Baltimore, also
placed his military command above civil government. In
May, Wallace ordered widespread confiscation of property
owned by Maryland secessionists. He justified his actions
as lawful measures against traitors who continued to draw
revenue from states occupied by Union forces. Soon, reports of the General's activities reached Bates, only a short
distance away in Washington. He stiffly reminded Wallace
of the provisions of the Confiscation Acts, which granted the
Attorney General sole responsibility in such cases, and
advised him to turn these cases over to local civil officers.
Wallace, however, refused to cooperate, and Bates, angered,
took the matter to Lincoln. The President agreed to ask
Wallace for an explanation, but no official measures were

[16] *Ibid.*, 394, 400-401; Bates to Broadhead, July 30, 1864, James
O. Broadhead Papers; Lincoln to Butler, August 9, 1864, Basler,
op. cit., VII, 487-88; Bates to Stanton, March 21, 1864, Attorney
General Letterbooks, C; Hans L. Trefousse, *Ben Butler, The South
Called Him Beast!* 169.

taken against the General, causing Bates to make another trip to the White House.[17]

Bates related,

> In conversation with the Pres[iden]t., I told him that I had not yet learned that the Secy. of War had issued the promised order, revoking Genl. Wallace's confiscation orders at Baltimore—I only knew that no public steps were taken to enforce them. He said yes, it had been issued—Stanton read him the letter to Wallace. . . . And so, it seems, that Genl. W[allace] ostentatiously published his orders, assuming very broad jurisdiction, and now, silently abstains from executing them—saying nothing about the revoking order. And thus without the spirit to enforce it.[18]

Ultimately, Bates discovered, little was done to check Wallace's activities.

Enervating struggles with army commanders, such as Butler and Wallace, and other vicissitudes of the long winter spent Bates physically and emotionally. By spring he became almost incapacitated. On April 29 he celebrated with his office staff the fiftieth anniversary of his migration to Missouri, but it was only a moment of release. He was more moody over his repeated clashes with the Army. In early May he suffered a mild stroke that affected his speech and forced him to remain at home in bed, unable even to sign papers. Added to his troubles was knowledge of the impending resignation of the trusted Coffey and the departure of one of his clerks, John M. Vaughan, who apparently had been victimized by unfounded rumors of disloyalty circulated against him. Bates decided to replace Coffey with J. Hubley Ashton, Assistant United States District Attorney of Eastern Pennsylvania, but the loss of his faithful aide and his own poor state of health drove him to private considerations concerning his future. At length he confided

[17] Bates to Wallace, May 25, 1864, Bates Papers.
[18] Beale, *Bates Diary*, 379.

to friends that he intended to take his son Barton's advice
and resign from the Cabinet.[19]

While resting at home, with Julia always at his side,
Bates rummaged through newspapers and maps to follow
the progress of war on all fronts. He was heartened by events
and began forecasting the fall of Richmond and the destruction of Lee's army within days. Since Coalter was in the
Wilderness with Grant, he hoped his predictions would come
true. He attempted to forget the daily tragedies of war by
making late evening social calls with Julia. On one occasion
at the Eames's, he met and talked with Julia Ward Howe,
the popular poet and composer and the wife of Samuel G.
Howe whose work with the blind, deaf, and dumb had
made him internationally renowned. He found Mrs. Howe
opinionated and aggressive, two traits he did not admire
in women, but thought her quite interesting. On other
evenings the elderly couple remained at home, Bates often
reading late into the night and Julia writing to the family
in Missouri. By the time their old friend James B. Eads
arrived in Washington toward the end of May, Bates had
begun to feel stronger, and, hoping that the end of the
war was in sight, he decided not to resign.[20]

It was not alone his struggles against the Army that had
exhausted Bates. Earlier in the year he had become involved
in the Fossat case, a complicated piece of litigation that
consumed much of his time and energy. This long, complicated case had plagued three of Bates's predecessors. In
1863 the Supreme Court finally ruled that the Castillero

[19] *Ibid.*, 361-63; Coffey to J. Hubley Ashton, May 3, 1864, Attor-
ney General Letterbooks, C; Bates to Eads, May 3, 1864, James
B. Eads Papers; Barton Bates to Edward Bates, May 13, 1864,
Bates Papers.

[20] Beale, *Bates Diary*, 366-67, 368, 370-71. Bates was an alert
listener at the social functions he attended in Washington. However, he was inclined to digest idle gossip which often proved
misleading.

title to the rich Almaden mine in California was fraudulent. Bates thought the disputes over California mining claims, including that concerning the New Almaden Mine, of vital importance to the government, since they involved lands regarded as public domain. As early as August, 1861, he wrote the chairman of the House Committee on Public Land Claims to urge a speedy settlement of California mine titles, maintaining that the government's right to much of the land was undisputable.[21]

Bates was concerned mainly with the activities of the New Almaden group, formed by the British-American syndicate of Barrow, Forbes and Company. This company laid claim to the mining rights of the rich New Almaden silver mine in California on the grounds that they had purchased it from Andres Castillero, the lawful owner and original founder of the New Almaden enterprise. Also, the syndicate had bought the Jose Reyos Berreyesa claim to the land on which the mine was located. In validating its title in court, however, the company ran into difficulty because a third claim, that of Justo Larios, was presented. Charles Fossat had bought part of the Larios claim and sold it to a group of speculators in the East, who formed the Quicksilver Mining Company. Successively, a California lower court in 1858 and the Supreme Court in 1863 had nullified the Castillero title, thus leaving the New Almaden Company in contention against the Quicksilver Mining Company on the basis of the Berreyesa claim and the actual operations of the mine. Convinced that the affair could be brought to an end after the Supreme Court's ruling, Bates recommended to Lincoln and to Secretary of the Interior John P. Usher that the government take immediate possession of the mine. Legally,

[21] U. S., *Congressional Globe*, 37th Cong., 1st Sess., XXXI, 455.

both the Fossat and Berreyesa claims now were represented as valid titles to the land.[22]

On July 8, 1863, the President followed the recommendations of Bates and of Stanton who, in 1858, had investigated the case for the government and also had represented the Quicksilver Mining interests. The President ordered seizure of the mine, pending the Court's decision. Next, he dispatched Leonard Swett as a special agent to California to make a full investigation of the conflicting claims. Swett, who carried a presidential writ closing the New Almaden mine, found the western mining interests greatly agitated over the government's intervention. He increased the furor by calling in troops to guard the mine. Agents of the interests involved spread word that the government intended to hold the mine and work it for its rich ore. Disturbed by these events, Lincoln directed Halleck to restore the mine to its former owners, the New Almaden Company, until the case could be settled in court. A former superintendent and stockholder in the New Almaden Mine as well as a partner in the law firm that represented the company, Halleck sent instructions which implied that the government had acted unwisely in occupying the grounds in the first place. To Bates, Halleck's message appeared as a personal affront, and he hinted at a conspiracy between the General and the speculators. Boldly, he charged corruption in high places, since the mine was under control of the New Almaden Company again. His suspicions included the likelihood of Swett and others having been bribed by the Quicksilver Mining interests, and the possible complicity of Stanton and Jeremiah S. Black, who had been retained as counsel by the company.

---

[22] Baltimore *Sun*, March 11, 1863; Leonard Ascher, "Lincoln's Administration and the New Almaden Scandal," *The Pacific Historical Review*, V, 38-41; Milton H. Shutes, "Abraham Lincoln and the New Almaden Mine," *California Historical Quarterly*, XV, 3-6. Forged documents and bribed witnesses were only a part of the background of the California claim cases.

Many persons in California, in fact, looked upon the government's action as favoring the Quicksilver Mining Company.[23]

The Fossat case, as it was called, came before the Supreme Court in early 1864 against a background of much public agitation and suspicion over the involvement of the Lincoln administration. Feeling he was personally implicated, Bates decided to argue the government's case. He thus appeared as chief counsel for the first time while attorney general. Facing him were two former attorneys general, Black and Caleb Cushing, representing the Quicksilver Mining claimants, as well as lawyers serving the New Almaden Company. The latter's claim appeared buttressed by a decision of the California district court in 1860 that had awarded the land now in question to the Berreyesa family. Both the Fossat, or Quicksilver, and Berreyesa, or New Almaden, interests therefore desired the title settled on the basis of land boundaries, in order to exclude the government's claim altogether.[24]

Convinced of corruption and chicanery in the case, Bates firmly held to his position that the land should be denied both claimants and revert to public ownership. On March 1, five days after the case began, he presented his first argument, in which he attacked the 1860 decision of the district court that awarded the mine to the Berreyesas on the basis that theirs was a valid title to the land. To prove the inconsistency of the decision rendered by the California court, he pointed to its subsequent ruling directing that a government survey be made. The result of the survey was to place

[23] Lincoln to Frederick F. Low, August 17, 1863, Basler, *op. cit.*, VI, 393-94; Bates to W. F. Otto, March 21, 1863, Attorney General Letterbooks, B; Beale, *Bates Diary*, 303-4; Howard K. Beale, ed., *The Diary of Gideon Welles, Secretary of the Navy under Lincoln and Johnson*, I, 397-98; Shutes, *op. cit.*, 8-9. As Attorney General, Black had dispatched Stanton to California to investigate the claim cases.

[24] Beale, *Bates Diary*, 339, 342; 2 *Wallace*, 653, 659, 668.

the location of the mine on the land claimed by the Fossat interests. The lower court, he insisted, had no right to order such a survey, since it had no power to determine the locality of a claim or to recognize as lawful the Surveyor General's report, which placed the mine on the Fossat land. Therefore, neither the Fossat group nor the Berreyesa claimants had valid title to the land in question. In presenting his argument, he also took care to keep the specter of corruption before the Court by describing the strategy of both Cushing and Black to exclude the government from the case. So heated did he become in court that he returned to his office thoroughly exhausted. He wrote the next day,

> This Fossat case is the first of any magnitude that I have argued. And, I do believe that my leaving most of the cases to be argued by retained counsel had spread widely at the bar and perhaps to some members of the Court, the belief that I was unable or afraid to encounter the leading members of the bar.[25]

The outcome of the Fossat case left Bates aghast. It had been, he noted, "that if there were a case first of all, the U.S. was a necessary party. But I proceeded to shew by analysis of the Statutes, that there is no case here." On April 4, however, Justice Samuel Nelson announced a majority opinion that upheld the Fossat claim and thus confirmed the Quicksilver Mining Company's ownership to both the mine and the land, excluding the government altogether. Stunned, Bates darkly speculated on the motives of the Court and privately agreed with the dissenting opinion of Clifford, who pronounced the outcome of the case a "monstrous result."[26]

The Fossat case provided Bates with what he thought was concrete evidence of the magnitude of corruption and in-

[25] Beale, *Bates Diary*, 339-40, 342; 2 *Wallace*, 678-81.

[26] Beale, *Bates Diary*, 342, 354; 2 *Wallace*, 712-13, 716-18, 727.

fluence-peddling. By midsummer, speculation and illegal trade in cotton added support to his conviction. The trade had grown ever since Lincoln's executive proclamation of July, 1861, permitting business transactions in confiscated cotton in areas occupied by Union armies. On July 2, 1864, Congress passed still another act, authorizing the Secretary of the Treasury to take charge of the sale of abandoned and captured property. Aimed primarily at securing cotton for Northern textile manufacturers, the legislation provided for the appointment of Treasury agents to purchase cotton from Southern plantation owners. Dispatched into the South to arrange for the transfer and sale of this cotton, Treasury agents often found ways to divert the proceeds from the crops into their own pockets. Also, under the provisions of the Captured Property Act, the Treasury continued to sell or lease plantations and, with the permission of the army commander involved, make arrangements for Northern investors to carry on a lucrative commercial intercourse with Southern merchants. As attorney general, Bates always had felt such illegal trade must be suppressed and the selling or leasing of confiscated or abandoned plantations to Northern investors curtailed if the Government was to spare itself charges of wartime graft. It was true that Lincoln's decree of April, 1863, had interdicted much of the commerce with states in rebellion and had helped to check unscrupulous cotton speculators, but Bates was convinced that the Administration unwittingly had helped large-scale corruption. He particularly thought Chase to be culpable. It was time, he believed, to bring "Mr. Chase's host of ignorant and rapacious swindlers" to justice.[27]

Basically, he took issue with the classification of confiscated plantations as "abandoned." He felt that if Lincoln's reconstruction plan was to work, Confederate property owners

[27] U. S., *Statutes at Large*, XIII, 375-78; Beale, *Bates Diary*, 382.

must be afforded legal protection against military seizure. Instead of dividing their estates among speculators, he recommended that the courts first decide whether or not the properties should be condemned or should be restored to the original owners. But neither the Army, which had seized the estates, nor the Treasury, whose agents were empowered to lease them out, Bates declared, had the right to give individuals an opportunity for personal gain. On the matter of securing the cotton, Bates recommended an expeditious compromise: Allow cotton growers to bring their product into the nearest Union military encampment, and then send it to collecting points where the purchase price would be paid. His assertions angered Stanton, who claimed that Bates's proposals virtually restored full property rights to Confederate owners. Though Bates refused to debate the point with the Secretary of War, he continued to protest permanent denial of property rights to those who had lost them in the war. No reconstruction program, he told the disturbed Stanton, could succeed if based on coercion and nurtured in bitterness. It was with some satisfaction that he witnessed the adoption of a modification of his plan when, in September, Lincoln placed the regulation of the cotton trade solely in the hands of the Secretary of the Treasury and designated several collecting points in the South where the transactions could be made.[28]

Privately, the old Whig discerned the influence of a Northeastern business-capitalist group whose viability had been strengthened by governmental favors. Though he reluctantly acknowledged the proposed Legal Tender bill to be constitutional, he regarded the issuance of paper money and deliberate inflation as a part of their spreading economic monopoly. But his official station permitted him little chance

[28] Beale, *Bates Diary*, 410-11; Bates to William J. Hough, Charles B. Sedgwick, and R. H. Gardner, September 5, 1864, Attorney General Letterbooks, C.

to act. On June 29 he attempted to devalue paper money by ruling that a resident of San Francisco, who had leased courtrooms to the government in 1861 under a contract that called for payment in gold, must be reimbursed in specie and not in the depreciated greenbacks.[29] In many ways he viewed the inflated currency system with the same disapprobation an old Jacksonian would have felt twenty-five years before, but, unlike his old foes, he could not strike it a mortal blow.

Bates acted in subtle ways against those who, he thought, were pursuing extremist policies; he used his patronage power quietly. In one case, he caused the removal of a United States marshal in Rhode Island for political reasons, though he coyly denied to Senator Henry B. Anthony of the same state that he had been involved in the matter. He also attempted to strengthen his patronage influence by suggesting to Senator Trumbull that he be given an extra appropriation to hire more legal assistants. Also, he blocked the appointment of radical attorneys in occupied Tennessee and the Montana territory. In addition, he replaced Rufus Waples, the district attorney in eastern Louisiana, and a United States marshal in the same area for cotton speculation.[30]

In the Cabinet, however, Bates felt helpless. He thought that the atmosphere of division and distrust exceeded that of earlier days. He no longer regarded Chase as an irascible colleague, but now looked on him as a conspiratorial agent of Republican business interests. "Chase's head," he had declared in late 1863, "is turned by his eagerness in the pursuit of the Presidency. For a long time back he has been filling all the offices in his own vast patronage, with extreme partisans, and contrived also to fill many vacancies

[29] Elbridge G. Spaulding, *History of Legal-Tender Paper Issued during the Rebellion*, 15-16; *Attorney General Opinions*, XI, 51.

[30] Beale, *Bates Diary*, 382.

properly belonging to other departments."[31] Now, in 1864, he believed that because of Chase's alliance with powerful groups of Northern manufacturers and financiers, the Treasury Department would be placed at the disposal of private business interests. Just as alarming was the knowledge that several congressmen schemed to cause a rupture in the Cabinet, either to rid the government of "border-state influence" or to thwart Lincoln's reconstruction program. It seemed obvious that Lincoln's various foes, relying on Chase's aid, expected to force Bates and Blair from the Cabinet.

Bates hoped a coalition between Lincoln men and the "better sort of Democrats" might salvage both the election and the war policies of the Administration. But his doubts about Lincoln's resoluteness grew, and the evidence he saw indicated that the President was losing ground to the Northeastern antislavery interest. He reflected,

> Upon the whole, the President seems very hopeful that the machinations of the radicals will fail, and that, in the matter of the nomination, his friends will be able to counteract them effectually. My chief fear is that the President's easy good nature will enable them to commit him to too many of their extreme measures, so that the wall of separation between them will be too thin to stop the fire of their bad principles, and save the constitution and laws, from their universal conflagration, which their measures plainly portend.[32]

To reassure himself, he talked occasionally with Lincoln after the hot, often protracted, Cabinet meetings during the summer. But much of the warm, relaxed relationship he had with Lincoln during the first year of the war was gone. Now he warned the President pontifically about the opposition's plans for the Republican national convention to be held in Baltimore. More than before, he was underestimating

[31] *Ibid.*, 310.

[32] *Ibid.*, 334.

Lincoln, failing to gauge accurately the President's penchant for political jousts and his success in organizing the party for an election. In despair, he revealed his innermost thoughts to the official painter, Francis B. Carpenter, who was busily sketching the Cabinet portraits for his depiction of the signing of the Emancipation Proclamation. Lincoln, Bates said, was almost the perfect man, but he lacked forcefulness. Yet, Bates privately feared any alternative to his chief. Lincoln, he concluded, "is immeasurably preferable to his opponents—Our only chance of a return to law and order—our only means to keep down the reckless, revolutionary spirit of the Radicals." But no doubt his image of a placid and tranquil chief executive, with little steel in his nature, disturbed Bates's thoughts.[33]

What Bates failed to realize was his own virtual isolation from party matters, which often left him uninformed about new political developments. Most surprising to him was public reaction to a circular issued in February by Senator Samuel G. Pomeroy of Kansas, Chairman of the National Executive Committee of the Republican party. In his circular, Pomeroy listed Lincoln's shortcomings and praised Chase as a much better candidate for the Presidency. Instead of aiding Chase, however, the "Pomeroy Circular" had a grievous effect on the Secretary's fortunes. Bates conceded now that Chase had little chance for the Presidency. But his naïvete about Lincoln and his distrust of both Stanton and Chase had greatly distorted his views about the future:

> I am beginning to grow old, and am a very old fashioned man; for in spite of the rushing current of new opinions, I still believe that we once had good old times, good old principles, and good old men to profess them and act them out, and a good Constitution worthy to be preserved to the latest posterity.[34]

[33] *Ibid.*, 350; Carpenter, *op. cit.*, 67-69; Benjamin P. Thomas, *Abraham Lincoln: A Biography*, 412-13.

[34] Beale, *Bates Diary*, 341, 349.

In the preconvention campaign, Bates also drew some erroneous conclusions from his talks with certain delegates on their way to the "National Union Convention" in Baltimore. He studiously ignored both the radical and the conservative delegates from his own state, especially the Drake Republicans who had just attended a convention in Cleveland that nominated Frémont. It dismayed him that the two Missouri delegations were seated at Baltimore; in his opinion, the intraparty confusion was a consequence of Lincoln's political ineptness and lack of direction. Such aberrations resulted, he thought, from Lincoln's willingness to compromise on any point in order to gain political allies.[35]

Naturally, Bates regarded the National Union convention, which adjourned on June 7, as a disaster for the Administration. "It [the convention] did indeed nominate Mr. Lincoln," he said, "but in a manner and with attendant circumstances, as if the object were to defeat their own nomination." He looked on the adoption of a platform that designated slavery as the basic cause of the war as a plot against the Administration. Also, it rankled him that the delegates did not nominate Lincoln by acclamation. In bitter humor he wrote,

> I shall tell the Pres[iden]t. in all frankness, that his best nomination is not at Baltimore, but his nomination spontaneously, by the People, by which the convention was constrained to name him. That if he chose to unite with his enemies, he and they can easily accomplish his defeat.[36]

On June 30 Bates's spirits lifted temporarily when he learned that Chase's long-awaited resignation had been submitted and accepted. He envisioned a conservative triumph

[35] *Ibid.*, 372-73; William F. Zornow, *Lincoln and the Party Divided*, 93-94; John G. Nicolay and John Hay, *Abraham Lincoln: A History*, IX, 68-70.

[36] Beale, *Bates Diary*, 374-75.

in the making, his vision being based on the hope of Stanton also being forced from the Cabinet. But he discerned a danger as well—Chase might become a martyr in the eyes of the Administration's foes and of the antislavery groups. That same evening he accompanied Montgomery Blair to Welles's residence. Far into the night the three men discussed the possible effects of Chase's resignation.[37]

Bates felt that the simultaneous fusing of the abortive Chase movement and the debates in Congress over reconstruction portended upheaval. It had bothered him when Stevens advocated the treatment of seceded states as conquered provinces, to be divided up as the North saw fit, and when Senator Sumner expounded on his favorite theory of "state suicide," which proposed to reduce the Confederacy, at the end of the war, to a vast territory. He strongly opposed any measures giving Congress the power to readmit the former Southern states to the Union. These ideas were anathema to him because he did not believe the Union had fought a war of conquest, and he did not wish to disturb the old social order of prewar years. He firmly insisted that if the rebellious states were not restored to the Union with their original constitutional and political status, the entire country would be consumed in vengeance and prolonged strife. Also, he feared that the settlement of the Negro question might be delayed in such an atmosphere.[38]

On July 2, 1864, Congress passed the Wade-Davis bill, a product of coalition politics between antislavery men and opponents of the President's plans for reconstruction. The act was an effort to check the President's program by ending all reconstruction measures until the fighting had stopped. It would empower provisional governors to enforce all laws— except those pertaining to slavery—that had been in effect

[37] *Ibid.*, 381; Beale, *Welles Diary*, II, 63.

[38] Beale, *Bates Diary*, 330-31, 382-83.

in 1860. All white male citizens except Confederate soldiers were to be enrolled, and when a number equal to one tenth of the votes cast in the 1860 election was reached, a new state convention would be called to draft a constitution. The new constitution was required to include prohibition of slavery and to exclude Confederate officials and officers from public service. Under the provisions of the bill, the state then might resume its former place in the Union. Implicit in the plan, however, was Sumner's theory of "state suicide" and the restriction of postwar executive pardon and amnesty.

At first, Bates was dismayed at the revolutionary implication in the proposed bill. He heartily supported Lincoln's refusal to sign the bill, which resulted in a pocket veto. Also, he agreed to help draft the President's explanatory reply to Congress. Upon careful examination, he found two sentences in the President's message that particularly interested him. In one, Lincoln expressed his approval of the Free State governments in Arkansas and Louisiana, and in a second, he questioned the power of Congress to legislate on slavery. Bates attempted to make Lincoln's meaning more clear by suggesting certain modifications. Since he did not sanction Lincoln's quasi approval of the Wade-Davis bill as a possible alternative to the Administration's plan, he substituted another statement. "For had the [Wade-Davis] bill been approved by the President," he added, "it would have been impossible, for want of time, to nominate provisional governors and to have them confirmed by the Senate, before its adjournment."[39] However, this sentence did not find its way into the message sent to Congress.

Although the decisions concerning reconstruction and the outcome of the election were serious matters to him, Bates's demeanor was not always so grim. In an attempt to inject

[39] Proclamation concerning Reconstruction, July 8, 1864, Basler, *op. cit.*, VII, 433-34; William B. Hesseltine, *Lincoln's Plan of Reconstruction*, 110-20.

some levity into Cabinet sessions he made himself the butt of a joke among his colleagues. At a session in July he announced that one "George Bates" was seeking the Presidency and desired to hold a convention in order to declare his candidacy. Lincoln, he teased, had a "formidable rival" in the field against him. He nailed George Bates's circular to the wall and caused much amusement by inferring a relationship to the misguided man.[40]

But the momentum of the McClellan and Frémont movements and the bickering in Congress over reconstruction during the summer gave Bates little inspiration for humor. In dismay he noted how many old conservative friends, such as Millard Fillmore and Francis Lieber, had joined anti-Lincoln camps. To him the great crusade to preserve the Union appeared to have degenerated into a disorderly mob. He said,

> I am more glad than ever that I belong to no party . . . there are in fact, no parties now, united by any common principle. Party-ties are so weakened that they no longer amount to an obligation; and party names are used only by crafty politicians, to juggle with, for electioneering purposes. Individuals seem bent only on the great work of taking care of themselves, and are ready to change sides, at short notice, and to enlist under any banner that promises higher pay and better hopes of plunder.

He looked on the movement to nominate McClellan as one inspired by venal politicians who would end the war on a stalemate. When the Democratic convention in Chicago nominated the discredited general on August 29, Bates sadly reflected that "the demoralized and effete Democratic Party" had little or no standards to bear, and few men to lead it.[41]

[40] George Bates to Bates, July 17, 1864, Bates Papers; Carpenter, *op. cit.*, 55.

[41] Beale, *Bates Diary*, 390-91, 408-9; Theodore C. Pease and James G. Randall, eds., *The Diary of Orville Hickman Browning, 1881*, I, 676.

As if to fulfill his prophecy, the Frémont campaign climaxed in a dramatic bargain. On September 23 he learned from the Postmaster General himself of Montgomery Blair's unexpected resignation from his post in the Cabinet when Blair revealed to Bates and Welles the contents of a letter he had received from Lincoln. The President requested his resignation, Blair told his startled colleagues, as part of a plan designed to bring about Frémont's withdrawal from the presidential race. Bates thought Blair had presented the facts as they really were, and he therefore sadly speculated on the outcome. He concluded,

> the result will, probably, be to ensure Mr. L[incoln]'s election over McClellan; and the Radicals, no doubt, hope that they will continue to govern the nation. In this view it is their shrewdest policy to abandon their separate organization, for in that they were foredoomed to defeat. But perhaps, their success is a melancholy defeat for their country.
>
> I think Mr. Lincoln could have been elected without them and in spite of them. In that event, the country might have been governed free from their malign influence, and more nearly in conformity to the Constitution.

But in spite of his bitterness, he contributed two hundred and fifty dollars to the Republican campaign fund and hoped Lincoln's re-election would make him a "freer and bolder man."[42]

Two weeks after Blair's resignation, another event caused Bates to reflect again on his own future. On October 12, Chief Justice Taney died. Only the night before, Bates had visited Taney's residence to inquire about the state of his health. He long had held the Chief Justice in awe and, throughout the war, had been fearful of the judicial power

[42] Beale, *Bates Diary*, 412-13, 422; Beale, *Welles Diary*, II, 156; Charles R. Wilson, "New Light on the Lincoln-Blair-Frémont 'Bargain' of 1864," *American Historical Review*, XLII, 74-78.

Taney might attempt to bring against the Administration. He wrote of Taney:

> He was a man of great and varied talents, a model of a presiding officer; and the last specimen within my knowledge, of a graceful and polished gentleman. The lustre of his fame, as a lawyer and judge, is for the present, dimmed by the bitterness of party feeling arising out of his unfortunate judgment in the Dred Scott case. That was a great error; but it ought not and will not, for long, tarnish his otherwise well earned fame. . . . He cannot be forgotten, for his life is interwoven with the history of his country, and, in a greater or lesser degree, must give tone and color to the eventful age in which he has lived.

Alone, he of all the Cabinet paid his last respects to the old Jacksonian by accompanying the funeral procession to nearby Frederick.[43]

Only a week before Taney's death, Bates had notified Lincoln of his intention to leave the Cabinet. He had refused Lincoln's offer of a district court judgeship in western Missouri because he secretly hoped to be appointed to the vacated Supreme Court post. On the day after Taney died, he decided to request the cherished appointment. In his letter to Lincoln he stated:

> I will only add, in asking for the Chief Justiceship, that I could not desire to close my public life more honorably, than by a brief term in the eminent position. . . . In fact, I desire it chiefly—almost wholly as the crowning, retiring honor of my life.[44]

Painfully Bates realized that he no longer had the close personal relationship with Lincoln that he once enjoyed. However, he believed that since the President wished him

[43] Beale, *Bates Diary,* 418-19.

[44] Tyler Dennett, ed., *Lincoln and the Civil War in the Diaries and Letters of John Hay,* 221-22; Bates to Lincoln, October 13, 1864, R. T. Lincoln Collection; Beale, *Bates Diary,* 419.

to remain in the Cabinet as Attorney General, he might grant him, ultimately, the appointment to the Supreme Court. He knew that political considerations forced Lincoln to look over other candidates, including Chase, Browning, Davis, and Stanton. Bates counted on his friend Browning, however, to support his eligibility for the high post. It would have been a cruel blow had he known of the curious change of heart on the part of Browning, who already had recommended Stanton for the position.[45]

Bates sincerely believed that his appointment to the Supreme Court would help bring about a moderate reconstruction program. As Attorney General, he knew he had little chance to check what he deemed was radical legislation or to contest the political measures of the more vindictive Republicans. With either Stanton or Chase on the Court, he feared a greater impetus toward a radical reconstruction program and the continuance of virtual wartime restraints on individuals. Too, his sense of history had not deserted him, and he wished to obtain the exalted office for reasons he admitted only privately. The longer he waited for Lincoln to make up his mind the more desirous he was to be made Chief Justice. Even the gossipy reports of Isaac Newton concerning the President's alleged efforts to free himself of political commitments in order to appoint his Attorney General to the Supreme Court increased his anxiety.[46]

Though tormented by his thoughts, he carried on the routine of office in a diligent manner. He worked on an official opinion concerning the Lake Erie pirates and performed many other daily tasks, since Ashton had gone to

[45] Samuel Miller to Davis, December 21, 1864, David Davis Papers; Burton J. Hendrick, *Lincoln's War Cabinet*, 461; Nicolay and Hay, *Lincoln*, IX, 343-46; Pease and Randall, *Browning Diary*, I, 688.

[46] Beale, *Bates Diary*, 427-28.

Philadelphia to be married. He saw to the completion of the project to line the walls of the attorney general's office with portraits of former occupants. But he was tense, irritable, and given to a quick, uncharacteristic anger. He fell into a trivial dispute with Fessenden over the allotment of additional space for his staff in the Treasury Building, and his quarrels with Seward in Cabinet sessions grew longer and more heated. Since the military news from Missouri concerning the activities of Confederates under Price was bad, he also brooded over the future of his state.[47]

Election Day found Bates with no news concerning the Supreme Court appointment. Without comment, he noted Lincoln's re-election in his diary. Two weeks later, in a letter to the Republican Clubs of New York, he hailed Lincoln's victory as a triumph for "lovers of legal liberty around the world." He dutifully prophesied that it would result in a "speedy restoration of peace and law and order." But, privately, he felt that the President had compromised too much, leaving him at the mercy of the forces that helped to re-elect him.[48]

By November 1 Bates had decided to resign from his post in the Cabinet. He had waited long enough for Lincoln to act on the appointment to the Supreme Court. First to know of his decision was his soldier son John Coalter, who recently had been promoted to the rank of captain. Wrangles with Seward over the blockade had wearied him, and his inner frustration over the Supreme Court appointment had enervated him. Mistakenly, he saw both Stanton and Seward in league with the Sumner-Stevens faction of the Republican leadership which, as it appeared to him, was on the verge

[47] Bates to Hitchcock, October 24, 1864, Ethan Allen Hitchcock Papers; Bates to Lt. Col. Benjamin R. Townsend, June 29, 1864, Bates to John A. Andrews, August 7, 1864, Bates to Fessenden, November 3, 1864, Attorney General Letterbooks, C.

[48] Bates to Republican Clubs of New York, November 22, 1864, in Washington *National Intelligencer*, November 26, 1864.

of gaining the final triumph over the executive branch. Though somewhat strangely indomitable regarding his own future, he feared only the worst for the country in the hands of the radical coalition that he imagined. And he felt helpless, aware that his influence in both the Cabinet and his state had waned as he became isolated from the party Republicans. In a stiffly polite letter to Lincoln, he thanked him for his "uniform and unvarying courtesy and kindness during the whole time in which we have been associated in the public service."[49]

Though his resignation became effective on November 30, Bates decided to remain in office until December 1 to conclude all of his affairs. On his last official day as Attorney General, he consulted with both Usher and Lincoln. Mostly they talked over the future financial needs of the office he was leaving. He also gave Lincoln a final and affirmative opinion on the question of retaining Mitchell as an adviser on immigration and colonization.

For days the Bates family had entertained old friends who were fleeing the South. As soon as their guests departed, Julia and Matilda left for West Point and one last visit with Charles Woodson Bates, the youngest son, who since early 1862 had been at the Academy. Nancy began arranging for the sale of the furniture in the house in "F" Street and saw to the crating of household goods to be shipped to Missouri.[50] On the night of December 1 she and her father moved to a temporary residence in the Metropolitan Hotel.

On the cold morning of December 3 Bates and his daughter left the capital, bound for St. Louis via Philadelphia, where

[49] Bates to Lincoln, November 24, 1864, R. T. Lincoln Collection; Beale, *Bates Diary*, 423-25, 426-28.

[50] Bates to Usher, November 30, 1864, Attorney General Letterbooks, C; Bates to Lincoln, November 30, 1864, R. T. Lincoln Collection; Beale, *Bates Diary*, 428-29.

they were to meet Julia and Matilda. Both still felt the
warmth of their friends' farewell on the preceding night in
their rooms at the Metropolitan. Earlier the previous day,
Bates had made a final visit to the White House. There he
had bade a rather sentimental farewell to Stanton, Seward,
Usher, and Welles. Lincoln fondly said goodbye to his de-
parting Attorney General and promised to write soon. But
when the train drew away from the platform in the Washington station, no one had come to bid him farewell; no
fulsome praises rang in Bates's ears. Only the editorial column
of the *New York Tribune* noted his leaving. His resignation
was, the editorialist wrote, the removal of the last conservative force in the Cabinet.[51]

[51] *New York Tribune,* November 26, 1864.

CHAPTER XII

A GENERATION
THAT HAD PASSED AWAY

*W*HEN Bates arrived in St. Louis, he found many changes in his beloved river town. To some, the war had been providential. Foundries, which supplied arms to the Union forces, enjoyed a prosperous business, as did various hemp and cotton factories, which furnished products needed for the vast conflict. St. Louis proper, in contrast to the stagnated river commerce and the ravaged countryside, was indeed rapidly growing into a major city, far removed in time and condition from the settlement Bates had first seen in 1814. Water-pipe factories, architectural iron works, and the successful St. Louis Gas Company were early evidences of the industrial city soon to rise. New houses and public buildings also indicated a growth in population commensurate with the economic change in St. Louis that Bates had long envisioned.

Bates, however, saw that all was far from well in the state so recently the scene of bloody fighting. Political controversy ran high as Missourians prepared to decide the momentous questions of reconstruction. The General Assembly, largely dominated by the Drake Republicans, had called for a state convention to abolish slavery and to determine postwar qualifications of voter and officeholder. Bates regarded the ambitious schemes of the Drake men as brazen attempts to consolidate their own control and to disfranchise potential political foes of more conservative persuasion. The convention delegates, he noted, "assume to remodel the State and dispose of all its interests. They do not condescend to amend the constitution, but assume to make a new one—the Declaration of Rights." Angrily he spoke out against the new party, charging it with acting in an unconstitutional manner to amend Missouri's instrument of government. Equating the convention to a national "radical" movement aimed at disbarring the Confederate states from full membership in the Union, disfranchising Confederate veterans, and implementing Negro equality, he saw an extension of the struggle he had fought in Washington.[1]

The initial successes of the state convention discouraged Bates because he had previously underestimated the strength of his foes and now tended to overestimate their popular acceptance. The Drake men pushed through an emancipation ordinance on January 11 and drafted a new constitution that provided for disqualification of Confederate sympathizers and a restrictive oath of allegiance designed to disfranchise almost all voters not of radical persuasion. Stung by their boldness in virtually abolishing the Constitution of 1820 and alerted by their impending victory, Bates attacked the Radical Republican program as illegal. He doggedly insisted that the

---

[1] Howard K. Beale, ed., *The Diary of Edward Bates, 1859-1866*, 439, 441-42, 443; Bates to Marie A. Carrington, February 25, 1865, Bates Papers; David D. March, "Charles D. Drake and the Constitutional Convention of 1865," *Missouri Historical Review*, XLVII, 111.

emancipation ordinance of 1863 was the manifestation of Missouri's popular will and that Negro suffrage was not part of that mandate. If the Drake forces should succeed, he warned, they would destroy the conservative nature of the state and would establish a minority government bent on revolution, not reconstruction.[2]

Increasingly concerned over the impending demise of the Provisional Government and the implementation of radical policies, Bates criticized publicly the convention proceedings. He also urged old conservative associates to resist the Drake group whom he characterized as a minority faction. Their fight, he maintained, was the same as the one being waged in Congress over the Southern officeholders and over voters' eligibility. His exhortations did not go unheeded; even his enemies, including Drake, realized that the former Attorney General might prove more than troublesome.[3]

An old political instinct told Bates that the Radicals meant to capitalize on their foes' disorganization and thus prevent true reconstruction. He looked on the continuance of martial law in Missouri, one of the policies endorsed by the Drake convention delegates, as highly unwarranted. His first thought was to rid Missouri of troops and military rule and thus destroy the police power of the Radical Republicans:

> I have constantly and openly, held—Officially at Washington and personally, everywhere—that martial law was not established in Mo. [Missouri]. That the military and provostal government, actually used here, was a bald usurpation of power—and every instance of its exercise, which concerned the civil rights of individuals and the jurisdiction of the Courts, was a manifest wrong, aggravated by the false pretense of lawful authority.

[2] Beale, *Bates Diary*, 453-54.

[3] Bates to James R. Doolittle, February 17, 1865, Bates Papers; Charles D. Drake Autobiography, XXXVII, 1072, 1089.

He thought prolonged martial law served only to aid those who proposed to bring about a political revolution during the reconstruction period in Missouri.[4]

In spite of his growing personal involvement in the convention proceedings, Bates, in early February, moved Julia, Nancy, and Matilda into a home on the corner of Morgan Street and Leffingwell Avenue. His modest savings had dwindled greatly, and he was forced to borrow money from Barton in order to make a down payment of $18,000 on the $23,000 home. The new atmosphere, however, was pleasant. He had enough space for a garden, and his friend Isaac Newton supplied him with seeds. Nancy and Matilda arranged a study for him, complete with a new writing desk. Much to his delight, his two daughters also began to sort his books and papers. The solitude of his leisure hours had turned his thoughts to writing a general history of the times through which he had lived and of the settlement of St. Louis and Missouri. He decided that the latter project was more immediately appropriate and began to contemplate the endeavors of a historian.[5]

Political affairs soon disrupted his literary plans, however. Discussions with Broadhead, Glover, and Judge Treat convinced him that he should devote time to an old stratagem of the past—a series of newspaper articles attempting to discredit the convention. After persuading the editor of the *Missouri Democrat* to publish his articles, he began writing "Letters to the People of Missouri." He intended to invert the Radical Republican argument, which held that opponents of the proposed constitution were "rebels," by demonstrating how confused and disloyal the Drake men were in their efforts to gain public support. His first "Letter to the People," submitted to the *Missouri Democrat* on April 4, attributed the Radicals' lack of popularity to the party's insistence on

[4] Beale, *Bates Diary*, 457.
[5] *Ibid.*, 443-44, 449, 450-51.

martial law. Swift political changes, he wrote, were not necessary to preserve internal order in Missouri, as no vacuum of political power need exist if people would demand a popular referendum on the so-called Drake Constitution. Laws "do confer upon the officers of government, national and state, all the powers which are necessary . . . to the peaceful rule of the country."[6]

A week later Bates, in his second letter, again examined the nature of martial law and the revolutionary character of the Missouri Constitutional Convention of 1865. The letter betrayed his feeling of urgency, for on April 8 the convention had voted to adopt their constitution. The delegates also had approved measures which continued martial law, vacated all judicial and civil offices, and disqualified those who would be disfranchised under the proposed constitution from voting for its ratification. Also, they passed the infamous "Ousting Ordinance," which allowed the governor to make new appointments to the state offices. These measures represented the complete Radical program, a program that Bates took to be an unconstitutional political reprisal. In his second letter he compared the Missouri Constitutional Convention of 1865 to the secessionist conventions held in 1860-1861 and found little difference. In all of these meetings, he asserted, the leaders were a radical minority who had fostered tragic revolution.[7]

While he was preparing his third and fourth letters for publication, reports of Lincoln's assassination arrived. Bates was stunned by the almost unbelievable news. Although he seldom revealed his innermost thoughts on the death of a friend or relative, he expressed a profound sadness over the President's untimely end. Aside from the loss of a man he

[6] *Ibid.*, 462, 467, 469-71; St. Louis *Missouri Democrat*, April 6, 1865; Thomas S. Barclay, *The Liberal Republican Movement in Missouri, 1865-1871*, 34-35, 37.

[7] St. Louis *Missouri Democrat*, April 12 and 28, 1865.

had wanted so much as a friend, he perceived the President's death to be a tragedy for the country. "I appreciated that character [Lincoln's], in beautiful simplicity of truth and kindness, and in its strength and goodness," he wrote. Lincoln had been the most logical and perceptive man he had ever known—logical because he had maneuvered both friend and foe alike; perceptive because he visualized the great changes coming in American government and society. Bates's praises, however sincere they may have been, were late. He evidently rated his former chief higher in death than he had in life.[8]

Bates viewed the advent of Andrew Johnson to the Presidency with little concern, for he thought that the former Governor of Tennessee was firmly committed to the policies of his great predecessor. However, he deplored the fact that Lincoln's death had stirred emotions of fanatical revenge that swept the country and led to a speedy military trial of the assassins. Angrily he condemned his successor, Attorney General James Speed, for lack of courage in failing to demand a civil trial for the accused conspirators. Much to his disgust, Speed had delivered his opinion justifying a military trial, after the assassins had been arraigned, convicted, and executed. He bitterly noted, too, that Speed had failed to provide for a possible commutation by President Johnson of the tribunal's final verdict.[9]

As had many War Democrats and moderate Republicans, Bates counted on Johnson's pursuing a gradual course toward political and social equality for the Negro. He devoted part of his final letter to the impending constitutional and social

[8] Beale, *Bates Diary*, 473, 474-75; St. Louis *Missouri Republican*, May 5, 1865. Titian J. Coffey related that Bates often returned from Cabinet meetings praising Lincoln. On one occasion, Coffey recollected, Bates said that Lincoln "is beyond question the master-mind of the cabinet." Coffey, in Ellen Thorndike Pike, ed., *Reminiscences of Abraham Lincoln*, 245.

[9] Beale, *Bates Diary*, 484, 499-500.

changes that he thought would be brought about in a struggle for Negro suffrage. The whole issue, he felt, was unrealistic. To grant voting rights to the Negro immediately, he warned, would be an unwise step that would lead to social and political tensions and create fears among many white communities that the United States was to become a mongrel civilization. Bates could not accept political equality for the Negro in its most basic form—suffrage for the freed slaves. He revealed, too, his anguished thoughts over the possibilities of assimilating the Negro into white society and hoped to hear soon that Johnson had rejected such goals and would allow the states to resume control over their domestic affairs, thereby ensuring that the constitutional order, which he loved, would be restored. Moreover, a con-ciliatory policy would allow the country ample time to stabil-ize itself and turn away from what he believed to be the extreme courses taken during the war. He regarded the direction that he wished the President to take as proper, but his frame of mind made him a preceptor of a later nineteenth-century philosophy that blended racism and na-tivism into a mixed defense of civil liberties and property rights.[10]

In order to defeat the proposed constitution, which brooked such great changes, and at the same time to affirm his loyalty to the Johnson administration, Bates launched a public campaign against the controversial test oath. He denounced the oath and its provision to remove the justices of the Su-preme Court of Missouri as illegal and without constitutional basis. By implementing the ousting ordinance and arresting and removing the supreme court justices who refused to take the oath, Bates charged, Governor Thomas C. Fletcher had acted wrongfully and was subject to prosecution. He also attacked the legality of using the oath as a determinant

[10] St. Louis *Missouri Democrat,* June 3, 1865.

of who might vote in the June election on the constitution. Convincingly, he described how the Radical Republicans themselves might be disqualified by the ordinance because of their long opposition to the Gamble government. As an answer to the Radicals' demands, he recommended that each district in Missouri keep an account of all persons disbarred from voting. Employing his old political wiliness, he also suggested a tactic of "pious perjury." All those who had not fought against the Union, he urged, should take the infamous ironclad oath, thus making them eligible to vote the Radical Republicans out of office.[11]

To aid the conservative cause in the bitter fight over ratification, Bates continued his public demand that court proceedings against Fletcher and the Radical Republican justices, who now sat on the state supreme court, be carried out. He also readied other arguments. The Drake men and the Radicals in Congress, he maintained, threatened State rights and the constitutional balance in government. If he could convince the voters that the Radicals lacked any appreciable popular support, he might decisively settle the controversy in the conservatives' favor. "I think we have gotten the Ultra-Radicals of Mo. [Missouri] ankle deep in the mire at the bottom of the pit which they had digged for us," he said. It seemed unbelievable that his foes could win on a platform based on martial law, Negro rights, and broad disfranchisement.[12]

Bates hopefully looked for a coalition of conservative Republicans and War Democrats under the leadership of the old St. Louis Whigs, represented by Broadhead, Rollins,

[11] Bates to Dr. M. L. Linton, May 29, 1865, in St. Louis *Missouri Republican*, May 31, 1865; Frederick W. Lehmann, "Edward Bates and the Test Oath," and Thomas K. Skinner, "The Removal of the Judges of the Supreme Court in Missouri in 1865," *Missouri Historical Society Collections*, IV, 390, 393-94; St. Louis *Missouri Republican*, June 19, 1865; Barclay, *op. cit.*, 41.

[12] Bates to Philip R. Fendall, June 11, 1865, Bates Papers.

and himself. Such a party appeared to be materializing when Glover and others organized a large and enthusiastic anti-constitution meeting in late May. For a few weeks afterward, signs of conservative unity were in evidence, and, by the time of the election, Bates was certain of the Radicals' defeat. The early election returns appeared to confirm his predictions, as the Drake forces fell behind. However, the soldiers' votes and possible chicanery at the counting places resulted in a narrow victory for the Drake Radicals. The certification of the constitution, leaving the conservatives de-moralized, put an end to Bates's hopes for a popular over-throw of the Republican extremists.[13]

The tension of the election and its frustrating climax over-taxed Bates's strength. Feeling ill, he restricted his activities and rested at home. A few weeks later he was better, and on Sunday, July 28, disregarding his doctor's advice, he took Julia and other members of the family to church. After the services he dined at a friend's house where General William T. Sherman was the guest of honor. The day's exertions proved too much. Upon his return home in the early after-noon, he suddenly became ill. By early evening his condition, complicated by a shortness of breath, had grown consider-ably worse. Julia summoned a doctor, who did not come immediately, and shortly afterward she sent word of their father's condition to Barton, Julian, and Fleming. By mid-night the family had gathered, apparently arriving in time to be deathbed witnesses. Bates had each relative come into his room for a farewell. Three hours passed in awful expectancy, and then the old patriarch fell asleep, still un-attended by a physician. In the morning the doctor finally arrived to find his patient seriously ill, but alive.[14]

[13] St. Louis *Missouri Republican,* May 29, 1865; Beale, *Bates Diary,* 486; David D. March, "The Campaign for the Ratification of the Constitution of 1865," *Missouri Historical Review,* XLVII, 231-32.

[14] Beale, *Bates Diary,* 495.

Days elapsed before Bates could sit up in bed, and weeks passed before he had recovered sufficiently to receive visitors. As soon as he began to recover, he made anxious inquiries about public affairs. He learned that many of the professional men who, under the provisions of the new constitution, were given until September 2 to take the loyalty oath, had refused to do so. Much to his delight, he heard too that the Missouri conservatives had re-formed their ranks and were planning for a convention in October. After a long talk with the Reverend Mr. James Mitchell, Commissioner of Emigration, who had stopped off in St. Louis, he was more convinced than ever that the conservatives were a political force. Excitedly, he wrote Senator James R. Doolittle of impending happenings. The war had begun with one revolution and its end had brought another, he informed the Wisconsin senator. The Radical "revolution," he suggested, "destroys the states, without whose separate action there can be no constitution [*sic*] government of the nation. It destroys the segregation of power ordained by the Constitution." It did not seem likely, he concluded, that such destructive power could long exist in a country of rational and free men. He clung to this belief, hoping that its fulfillment would put an end to the disruptive tendencies of a new political-social group intent on the maintenance of their own power.[15]

Ill as he was, Bates watched the Missouri convention's deliberations with great interest. It dismayed him to see no practical course of action emerging from their councils, and so he wrote Johnson, asking the President to call a national conservative convention. He assured Johnson that such a convention would be warmly supported by western conservatives, but, to ensure the eventual defeat of the

[15] Bates to Doolittle, October 10, 1865, Bates Papers.

radicals, he suggested that the President issue an executive order dissolving military courts and martial law everywhere. He advised him, as he once had Lincoln, to act boldly as the guardian of the Constitution. Altering some of his recollections, he pictured Lincoln as a strong leader when the occasion demanded it. Now, he implored, Johnson must stand, as his predecessor had done, against the spread of martial law and of radical political strength. He must allow the old leadership of both the North and the South to re-assert itself.[16]

Bates characteristically regarded the political struggle as one for the preservation of the Constitution and for the maintenance of white supremacy. Johnson's veto of the Civil Rights bill, his attack on the Fourteenth Amendment, which guaranteed citizenship rights, and the calling of a National Union convention at Philadelphia appeared to Bates as signals of the long-awaited conservative offensive. Encouraged by the prospects, he held frequent talks with Broadhead, Glover, and Eads about the political situation in Missouri and in the nation. Anxiously, however, he watched for some sign from Johnson, for he knew the actions of the President were the key to a conservative counteroffensive against what he visualized as the consolidated forces of antislavery, industrial consolidation, and social and political change. He inquired eagerly of Johnson's plans from such distinguished guests as Generals Meade, Sherman, and Thomas, who came to visit him, and even wrote to Johnson, promising that Missouri followers were "organizing (and expected soon to be perfectly organized) and fully resolved to fight the great

[16] Beale, *Bates Diary*, 488, 512-13; Bates to Fendall, November 25, 1865, Bates Papers; Bates to Johnson, February 10, 1866, Andrew Johnson Papers.

battle for the Constitution."[17] As in the past, he again saw political foes as the advocates of anticonstitutional government.

Bates also kept in close contact with Egbert E. Brown, who presided over the Missouri convention, frequently offering him advice on resolutions or political strategy. He thought it would be wise for the conservatives of the state to adopt the same strategy he had used at the time the constitution was ratified: a state-wide petition calling for a general election in which all persons who had suffrage rights prior to the adoption of the Drake constitution were eligible to vote.[18]

Sincere as his fight against the radical minority was, Bates once again displayed a lack of realism in his assessment of the political situation. He little comprehended the basic economic and social changes taking place in the country and the shifting of political power to more populous and urbanized states. The Fourteenth Amendment and the Civil Rights Act, along with the Second Freedmen's Bureau Bill, passed over Johnson's veto and added weight to the cause of equality for the Negro. These measures appeared to him, however, as legislation spawned by men like Fletcher and William G. (Parson) Brownlow, wartime governor of Tennessee, who preached mass democracy while dividing up the spoils of war. He demonstrated a shortcoming that had hampered him in the past, for he had scant knowledge of new political forces in operation and of a new economic order founded

[17] Bates to Doolittle, February 17, 1866, Bates Papers; Beale, *Bates Diary,* 528, 554, 478, 495, 530, 536, 562; Bates to Johnson, July 12, 1866, Johnson Papers. For the newest interpretation of Johnson and the attempted formation of a national conservative coalition, see LaWanda Cox and John H. Cox, *Politics, Principle and Prejudice, 1865-1866: Dilemma of Reconstruction America,* 221-27.

[18] Beale, *Bates Diary,* 563; M. Schuyler to Doolittle, April 28, 1866, James R. Doolittle Collection.

on large aggregates of capital and the audacity of adventure-
some entrepreneurs. In postwar reconstruction he saw only
a struggle unchanged between good and evil or, more
precisely, between the same political factions of the prewar
days arguing over the same issues which once had split
Democrats and Whigs. Somewhat analogous to countless
persons in the South, and yet detached from them by a
war, Bates remained an unreconstructed border-state conservative. But, curiously, his reaction to the postwar chaos
returned him to the defense of a government and society
Jeffersonian in simplicity and style, and archaic in concept.
Frustrated by the new order, he fell back into a defensive
position ringed with a concept of laissez-faire economics,
State rights, and a theory of political dominance by an in-
trenched middle class who adhered to the traditions of bygone
days.

In spite of his weakened condition, Bates mustered enough
strength to help plan a reception in honor of President
Johnson, who was to visit Missouri prior to the fall congressional elections. A few weeks before, the conservatives had
left their National Union convention in Philadelphia, filled
with great hopes, not the least factor of which was Johnson's
projected trip around the country to defend his policies. As
part of their campaigns, local conservative committees prepared to greet Johnson on his swing around the circle, shortly
before the elections. Bates was too ill to leave home, but
with Broadhead and Glover he made preparations to make
Johnson's visit to St. Louis successful.[19]

On September 8 Johnson arrived in St. Louis from Alton,
Illinois. A formal reception, including a fleet of thirty-six
vessels, had been readied for the President and his party
composed of such dignitaries as Grant, Seward, and Welles.
Johnson, upon his arrival, addressed his St. Louis audience,

[19] Beale, *Bates Diary*, 565-66.

but was jeered by foes who had stationed themselves at
strategic points. Angered by their catcalls, he launched into
a diatribe on the sins of radicalism. The opposition press, in
reporting the event, depicted the President's outburst as the
ravings of a drunkard or of a man too inarticulate to make
a coherent speech.[20] The incident contributed to Johnson's
decline in popularity with the electorate and made his first
day in St. Louis certainly an inauspicious one.

The next day Bates received Johnson, Seward, and Welles
at his residence, in the presence of various members of his
family. Though very ill from a lung condition that was now
malignant, the former Attorney General greeted his old Cabinet colleagues, Welles and Seward, and warmly welcomed
the President. Seward returned Bates's hospitality by paying
him a particularly moving tribute, remarking how seriously
his services were needed once more in the Cabinet. Bates
tearfully responded to the man he once considered so dangerous, and for a few minutes there was an embarrassing
silence. Believing him to be on the verge of death, Welles
spoke up, expressing his high professional regard for his
old friend. By the time he had finished, Bates had recovered
his composure and joined in a lively conversation with the
three men for the better part of the afternoon. As he was
leaving, Johnson thanked Bates for his efforts in the campaign and floridly declared him to be one of the great
American patriots. All over St. Louis and the state of Missouri there was a flush of pride for the old citizen who
was apparently held in great esteem by men in high office.[21]

The 1866 congressional elections, however, which resulted
in defeat for the Johnson conservatives, were a severe blow
to Bates and brought his political activities to a close.
Although he should have been heartened by the decisions

[20] St. Louis *Missouri Republican*, September 9, 1866.

[21] *Chicago Tribune*, September 11, 1866; *Liberty Weekly Tribune*, September 14, 1866.

of the Supreme Court on *Cummings* and on *Garland,* which declared the Test Oath Act unconstitutional, he was stunned by the successes of the radicals in the election and what he believed to be the beginning of racial amalgamation in America. He discontinued writing in his diary, an endeavor he had pursued periodically since 1842, and much of his public activity. The last entry in his diary is a comment on a newspaper clipping, comparing the number of words in the newly adopted Missouri constitution to the number in the United States Constitution, which contained much less verbiage. "A fair contrast," Bates concluded, "between the patriots and the Statesmen of the Revolution and the Radical Demagogues of our own time."[22] His vision of the Revolutionary period remained unchanged; its virtues, he believed, had been lost in the cruel tides of history.

Life was not over for Bates, however. He spent much time in the company of his family, including John Coalter, who had advanced to the rank of lieutenant colonel in the Army and was now stationed in St. Louis. Fleming, the one son who had served in the Confederate Army, had also returned home with his family to a forgiving father. Not so pleasant was the presence of Woodson, whose failure at West Point dismayed Bates so deeply that the younger son was virtually in disgrace. The children of Barton, Julian, and Fleming, however, made up for this unpleasantness, often visiting their grandfather and remaining overnight at his home. Although Bates occasionally entertained friends at his home, most of his time was reserved for his immediate family.[23]

[22] Beale, *Bates Diary,* 570; Bates to Eads, November 23, 1866, James B. Eads Papers.

[23] Beale, *Bates Diary,* 491, 505, 510, 516, 520, 528, 530, 537, 555, 560, 563. John Coalter Bates remained in the Army and fought in Cuba and in the Philippines. In 1902 he became a major general, and, in 1906, upon rising to the position of Army Chief of Staff, he was promoted to lieutenant general. He died in 1919.

As he spent nearly all of his days at home, Bates found that his weakened condition made it difficult to maintain contacts with old political friends and acquaintances. Too, he was more and more saddened by the realization that time and circumstances had separated him from associates of long ago. Especially poignant was the alienation of Charles Gibson, who had deserted Lincoln for McClellan in the 1864 presidential campaign. Occasionally, Bates talked with Broadhead or Eads when he made a trip into the city, and for a while he derived much satisfaction from being one of the founders and acting as a vice-president of the Missouri Historical Society. As often as he could, he journeyed downtown to attend meetings of the society and to hold brief talks with other senior residents in the St. Louis community.[24]

Although retired from public life, Bates could not resist the controversy that split the Presbyterian church in St. Louis. He had continued to associate with churchmen, including Father Peter J. De Smet, the famous missionary to the Indians; the Reverend Mr. James McCosh, the Scotch Presbyterian; and Dr. Henry A. Boardman, noted churchman of Philadelphia, long after his abandonment of professional and political relationships. It displeased him greatly, therefore, when the Old and New Assemblies in the St. Louis Presbyterian church identified themselves with the conservative and radical political factions, respectively, and began warring with each other. He thought it deplorable for church members to equate their politics with religion, their mortal activities with divine sanction. "If the Church can survive the shock of this epidemic madness—this wicked defection of so many of its members," he wrote, "it must be on account of its own intrinsic excellency and the persevering courage of a few of its members who still remain faithful, and whose salt has not lost its savor, in the midst of this general decay."

[24] *Ibid.*, 528; J. Thomas Scharf, *History of St. Louis, City and County*, I, 896-97.

He painfully discovered that his exhortations could not reconcile the two factions.[25]

Aside from the religious schism within his own denomination, Bates, in the last stages of his life, confronted financial troubles. Having used all of his available capital to buy the house and five lots on Morgan Street, he continued to deal in small land sales as his resources gradually dwindled. He sold Grape Hill for $8,000 in order to pay his debts and by 1868 had to borrow an additional $3,366 from Barton to meet new ones. Eventually, he sold both his sister's home in St. Charles and his interest in the family home in Florissant. By July 1, 1868, the mounting burden of his financial difficulties and the increasing seriousness of his illness led him to the decision of making his will. In it he bequeathed his estate and property to Julia, whom he appointed executor. In order to repay Barton he willed to him title to the common field lands he held in Carondolet.[26]

Bates had acted none too soon. In early December of 1868 his health steadily worsened. The new year brought no improvement, and, by early March, his doctors had notified the family that this would be his final illness. He was awake only a portion of the time, as the weakness of his pain-racked chest frequently caused him to lapse into unconsciousness.[27] For a brief period he rallied, in which time he sent his salutations to the National Waterways Convention of 1869. With Julia and his favorite grandchild Onward faithfully by his bed, he lay reminiscing of a time long ago when he had crossed the great Mississippi to begin a new and promising career as a young territorial lawyer and politician. Days

[25] Beale, *Bates Diary*, 554, 557-60.

[26] *Ibid.*, 475; Barton Bates Memo Book, December, 1868, Bates Papers; Edward Bates's Will, May 20, 1869, Bates Papers (State Historical Society of Missouri).

[27] Barton Bates to Eads, December 23, 1868, Eads Papers.

passed thus, with some family members always present. On March 25, 1869, the final hours came, and he died peacefully, surrounded by relatives and friends.[28]

Bates lived and died a "Jeffersonian Republican," a spokesman of the democratic faith, editorialized the *Missouri Republican*. At a meeting of the St. Louis bar called by James Broadhead, other eulogies were delivered. Most of the speeches approached deification of the departed politician and lawyer. Glover described Bates as one of the two or three truly great Western statesmen. John Darby, remembering particularly the Chicago convention of 1847, lauded his long career as a political leader and organizer. Judge Breckenridge spoke of him as a great lawyer and public servant, and James O. Broadhead concluded with the statement that the man they honored was undoubtedly the soul of early Missouri.[29] Simplicity marked the religious service at the Bates home on Morgan Street, and simplicity characterized the most appropriate comment on Bates's life. Fittingly, an anonymous observer delivered the final epitaph. Turning to Glover, who rode alongside him in the funeral procession on the way to Bellefontaine Cemetery, he quietly remarked that Edward Bates "belonged to a generation that had passed away."[30]

[28] Barton Bates Memo Book, March, 1869, Hester Bates to Mrs. Barton Bates, March 27, 1869, Bates Papers.

[29] St. Louis *Missouri Republican*, March 26, 30, and 31, 1869.

[30] *Ibid.*, March 30, 1869; Julian Bates to H. J. Seever, December 8, 1899, Bates Papers. Edward Bates was buried at Bellefontaine Cemetery in St. Louis County, two miles northwest of Florissant.

BIBLIOGRAPHY

Manuscript Sources

I.   U. S. OFFICIAL PAPERS

Attorney General. Letterbooks. National Archives, Washington, D. C.

Attorney General. Papers. National Archives, Washington, D. C.

Department of the Interior. Letterbooks. National Archives, Washington, D. C.

II.   PRIVATE PAPERS

David Rice Atchison Papers. Western Historical Manuscripts Collection, University of Missouri, Columbia.

Edward Bates Diary, 1846-1852. Missouri Historical Society, St. Louis.

Edward Bates Diary, 1859-1866. Library of Congress.

Edward Bates Papers. Missouri Historical Society, St. Louis.

Edward Bates Papers. State Historical Society of Missouri, Columbia.

Thomas Hart Benton Papers. Missouri Historical Society, St. Louis.

Jeremiah S. Black Papers. Library of Congress.

Blair Family Papers. Library of Congress.

James O. Broadhead Papers. Missouri Historical Society, St. Louis.

Orville H. Browning Letters. Illinois State Historical Library, Springfield.

Simon Cameron Correspondence. Library of Congress.

Salmon P. Chase Collection. Pennsylvania Historical Society, Philadelphia.

Schuyler Colfax Collection. Illinois State Historical Library, Springfield.

Philip St. George Cooke Collection. Southern Historical Collection, University of North Carolina, Chapel Hill.

Thomas Corwin Papers. Library of Congress.

J. E. D. Couzins Papers. Missouri Historical Society, St. Louis.

John F. Darby Papers. Missouri Historical Society, St. Louis.

David Davis Papers. Illinois State Historical Library, Springfield.

James R. Doolittle Collection. Missouri Historical Society, St. Louis.

Charles D. Drake Autobiography. State Historical Society of Missouri, Columbia.

Daniel Dunklin Collection. Western Historical Manuscripts, University of Missouri, Columbia.

James B. Eads Papers. Missouri Historical Society, St. Louis.

Rufus Easton Papers. Missouri Historical Society, St. Louis.

William Greenleaf Eliot Collection. Missouri Historical Society, St. Louis.

William M. Evarts Correspondence. Library of Congress.

Thomas Ewing Papers. Library of Congress.

Philip R. Fendall Papers. Duke University Library, Durham, North Carolina.

William Pitt Fessenden Correspondence. Library of Congress.

Filley Family Papers. Missouri Historical Society, St. Louis.

Millard Fillmore Papers. Buffalo Historical Society, Buffalo, New York.

Hamilton Fish Correspondence. Library of Congress.

Hamilton R. Gamble Papers. Missouri Historical Society, St. Louis.

Charles Gibson Papers. Missouri Historical Society, St. Louis.

Horace Greeley Collection. New York Public Library.

John Hanna Collection. Indiana University Library, Bloomington.

Ethan Allen Hitchcock Papers. Library of Congress.

Andrew Johnson Papers. Library of Congress.

Reverdy Johnson Papers. Library of Congress.

Julian-Giddings Collection. Library of Congress.

Kennett Family Papers. Missouri Historical Society, St. Louis.

Richard Lathers Papers. Library of Congress.

Abiel Leonard Papers. State Historical Society of Missouri, Columbia.

Francis Lieber Collection. Henry E. Huntington Library, San Marino, California.

Abraham Lincoln Collection. Abraham Lincoln National Life Foundation, Fort Wayne, Indiana.

Abraham Lincoln Collection. Allegheny College, Meadsville, Pennsylvania.

Abraham Lincoln Collection. Brown University Library, Providence, Rhode Island.

Abraham Lincoln Collection. Chicago Historical Society, Chicago.

Abraham Lincoln Collection. Chicago Public Library, Chicago.

Abraham Lincoln Collection. Henry E. Huntington Library, San Marino, California.

Abraham Lincoln Collection. Maryland Historical Society, Baltimore.

Abraham Lincoln Collection. Massachusetts Historical Society, Boston.

Abraham Lincoln Collection. Yale University Library, New Haven, Connecticut.

Abraham Lincoln Papers. Missouri Historical Society, St. Louis.

Robert Todd Lincoln Collection. Library of Congress.

Corbin A. Maupin Papers. Alderman Library, University of Virginia, Charlottesville.

Edwin D. Morgan Papers. New York State Library, Albany.

John G. Nicolay Correspondence. Library of Congress.

Wyndham Robertson Collection. University of Chicago Library, Chicago.

Dr. John Sappington Manuscripts. State Historical Society of Missouri, Columbia.

William H. Seward Papers. Rochester University Library, Rochester, New York.

Sol Smith Collection. Missouri Historical Society, St. Louis.

General Thomas Smith Collection. State Historical Society of Missouri, Columbia.

John F. Snyder Collection. Missouri Historical Society, St. Louis.

Edwin M. Stanton Papers. Library of Congress.

Samuel Treat Papers. Missouri Historical Society, St. Louis.

Lyman Trumbull Papers. Library of Congress.

Justin H. Turner Collection. Illinois State Historical Library, Springfield.

Benjamin F. Wade Papers. Library of Congress.

Gideon Welles Papers. Library of Congress.

Henry Wilson Papers. Library of Congress.

William Wirt Papers. Maryland Historical Society, Baltimore.

Published Sources

I. UNITED STATES PUBLIC DOCUMENTS

American State Papers, Public Lands. Vols. IV, V, 1859-1860.

Black, J. S., *Reports of Cases Argued and Determined in the Supreme Court, 1861-1862.* Washington, 1862-1863. 2 vols.

A Compilation of the Messages and Papers of the Presidents, 1789-1897. Edited by James D. Richardson. Washington, 1907. 10 vols.

Congress, *Annals of Congress.* 17th Cong., 2d Sess., 1855.

Congress, *Congressional Debates.* 20th Cong., 1st Sess., Vol. IV, 1828.

Congress, *Congressional Debates.* 20th Cong., 2d Sess., Vol. V, 1830.

Congress, *Congressional Debates.* 21st Cong., 1st Sess., Vol. VI, 1830.

Congress, *Congressional Globe.* 37th Cong., 1st Sess., Vol. XXXI, 1861.

Congress, *Congressional Globe.* 37th Cong., 2d Sess., Vol. XXXII, 1862.

Congress, *Congressional Globe.* 37th Cong., 3d Sess., Vol. XXXIII, 1863.

Congress, House of Representatives, *Miscellaneous Documents.* 37th Cong., 1st Sess., 1861.

Congress, House of Representatives, *Miscellaneous Documents*. 37th Cong., 2d Sess., 1862.
Congress, House of Representatives, *Miscellaneous Documents*. 70th Cong., 2d Sess., 1929.
Congress, House of Representatives, *Reports*. 20th Cong., 2d Sess., 1830.
Congress, Senate, *Executive Documents*. 37th Cong., 2d Sess., 1862.
Federal Cases, 1789-1879. St. Paul, Minnesota, 1894-1895. 31 vols.
Opinions of the Attorneys General of the United States. Washington, 1852.
Prize Cases Decided in the United States Supreme Court, 1789-1918. Edited by James B. Scott. Oxford, 1923. 3 vols.
Statutes at Large. Boston, 1848-   . 77 vols.
The Territorial Papers of the United States, Arkansas Territory. Edited by Clarence E. Carter. Vol. XX. Washington, 1954.
Wallace, James. *Cases Argued and Adjudged in the Supreme Court, 1863-1874*. Washington, 1864-1876. 23 vols.
The War of the Rebellion: A Compilation of the Official Records of the Union and Confederate Armies. Edited by Richard Rush and others. Washington, 1894-1914. 128 vols.

II.   STATE OF MISSOURI PUBLIC DOCUMENTS

Journal of the House of Representatives of the State of Missouri. Second General Assembly. St. Charles, 1823.
Journal of the House of Representatives of the State of Missouri. Eighth General Assembly. Fayette, 1835.
Journal of the Senate of the State of Missouri. Sixth General Assembly. Fayette, 1831.
The Messages and Proclamations of the Governors of the State of Missouri. Edited by Buel Leopard, Floyd C. Shoemaker, and others. Columbia. 19 vols.
Missouri State Convention Journal. St. Louis, 1820.

III.   PUBLISHED COLLECTIONS

Basler, Roy P., ed., *The Collected Works of Abraham Lincoln*. New Brunswick, New Jersey, 1953. 8 vols.
Chase, Salmon P., "Diary and Correspondence of Salmon P.

Chase." *The Annual Report of the American Historical Association for the Year 1902,* II (Washington, 1903), 45-522.

Evarts, Sherman, ed., *Arguments and Speeches of William Maxwell Evarts.* New York, 1919. 3 vols.

Ford, Worthington C., ed., *Letters of Henry Adams, 1858-1891.* Boston, 1930. 2 vols.

Johnson, Robert U., and Clarence C. Buel, eds., *Battles and Leaders of the Civil War.* New York, 1956. 2 vols.

Larsen, Arthur J., ed., *Crusader and Feminist: Letters of Jane Grey Swisshelm, 1858-1865.* St. Paul, Minnesota, 1934.

Marshall, Thomas M., *The Life and Papers of Frederick Bates.* St. Louis, 1925. 2 vols.

Meneely, A. Howard, "Three Manuscripts of Gideon Welles." *American Historical Review,* XXXI (1925-1926), 484-94.

Rollins, Curtis B., ed., *Letters of George Caleb Bingham to James S. Rollins.* Columbia, Missouri, 1937-1939.

IV. DIARIES AND MEMOIRS

Adams, Charles Francis, ed., *Memoirs of John Quincy Adams.* Philadelphia, 1874-1877. 12 vols.

Ambler, Charles H., ed., *Recollections of War and Peace, 1861-1868.* New York, 1938.

Bates, Edward, *Edward Bates against Thomas Hart Benton.* St. Louis, 1828.

Bates, Edward, "Frederick Bates Biographical Sketch." *Michigan Pioneer and Historical Society Collections,* VIII (1885), 563-65.

Bates, Onward, *Bates et al of Virginia and Missouri.* Chicago, 1914.

Bay, William V. N., *Reminiscences of the Bench and Bar of Missouri.* St. Louis, 1878.

Beale, Howard K., ed., *The Diary of Edward Bates, 1859-1866.* The Annual Report of the American Historical Association for the Year 1930, IV. Washington, 1933.

———, ed., *The Diary of Gideon Welles, Secretary of the Navy under Lincoln and Johnson.* New York, 1960. 3 vols.

Blaine, James G., *Twenty Years of Congress.* Norwich, Connecticut, 1884. Vol. I.

Brackenridge, Henry M., *Recollections of Places and Persons in the West.* Philadelphia, 1886.

Broadhead, James O., "Recollections," in A. J. D. Stewart, ed., *Bench and Bar of Missouri.* St. Louis, 1898.

Carpenter, Francis B., *Six Months at the White House with Abraham Lincoln.* New York, 1866.

Chittenden, Lucius E., *Recollections of President Lincoln and His Administration.* New York, 1901.

Darby, John F., *Personal Recollections.* St. Louis, 1880.

Dennett, Tyler, ed., *Lincoln and the Civil War in the Diaries and Letters of John Hay.* New York, 1939.

Donald, David, ed., *Inside Lincoln's Cabinet: The Civil War Diaries of Salmon P. Chase.* New York, 1954.

Dudley, Thomas H., "The Inside Facts of Lincoln's Nomination." *Century Magazine,* XL (1890), 477-79.

Greeley, Horace, *Recollections of a Busy Life.* New York, 1869.

Gurowski, Adam, *Diary, March 4, 1861-November 2, 1862.* Boston, 1862.

Julian, George W., *Political Recollections, 1840-1872.* Chicago, 1884.

Lamon, Ward Hill, *Recollections of Abraham Lincoln, 1847-1865.* Chicago, 1895.

Lucas, John B. C., ed., *Letters of Honorable John B. C. Lucas from 1815 to 1836.* St. Louis, 1905.

McClellan, George B., *McClellan's Own Story.* New York, 1887.

McClure, Alexander, *Abraham Lincoln and Men of War Times.* Philadelphia, 1892.

————, *Recollections.* Philadelphia, 1903.

McCormack, Thomas J., ed., *Memoirs of Gustave Koerner, 1809-1896.* Cedar Rapids, Iowa, 1909. 2 vols.

Meigs, Montgomery C., "General M. C. Meigs on the Conduct of the Civil War." *American Historical Review,* XXVI (1920-1921), 285-303.

Nevins, Allan, and M. H. Thomas, eds., *The Diary of George Templeton Strong.* New York, 1952. 4 vols.

Pease, Theodore C., and James G. Randall, eds., *The Diary of Orville Hickman Browning, 1850-1881.* Springfield, Illinois, 1925-1933. 2 vols.

Pike, Allen Thorndike, ed., *Reminiscences of Abraham Lincoln.* New York, 1888.

Poore, Ben Perley, *Perley's Reminiscences of Sixty Years in the National Metropolis.* Philadelphia, 1886. 2 vols.

Rice, Allen T., ed., *Reminiscences of Abraham Lincoln.* New York, 1888.

Rockwell, Rufus, ed., *Intimate Memories of Abraham Lincoln.* Elmira, New York, 1945.

Russel, William H., *My Diary North and South.* Boston, 1863.

Schurz, Carl, *Reminiscences.* New York, 1907-1908. 3 vols.

Townsend, E. D., *Anecdotes of the Civil War in the United States.* New York, 1884.

Usher, John P., *President Lincoln's Cabinet.* Omaha, Nebraska, 1925.

Villard, Harold G., and Oswald G. Villard, eds., *Lincoln on the Eve of '61.* New York, 1941.

Weed, Harriet A., ed., *Autobiography of Thurlow Weed.* Boston, 1883.

Welles, Gideon, "Administration of Abraham Lincoln." *The Galaxy,* XXIV (1877-1878), 437-50, 608-24, 733-45.

Wilson, Rufus R., ed., *Intimate Memories of Lincoln.* Elmira, New York, 1945.

V.   NEWSPAPERS AND PERIODICALS

Periodicals:

American Review, VII (1847).

Appletons' American Annual Cyclopedia. Vols. I-V. New York, 1864-1867.

Fergus, Robert, *Chicago River and Harbor Convention.* No. 18, Fergus Historical Series. Chicago, 1882.

Hunt's Merchant Magazine and Commercial Review, XVII (1847).

Paxton, John, "St. Louis Directory and Register, 1821." *St. Louis Directory for 1854-1855.* St. Louis, 1854.

The following newspaper is in the Missouri Historical Society at St. Louis:
Missouri Democrat, St. Louis, Missouri

The following newspapers are in the University of Missouri Library at Columbia:
Boston Evening Transcript, Boston, Massachusetts
Chicago Tribune, Chicago, Illinois
Constitution, Washington, D. C.
Daily Picayune, New Orleans, Louisiana

Evening Star, Washington, D. C.
National Intelligencer, Washington, D. C.
New York Times, New York
New York Tribune, New York
Pittsburgh Post, Pittsburgh, Pennsylvania
Richmond Enquirer, Richmond, Virginia
Sun, Baltimore, Maryland

The following newspapers, published in Missouri, are in the library of the State Historical Society of Missouri at Columbia:
Daily Union, St. Louis
Hannibal Messenger, Hannibal
Independent Patriot, Jackson
Jefferson Inquirer, Jefferson City
Jeffersonian Republican, Jefferson City
Liberty Weekly Tribune, Liberty
Missouri Argus, St. Louis
Missouri Gazette, St. Louis
Missouri Intelligencer, Columbia
Missouri Intelligencer, Fayette
Missouri Intelligencer, Franklin
Missouri Republican, St. Louis
Missouri State Times, Jefferson City
Missouri Statesman, Columbia
Missouri Whig, Palmyra
St. Louis Beacon, St. Louis
St. Louis Enquirer, St. Louis
St. Louis Evening News, St. Louis
St. Louis Globe-Democrat, St. Louis
St. Louis Intelligencer, St. Louis
Southern Sentinel, Palmyra
Tri-Weekly Messenger, Hannibal
Weekly Sentinel, Palmyra
Western Monitor, Fayette

VI.   BOOKS AND ARTICLES

Adams, Charles F., *Richard Henry Dana, Jr.* New York, 1891.
Adams, Ephraim D., *Great Britain and the American Civil War.* New York, 1925. 2 vols.
Ambler, Charles H., *Francis H. Pierpont, Union War Governor*

of Virginia and Father of West Virginia. Chapel Hill, North Carolina, 1939.

Anderson, Hattie M., "Frontier Economic Problems in Missouri." *Missouri Historical Review,* XXXIV (1939-1940), 301-34.

Angle, Paul M., ed., "The Western Trip of Philip Hone." *Journal of the Illinois State Historical Society,* XXXVIII (1945), 277-94.

Ascher, Leonard, "Lincoln's Administration and the New Almaden Scandal." *The Pacific Historical Review,* V (1936), 38-51.

Auchampaugh, Philip G., *James Buchanan and His Cabinet on the Eve of Secession.* Lancaster, Pennsylvania, 1926.

Baker, Olive, "Paper Read before Montgomery County Club of St. Louis." *Missouri Historical Review,* VII (1912-1913), 200-23.

Ballantine, Henry W., "Martial Law." *Columbia Law Review,* XII (1912-1913), 529-38.

Bancroft, Frederick, *The Life of William H. Seward.* New York, 1900.

Barclay, Thomas S., *The Liberal Republican Movement in Missouri, 1865-1871.* Columbia, Missouri, 1926.

Baringer, William E., *A House Dividing: Lincoln as President-Elect.* Springfield, Illinois, 1945.

———, *Lincoln's Rise to Power.* Boston, 1937.

Barrows, Chester L., *William Maxwell Evarts, Lawyer, Diplomat, Statesman.* Chapel Hill, North Carolina, 1941.

Baxter, James P., "The British Government and Neutral Rights, 1861-1865." *American Historical Review,* XXXIV (1928-1929), 9-29.

Baxter, Maurice G., *Orville H. Browning, Lincoln's Friend and Critic.* Bloomington, Indiana, 1957.

Beale, Howard K., *The Critical Year: A Study of Andrew Johnson and Reconstruction.* New York, 1930.

Beck, Warren A., "Lincoln and Negro Colonization in Central America." *The Abraham Lincoln Quarterly,* VI (1950-1951), 162-83.

Bernard, Kenneth A., "Lincoln and Civil Liberties." *Abraham Lincoln Quarterly,* VI (1950-1951), 375-99.

Broadhead, Garland C., "A Few of the Leading People and

Events of Missouri History." *Missouri Historical Review,* I (1906-1907), 284-92.

Bryan, William S., and Robert Rose, *A History of the Pioneer Families of Missouri.* St. Louis, 1876.

Cain, Marvin R., "Edward Bates and Hamilton R. Gamble: A Wartime Partnership." *Missouri Historical Review,* LVI (1962), 146-55.

Carmen, Harry J., and Reinhard H. Luthin, *Lincoln and the Patronage.* New York, 1943.

Carpenter, A. H., "Military Government of Southern Territory, 1861-1865." *The Annual Report of the American Historical Association for the Year 1900,* I (Washington, 1901), 467-98.

Castel, Albert, "The Fort Pillow Massacre: A Fresh Examination of the Evidence." *Civil War History,* IV (1958), 37-50.

Catton, Bruce, *Grant Moves South.* New York, 1960.

Chambers, William N., *Old Bullion Benton: Senator from the New West.* Boston, 1956.

Claussen, Martin P., "Peace Factors in Anglo-American Relations, 1861-1865." *Mississippi Valley Historical Review,* XXVI (1940), 511-22.

Cleven, Andrew N., "Some Plans for Colonizing Liberated Negro Slaves in Hispanic America." *The Journal of Negro History,* XI (1926), 35-49.

Cole, Arthur C., "Lincoln's Election an Immediate Menace to Slavery in the States?" *American Historical Review,* XXXVI (1930-1931), 740-67.

Cox, LaWanda, and John H. Cox, *Politics, Principle and Prejudice, 1865-1866: Dilemma of Reconstruction America.* New York, 1963.

Craven, Avery, *The Coming of the Civil War.* New York, 1942.

———, *The Growth of Southern Nationalism, 1848-1861.* Baton Rouge, 1953.

———, ed., *Essays in Honor of William E. Dodd.* Chicago, 1935.

Culmer, Frederick A., "Abiel Leonard." *Missouri Historical Review,* XXVII (1932-1933), 113-31, 217-39, 315-36.

Current, Richard H., *Old Thad Stevens: A Story of Ambition.* Madison, 1942.

Curry, Richard O., "A Reappraisal of Statehood Politics in West Virginia." *Journal of Southern History,* XXVII (1962), 403-21.

Deener, David R., *The United States Attorneys General and International Law*. The Hague, 1957.

Dennett, Tyler, "Lincoln and the Campaign of 1864." *Abraham Lincoln Association Papers* (1935).

Donald, David, *Lincoln Reconsidered: Essays on the Civil War*. New York, 1959.

————, ed., *Why the North Won the Civil War*. Baton Rouge, 1960.

Dorris, Jonathan T., *Pardon and Amnesty under Lincoln and Johnson: The Restoration of the Confederates to their Rights and Privileges, 1861-1898*. Chapel Hill, 1953.

Douglas, Walter B., "Manuel Lisa," *Missouri Historical Society Collections*, III (1908-1911), 367-406.

Edwards, Richard, and M. Hopewell, *Edwards' Great West*. St. Louis, 1860.

Elliott, Charles W., *Winfield Scott, the Soldier and the Man*. New York, 1937.

Fehrenbacher, Don E., *Prelude to Greatness: Lincoln in the 1850's*. Stanford, 1962.

Fessenden, Francis, *Life and Public Services of William Pitt Fessenden*. Boston, 1907.

Fisher, Sidney G., "The Suspension of Habeas Corpus during the War of the Rebellion." *Political Science Quarterly*, III (1888), 454-88.

Fite, Emerson D., *The Presidential Campaign of 1860*. New York, 1911.

Franklin, John H., *The Emancipation Proclamation*. New York, 1963.

Freidel, Frank, *Francis Lieber, Nineteenth-Century Liberal*. Baton Rouge, 1947.

Garraty, John A., *Silas Wright*. New York, 1949.

Gates, Paul W., "The Struggle for Land and the Irrepressible Conflict." *Political Science Quarterly*, LX (1951), 248-71.

Gernon, Blaine B., "Chicago and Abraham Lincoln." *Journal of the Illinois State Historical Society*, XXVII (1934-1935), 243-84.

Gibson, Charles, "Edward Bates." *Missouri Historical Society Collections*, II (1900), 52-56.

Gorham, George C., *Life and Public Services of Edwin M. Stanton*. New York, 1899. 2 vols.

Gray, Wood, *The Hidden Civil War: The Story of the Copper-heads.* New York, 1942.

Greeley, Horace, *The American Conflict.* Hartford, Connecticut, 1864-1866. 2 vols.

Green, Constance M., *Washington: Village and Capital, 1800-1878.* Princeton, 1962.

Gregory, Charles N., "Samuel Freeman Miller: Associate Justice of the Supreme Court of the United States." *Yale Law Journal,* XV (1907-1908), 422-42.

Griffis, William O. E., *Millard Fillmore.* Ithaca, New York, 1915.

Haines, Charles G., *The American Doctrine of Judicial Supremacy.* New York, 1959.

Halbert, Sherrill, "The Suspension of the Writ of Habeas Corpus by President Lincoln." *The American Journal of Legal History,* II (1958), 95-116.

Hamilton, Holman, *Zachary Taylor: Soldier in the White House.* Indianapolis, 1951.

Hamilton, W. J., "The Relief Movement in Missouri." *Missouri Historical Review,* XXII (1927-1928), 51-92.

Hamlin, Charles E., *The Life and Times of Hannibal Hamlin.* Cambridge, Massachusetts, 1899.

Hammond, Bray, *Banks and Politics in America from the Revolution to the Civil War.* Princeton, New Jersey, 1957.

———, "The North's Empty Purse, 1861-1862." *American Historical Review,* LXVII (1961), 1-18.

Harding, Samuel B., "Missouri Party Struggles in the Civil War Period." *The Annual Report of the American Historical Association for the Year 1900,* I (Washington, 1901), 85-104.

Hart, Albert B., *Salmon Portland Chase.* Cambridge, Massachusetts, 1899.

Hassler, Warren W., Jr., *General George B. McClellan, Shield of the Union.* Baton Rouge, 1957.

Hendrick, Burton J., *Lincoln's War Cabinet.* Boston, 1946.

Herriott, Frank I., "Memories of the Chicago Convention of 1860." *Annals of Iowa,* XII (1915-1921), 446-66.

———, "The Conference in the Deutsches Haus, Chicago, May 14-15, 1860." *Transactions of the Illinois State Historical Society,* XXXV (1928), 101-91.

Hesseltine, William B., *Lincoln and the War Governors.* New York, 1948.

——, *Lincoln's Plan of Reconstruction.* Tuscaloosa, Alabama, 1960.

Hodder, Frank H., "The Railroad Background of the Kansas-Nebraska Act." *Mississippi Valley Historical Review,* XII (1925-1926), 3-22.

Hollister, O. J., *Life of Schuyler Colfax.* New York, 1886.

Holtzoff, Alexander, "Some Phases of the Law of Blockade." *The American Journal of International Law,* X (1916), 53-64.

Hopkins, Vincent C., *Dred Scott's Case.* New York, 1957.

Horner, Harlan H., *Lincoln and Greeley.* Urbana, 1953.

Houck, Louis, *History of Missouri.* Chicago, 1908. 3 vols.

Jellison, Charles A., *Fessenden of Maine: Civil War Senator.* Syracuse, New York, 1962.

Johnson, Charles W., *Proceedings of the First Three Republican National Conventions, 1856, 1860, and 1864.* Minneapolis, 1893.

Johnson, Ludwell H., *Red River Campaign: Politics and Cotton in the Civil War.* Baltimore, 1958.

King, Willard L., *Lincoln's Manager: David Davis.* Cambridge, Massachusetts, 1960.

Kirkland, Edward C., *The Peacemakers of 1864.* New York, 1927.

Klement, Frank L., *The Copperheads in the Middle West.* Chicago, 1960.

Laughlin, Sceva B., "Missouri Politics During the Civil War." *Missouri Historical Review,* XXIII (April, 1929), 400-426; (July, 1929), 583-618, XXIV; (October, 1929), 87-113; (January, 1930), 261-84.

Lehmann, Frederick W., "Edward Bates and the Test Oath." *Missouri Historical Society Collections,* IV (1912-1923), 389-401.

Livermore, William R., "The Emancipation Pen." *Proceedings of the Massachusetts Historical Society,* XLIV (1910-1911), 595-604.

Lonn, Ella, *Desertation During the Civil War.* New York, 1928.

Luthin, Reinhard, *The First Lincoln Campaign.* Cambridge, Massachusetts, 1944.

MacArtney, Clarence E., *Lincoln and His Cabinet.* New York, 1931.

McCarthy, Charles H., *Lincoln's Plan of Reconstruction*. New York, 1901.

McClure, Clarence H., *Opposition in Missouri to Thomas Hart Benton*. Nashville, 1927.

McElroy, John, *The Struggle for Missouri*. Washington, 1909.

McLaughlin, Andrew C., *A Constitutional History of the United States*. New York, 1935.

Mallam, William D., "Lincoln and the Conservatives." *Journal of Southern History*, XXVIII (1962), 31-45.

March, David D., "Charles D. Drake and the Constitutional Convention of 1865." *Missouri Historical Review*, XLVII (1952-1953), 110-23.

———, "The Campaign for the Ratification of the Constitution of 1865." *Missouri Historical Review*, XLVII (1952-1953), 223-32.

Marshall, John A., *American Bastille*. Philadelphia, 1883.

Martin, Edward S., *The Life of Joseph Hodges Choate*. New York, 1920. 2 vols.

Milton, George Fort, *Abraham Lincoln and the Fifth Column*. New York, 1942.

Moore, Glover, *The Missouri Controversy, 1818-1821*. Lexington, Kentucky, 1953.

Moore, John B., *A Digest of International Law*. Washington, 1906. 8 vols.

Nevins, Allan, *Frémont, the West's Greatest Adventurer*. New York, 1928. 2 vols.

———, *Ordeal of the Union*. New York, 1947. 2 vols.

———, *The Emergence of Lincoln*. New York, 1951. 2 vols.

———, *The War for the Union: The Improvised War*. New York, 1959.

———, *The War for the Union: War Becomes Revolution*. New York, 1960.

Nichols, Roy F., *The Disruption of American Democracy*. New York, 1948.

———, "The Kansas-Nebraska Act: A Century of Historiography." *Mississippi Valley Historical Review*, XLIII (1956-1957), 187-212.

Nicolay, Helen, "Lincoln's Cabinet." *Abraham Lincoln Quarterly*, V (1949), 260-68.

Nicolay, John G., and John Hay, *Abraham Lincoln: A History*. New York, 1890. 10 vols.

O'Connor, Thomas H., "Lincoln and the Cotton Trade." *Civil War History,* VII (1961), 20-35.

Oldroyd, Osborn H., *Lincoln's Campaign or the Political Revolution of 1860.* Chicago, 1896.

Parrish, William E., *Turbulent Partnership: Missouri and the Union, 1861-1865.* Columbia, Missouri, 1963.

———, *David Rice Atchison of Missouri: Border Politician.* Columbia, Missouri, 1961.

Perry, Thomas S., *The Life and Letters of Francis Lieber.* Boston, 1882.

Pitkin, Thomas M., "Western Republicans and the Tariff in 1860." *Mississippi Valley Historical Review,* XXVII (1940-1941), 401-20.

Potter, David M., *Lincoln and His Party in the Secession Crisis.* New Haven, 1942.

Primm, James N., *Economic Policy in the Development of a Western State: Missouri, 1820-1860.* Cambridge, Massachusetts, 1954.

Quarles, Benjamin, *The Negro in the Civil War.* Boston, 1953.

———, *Lincoln and the Negro.* New York, 1962.

Randall, James G., "Some Legal Aspects of the Confiscation Acts of the Civil War." *American Historical Review,* XVIII (1912-1913), 79-86.

———, *The Confiscation of Property During the Civil War.* Indianapolis, 1913.

———, "The Indemnity Act of 1863: A Study in the War-Time Immunity of Governmental Officers." *Michigan Law Review,* XX (1921-1922), 589-613.

———, "Lincoln in the Role of Dictator." *South Atlantic Quarterly,* XXVIII (1929), 236-52.

———, "Has the Lincoln Theme Been Exhausted?" *American Historical Review,* XLI (1936), 270-94.

——, "The Civil War Restudied." *Journal of Southern History,* VI (1940), 439-57.

———, "Civil and Military Relationships under Lincoln." *The Pennsylvania Magazine of History and Biography* (1945), 199-206.

———, *Lincoln, the President.* New York, 1945-1953. 3 vols.

———, *Lincoln and the South.* Baton Rouge, 1946.

———, *Lincoln, the Liberal Statesman.* New York, 1947.

————, *Constitutional Problems under Lincoln*. New York, 1951.

————, *The Civil War and Reconstruction*. Boston, 1953.

Randall, James G., and Richard N. Current, *Lincoln, the President: Last Full Measure*. New York, 1955. Vol. IV.

————, *Mr. Lincoln*. New York, 1957.

Richardson, Lemont K., "Private Land Claims in Missouri." *Missouri Historical Review*, L (1955-1956), 387-99.

Riddle, Donald W., *Congressman Abraham Lincoln*. Urbana, 1957.

Robinson, William M., Jr., *The Confederate Privateers*. New Haven, 1928.

Russel, Robert R., "The Pacific Railroad Issue in Politics Prior to the Civil War." *Mississippi Valley Historical Review*, XII (1925-1926), 187-201.

Ryle, Walter H., *Missouri: Union or Secession*. Nashville, 1931.

————, "Slavery and Party Realignment in Missouri in the State Election of 1856." *Missouri Historical Review*, XXXIX (1944-1945), 320-32.

Sandburg, Carl, *Abraham Lincoln: The War Years*. New York, 1936-1939.

Scharf, J. Thomas, *History of St. Louis, City and County*. Philadelphia, 1883. 2 vols.

Scott, Eben C., *Reconstruction during the Civil War in the United States of America*. New York, 1895.

Sellers, Charles G., Jr., *James K. Polk, Jacksonian, 1795-1843*. Princeton, New Jersey, 1957.

Sellery, George C., *Lincoln's Suspension of Habeas Corpus as Viewed by Congress*. Madison, 1907.

Shanks, Henry T., *The Secession Movement in Virginia, 1847-1861*. Richmond, 1934.

Shapiro, Samuel, *Richard Henry Dana, Jr., 1815-1882*. East Lansing, Michigan, 1961.

Sharp, James R., "Governor Daniel Dunklin's Jacksonian Democracy in Missouri, 1832-1836." *Missouri Historical Review*, LVI (1961-1962), 217-29.

Shepard, Elihu, *The Early History of St. Louis and Missouri from Its First Exploration by White Men, 1773 to 1843*. St. Louis, 1870.

Shoemaker, Floyd C., *Missouri's Struggle for Statehood, 1804-1821*. Jefferson City, 1916.

Shuckers, Jacob W., *The Life and Public Services of Salmon Portland Chase*. New York, 1874.

Shutes, Milton H., "Abraham Lincoln and the New Almaden Mine." *California Historical Quarterly*, XV (1936), 3-20.

Silver, David M., *Lincoln's Supreme Court*. Urbana, 1956.

Skinner, Thomas K., "The Removal of the Judges of the Supreme Court of Missouri in 1865." *Missouri Historical Society Collections*, IV (1912-1923), 243-74.

Smith, Edward C., *The Borderland in the Civil War*. New York, 1927.

Smith, Willard H., *Schuyler Colfax: The Changing Fortunes of a Political Idol*. Indianapolis, 1952.

Smith, William E., *The Francis Preston Blair Family in Politics*. New York, 1933. 2 vols.

Spaulding, Elbridge G., *History of Legal-Tender Paper Issued during the Rebellion*. Buffalo, New York, 1897.

Sproat, John G., "Blueprint for Radical Reconstruction." *Journal of Southern History*, XXIII (1957), 25-44.

Stampp, Kenneth M., "Lincoln and the Strategy of Defense in the Crisis of 1861." *Journal of Southern History*, XI (1945), 297-323.

———, *And the War Came: The North and the Secession Crisis, 1860-1861*. Baton Rouge, 1950.

Staudenraus, P. J., *The African Colonization Movement, 1816-1865*. New York, 1961.

Stedman, Laura, and George W. Gould, *The Life and Letters of Edmund Clarence Stedman*. New York, 1910. 2 vols.

Stevens, Walter B., "Lincoln and Missouri." *Missouri Historical Review*, X (January, 1916), 63-119.

———, "Alexander McNair." *Missouri Historical Review*, XVII (1922-1923), 3-21.

Swisher, Carl B., *Roger B. Taney*. New York, 1935.

———, *American Constitutional Development*. New York, 1951.

Tegeder, Vincent G., "Lincoln and the Territorial Patronage: The Ascendancy of the Radicals in the West." *Mississippi Valley Historical Review*, XXXV (1948-1949), 77-90.

Thomas, Benjamin P., *Abraham Lincoln: A Biography*. New York, 1952.

———, and Harold M. Hyman, *Stanton, The Life and Times of Lincoln's Secretary of War*. New York, 1962.

Trefousse, Hans L., *Ben Butler, The South Called Him Beast!* New York, 1957.

———, *Benjamin Franklin Wade: Radical Republican from Ohio.* New York, 1963.

Trexler, Harrison A., *Slavery in Missouri, 1804-1865.* Baltimore, 1914.

Van Deusen, Glyndon C., *Horace Greeley: Nineteenth-Century Crusader.* Philadelphia, 1953.

———, "Thurlow Weed's Analysis of William H. Seward's Defeat in the Republican Convention of 1860." *Mississippi Valley Historical Review,* XXXIV (1947-1948), 101-4.

Van Ravenswaay, Charles, "The Tragedy of David Barton." *Bulletin of the Missouri Historical Society,* VII (1950-1951), 35-56.

Warren, Charles, *The Supreme Court in United States History.* Boston, 1937. 2 vols.

West, Richard S., Jr., *Gideon Welles, Lincoln's Navy Department.* New York, 1943.

Williams, Mentor L., "The Chicago River and Harbor Convention, 1847." *Mississippi Valley Historical Review,* XXV (1948-1949), 607-26.

Williams, T. Harry, *Lincoln and the Radicals.* Madison, 1941.

Wilson, Charles R., "New Light on the Lincoln-Blair-Frémont 'Bargain' of 1864." *American Historical Review,* XLII (1936-1937), 71-78.

Woodburn, James A., "The Attitude of Thaddeus Stevens toward the Conduct of the War." *American Historical Review,* XII (1906-1907), 567-83.

Zornow, William F., "The Missouri Radicals and the Election of 1864." *Missouri Historical Review,* XLV (July, 1951), 354-70.

———, *Lincoln and the Party Divided.* Norman, Oklahoma, 1954.